POWER

Learning

Strategies for Success in Higher Education and Life

Second Canadian Edition

Robert S. Feldman

University of
Massachusetts—Amherst

Sheila Chick

Fanshawe College

 **McGraw-Hill Ryerson**

Toronto   Montréal   Boston   Burr Ridge, IL   Dubuque, IA   Madison, WI   New York
San Francisco   St. Louis   Bangkok   Bogotá   Caracas   Kuala Lumpur   Lisbon   London   Madrid
Mexico City   Milan   New Delhi   Santiago   Seoul   Singapore   Sydney   Taipei

McGraw-Hill Ryerson

P.O.W.E.R. Learning
Second Canadian Edition

ISBN: 0-07-091977-1

1 2 3 4 5 6 7 8 9 10 QPD 0 9 8 7 6

Printed and bound in the United States of America

Statistics Canada information is used with the permission of the Minister of Industry, as Minister responsible for Statistics Canada. Information on the availability of the wide range of data from Statistics Canada can be obtained from Statistics Canada's Regional Offices, its World Wide Web site at http://www.statcan.ca, and its toll free access number 1-800-263-1136.

Care has been taken to trace ownership of copyright material contained in this text; however, the publisher will welcome any information that enables them to rectify any reference or credit for subsequent editions.

Sponsoring Editor: Leanna Maclean
Developmental Editor: Christine Gilbert
Marketing Manager: Dawn Doherty
Supervising Editor: Jaime Smith
Copy Editor: Erin Moore
Senior Production Coordinator: Jennifer Wilkie
Page Layout: Sharon Lucas
Cover Design: Sharon Lucas
Printer: Quebecor Printing Dubuque, Inc.

Library and Archives Canada Cataloguing in Publication

Feldman, Robert S. (Robert Stephen), 1947-
        P.O.W.E.R. learning / Robert S. Feldman, Sheila Chick. — 2nd Canadian ed.

Includes bibliographical references and index.
ISBN 0-07-091977-1

        1. College student orientation. 2. Study skills. 3. College students—Life skills guides. I. Chick, Sheila II. Title.

LB2343.3.F44 2005   378.1'98   C2004-907320-6

Contents

Preface iii

About the Authors xxii

Acknowledgments xviii

Part One: Getting Started

1 P.O.W.E.R. Learning: Becoming a Successful Student 1

Looking Ahead 2

Why Go to College or University? 3

Try It! 1: Why Am I Going to College or University? 4

Journal Reflections: My School Experiences 5

P.O.W.E.R. Learning: The Five Key Steps to Achieving Success 5

Prepare 6

Try It! 2: How I Can Benefit from My Student Success Course 7

Try It! 3: Course Goals 8

Organize 9

Try It! 4: Course Goals, Revisited 10

Work 11

Evaluate 13

Try It! 5: Examine the Causes of Success and Failure 14

Rethink 15

Try It! 6: The Good and The Bad 16

Are You Ready to Become a P.O.W.E.R. Learner? 17

Career Connections: P.O.W.E.R. Learning Meets the World of Work 18

Try It! 7: Employability Skills Profile 19

Looking Back 21

Try It! 8: Are You Afraid of Success? 22

Speaking of Success: Roberta Bondar 23

P.O.W.E.R. Portfolio: Employability Skills 24

Resources 24

The Case of . . . No Clue 26

2 Making the Most of Your Time 27

Looking Ahead 28

Time for Success 29

Prepare: Learning Where Time Is Going 29

Try It! 1: Create a Time Log 30

Journal Reflections: Where Does My Time Go? 31

Try It! 2: Identify the Black Holes of Time Management 32

Try It! 3: Set Priorities 34

Organize: Mastering the Moment 35

Work: Controlling Time 41

Try It! 4: Build a Daily To-Do List 41

Try It! 5: Find Your Procrastination Quotient 44

Career Connections: Career Planning 46

Evaluate: Checking Your Time 46

Rethink: Reflecting on Your Personal Style of Time Management 48

Speaking of Success: Emm Gryner   50

Looking Back   51

P.O.W.E.R. Portfolio: Goal-Setting Models   51

Resources   56

The Case of . . . Where Does the Time Go?   57

3 Recognizing How You Learn, Who You Are, and What You Value   59

Looking Ahead   60

Discovering Your Learning Styles   61

Are You a Primarily Visual, Auditory, or Tactile Learner?   62

Handling Information: Do You Focus on Pieces or the Whole?   62

Try It! 1: Learning Style Inventory: Are You a Visual, an Auditory, or a Kinesthetic Learner?   63

Journal Reflections: How I Learn   65

Multiple Intelligences   65

Try It! 2: Assess Your Analytical and Relational Learning Styles   66

Personality Styles   67

Try It! 3: You and Your Multiple Intelligences   68

Experiential Learning   72

Facts to Remember about Learning, Personality, Experiential, and Processing Styles   73

Try It! 4: Learning Style Indicator   74

Try It! 5: What I Know About My Learning Styles   76

Self-Concept: "Who Am I?"   78

Self-Concept and Self-Fulfilling Prophecies   78

Make Sure Your Self-Concept Is Yours   80

Self-Esteem: Building a Positive View of Yourself   81

Why Self-Esteem Matters   81

Try It! 6: Measure Your Self-Esteem   82

Preparing a Personal Mission Statement   85

Prepare: Identifying Your Values   85

Organize: Placing Order on What Motivates You   86

Work: Creating a Personal Mission Statement   87

Try It! 7: Organize Your Needs   88

Evaluate: Assessing Your Personal Mission Statement   89

Try It! 8: Write a Mission Statement   90

Rethink: Reconsidering Your Options   91

Career Connections: Personality Assessments on the Job   91

To Thine Own Self Be True: No One Is Responsible for Your Life but You   92

Speaking of Success: Todd Currie   93

Looking Back   94

P.O.W.E.R. Portfolio: Self-Improvement   94

Resources   95

The Case of . . . The Instructor Who Spoke Too Much   96

Part Two: Using P.O.W.E.R. in the Classroom

4 Using Technology for Information Management   97

Looking Ahead   98

You and Computers   99

Journal Reflections: How I Feel about Computers   99

Word-Processing Programs: Spreading the Word   99

Try It! 1: Express Yourself   100

Presentation Programs: Looking Good 101
  Try It! 2: Presenting. . . 102

Spreadsheet Programs: Crunching the Numbers 102

Using E-Mail Effectively 103

Writing and Responding to E-Mail 103

Netiquette: Showing Civility in E-Mail 104

Distance Learning: Classes Without Walls 105
  Try It! 3: Assess Your Course-Taking Style 106
  Prepare: Identifying Distance Learning Course Possibilities 107
  Try It! 4: Get Some Distance on the Problem 108
  Organize: Obtaining Access to Technology 108
  Work: Participating in a Distance Learning Class 109
  Evaluate: Considering Your "Classroom" Performance 109
  Rethink: Reflecting on What and How You Have Learned 110

Locating the Information You Need 110

Becoming Acquainted with Information Sources 110
  Try It! 5: Test Drive the Library Catalogue 113
  Try It! 6: Information, Please! 116
  Try It! 7: Work the Web 117

Career Connections: Researching Careers on the Web 118

Narrowing Your Search 119

Using the Information You Find 120
  Try It! 8: Summarize, Don't Plagiarize 124

Remembering That Not All Sources of Information Are Equal 125

Placing Information in Context 126

Speaking of Success: Shawn Thomson 126

Looking Back 128

P.O.W.E.R. Portfolio: High-Tech Skills 128

Resources 129

The Case of . . . The Unsuspecting Plagiarist 131

---

5 Taking Notes   133

Looking Ahead 134

Taking Notes in Class 135
  Prepare: Considering Your Goals 135
  Try It! 1: Identify Course Goals 136
  Organize: Getting Your Notetaking Tools Together 137
  Journal Reflections: How Do I Take Notes? 139
  Work: Processing—Not Copying—Information 140
  Try It! 2: Outline a Lecture 143
  Try It! 3: Take Notes During Discussions 144
  Evaluate: Thinking Critically about Your Notes 147
  Try It! 4: Evaluate Your Class Notes 148
  Rethink: Activating Your Memory 149

  Try It! 5: Practise Your Notetaking Skills 151

Taking Notes: Multimedia Technology 152

Taking Notes as You Study 152

Speaking of Success: Kofi Boateng 153

Taking Notes on Material You Can Write On 154

Career Connections: Notetaking on the Job: Taking Minutes 154

Taking Study Notes on Material You Can't Write On 155

Looking Back 156

P.O.W.E.R. Portfolio: Take Note 156

Resources 157

The Case of . . . A Clean Sweep 158

Looking Ahead 160

Getting Ready 161

Journal Reflections: How I Feel about Tests 161

Prepare: Readying Your Test-Taking Strategies 162

Try It! 1: Complete a Test-Preparation Checklist 163

Organize: Facing the Day of the Test 168

Taking the Test 169

Work: Tackling the Test 169

Try It! 2: Understand Action Verbs in Essay Questions 172

Career Connections: Professional Tests: More Exams and Tests 175

Evaluate: Taking Your Own Final Examination 175

Try It! 3: Take a Test-Taking Test 177

Rethink: Reflecting on the Real Test of Learning 179

Try It! 4: Analyze Returned Tests 180

What If You Fail? 182

Looking Back 182

Speaking of Success: Asta Kovanen 183

P.O.W.E.R. Portfolio: Put It to the Test 184

Resources 185

The Case of . . . Too Many Questions, Too Little Time 186

Part Three: P.O.W.E.R. Foundations of Success

 7 Building Your Reading and Listening Skills **187**

Looking Ahead 188

Sharpen Your Reading Skills 189

Read for Retention, Not Speed 189

Journal Reflections: How I Read 189

Prepare: Approaching the Written Word 190

Try It! 1: Discover How Advance Organizers Help 191

Try It! 2: Read the Frontmatter 192

Organize: Gathering the Tools of the Trade 192

Try It! 3: Create an Advance Organizer 193

Work: Getting the Most Out of Your Reading 194

Try It! 4: Discover Your Attention Span 195

Try It! 5: Mark up a Book Page 199

Evaluate: Considering What It Means and What You Know 200

Rethink: Getting It the Second Time 201

Dealing with Learning Disabilities 202

Try It! 6: Make a Concept Map 203

Building Listening Skills 204

Tips for Active Listening: Listen Up! 204

Career Connections: Active Listening In the Workplace: A Matter of Life and Death 205

Breaking the Ice: Tips for Getting over Stage Fright and Asking Questions in Class 207

The Problem Instructor 207

Speaking of Success: Rachel Trail 209

Looking Back 210

P.O.W.E.R. Portfolio: Reading and Listening 210

Resources 211

The Case of . . . What's Wrong with this Picture? 212

8 Writing and Speaking

Looking Ahead 214

The Writing Process 215

Prepare: Confronting the Blank Page 215

Journal Reflections: How I Feel About Writing 217

Try It! 1: Set Yourself Free: Freewriting 218

Try It! 2: Get Your Brain Storming: Using Brainstorming to Generate Ideas 219

Organize: Constructing a Scaffold 220

Try It! 3: Make Your Point: Write a Thesis Statement 222

Work: Writing the Work 223

Evaluate: Acting as Your Own Best Critic 228

Rethink: Reflecting on Your Accomplishment 228

Speaking Your Mind 229

Try It! 4: Thinking Critically About Writing 230

Meeting the Challenge of Public Speaking 230

Career Connections: Write Away 231

Try It! 5: Let's Talk 232

Journal Reflections: How I Feel About Public Speaking 233

Try It! 6: Prop Yourself Up 235

Speaking Off-the-Cuff: Extemporaneous Speaking 236

Try It! 7: Put Yourself on the Spot 237

Remember: You're Already an Accomplished Public Speaker 237

Speaking of Success: John Lu 238

Looking Back 239

P.O.W.E.R. Portfolio: Writing and Speaking 239

Resources 242

The Case of . . . the Reluctant Speaker 243

9 Improving Your Memory

Looking Ahead 246

The Secret of Memory 247

The Value of Forgetting 247

Try It! 1: Remember Details 248

Prepare: Determining What You Need to Remember 249

Organize: Relating New Material to What You Already Know 249

Work: Using Proven Strategies to Memorize New Material 250

Journal Reflections: What Sort of Memory Do I Have? 251

Try It! 2: Organize Your Memory 252

Try It! 3: Do It Yourself Acronyms and Acrostics 254

Try It! 4: Peg the Memory 257

Try It! 5: Visualize the Possibilities 259

Career Connections: Memory on the Job 260

Evaluate: Testing Your Recall of New Information 260

Rethink: Consolidating Memories through Repeated Review 261

Try It! 6: Remember Demain 262

Speaking of Success: Elaine Hudson 263

Looking Back 264

P.O.W.E.R. Portfolio: Keep It in Mind 264

Resources 265

The Case of . . . the Group of Seven 266

Part Four: Life Beyond the Classroom

10 Making Decisions That Are Right for You 267

Looking Ahead 268

Making Good Decisions:
A Framework 269

Prepare: Identifying Your Goals 269

Organize: Considering and Assessing
the Alternatives 270

Journal Reflections: My Decision Crossroads 271

Work: Making and Carrying out the
Decision 272

Career Connections: Weighing
Career Possibilities 273

Evaluate: Considering the Outcomes 275

Rethink: Reconsidering Your Goals and
Options 275

Problem Solving: Applying Critical
Thinking to Find Solutions 276

What's the Problem? 276

Strategies for Working on Life's
Messier Problems 277

Assessing Your Potential Solutions 279

Reflect on the Process of Problem
Solving 279

Don't Fool Yourself: Avoiding
Everyday Problems in Critical
Thinking 279

Try It! 1: Exercise Your Problem-Solving
Skills 280

Try It! 2: Fact versus Opinion 283

Try It! 3: What's Wrong with This Picture?
Identify the Faulty Reasoning 284

Speaking of Success: Jeff Goplin 285

Looking Back 286

P.O.W.E.R. Portfolio: Decision
Making and Critical Thinking 286

Resources 287

The Case of . . . Left Holding the
Lease 289

11 Making Academic Choices 291

Looking Ahead 292

Making Academic Choices 293

Prepare: Becoming Familiar with Your
Options and Requirements 293

Organize: Examining What You Have
Done and What You Need to Do 295

Try It! 1: Create a List of Course
Requirements 296

Work: Choosing Next Term's Courses 297

Evaluate: Deciding Whether You Are in
the Classes You Need 298

Try It! 2: Choose Your Courses 299

Rethink: Learning What You Love and
Liking What You Learn 302

Try It! 3: Reflect on Your College or
University Experience 303

Choosing a Program or Major 304

Try It! 4: Identify Major Attractions 306

Career Connections: Choosing a
Job That's Right for You 308

Dealing with Academic Failure—
and Success 309

Journal Reflections: Focus on Your Interests 309

Speaking of Success:
Dr. Anthony Brissett 311

Looking Back 312

P.O.W.E.R. Portfolio: Choosing Your
Courses and Major 312

Resources 313

The Case of . . . No Clear Decision 315

Looking Ahead 318

Becoming Comfortable in a
Multicultural, Diverse World 319

Race, Ethnicity, and Culture 319

*Try It! 1: Determine the Multicultural
Diversity of Your Campus Community* 320

Building Cultural Competence 321

*Prepare: Accepting Multiculturalism and
Diversity as a Valued Part of Your Life* 321

Career Connections: Cultural
Competence in the Workplace 322

*Organize: Exploring Your Own Prejudices
and Stereotypes* 322

*Journal Reflections: Thinking about Race,
Ethnicity, and Culture* 323

Try It! 2: Check Your Stereotype Quotient 324

Work: Developing Cultural Competence 324

*Evaluate: Checking Your Progress in
Attaining Cultural Competence* 327

*Rethink: Understanding How Your Own
Racial, Ethnic, and Cultural Background
Affects Others* 327

Building Lasting Relationships 328

Making Friends 328

Try It! 3: Define Friendship 329

The R-Word: Relationships 330

Communicating in Relationships 331

*Being a Good Listener: The Power of
Supportive Silence* 331

Loneliness 333

*It's Not Just Talk: Avoiding and
Handling Conflicts in Relationships* 334

Try It! 4: Switch "You" to "I" 335

*Changing Relationships: Surviving
Endings* 337

Try It! 5: Resolve That Conflict 338

Speaking of Success: Jenny Zhang 339

Looking Back 340

P.O.W.E.R. Portfolio: Getting Along
with Others 341

Resources 341

The Case of . . . Answering for All 343

13 Money Matters

345

Looking Ahead 346

Managing Your Money 347

Career Connections: Budgeting
on the Job 348

Prepare: Identifying Your Financial Goals 348

*Organize: Determining Your Expenditures and
Income* 349

Journal Reflections: My Sense of Cents 349

Try It! 1: Identify Your Financial Goals 350

Work: Making a Budget That Adds Up 353

Try It! 2: Determine Your Saving Style 355

Evaluate: Reviewing Your Budget 356

Rethink: Reconsidering Your Financial Options 356

Credit Cards 357

Try It! 3: Maintain Your Interest 359

*Try It! 4: I Know What You Did Last
Summer: Learn What Your Credit
History Shows* 360

Student Housing 361

Paying for Your Postsecondary
Education 362

*Identifying the Different Types of
Funding Available* 363

*Researching Possible Sources of
Financial Aid* 364

Applying for Financial Aid 365

*Try It! 5: Discover Your Personal Financial
Philosophy* 366

*Show Me the Money: Building a
Financial Philosophy* 365

Looking Back 368

P.O.W.E.R. Portfolio: Money Matters 354
Speaking of Success: Murray Baker 369
Resources 370

The Case of . . . Overdrawn,
Overwrought, and Over Her Head 372

14 Stress, Health, and Wellness 373

Looking Ahead 374
Living with Stress 375
*What Is Happening When We Are
Stressed Out* 375
Handling Stress 376
   Prepare: Readying Yourself Physically 376
   *Organize: Identifying What Is Causing
   You Stress* 377
   *Work: Developing Effective Coping
   Strategies* 378
   *Try It! 1: Assess Your Susceptibility to
   Stress-Related Illness* 378
   Try It! 2: Look for the Silver Lining 381
   *Evaluate: Asking Whether Your Strategies
   for Dealing with Stress Are Effective* 382
   Try It! 3: Use Progressive Relaxation 382
   Rethink: Placing Stress in Perspective 383
Keeping Well 383
Eating Right 384
Making Exercise a Part of Your Life 385
Getting a Good Night's Sleep 385
Career Connections: Anticipating
Job Stress 386

Staying Safe on the Job 387
Drug Abuse 387
Alcohol and Its Allure 387
   *Journal Reflections: College Drinking
   Experiences* 388
Nicotine 388
   *Try It! 4: Personal Styles: Consider Your
   Drinking Style* 389
Illegal Drugs 390
Sexual Health and Decision Making 392
   Try It! 5: Tap into Campus Resources 393
Preventing Unwanted Pregnancy 393
What You Can Do If You Are Pregnant 395
*What You Can Do to Avoid Sexually
Transmitted Diseases* 396
Date Rape 397
Speaking of Success: Krista Bailey 398
Looking Back 399
P.O.W.E.R. Portfolio: Stress, Health,
and Growth 400
Resources 400
The Case of . . . Grievous Bodily
Harm 402

Conclusion 403
A Final Word 403
Endnotes 404
Acknowledgments 405
Photo Credits 406
Index 408

Introducing *P.O.W.E.R. Learning: Strategies for Success in Higher Education and Life, Second Canadian Edition*

This Canadian text is designed to be used by students in first-year experience courses. For many students, the first-year experience course is a literal lifeline. It provides the means to learn what it takes to achieve academic success and to make a positive social adjustment to the campus community. If students learn how to do well in their first term of college or university, they build a foundation that will last a lifetime.

P.O.W.E.R. Learning provides a framework that students can begin to use immediately to become more effective students. Having taught first-year experience courses many times, we know this framework had to meet several important criteria. Specifically, it had to be:

- Clear, easy-to-grasp, logical, and compelling, so that students could readily see its merits.

- Effective for a variety of student learning styles—as well as a variety of teaching styles.

- Workable within a variety of course formats.

- Transferable to settings ranging from the classroom to the dorm room to the board room.

- Effective in addressing both the mind *and* the spirit, presenting cognitive strategies and skills, while engaging the natural enthusiasm, motivation, and inclination to succeed that students carry within them.

Based on comprehensive, detailed feedback obtained from both instructors and students, the Second Canadian Edition of *P.O.W.E.R. Learning: Strategies for Success in Higher Education and Life* meets these criteria. The book will help students confront and master the numerous challenges of the postsecondary experience through use of the P.O.W.E.R. learning approach, embodied in the five steps of the acronym *P.O.W.E.R.* (*P*repare, *O*rganize, *W*ork, *E*valuate, and *R*ethink). Using simple—yet effective—principles, *P.O.W.E.R. Learning* teaches the skills needed to succeed in college or university and careers beyond.

The Goals of the Book

P.O.W.E.R. Learning: Strategies for Success in Higher Education and Life, Second Canadian Edition **addresses five major goals.**

1. **To provide a systematic framework for organizing the strategies that lead to success.** First and foremost, the book provides a systematic, balanced presentation of the skills required to achieve student success. Using the *P.O.W.E.R.* framework and relying on proven strategies, *P.O.W.E.R. Learning* provides specific, hands-on techniques for achieving success as a student.

2. **To offer a wide range of skill-building opportunities.** *P.O.W.E.R. Learning* provides a wealth of specific exercises, diagnostic questionnaires, case studies, and journal writing activities to help students to develop and master the skills and techniques they need to become effective learners and problem solvers. *Readers learn by doing.*

3. **To demonstrate the connection between academic success and success beyond the classroom.** Stressing the importance of *self-reliance* and *self-accountability,* the book demonstrates that the skills required to be a successful student are tied to career and personal success as well.

4. **To develop critical thinking skills.** Whether to evaluate the quality of information found on the Internet or in other types of media, or to judge the merits of a position taken by a friend, colleague, or politician, the ability to think critically is more important than ever in this age of information. Through frequent questionnaires, exercises, journal activities, and guided group work, *P.O.W.E.R. Learning* helps students to develop their capacity to think critically.

5. **To provide an engaging, accessible, and meaningful presentation.** The fifth goal of this book underlies the first four—to write a student-friendly book that is relevant to the needs and interests of its readers and that will promote enthusiasm and interest in the process of becoming a successful student. Learning the strategies needed to become a more effective student should be a stimulating and fulfilling experience. Realizing that these strategies are valuable outside the classroom as well will provide students with an added incentive to master them.

In short, *P.O.W.E.R. Learning: Strategies for Success in Higher Education and Life* is designed to give students a sense of mastery and success as they read the book and work through its exercises. It is meant to engage and nurture students' minds and spirits, stimulating their intellectual curiosity about the world and planting a seed that will grow throughout their lifetime.

Achieving the Goals of the Book

The goals of *P.O.W.E.R. Learning: Strategies for Success in Higher Education and Life,* Second Canadian Edition are achieved through a consistent, carefully devised set of features common to every chapter. Students and faculty endorsed each of these elements. They include the following:

Chapter-opening scenarios.

Each chapter begins with a short vignette, describing an individual grappling with a situation that is relevant to the subject matter of the chapter. Readers will be able to relate to these vignettes, which feature students running behind schedule (Chapter 2), figuring out a way to keep up with reading assignments (Chapter 7), or facing a long list of French vocabulary words to memorize (Chapter 9).

Looking Ahead sections.

These sections provide a bridge between the opening vignettes and the remainder of the chapter and include orienting questions that lay out the chapter's objectives.

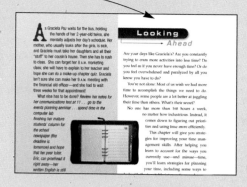

P.O.W.E.R. Plan.

Every chapter includes a figure that summarizes the key activities related to each step of the P.O.W.E.R. process for the major topic discussed in the chapter. The P.O.W.E.R. Plan figures are especially helpful to visually oriented learners.

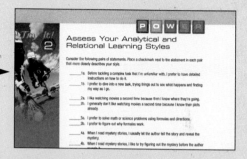

Try It! activities.

These sections, interspersed throughout the chapter, include written exercises of all types. These activities are keyed to one or more of the steps of P.O.W.E.R.; the relevant steps are indicated by highlighted letters at the top of each *Try It!* There are at least five *Try It!* activities in every chapter, and at least one of these is designated as an in-class, group exercise. Examples of *Try It!* exercises include "Assess Your Analytical and Relational Learning Styles" (Chapter 3), "Take a Test-Taking Test" (Chapter 6), "Discover Your Attention Span" (Chapter 7), and "Identify Your Financial Goals" (Chapter 13).

Speaking of Success.

Every chapter includes interviews with individuals who exemplify academic success. Many of these individuals have struggled to overcome difficulties in their personal lives or in school before achieving academic or career success. Students will be able to relate to or identify with the stories told by the people profiled in these sections; some accounts may inspire readers to realize their goals and aspirations.

Career Connections.

This feature links the material in the chapter to the world of work, demonstrating how the strategies discussed in the chapter are related to career choices and success in the workplace. Topics addressed in these sections include narrowing career choices, applying for jobs, and developing workplace listening skills.

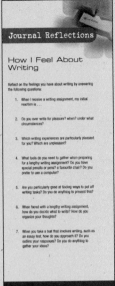

Journal Reflections.

This feature provides students with the opportunity to keep an ongoing journal, making entries relevant to the chapter content. Students are asked to reflect and think critically about related prior experiences. For example, the Journal Reflections in Chapter 8, "How I Feel About Writing," asks students to reflect on their feelings about the writing process and the one in Chapter 13, "My Sense of Cents" asks students to evaluate their financial savvy after performing a few simple but eye-opening exercises (e.g., "How much money do you now have in your pockets and wallet? [Guess first, and then look.] How close did you come?").

Running Glossary.

Key terms appear in boldface in the text and are defined in the margins. Key terms are highlighted in colour in the index.

End-of-chapter material.

Each chapter ends with a summary (Looking Back), organized around the orienting questions featured in the Looking Ahead section; a P.O.W.E.R. Portfolio section with suggestions for portfolio submissions; and an annotated list of student resources. These resources include campus offices, relevant supplemental readings, and World Wide Web sites. This material helps students study and retain important concepts presented in the chapter, as well as guiding future inquiry.

P.O.W.E.R. Portfolio.

Each section includes suggestions for submissions to a learning or skills portfolio. This feature allows students to compile a portfolio, which can be used as an evaluation tool for the whole course. Some submissions are revised and edited assignments from the chapters, for example, the Personal Mission Statement from Chapter 3. Students will be able to understand and learn the skills of developing a portfolio, an important tool in goal setting, evaluation, and career development.

Case Study.

Each chapter ends with a case study (The Case of . . .) to which the principles described in the chapter can be applied. Case studies are based on situations that students might themselves encounter. Each case provides a series of questions that encourage students to consider what they've learned and to use critical thinking skills in responding to these questions.

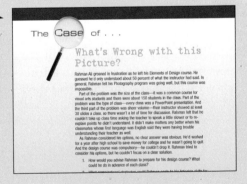

What's New and Updated in the Second Canadian Edition?

- Emphasis in *Chapter 1: P.O.W.E.R. Learning: Becoming a Successful Student* revised to focus on benefits of student success/first year experience courses, along with a discussion of ethics as it relates to plagiarism and academic responsibility.

- Goals-Setting Models revised and expanded in *Chapter 2: Making the Most of Your Time.*

- New section on Multiple Intelligences added in *Chapter 3*, including two new *Try It!* exercises.

- *Chapter 4: Using Technology for Information Management* revised to include more information on using technology and how it can help with your studies and research. Includes updated and expanded sections on e-mail etiquette, presentation programs, plagiarism, and distance learning.

- The section on note-taking styles in *Chapter 5* revised to include the Cornell Method. Other revisions include expanded sections on using laptops in class, and a new section on using Multimedia Technology (i.e. Power Points) for note-taking.

- *Chapter 6: Taking Tests* includes revisions to the sections on study groups, practicing tests, and failure with a new *Try It!* — Analyzing Returned Tests.

- Highlights in *Chapter 7: Building Your Reading and Listening Skills* include an updated Reading for Retention section with a discussion of Common Reading Problems.

- New *Try It!* on Evaluating Writing Styles added to *Chapter 8* to further practice the "Rethink" and "Evaluate" portions of the P.O.W.E.R. method. New section on Writing a Resume added, including a sample resume.

- *Chapter 9: Improving Your Memory* revised to include a new discussion on reviewing notes within 48 hours as a memorization method.

- New exercises added in *Chapter 10: Making Decisions That Are Right for You.*

- *Chapter 11: Making Academic Choices* revised to reflect that every academic institution has its own unique system for making academic choices. Links to online inventory websites have also been included.

- *Chapter 12: Getting Along with Others* revised and updated to include further discussion on race, ethnicity and culture.

- *Chapter 13: Money Matters* contains expanded information on credit card debt, child care and student loans, along with a brand new section on student housing.

- New section on stress added to *Chapter 14: Stress, Health and Wellness*, along with discussions of diet fads and alcohol (including a new feature, *Personal Styles Try It!* — "Considering Your Drinking Style")

- Nine new Speaking of Success features have been added, with others updated with new information on these Canadian success stories.

- All end of chapter resources revised and updated.

- The Case of ... feature has been revised in five chapters, with the feature in *Chapter 4* updated to address plagiarism.

P.O.W.E.R. Tools for Instructors and Students

The same philosophy and goals that guided the writing of *P.O.W.E.R. Learning: Strategies for Success in Higher Education and Life*, Second Canadian Edition have informed the development of a *comprehensive, first-rate* set of teaching aids. Through a series of focus groups, questionnaires, and surveys, we asked instructors what they needed to optimize their courses. We also analyzed what other publishers provided in the way of teaching aids to make sure that the ancillary materials accompanying *P.O.W.E.R. Learning* would surpass the level of support to which instructors are accustomed.

As a result of the extensive research that went into devising the teaching aids, we are confident that whether you are an instructor with long experience, or are teaching the course for the first time, this book's instructional package will enhance classroom instruction and provide guidance as you prepare for and teach the course.

Canadian Supplements and Services

An extensive selection of Canadian supplements is available to complement *P.O.W.E.R Learning*, Second Canadian Edition.

Your Integrated Learning Sales Specialist is a McGraw-Hill Ryerson representative who has the experience, product knowledge, training, and support to help you assess and integrate any of the below-noted products, technology, and services into your course for optimum teaching and learning performance. Whether helping your students improve their grades or putting your entire course online, your *i*Learning Sales Specialist is there to help you do it. Contact your local *i*Learning Sales Specialist today to learn how to maximize all of McGraw-Hill Ryerson's resources!

McGraw-Hill Ryerson offers a unique *i*Services package designed for Canadian faculty. Our mission is to equip providers of higher education with superior tools and resources required for excellence in teaching. For additional information visit http://www.mcgrawhill.ca/highereducation/iservices.

Instructor's Manual and Test Bank The Second Canadian edition of this manual contains suggestions for teaching each topic in the text, tips on teaching student success, handouts and transparency masters, audio-visual resources, sample syllabi, tips on the Web, and chapter quizzes.

Online Learning Centre (www.mcgrawhill.ca/college/power) The Instructor Centre includes provides vital support for learning and teaching online. Downloadable supplements such as CBC Videos, the Instructor's Manual and Power Point Slides are available. The Instructor Centre is password protected.

For students, the site includes interactive quizzes, weblinks, and CBC Videos, along with other useful study resources.

PageOut Visit www.mhhe.com/pageout to create a Web page for your course using our resources. PageOut is the McGraw-Hill Ryerson website development centre. This Web page-generation software is free to adopters and is designed to help faculty create an online course, complete with assignments, quizzes, links to relevant websites, and more—all in a matter of minutes.

In addition, content cartridges are available for the course management systems **WebCT** and **Blackboard**. These platforms provide instructors with user-friendly, flexible teaching tools. Please contact your local McGraw-Hill Ryerson *i*Learning Sales Specialist for details.

Full-Colour Customization The Second Canadian edition of *P.O.W.E.R. Learning* can be custom published for your course, either as a briefer text for shorter courses, or expanded with your own course material included. You can add a campus map, calendar, or anything else specific to your school, or readings, articles, or any other material you use in your course. Please contact your McGraw-Hill Ryerson *i*Learning Sales Specialist for details.

Workshops Workshops are available on a variety of topics, including student success, integrating technology into your course, and teacher training. Contact your McGraw-Hill Ryerson *i*Learning Sales Specialist for more information.

Additional Media Resources Available:

For a description of additional media resources available, such as CD-ROMs and video series, please go to the Online Learning Centre at www.mcgrawhill.ca/college/power.

About the Authors

To my students, who make teaching a joy.

Robert S. Feldman is a Fellow of both the American Psychological Association and the American Psychological Society. He is a winner of a Fulbright Senior Research Scholar and Lecturer award and has written some 100 scientific articles, book chapters, and books. His books, some of which have been translated into Spanish, French, Portuguese, and Chinese, include *Fundamentals of Nonverbal Behavior, Development of Nonverbal Behavior in Children, Understanding Psychology, 6/e,* and *Development Across the Life Span, 3/e.* His research interests encompass the study of honesty and truthfulness in everyday life, development of nonverbal behaviour in children, and the social psychology of education. His research has been supported by grants from the National Institute of Mental Health and the National Institute on Disabilities and Rehabilitation Research.

With the last of his three children starting college last fall—and facing the proverbial empty nest—Professor Feldman occupies his spare time with serious cooking and earnest, but admittedly unpolished, piano playing. He also loves to travel with his wife, who is also a college professor. He lives with her in a home that looks out on the Holyoke mountain range in Amherst, Massachusetts.

For Penny — artist, teacher, learner, friend, and milagro.

Sheila Chick teaches at Fanshawe College in London, Ontario, where she is a professor in the General Studies Division. She has taught communication, student success, popular culture, English as a Second Language, career development, and instructional design courses.

Sheila is a graduate of Toronto Teachers' College, the University of Western Ontario (King's College) and the University of Calgary, where her focus was on the use of portfolios for career development. Her areas of research and interest are in instructional design, workplace learning, and faculty evaluation.

An avid gardener, painter, traveller, and swimmer, Sheila lives in London, Ontario with her husband, Errol Cochrane, and daughter, Caitlin.

Acknowledgments

I am grateful to the reviewers for the Second Canadian edition for their insightful feedback on the changes necessary to serve Canadian learners well. I appreciate the time you took to carefully identify areas that needed attention and acknowledge those sections that worked. Knowing the busy and multi-tasking nature of your jobs, I am thankful for your opinions, experience, and knowledge.

Sue Adams, *Sheridan College*
Penny Biles, *Sheridan College*
Beverley Davies, *Niagara College*
Dawn Firth, *Sprott-Shaw Community College*
Dr. Denis Hlynka, *University of Manitoba*
Philip Jones, *Algonquin College*
Selia Karsten, *Seneca College*

Crystal Kotow-Sullivan, *St. Clair College*
Alexandra Pawlowsky, *University of Manitoba*
Penny Poole, *Fanshawe College*
Hyacinth Randall, *Seneca College*
Cynthia Riley, *Seneca College*
Frank Robbins, *Seneca College*
Harvey Starkman, *Seneca College (York Campus)*

I also appreciate the enthusiasm of the individuals profiled in the "Speaking of Success" features, for their interest in the book, their willingness to participate in the adapting and revision of P.O.W.E.R. Learning, and their great senses of humour. It was a delight to meet you all, personally or virtually, as a result of this project. Thank you to Dr. Roberta Bondar, Emm Gryner, Todd Currie, Shawn Thomson, Kofi Boateng, Asta Kovanen, Rachel Trail, John Lu, Elaine Hudson, Jeff Goplin, Dr. Anthony Brissett, Jenny Zhang, Murray Baker, and Krista Bailey.

I am also indebted to colleagues in the General Studies Division at Fanshawe College who have taught me many valuable lessons, especially about collegiality, teamwork, and communicating in an intense academic environment. Special thanks to Kim Cechetto for her friendship, honesty, and wisdom; to Penny Poole for her continued love and support; to Kim Dugan, Rita Terron, and Stephanie Ketley for their lessons of friendship; and Michelle Squire for continuing to be a fount of wisdom. A special thank you to my colleagues in the ESL Division. You make it fun to come to work each day!

My gratitude is extended to the McGraw-Hill Ryerson editorial and production team who have patiently shepherded this revision to completion: Leanna Maclean, Sponsoring Editor; Christine Gilbert, Developmental Editor; Jaime Smith, Supervising Editor; and Erin Moore, Copy Editor. The Media Technology team who develops and maintains the P.O.W.E.R. Learning website do a wonderful job and should be commended!

I am most grateful to all the students I have had the honour of teaching and learning from over the past 20 years at Fanshawe College. I consider myself lucky to have known you. I especially want to thank my second-language learners, who have taught me much about broadening my perspectives and informing my teaching to reflect the multicultural perspective that makes Canada so unique.

Finally, thanks to my friends and family, especially Errol, Cait, Max, and Billy.

Sheila Chick
schick@fanshawec.on.ca

Technology Solutions

Online Learning Centre

More and more students are studying online. That is why we offer an Online Learning Centre (OLC) that follows *P.O.W.E.R. Learning* chapter by chapter. You don't have to build or maintain anything and it's ready to go the moment you and your students type in the URL:

www.mcgrawhill.ca/college/power

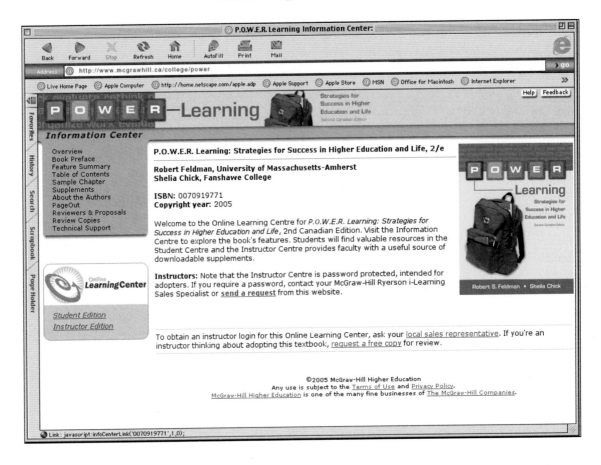

As your students study, they can refer to the OLC website for such benefits as:

- Study Quizzes
- CBC Video Segments
- Cross Word Puzzles
- Flashcards
- Chapter Outlines
- Weblinks

- P.O.W.E.R. Map
- Personality Type Explorer
- Interactive Exercises such as *Try Its* and Journal Reflections
- Glossary and Key Terms

Remember, the *P.O.W.E.R. Learning* OLC content is flexible enough to use with any course management platform currently available. If your department or school is already using a platform, we can help. For information on our course management services, contact your *i*Learning Sales Specialist or see "Canadian Supplements and Services" on page xvi.

P.O.W.E.R. Learning: Becoming a Successful Student

1

Why Go to College or University?

Journal Reflections: My School Experiences

P.O.W.E.R. Learning: The Five Key Steps to Achieving Success

Prepare

Organize

Work

Evaluate

Rethink

Are You Ready to Become a P.O.W.E.R. Learner?

Career Connections: P.O.W.E.R. Learning Meets the World of Work

Speaking of Success: Roberta Bondar

The Case of . . . No Clue

The first day of school started with a bang—literally. Miriam Motumba was easing out of bed, trying not to waken the baby, when *bang!*—she heard the door slam. Her 7- and 8-year-old sons were up and arguing already. Miriam had hoped to have a quick shower before making lunches and getting breakfast ready, but that hope was now dashed. She quickly separated the boys, sitting them at opposite ends of the room, and went to wake up her daughter. Miriam wondered whether she was doing the right thing. She had been out of school for 10 years and had four kids—two in school and two in daycare. Could she succeed in getting a decent education and providing a better life for herself and her kids?

As Kendra Jackson sat in her car, waiting for a parking space on her first day of classes, the car behind her suddenly bumped into her—bang! Already tense, afraid she would be late, and not even knowing where her classrooms were, Kendra burst into tears. The accident was minor, but Kendra took it as a bad omen. She didn't know whether she was doing the right thing by moving to the city and studying environmental technology. She knew her parents were counting on her, but right then Kendra wanted to go home and forget about college.

Jamie Stuart glanced up at the clock, wondering how much time was left in his night shift, as—bang!—the stamping machine came down on another sheet of metal. Jamie was on automatic pilot, having performed the same manoeuvre all night, and he stifled a huge yawn. He needed the extra shifts, because his student loan hadn't arrived yet, and he had to buy his paramedic textbooks, equipment, and uniform this week. Jamie had taken extra science courses to be accepted into the paramedic program, and he was excited about saving lives, but Jamie didn't know whether he could afford to stay in school.

As Jing Zhou struggled to find her bus pass on the crowded bus, she lost her grip on her coffee and—bang!—it fell to the floor, splattering everyone. Mortified, Jing tried to apologize, but she couldn't; all her English words had deserted her. Although she had been in Canada for a few weeks, her confidence when speaking was low. As she glanced at the strangers on the bus, she worried about how she was ever going to succeed in a school with English-speaking students. How was she going to make friends and feel included?

Looking Ahead

Whether academic pursuits are a struggle or come easily to you, whether you live on campus or commute, whether you are fresh out of high school or are returning to school years after high-school graduation, postsecondary education is a challenge. Student success courses are offered by a growing number of Canadian colleges and universities because the transition from high school or university is real and not always easy. You might think you don't need a student success course because you always did well in high school. Or perhaps you are a parent with children and so you know what is necessary to do well in school. Or perhaps you have been working for a while, and you know what it takes to be successful in the world of work. Think again! Student success courses help postsecondary students focus on proven strategies that assist them in this challenging transition.

P.O.W.E.R. Learning is designed to help you learn the most effective ways to approach challenges. It will teach you practical strategies, hints, and tips that can lead you to success, all centred on an approach to achieving student success: P.O.W.E.R. Learning.

This book presents information in a hands-on format. P.O.W.E.R. Learning is meant to be *used*, not just read. Write on it, underline words and sentences, use a highlighter, circle key points, and complete the questionnaires right in the book. Remember, this is a book to help you with your course work throughout your postsecondary career. Invest some time now. Mastering these learning techniques, making them second nature, will provide an enormous payoff.

After reading this chapter, you'll be able to answer these questions:

- **What are the benefits of a postsecondary education?**

- **What are the basic principles of P.O.W.E.R. Learning?**

- **How do expert students use P.O.W.E.R. Learning?**

Why Go to College or University?

Congratulations! You're in a community college, a university, an institute of technology, or a university college. Students in Canada have many options for higher education and the reasons for furthering their education are just as numerous. For Miriam Motumba, proving that she can succeed in school is almost as important as improving her socioeconomic situation. Kendra Jackson's parents want her to be the first in her family to get a college diploma, but in reality, the options in her small hometown are limited—she really doesn't know what else to do with her life. Jamie Stuart wants a better job; paramedicine will not only allow him to make more money than at his factory job, but will also give him a career with more action, variety, and excitement. Jing Zhou, a recent immigrant, wants to learn more about her adopted country and gain the academic skills necessary to succeed, and she wants to develop a different way of looking at things. Consider your own reasons for attending college or university as you complete Try It! 1, "Why Am I Going to College or University?"

Typically, improving opportunities for employment or making more money are part of most students' responses, and it's not wrong to expect that having a postsecondary education helps people find better jobs. The average person with a diploma or degree earns from 30 to 50 percent more each year than the average person with only a high-school education. As jobs become increasingly complex and technologically sophisticated, a postsecondary education will become more of a necessity.

But the value of a postsecondary education extends far beyond salaries. Consider these added reasons for pursuing a higher education:

- **You'll learn to think and communicate better.** Here's what one student said about his postsecondary experience after he graduated: "It's not about what you major in or which classes you take. . . . It's really about learning to *think* and to *communicate*. *Wherever* you end up, you'll need to be able to analyze and solve problems—to figure out what needs to be done and do it."[1]

  Education improves your ability to understand the world as it is now and as it will be. By helping you to develop your capacity for critical and creative thinking, education increases your abilities to think clearly and to communicate more effectively with others.

- **You'll be able to better deal with advances in knowledge and technology that are changing the world.** Innovations such as genetic engineering, drugs to reduce forgetfulness, and computers that respond to our voices illustrate how rapidly the world is changing.

  No one knows what the future holds, but education can provide intellectual tools that you can apply regardless of the specific situation in which you find yourself. You can't anticipate what the future holds, but you can prepare for it through a postsecondary education.

- **You'll be better prepared to live in a world of diversity.** Canada is changing rapidly. Our cultural mosaic includes people from many different races, religions, and ethnic backgrounds. You'll be working and living with people whose backgrounds, lifestyles, and ways of thinking are different from your own.

Why Am I Going to College or University?

Place a 1, 2, and 3 by the three most important reasons that you have for attending college or university:

_____ I want to get a good job when I graduate.
_____ My parents want me to go.
_____ I couldn't find a job.
_____ I want to get away from home.
_____ I want to get a better job.
_____ I want to gain a general education and appreciation of ideas.
_____ I want to improve my reading and study skills.
_____ I want to become a more cultured person.
_____ I want to make more money.
_____ I want to learn more about things that interest me.
_____ A mentor or role model encouraged me to go.
_____ I want to prove to others that I can succeed.
_____ I want to feel better about myself.
_____ I want to improve life for my family and me.
_____ I want to prove to myself that I can do it.
_____ I want to grow up.
_____ _____
_____ _____

What do your answers tell you about yourself? Did you think about these reasons when you filled out your application form? How do your reasons compare with those of your classmates?

The focus on multiculturalism in Canada, along with the fact that we live in a global society, necessitates a deeper understanding of other cultures. Culture provides a lens through which people view the world. You won't be prepared for the future unless you understand others and their cultural backgrounds—as well as how your own cultural background affects you.

- **You'll make learning a lifelong habit.** Higher education isn't the end of your education. If you make the most of college or university, you will develop a thirst for more knowledge, a lifelong quest that can never be fully satisfied. Education will build on your natural curiosity about the world, and it will make you aware that learning is a rewarding and never-ending journey.

- **You'll understand the meaning of your own contributions to the world.** You are poised to make your own contributions to society and the world. Higher education provides you with a window to the past, present, and future, and it allows you to understand the significance of your own contributions. Postsecondary education provides you with a compass to discover who you are, where you've been, and where you're going.

P.O.W.E.R. Learning
A system designed to help people achieve their goals, based on five steps: prepare, organize, work, evaluate, and rethink

_____

Now it's time to introduce you to a process that will help you achieve your goal of obtaining a college or university education, and help you succeed in life beyond school: P.O.W.E.R. Learning.

P.O.W.E.R. Learning: The Five Key Steps to Achieving Success

P.O.W.E.R. Learning itself is merely an acronym—a word formed from the first letters of a series of steps (see the P.O.W.E.R. Plan on the next page) that will help you take in, process, and use information you are exposed to in school. It will help you to achieve your goals, both while you are in school and after you graduate. The steps in P.O.W.E.R. Learning serve as a strategy for accomplishing what you want to—and sometimes have to—accomplish.

Prepare, **O**rganize, **W**ork, **E**valuate, and **R**ethink: that's it. It's a simple but effective framework that will increase your chances of success at any task, from writing an essay to purchasing groceries.

Keep this in mind: P.O.W.E.R. Learning isn't a product that you can simply pull down off the bookshelf and use without thinking. P.O.W.E.R. Learning is a *process*, and *you* are the only one who can make it work. Without your personal investment, P.O.W.E.R. Learning is just words on paper. You will have to supply the effort and practice to make it work for you.

Relax—you already know each element of P.O.W.E.R. Learning. You've graduated from high school and been accepted into college or university. You've also probably held a job, had a first date, and gotten your driver's licence. Each accomplishment required that you use strategies of P.O.W.E.R. Learning. What you'll be doing throughout this book is becoming more aware of these strategies and how you can use them to help you in school and beyond.

Prepare

Chinese philosopher Lao Tzu said that travellers taking a long journey must begin with a single step.

P.O.W.E.R Plan

Before they take that first step, travellers need to know several things: what their destination is, how they're going to get there, how they'll know when they reach the destination, and what they'll do if they have trouble along the way.

In the same way, you need to know where you're headed as you embark on the intellectual journeys involved in higher education. Whether it be a major, long-term task, such as graduating, or a more limited activity, such as getting ready to write a paper, you'll need to prepare for the journey. To see this for yourself, complete Try It! 2, "How I Can Benefit from My Student Success Course."

Setting Goals Before we seek to accomplish any task, we all do some form of planning. The trouble is that such planning is often done unconsciously, as if we are on autopilot. However, the key to success is to ensure that planning is systematic.

The best way to plan systematically is to use *goal-setting strategies*. In many cases, goals are clear and direct. It's obvious that our goal in washing dishes is to have the dishes end up clean and dry. We know that our goal at the gas station is to fill the car's tank with gas.

Other goals are not so clear-cut. In fact, often the more important the task, the less obvious are our goals.

Let's use taking a college or university course as an example. You probably have several goals for each course you are taking this term. To see this, complete the activity in Try It! 3, "Course Goals."

What's the best way to set appropriate goals? Here are some guidelines:

Long-term goals
Aims relating to major accomplishments that take some time to achieve

Short-term goals
Relatively limited steps toward the accomplishment of long-term goals

- **Set both long-term and short-term goals. Long-term goals** are aims relating to major accomplishments that take some time to achieve. **Short-term goals** are relatively limited steps you take on the road to accomplishing your long-term goals. For example, one of the primary reasons you're in a postsecondary institution is to achieve the long-term goal of getting a diploma or degree. But to reach that goal, you have to accomplish a series of short-term goals, such as completing a set of required courses, taking a series of elective courses, and choosing a major. Furthermore, even these short-term goals can be broken down into shorterterm goals. To complete a required course, for instance, you have to accomplish short-term goals such as completing a paper and taking several tests.

- **Recognize that who you are determines your goals.** Goal setting starts with knowing yourself. As you'll see when we focus on understanding yourself in Chapter 3, it is self-knowledge that tells you what is and is not important to you, and this knowledge will help you keep your goals in focus and keep your motivation high when things get tough.

How I Can Benefit from My Student Success Course

Academic journeys are similar to other major trips and they require the same sort of preparation. Think of the student success course as "The Lonely Planet Guide to Higher Education." Just as if you were planning to go to Nepal or Ecuador, some things you know; some things you think you know; some things you have heard about; and some things are totally foreign to you. Your student success course will help orient you to the new culture and expectations of postsecondary education. As you go through the table of contents, think about and identify:

What I Know	What I Think I Know	What I've Heard About	What's Totally New to Me
_____	_____	_____	_____
_____	_____	_____	_____
_____	_____	_____	_____
_____	_____	_____	_____
_____	_____	_____	_____
_____	_____	_____	_____

Attitude Check!
Just as your attitude can make the difference between a great trip and a disaster, the same is true at college or university. Is your attitude going to ensure your student success course is a positive experience? If so ... cool! If not ... adjust it!

Working in a Group: Compare your lists with others in your group. Discuss what you have learned, where you have learned it, how you used the learning, and your goals for this course.

- **Make goals realistic and attainable.** Someone once said, "A goal without a plan is but a dream." We'd all like to win gold medals at the Olympics or star in rock videos or write best-selling novels; few of us are likely to achieve such goals.

  Be honest with yourself. There is nothing wrong with having big dreams, but it is important to be realistically aware of what it takes to achieve them. If our long-term goals are unrealistic and we don't achieve them, the big danger is that we may wrongly believe that we are inept and lack ability and use this belief as an excuse for giving up. Instead, we should realize that the problem has less to do with our abilities than with poor goal-setting strategies. If goals are realistic, we can develop a plan to attain them, spurring us on to attain more.

- **State goals in terms of behaviour that can be measured against current accomplishments.** Goals should represent some *measurable* change from

Try It!

3

Course Goals

Think about one of the classes that you are taking this term. List as many goals as you can think of for taking the class:

_____

_____

_____

_____

_____

_____

_____

_____

_____

_____

The goals you've listed most likely range from the specific ("passing the class with a good grade") to the more general and vague ("becoming educated in the subject matter of the class").

Now, rank order them to determine which are the most important to you. Note that some of these goals may be short-term goals ("get a decent grade") and some represent longer-term goals ("complete all program requirements"). In addition, your goals may be specific ("get an A in the course") or relatively vague ("do well in the class").

What is the difference between those goals that are most important to you and those least important to you? Are your goals mostly short-term or long-term? How specific are your goals? What implications might your different goals have for your future success in the course?

Working in a Group: Compare *your* goals for the course with those of other students and consider the similarities and differences.

a current set of circumstances. We want our behaviour to change in some way that can usually be expressed in terms of numbers—to show an increase ("raise my grade point average 10 percent") or a decrease ("reduce wasted time by two hours each week"), or to be maintained ("keep in touch with my out-of-town friends by writing four e-mail messages each month"), developed ("participate in one workshop on critical thinking"), or restricted ("reduce my phone expenses 10 percent").

- **Ensure your goals involve behaviour over which you have control.** We all want world peace and an end to poverty. Few of us have the resources or capabilities to bring either about. However, it is realistic to want to work in small ways to help others, such as by becoming a Big Brother or Big Sister or by volunteering at a local food bank.

- **Take ownership of your goals.** Make sure that the goals you choose are *your* goals and not the goals of your parents, teachers, brothers, sisters, or friends. Trying to accomplish goals that "belong" to others is a recipe for disaster. If you're attending school only because others have told you to, and you have no commitment of your own, you'll find it hard to maintain the enthusiasm—not to mention the hard work—required to succeed.

- **Identify how your short-term goals fit with your long-term goals.** Your goals should not be independent of one another. Instead, they should fit together into a larger vision of who you want to be. Periodically, step back and consider how what you're doing today relates to the kind of person you would ultimately like to be. Complete the activity in Try It! 4, "Course Goals, Revisited."

A Word About Ethics

Ethics . . . academic honesty . . . character. During your college or university career, you will be faced with many choices. Just as your short-term goals lead to your long-term objectives, the small choices about everyday ethics—*Should I lie to my professor when my assignment is late? Should I take the easy way out and copy that section of a website to include in my essay? Should I blow off a team meeting for a project when I know everyone will get the same mark anyway?*—all contribute to your development as a nurse, a firefighter, a landscape architect, an engineer, a teacher, a journalist, a business manager . . . as a human being. As you prepare for your exams, write your essays, and work on your projects, don't forget about your character development.

> "After working a couple of years after high school, I realized that with no education, my growth in the company and as a person would be very limited. After completing my first year at another college, I had a better understanding of what I wanted out of a school, so I investigated the school I am currently at. I realized that it held the best options for me to learn and be involved with the sorts of things that I wanted to do."
>
> Paul Miles, Student, Sir Sanford Fleming College

O rganize

By determining where you want to go and expressing your goals in measurable terms, you have already made progress. Having a distinct destination will make clearer the various options you have for reaching it and will also help you know when you've arrived. You might think you're now ready to head out and begin the intellectual trip to student success, but there's another step you must take first. You now have to *organize* the resources you'll need to reach your goal.

The second step in P.O.W.E.R. Learning is to *organize* the tools you'll need to accomplish your goals. Building on the goal-setting work you've undertaken in the *preparation* stage, it's time to determine the best way to accomplish the goals you've identified.

How do you do this? Suppose you've decided to build a set of bookshelves for one room in your house. Let's say that you've already determined the kind of bookshelves you like and figured out the basic characteristics of the ones you will build (the preparation step in P.O.W.E.R. Learning). The next stage involves gathering the necessary tools, buying the wood and other building materials, sorting the construction supplies, and preparing the room for the shelving project—all aspects of organizing for the task.

Try It! 4

Course Goals, Revisited

Given the goal-setting guidelines we've discussed, let's revisit the goals that you listed earlier regarding a specific course in which you are enrolled. Rewrite each of those goals in terms that are realistic, measurable, and under your control.

_____

_____

_____

_____

_____

_____

_____

_____

_____

_____

_____

Do the goals, as restated, seem more or less attainable? Do the restated goals give you greater clarity into how you can achieve them? Are there any goals that now seem unattainable?

Working in a Group: Exchange your list of goals with your classmates and ask them to evaluate them on realism and measurability.

Similarly, your academic success will hinge to a large degree on the thoroughness of your organization for each academic task that you face. In fact, one of the biggest mistakes that postsecondary students make is plunging into an academic project—studying for a test, writing a paper, completing an in-class assignment—without being organized.

There Are Several Kinds of Organization On a basic level is organization involving the *physical aspects* of task completion. For instance, you need to ask yourself whether you have the appropriate tools for a project, such as pens, paper, and a calculator. If you're using a computer, do you have access to a printer? Is the printer working? Do you have disks to back up your files? Do you have the books and other materials you'll need to complete the assignment? Will the campus bookstore be open if you need anything else? Will the library be open when you need it?

Intellectual organization is even more critical. Intellectual organization is accomplished by considering and reviewing the academic skills that you'll need to successfully complete the task at hand.

For example, if you're working on a math assignment, you'll want to consider the basic math skills that you'll need and brush up on them. Just actively thinking about this will help you organize intellectually. Recalling and reviewing fundamental math skills, such as how to figure percentages and use decimals, will organize your thinking when you begin a new assignment. Similarly, you'd want to mentally review your understanding of the causes of the American Revolution before beginning an assignment on the relocation of United Empire Loyalists in what is now Canada.

Why does creating an intellectual organization matter? The answer is that it provides a context for when you actually begin to work. Organizing in advance paves the way for better learning of new material. The better your intellectual (and physical) organization for a task, the more successful you'll be.

Too often, students are in a hurry to meet a deadline and figure they'd better just dive in and get it done. Organizing in advance can actually *save* you time, because you're less likely to end up losing your way as you work to complete your task.

Much of this book is devoted to strategies for determining—*before* you begin work on a task—how to develop the intellectual tools for completing an assignment. However, as you'll see, these strategies share a common theme: success comes not from a trial-and-error approach but from following a systematic plan for achievement. Of course, this does not mean that there will be no surprises along the way, nor that sheer luck is never a factor in great accomplishments. It does mean that we often can make our own luck through careful preparation and organization.

College or university is not an endpoint but part of a lifelong educational journey.

W ork

You're ready. The preliminaries are out of the way. You've *prepared* and you've *organized*. Now it's time to actually do the work.

In some ways *work* is the easy part, because—if you conscientiously carried out the preparation and organization—you should know exactly where you're headed and what you need to do to get there.

It's not quite so easy, of course. How effectively you get down to business depends on many factors. Some may be out of your control. There may be a power outage that closes down the library or a massive traffic jam that delays your getting to campus. But most factors are—or should be—under your control. Instead of getting down to work, you may find yourself thinking up "useful" things to do—like finally hanging that poster that's been rolled up in a corner for three months—or simply sitting captive in front of the TV. This kind of obstacle to work relates to motivation.

Finding the Motivation to Work   "If only I could get more motivated, I'd do so much better with my _____" (insert *schoolwork, diet, exercising*, or the like—*you* fill in the blank).

All of us have said something like this at one time or another. We use the concept of **motivation**—or its lack—to explain why we just don't work hard at a task. But when we do that, we're fooling ourselves. We all have *some* motivation, that inner power and psychological energy that directs and fuels our behaviour and allows us to persist, even when the going gets rough. Without any motivation, we'd never get out of bed in the morning and accomplish anything.

Motivation

The inner power and psychological energy that directs and fuels behaviour

We've all seen evidence of how strong our motivation can be. Perhaps you're an avid basketball player and you love to practise after school and play on an intramural team. Or maybe your love of music helped you learn to play the guitar, making practising for hours a pleasure rather than a chore. Or perhaps you're a single mother, juggling work, school, and family, and you get up early every morning to make breakfast for your kids before they go to school.

All of us are motivated. The key to success inside and outside the classroom is to tap into, harness, and direct that motivation.

Thought of in this way, motivating ourselves becomes a little less intimidating. If we assume that we already have all the motivation we need, P.O.W.E.R. Learning becomes a matter of turning the skills we already possess into a habit. It becomes a matter of redirecting our psychological energies toward the *work* we want to accomplish.

Most of us have to learn how to do this, and that's where this book comes in. In a sense, everything you'll encounter in this book will help you to improve your use of the motivation that you already have. But there's a key concept that underlies the control of motivation—viewing success as a result of effort. *Effort is the cause of success.*

Suppose, for example, you've earned a good grade on your midterm. The instructor beams at you as she hands back your test. How do you feel?

You will undoubtedly be pleased, of course. But at the same time you might think to yourself, "Better not get a swollen head about it. It was just luck." Or perhaps you explain your success by thinking, "Pretty easy test."

If you often think this way, you're cheating yourself. Patting yourself on the back and thinking with satisfaction, "All my hard work really paid off," is sure to reinforce your future success. A great deal of psychological research has shown that thinking you have no control over what happens to you sends a powerful and damaging message to your self-esteem that you are powerless to change things. Just think of how different it *feels* to say to yourself, "Wow, I worked at it and did it," as compared with "I lucked out," or "It was so easy that anybody could have done well."

In the same way, we can delude ourselves when we try to explain our failures. People who see themselves as the victims of circumstance may tell themselves, "I'm just not smart enough," when they don't do well on an academic task. Or they might say, "Those other students don't have to work five hours a day." By making these kinds of excuses, they have disconnected themselves from their own motivation to do better.

The way in which we view the cause of success and failure is, in fact, directly related to our success. Students who generally see effort and hard work as the reasons behind their performance usually do better in school. It's not hard to see why: When they are working on an assignment, they feel that the greater the effort they put forth, the greater their chances of success. So they work harder. They

> "Education is not merely a means for earning a living or an instrument for the acquisition of wealth. It is an initiation into a life of spirit, a training of the human soul in the pursuit of truth and the practice of virtue."
>
> Vijaya Lakshmi Pandit

are positive thinkers, believing that they have control over their success. If they fail, they believe they can do better in the future. Failure just makes them try harder.

Here are some tips for keeping your motivation alive, so you can *work* with your full energy behind you:

- **Take responsibility for your failures—and successes.** When you do poorly on a test, don't blame the professor, the textbook, or a job that kept you from studying. Analyze the situation, and see how you could have changed what you did to be more successful in the future. At the same time, when you're successful, think of the things you did to bring about that success.

- **Think positively.** Assume that the strengths that you have will allow you to succeed and that, if you have difficulty, you can figure out what to do. Your attitude plays a major role in your success.

- **Accept that you can't control everything.** Sometimes things are out of your control. Seek to understand which things can be changed and which cannot. You might be able to get an extension on a paper due date, but you are probably not going to be excused from a requirement that all students must comply with.

To further explore the causes of academic success, consider the questions in Try It! 5, "Examine the Causes of Success and Failure," and discuss them with your classmates.

valuate

"Great, I'm done with the work. Now I can move on."

It's natural to feel relief when you've finished the work necessary to fulfill the basic requirements of an assignment. After all, if you've written the five double-spaced pages required for an assignment, why shouldn't you heave a sigh of relief and just hand in your paper?

The answer is that if you stop at this point, you'll almost be guaranteed a mediocre grade. Did Shakespeare dash off the first draft of *Hamlet* and, without another glance, send it off to the Globe Theatre for production? Do professional athletes just put in the bare minimum of practice to get ready for a big game?

In both cases, the answer is no. Even the greatest work does not spring forth as the embodiment of perfection.

Consequently, the fourth step in the P.O.W.E.R. process is **evaluation,** which consists of determining how well the work we have produced matches our goals for it. Let's consider some steps to follow in evaluating what you've accomplished:

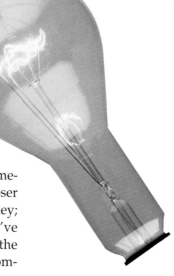

- **Take a moment to congratulate yourself and feel some satisfaction.** Whether it's been studying for a test, writing a paper, preparing a review sheet, or reading an assignment, you've done something important. You've moved from ground zero to a spot that's closer to your goal. Maybe you've reached the midpoint of your journey; maybe you're just about where you want to be. Whatever spot you've reached, the fact that you've already *prepared, organized,* and done the *work* means that you've navigated through many difficulties and completed the greater part of the journey.

Evaluation
An assessment of the match between a product or activity and the goals it was intended to meet

Try It! 5

👥 Working in a Group: Examine the Causes of Success and Failure

Consider, in a group, the following situations:

1. Although he studied for a few hours the night before the test, Jack gets a D on a midterm. When he finds out his grade, he is disgusted and says to himself, "I'll probably never do any better in this course. I better just blow it off for the rest of the term and put my energies into my other classes."

2. Chen receives an A– on her anatomy exam. She is happy, but when her instructor tells the class that they did well as a group and that the average grade was B+, she decides that she did well only because the exam was so easy.

3. Andy gets a C on his first math quiz. Because he didn't do as well as he had expected, he vows to perform better the next time. He doubles the amount of time he studies for the next quiz, but still his grade is only slightly higher. Distressed, he considers dropping the class because he thinks that he'll never be successful in math.

In a group, consider the following questions about each of the situations:

1. What did each student conclude was the main cause of his or her performance, and what effect will this conclusion probably have on the student?

2. Taking an outsider's point of view, what do *you* think was probably the main cause of the student's performance?

3. What advice would you give each student?

Now consider these broader questions:

1. What are the most important reasons some students are more academically successful in their postsecondary education than others?

2. How much does ability determine success? How much does luck determine success? How much do circumstances determine success?

3. If someone performs poorly on an exam, what are the possible reasons for that performance? If someone performs well on an exam, what are the possible reasons for that performance? Why is it harder to find reasons for good compared with poor performance?

- **Compare what you've accomplished with the goals you're trying to achieve.** Think about the goals, both short-term and long-term, that you're trying to accomplish. How closely does what you've done match what you're aiming to do? Focus on your short-term goal for the task, and see how close you've come. For instance, if your short-term goal is to complete a statistics problem set with no errors, you'll need to check the paper carefully to ensure you haven't made any mistakes.

- **Evaluate your accomplishments as if you were a respected teacher from your past.** If you've written a paper, reread it from the perspective of that teacher. If you've completed a worksheet, think about what comments you'd write across the top if you were that teacher.

- **Evaluate what you've done as if you were your current instructor.** This time, consider what you're doing from the perspective of the instructor who gave you the assignment. How would the instructor react to what you've done? Have you followed the assignment to the letter? Can you figure out which aspects of your work are particularly important? Is there anything you've missed?

- **Revise your work based on your evaluation.** If you're honest with yourself, it's unlikely that your first work will satisfy you. None of us can produce our best work initially. So go back to *work* and revise what you've done. Don't think of it as a step back: Revisions you make based on your evaluation bring you closer to your final goal. Going back moves you forward. Complete the activity in Try It! 6, "The Good and The Bad."

R ethink

They thought it was perfect, but they were wrong.

In fact, it was a $1.5 billion mistake. The finely ground mirror of the Hubble space telescope, designed to provide an unprecedented glimpse into the vast reaches of the universe, was not so finely ground after all.

Despite an elaborate system of evaluation designed to catch any flaws, the mirror had a tiny blemish that was not detected until the telescope had been launched into space and had started to send back blurry photographs. By then, it seemed too late to fix the mirror.

Or was it? NASA engineers rethought the problem for months, devising, and discarding, one potential fix after another. Finally, after looking at the situation with fresh eyes, they formulated a daring solution that involved sending a team of astronauts into space. Once there, they would install several new mirrors in the telescope, which would refocus the light and compensate for the original flawed mirror.

Although the engineers could not be certain that the $629 million plan would work, it seemed like a good solution, at least on paper. It was not until the first photos were beamed back to earth, though, that NASA knew their solution was successful. These photos were spectacular.

It took months of reconsideration before NASA scientists could figure out what went wrong and devise a solution to the problem they faced. Their approach exemplifies—on a grand scale—the final step in P.O.W.E.R. Learning: rethinking.

To *rethink* what you've accomplished earlier means looking at what you've done with fresh eyes. It includes using **critical thinking,** thinking that involves reanalyzing, questioning, and challenging our underlying assumptions. While evaluation means considering how well what we have done

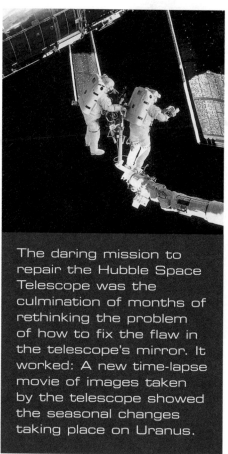

The daring mission to repair the Hubble Space Telescope was the culmination of months of rethinking the problem of how to fix the flaw in the telescope's mirror. It worked: A new time-lapse movie of images taken by the telescope showed the seasonal changes taking place on Uranus.

Critical thinking
A process involving reanalyzing, questioning, and challenging underlying assumptions

The Good and The Bad

Suppose your instructor asked you to write a paragraph about your best or worst moment in college or university so far. Write a first draft of that paragraph below.

_____

_____

_____

_____

_____

_____

Now, evaluate the paragraph you've written. Is the grammar correct? Is every word spelled correctly? Does the paragraph flow nicely? Did you use vivid language? Do you think your instructor will find it acceptable?

When you consider all these factors, you'll probably find the paragraph falls short of what you'd like it to be. Consequently, rewrite it below, trying to make it conform more closely to your ideal.

_____

_____

_____

_____

_____

_____

What things did you learn from the evaluation step that you didn't know before you did it? Does evaluation get you closer to the goal of perfecting the paragraph?

Working in a Group: Have a classmate evaluate your initial paragraph. How does your classmate's evaluation compare to your own?

matches our initial goals, rethinking means reconsidering not just the outcome of our efforts, but the ideas and the process we've used to get there.

We'll be considering critical thinking throughout this book, examining specific strategies in every chapter. For the moment, the following steps provide a general framework for using critical thinking to rethink what you've accomplished:

1. **Reanalyze, reviewing how you accomplished the task.** Consider the approach and strategies you used. What worked best? Are there any alternatives that might work better the next time?

2. **Question the outcome.** Take a "big picture" look at what you have accomplished. Are you pleased and satisfied? Is there anything you missed?

3. **Identify your underlying assumptions and challenge them.** Consider the assumptions you made in approaching the task. Are these underlying assumptions reasonable? If you had used different assumptions, would the result have been similar or different?

4. **Consider alternatives rejected earlier.** You likely discarded possible strategies and approaches before completing your task. Now's the time to think about those approaches once more and determine whether they might have been more appropriate than the road you followed. It's still not too late to change course.

Completing the Process The rethinking step of P.O.W.E.R. Learning is meant to help you understand your process of work and to improve the final product if necessary. But mostly it is meant to help you grow, to become better at whatever it is you've been doing.

- **Know that there's always another day.** Your future success does not depend on any single assignment, paper, or test. Don't fall victim to self-defeating thoughts such as "If I don't do well, I'll never graduate" or "Everything is riding on this one assignment." You almost always have an opportunity to recover from a failure.

- **Realize that deciding when to stop work is often as hard as getting started.** For some students, knowing when enough is enough is as hard as taking the first step on an assignment. Knowing when you have put in enough time studying for a test or have revised a paper sufficiently is as much a key to success as preparing properly. If you've carefully evaluated what you've done and have seen that there's a close fit between your goals and your work, it's time to stop work and move on.

Are You Ready to Become a P.O.W.E.R. Learner?

It's a bother. You've done things a certain way all your life, and it's worked reasonably well. It won't matter in the long run.

Are such excuses running through your head as you contemplate P.O.W.E.R. Learning? Are you thinking to yourself that P.O.W.E.R. Learning doesn't seem worth the effort and, even if it works with other people, it probably won't work with you?

Such thoughts are a natural reaction to being challenged. For most of us, change is uncomfortable, and when we're confronted with new ways of doing things, we may react with anxiety, defensiveness, fear, or even anger. Why? Because we're creatures of habit, and the feeling of familiarity we get from our routine style of doing things is as comforting as an old, worn comfortable pair of jeans.

Ironically, sometimes we may reject change because it can bring about more success than we're ready to handle. Some people have a **fear of success**—they are reluctant to excel and thus actively avoid getting into situations in which success is likely. (To determine whether you have a fear of success, complete Try It! 8, "Are You Afraid of Success?" on page 22.)

If you do fear success to some degree, you're not alone. Many people feel they don't deserve to do well. Some people who have already achieved

Fear of success
Reluctance to excel and avoidance of situations in which success is likely

Career Connections

P.O.W.E.R. Learning Meets the World of Work

Although success in higher education is about more than getting a good job, there is a lot of transferability between academic and career skills. The Conference Board of Canada's Employability Skills Profile 2000+ identifies key skills required in Canadian workplaces.[2] After looking at the list, complete Try It! 7 for a self-assessment of these important skills. Don't worry if your self-assessment isn't strong in all areas—these can become goals.

Fundamental Skills

You will be better prepared to progress in the world of work when you can

Communicate
- read and understand information presented in a variety of forms (e.g., words, graphs, charts, diagrams)
- write and speak so others pay attention and understand
- listen and ask questions to understand and appreciate the points of view of others
- share information using a range of information and communications technologies (e.g., voice, e-mail, computers)
- use relevant scientific, technological, and mathematical knowledge and skills to explain or clarify ideas

Manage Information
- locate, gather, and organize information using appropriate technology and information systems
- access, analyze and apply knowledge and skills from various disciplines (e.g., the arts, languages, science, technology, mathematics, social sciences, and the humanities)

Use Numbers
- decide what needs to be measured or calculated
- observe and record data using appropriate methods, tools, and technology
- make estimates and verify calculations

Think & Solve Problems
- assess situations and identify problems
- seek different points of view and evaluate them based on facts
- recognize the human, interpersonal, technical, scientific, and mathematical dimensions of a problem
- identify the root cause of a problem
- be creative and innovative in exploring possible solutions
- readily use science, technology and mathematics as ways to think, gain and share knowledge, solve problems and make decisions
- evaluate solutions to make recommendations or decisions
- implement solutions
- check to see if a solution works, and act on opportunities for improvement

Personal Management Skills

You will be able to offer yourself greater possibilities for achievement when you can

Demonstrate Positive Attitudes & Behaviours
- feel good about yourself and be confident
- deal with people, problems, and situations with honesty, integrity, and personal ethics
- recognize your own and other people's good efforts
- take care of your personal health
- show interest, initiative, and effort

Be Responsible
- set goals and priorities balancing work and personal life
- plan and manage time, money, and other resources to achieve goals
- assess, weigh, and manage risk
- be accountable for your actions and the actions of your group
- be socially responsible and contribute to your community

Be Adaptable
- work independently or as a part of a team
- carry out multiple tasks or projects
- be innovative and resourceful: identify and suggest alternative ways to achieve goals and get the job done
- be open and respond constructively to change
- learn from your mistakes and accept feedback
- cope with uncertainty

Learn Continuously
- be willing to continuously learn and grow
- assess personal strengths and areas for development
- set your own learning goals
- identify and access learning sources and opportunities
- plan for and achieve your learning goals

Work Safely
- be aware of personal and group health and safety practices and procedures, and act in accordance with these

Teamwork Skills

You will be better prepared to add value to the outcomes of a task, project, or team when you can

Work with Others
- understand and work within the dynamics of a group
- ensure that a team's purpose and objectives are clear
- be flexible: respect, be open to and supportive of the thoughts, opinions, and contributions of others in a group
- recognize and respect people's diversity, individual differences, and perspectives
- accept and provide feedback in a constructive and considerate manner
- contribute to a team by sharing information and expertise
- lead or support when appropriate, motivating a group for high performance
- understand the role of conflict in a group to reach solutions
- manage and resolve conflict when appropriate

Participate in Projects & Tasks
- plan, design or carry out a project or task from start to finish with well-defined objectives and outcomes
- develop a plan, seek feedback, test, revise, and implement
- work to agreed quality standards and specifications
- select and use appropriate tools and technology for a task or project
- adapt to changing requirements and information
- continuously monitor the success of a project or task and identify ways to improve

The Conference Board of Canada
Insights You Can Count On

Employability Skills Profile

Skill Area	Self-Rating	Demonstration and Evidence

Fundamental Skills
Communicate

1. I read and understand information in a variety of forms — 1 _____ 10
2. I write and speak so others pay attention and understand — 1 _____ 10
3. I listen and ask questions to understand and appreciate other points of view — 1 _____ 10
4. I share information using information technology — 1 _____ 10
5. I use knowledge and skills to explain or clarify ideas — 1 _____ 10

Manage Information

6. I locate, gather, and organize information using technology and information systems — 1 _____ 10
7. I access and apply knowledge and skills from various disciplines — 1 _____ 10

Use Numbers

8. I decide what needs to be measured or calculated — 1 _____ 10
9. I observe and record data using methods, tools, or technology — 1 _____ 10
10. I make estimates and verify calculations — 1 _____ 10

Think and Solve Problems

11. I assess situations and identify problems — 1 _____ 10
12. I seek different points of view and evaluate them on fact — 1 _____ 10
13. I recognize all dimensions of a problem — 1 _____ 10
14. I identify the root cause of a problem — 1 _____ 10
15. I am creative and innovative in exploring solutions — 1 _____ 10
16. I use science, technology, and math to think, gain and share knowledge, solve problems, and make decisions — 1 _____ 10
17. I evaluate solutions — 1 _____ 10
18. I implement solutions — 1 _____ 10
19. I check solutions and improve them — 1 _____ 10

Personal Management Skills
Demonstrate Positive Attitudes and Behaviours

20. I feel good about myself and am confident — 1 _____ 10
21. I deal with people, problems, and situations with honesty, integrity, and ethics — 1 _____ 10
22. I recognize my own and others' good efforts — 1 _____ 10
23. I take care of my personal health — 1 _____ 10
24. I show interest, initiative, and effort — 1 _____ 10

Be Responsible

25. I set goals and priorities, balancing work and personal life — 1 _____ 10
26. I plan and manage time and money to achieve goals — 1 _____ 10

(continued on next page)

Employability Skills Profile— Continued

Skill Area	Self-Rating	Demonstration and Evidence
27. I assess, weigh, and manage risk	1 ____ 10	_____
28. I am accountable for my and my group's actions	1 ____ 10	_____
29. I am socially responsible and contribute to the community	1 ____ 10	_____

Be Adaptable

30. I work independently or as part of a team	1 ____ 10	_____
31. I carry out multiple tasks and projects	1 ____ 10	_____
32. I am innovative and resourceful and seek alternative ways to get the job done	1 ____ 10	_____
33. I am open and respond constructively to change	1 ____ 10	_____
34. I learn from mistakes and accept feedback	1 ____ 10	_____
35. I cope with uncertainty	1 ____ 10	_____

Learn Continuously

36. I am willing to continuously learn and grow	1 ____ 10	_____
37. I assess personal strengths and areas for development	1 ____ 10	_____
38. I set my own learning goals	1 ____ 10	_____
39. I identify and access learning sources and opportunities	1 ____ 10	_____
40. I plan for and achieve my learning goals	1 ____ 10	_____

Work Safely

41. I am aware of personal and group health and safety practices and procedures, and act in accordance with these	1 ____ 10	_____

Teamwork Skills
Work with Others

42. I understand and work within group dynamics	1 ____ 10	_____
43. I ensure my team's purpose and objectives are clear	1 ____ 10	_____
44. I am flexible and respect the thoughts, opinions, and contributions of others in a group	1 ____ 10	_____
45. I recognize and respect people's diversity, differences, and perspectives	1 ____ 10	_____
46. I accept and provide constructive feedback	1 ____ 10	_____
47. I contribute by sharing information and expertise	1 ____ 10	_____
48. I lead or support where appropriate	1 ____ 10	_____
49. I understand the role of conflict in group decision making	1 ____ 10	_____
50. I manage and resolve conflict when appropriate	1 ____ 10	_____

Participate in Projects and Tasks

51. I plan, design, carry out, and complete projects	1 ____ 10	_____
52. I plan, seek feedback, test, revise, and implement	1 ____ 10	_____
53. I work to agreed quality standards	1 ____ 10	_____
54. I select and use appropriate technology for projects	1 ____ 10	_____
55. I adapt to changing requirements and information	1 ____ 10	_____
56. I monitor the success of a project or task and improve	1 ____ 10	_____

success feel they don't deserve it; instead, they believe their success was un-earned or unwarranted.

However, such negative thinking is inappropriate, and you should try and overcome the idea that you are unworthy of success. Becoming an accomplished student depends on your willingness to embrace success and to accept wholeheartedly the possibility of change in yourself. The techniques for doing this are in this book, but only you can implement them. The road to success may not be simple or direct, but few goals are more important in life than receiving a postsecondary education.

Looking
Back

What are the benefits of a postsecondary education?

- The reason first-year students most often cite for attending college or university is to get a better job, and postsecondary graduates do earn more on average than nongraduates.

- College and university also provide many other benefits. These include becoming well educated, understanding the interconnections between different areas of knowledge and our place in history and the world, and understanding diversity and multiculturalism.

What are the basic principles of P.O.W.E.R. Learning?

- P.O.W.E.R. Learning is a systematic approach people can easily learn, using abilities they already possess, to acquire successful habits for learning and achieving personal goals.

- P.O.W.E.R. Learning involves preparation, organization, work, evaluation, and rethinking.

Are You Afraid of Success?

Answer each of the following yes/no questions:[3]

1. I am sometimes afraid to do things as well as I know I could. _____ Yes _____ No

2. I never worry about the possibility of being disliked by others for doing well at something. _____ Yes _____ No

3. I sometimes do less than my very best so that no one will be threatened. _____ Yes _____ No

4. I often worry about the possibility that others will think I am a showoff. _____ Yes _____ No

5. I never worry abut the possibility that others may think I work too hard. _____ Yes _____ No

6. I would find it nerve-racking to be regarded as one of the best in my field. _____ Yes _____ No

7. I seem to be more anxious after succeeding at something than after failing at something. _____ Yes _____ No

8. I do not like competing with others if there is a possibility that hard feelings toward me may develop. _____ Yes _____ No

9. If I were outstanding at something, I would worry about the possibility of others making fun of me behind my back. _____ Yes _____ No

10. I worry that I may become so knowledgeable that others will not like me. _____ Yes _____ No

Scoring: Use the key below to score the assessment. Give yourself one point for each matching answer.
1. Yes; 2. No; 3. Yes; 4. Yes; 5. No; 6. Yes; 7. Yes; 8. Yes; 9. Yes; 10. Yes.

If you scored 5 or below, you have little fear of success and are ready to move toward becoming a more successful student. However, if your total score is greater than 5, you have some degree of anxiety about success.

Does your score surprise you? Do you think your fear of success may have hindered you in the past? How might your fear of success have developed during earlier stages of life? Can you speculate on ways that you might overcome your fear of success?

Speaking of Success

Roberta Bondar

B.Sc., University of Guelph; M.Sc., University of Western Ontario; Ph.D., University of Toronto; M.D., McMaster University; F.R.C.P. (Neurology), University of Western Ontario

Scientist, physician, astronaut, teacher, author, and photographer are just some of the careers that Dr. Roberta Bondar has held.

Dr. Roberta Bondar, Canada's first woman and first physician in space, has received more than 20 honorary doctorates and many prestigious awards, such as the Order of Ontario and the Order of Canada, for her accomplishments. She continues her tradition of achievement and excellence as a nature and landscape photographer. Her recent exhibit, *Passionate Vision*, a series of more than 100 photographs of Canada's 41 national parks, was created after two-and-a-half years travelling by plane, helicopter, skidoo, horse, canoe, car, and on foot in Canada's pristine wilderness.

Following her 1992 flight on the shuttle *Discovery*, Roberta returned from space with a desire to photograph the Earth, and to encourage others to love, respect, and protect our planet.

Although Roberta believes that passion and dreams are very important in achieving goals, she encourages students to remember the realities of life, which involve participating in certain ways, respecting social mores, and following required patterns. For example, in talking about realizing her own lifelong dream of becoming an astronaut, she says, "It wasn't just a dream to go into space. It was work. It was hard work. It was death-

UNIVERSITY of GUELPH

defying work. It was something that when I first had the dream, I would never have known I had to do all those things."

Speaking personally about challenges, Roberta says, "Our challenges define our strength. They make us identify the kinds of things that we find that are weak about ourselves and we have to address them because we cannot be the weakest link in the chain."

For Roberta, support systems are the most important things a young person can have when faced with challenges. She feels that choosing knowledgeable and wise people—whether as peers, role models, or mentors—is essential. She credits her success to her mother, Mildred Bondar, for being a teacher, a friend, and a mentor who was able to impart knowledge and deliver it with humour and passion. Roberta tries to emulate her mother, feeling that if you want someone to learn and remember, you must present the subject with passion and with truth.

Roberta has already set her next goal: *Passionate Vision II*, for which she is exploring and photographing Canada's newest national parks and other parts of the world. It's an admirable goal for someone who has already accomplished so much.

How do expert students use P.O.W.E.R. Learning?

- To *prepare,* learners set both long-term and short-term goals, making sure their goals are realistic, measurable, under their control, and will lead to their final destination.

- They *organize* the tools they will need to accomplish those goals.

- They get down to *work* on the task at hand. Using their goals as motivation, expert learners also understand that success depends on effort.

- They *evaluate* the work they've done, considering what they have accomplished in comparison with the goals they set for themselves during the preparation stage.

- Finally, they *rethink,* reflecting on the process they've used and taking a fresh look at what they have done.

P.O.W.E.R. Portfolio

Employability Skills

Using your information from Try It! 7, "Employability Skills Profile," begin developing an employability skills section for your portfolio. Look at the evidence and demonstrations you identified for each of the 56 skill areas and compile them for inclusion in your portfolio. Using goal-setting suggestions from this chapter, identify short-term goals for yourself in these areas and create specific plans of action to accomplish them. For example, Garry is a first-year student studying earth sciences. Scientific terminology is quite new for him, so he gives himself a 5.5.

I read and understand information in a variety of forms   1 _____ 10

Maintaining a B in Geology (multiple choice tests/flash cards)
- *GOAL B+ or A (next quiz – Fri) Improving scientific pronunciation (study group)*
- *GOAL B+ on oral presentation (2 weeks)*

By the end of the semester, Garry will undoubtedly be more confident in this area, as will you! At the end of this course, assess yourself again and see whether you've made any progress in developing your employability skills profile.

Resources

On Campus

If you are commuting to school, your first "official" encounters on campus are likely to be with representatives of the Student Affairs Office or its equivalent. The Student Affairs Office has the goal of maintaining the quality of student life, helping to ensure that students receive the help they need.

If you are living on campus, your first encounter will more likely be with representatives of the student residence. Their job is to help you settle in and orient you to the campus. Your residence also probably has student residential advisers living on every floor; they can give you an insider's view of life on campus.

During your first days of college or university, don't feel shy about asking whatever school representative you encounter questions regarding what you may expect, how to find things, and what you should be doing.

In future chapters you'll find specific information about which college officials you should turn to. Seek them out if you are experiencing difficulties. They are there to help you get the most out of your higher education.

In Print

Virginia N. Gordon and T.L. Minnick's helpful book, *Foundations: A Reader for New College Students* (Wadsworth Publishing; 2nd edition, 2001) includes articles and essays on the most important topics that a college or university student faces. A number of different perspectives are presented, fostering critical thinking.

Navigating Your Freshman Year (Students Helping Students Series), by Allison Lombardo (Natavi Guides; 1st edition, 2003) is a compilation of student advice to incoming college or university students on such diverse topics as budgeting, developing university-employee contacts, roommate ground rules, and writing your first college or university essay.

On the Web

The following sites on the World Wide Web provide the opportunity to extend your learning about the material in this chapter. Although the Web addresses were accurate at the time the book was printed, check the P.O.W.E.R. Learning website, <www.mcgrawhill.ca/college/power>, for any changes that may have occurred.

www.campusaccess.com
This site provides links to all the colleges and universities in Canada and contains many useful articles of interest for postsecondary students.

www.topachievement.com/articles.html
On this page, you'll find several articles on motivation and goal setting.

www.careerintern.ca/Career_Center/employability_portfolio.htm
This site houses a wealth of information on employability portfolios, including a dozen links to other employability portfolio sites.

The Case of . . .

No Clue

It was during the second week of classes that the questioning started. Until then, Roger hadn't thought much about his decision to attend a large community college in a Vancouver suburb. It had seemed like a good idea, and he was excited when he was accepted, but he couldn't really pinpoint why he was there.

That was becoming a problem. As he was walking to class, he began to think about all that had happened to him in the last few weeks. First-year orientation . . . meeting his roommate and trying to deal with his odd neatness . . . enrolling for classes . . . finding his way around campus . . . meeting a huge number of new people and trying to figure out where he fit in. Everyone else seemed to know what they were doing. Why didn't he?

It was overwhelming. He wanted to run that minute and call his parents and tell them to come pick him up. He needed to lie on his bed in his room where it was familiar and comfortable and try to figure out what he should do. Nothing seemed to make sense. He began to question his decision to attend college. What was he going to do with his life? The question made him feel even more overwhelmed. Did he really need a college diploma? With his computer skills, he could probably get a job right away. Hadn't his father's friend told him that he had a job waiting for him whenever he wanted it? At least then he'd be making money.

"Why bother?" he thought to himself. "What an expense, and what a hassle. For what?" He realized, to his surprise, he had no real clue as to why he was in college.

1. What arguments could you provide Roger as to the value of a college education?

2. Do you think that Roger's doubts are common? Do people often attend college or university without thinking about it very much?

3. What might you suggest that Roger do to help deal with his doubts about the value of higher education?

4. Why might a student's doubts about the value of postsecondary education be especially strong during the beginning weeks of school?

5. Do you share any of Roger's concerns about the value of higher education? Do you have additional ones? Did you think carefully about the reasons for attending school before you enrolled?

Making the Most of Your Time

2

Time for Success

Prepare: Learning Where Time Is Going

Journal Reflections: Where Does My Time Go?

Organize: Mastering the Moment

Work: Controlling Time

Evaluate: Checking Your Time

Career Connections: Career Planning

Rethink: Reflecting on Your Personal Style of Time Management

Speaking of Success: Emm Gryner

The Case of . . . Where Does the Time Go?

As Graciela Paz waits for the bus, holding the hands of her 2-year-old twins, she mentally adjusts her day's schedule. Her mother, who usually looks after the girls, is sick, and Graciela must take her daughters and all their "stuff" to her cousin's house. Then she has to rush to class. She can forget her 8 A.M. marketing class; she will have to explain to her teacher and hope she can do a make-up chapter quiz. Graciela isn't sure she can make her 9 A.M. meeting with the financial aid officer—and she had to wait three weeks for that appointment!

What else has to be done? *Review her notes for her communications test at 11 . . . go to the events planning seminar . . . spend time in the computer lab finishing her mature students' column for the school newspaper (the deadline is tomorrow) and hope that her peer tutor, Eric, can proofread it right away—her written English is still not perfect—meet with her group to rehearse their human relations presentation . . .* Graciela has a nagging suspicion something else needs to be done, but she can't put her finger on it.

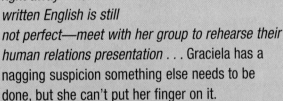

After waiting longer than expected, Graciela finally gets on the bus. Nikki, who wouldn't eat her breakfast this morning, is crying and Raquel is insisting that she didn't hit her sister. So much for collecting her thoughts on the bus. She has been up for a little over an hour and already Graciela is running way behind schedule.

Are your days like Graciela's? Are you constantly trying to cram more activities into less time? Do you feel as if you never have enough time? Or do you feel overwhelmed and paralyzed by all you know you have to do?

You're not alone: Most of us wish we had more time to accomplish the things we need to do. However, some people are a lot better at juggling their time than others. What's their secret?

No one has more than 168 hours a week, no matter how industrious. Instead, it comes down to figuring out priorities and using time more efficiently.

This chapter will give you strategies for improving your time management skills. After helping you learn to account for the ways you currently use—and misuse—time, you'll learn strategies for planning your time, including some ways to deal with the inevitable interruptions and counterproductive personal habits that can sabotage your best intentions.

We also consider techniques for dealing with competing goals. Special challenges are involved in juggling the priorities of college work with other aspects of life, especially when they include childrearing or holding a job.

After reading this chapter, you'll be able to answer these questions:

- **How can I manage my time most effectively?**

- **How can I better deal with surprises and distractions?**

- **How can I balance competing priorities?**

Time for Success

Without looking up from the page, answer this question: What time is it?

You've probably got some idea of the current time. In fact, most people are pretty accurate in their answer. If you don't know for sure, it's very likely that you can find out quickly. You may have a watch on your wrist; there may be a clock on the wall, desk, or computer screen.

Time is something from which we can't escape. Even if we ignore it, it's still going by, ticking away. Our lives are moving forward in time whether we choose to pay attention to it or not. So the main issue in using your time well is, "Who's in charge?" We can allow time to slip by and let it be our enemy, or we can take control of it and make it our ally.

By taking control of how you spend your time, you'll increase your ability to do the things you must do to be successful as a student. More than that, the better you are at managing the time you devote to your studies, the more time you will have to spend pursuing your interests.

We all know people who seem to be able to find time to do everything. Successful time managers make conscious choices about how they spend their time. Being in control of their time enables them to shape their future in the way *they* want, rather than feeling as if they are running around trying to keep up with a timetable set by others or by circumstance.

The goal of time management is not to schedule every waking moment of the day. Instead, the goal is to make informed choices as to how we use our time. Rather than letting the day slip by, largely without our awareness, the time management procedures we'll discuss can make us more aware of time's passage and better able to harness time for our own ends.

"I'm too busy going to college to study."

![P] repare: Learning Where Time Is Going

Before you get somewhere, you need to know where you're starting from and where you want to go. So the first step in improving your time management skills is figuring out how you're managing your time now.

What follows are some ways to figure out how you are now spending your time.

Create a Time Log "Where did the day go?" If you've ever said this to yourself, one way of figuring out where you've spent your time is to create a **time log.** A time log is the most essential tool for improving your use of time.

Time log
A record of how time is spent

Try It!
1

Create a Time Log

Keep track of seven days on a log like this one. Be sure to make copies of this sheet before you fill it in.

Day of the week and date: _____

	hygiene	food	classes	studies	work	TV	recreation	personal	sleep	social
12:00 A.M. (MIDNIGHT) to 1:00 A.M.										
1:00 A.M. to 2:00 A.M.										
2:00 A.M. to 3:00 A.M.										
3:00 A.M. to 4:00 A.M.										
4:00 A.M. to 5:00 A.M.										
5:00 A.M. to 6:00 A.M.										
6:00 A.M. to 7:00 A.M.										
7:00 A.M. to 8:00 A.M.										
8:00 A.M. to 9:00 A.M.										
9:00 A.M. to 10:00 A.M.										
10:00 A.M. to 11:00 A.M.										
11:00 A.M. to 12:00 P.M. (NOON)										
12:00 P.M. (NOON) to 1:00 P.M.										
1:00 P.M. to 2:00 P.M.										
2:00 P.M. to 3:00 P.M.										
3:00 P.M. to 4:00 P.M.										
4:00 P.M. to 5:00 P.M.										
5:00 P.M. to 6:00 P.M.										
6:00 P.M. to 7:00 P.M.										
7:00 P.M. to 8:00 P.M.										
8:00 P.M. to 9:00 P.M.										
9:00 P.M. to 10:00 P.M.										
10:00 P.M. to 11:00 P.M.										
11:00 P.M. to 12:00 A.M. (MIDNIGHT)										
Total Hours										

Analyze your log

After you complete your log for a week, analyze how you spend your time according to the major categories on the log. Add up the amount of time you spend on (1) hygiene (showering, brushing teeth, etc.), (2) food (cooking, eating, shopping), (3) taking classes, (4) studying, (5) work, (6) TV, (7) recreation and leisure (sports, concerts, exercise), (8) personal (writing, religious activities, family activities), (9) sleep, and (10) social (friends, dating, telephone). You can also create other broad categories that eat up significant amounts of time.

What do you spend most of your time on? Are you satisfied with the way that you are using your time? Are there any areas that seem to use up excessive amounts of time? Do you see some simple fix that will allow you to use time more effectively?

Working in a group: Compare *your* use of time during an average week with that of your classmates. What are the major differences and similarities in the use of time?

Figure 2.1

List of Priorities

Priority	Priority Index
Study for each class at least 30 minutes/day	1
Start each major paper 1 week in advance of due date	2
Hand in each paper on time	1
Review for test starting a week before test date	2
Be on time for job	2
Check in with Mom once a week	3
Work out 3 x/week	3

Set Your Priorities   By this point you should have a good idea of what's taking up your time. But you may not know what you should be doing instead.

To figure out the best use of your time, you need to determine your priorities. **Priorities** are the tasks and activities you need and want to do, rank-ordered from most important to least important. There are no right or wrong priorities; you have to decide for yourself what you want to accomplish. Maybe spending time on your studies is most important to you, or maybe your top priority is spending time with your family. Only you can decide.

To effectively manage your time in college or university, the best procedure is to identify priorities for an entire term. What do you need to accomplish? Don't just choose obvious, general goals, such as "passing all my classes." Instead, think about your priorities in terms of specific, measurable activities, such as "studying 10 hours before each chemistry exam." (Look at the example of a priority list in Figure 2.1.) Keep in mind that your program and course selection will determine many of your course priorities. Career-focused programs, such as engineering or nursing, will require many more in-class or lab hours than the average arts or humanities program. On the other hand, an arts course may require many hours of research time to effectively develop essays. Some courses are reading intensive; others are problem-based. However, to a certain extent, the nature of your courses will determine your priorities.

Write your priorities on the chart in Try It! 3, "Set Priorities." After you've filled out the chart, organize it by giving each priority a "priority index" number from 1 to 3. A "1" represents a priority that absolutely must be done. For instance, a paper with a fixed due date should receive a "1" for a priority ranking; carving out time to take those guitar lessons you always wanted to take might be ranked a "3" in terms of priority. The important point is to rank order your priorities to reveal what is and is not important to accomplish during the term.

Setting priorities will help you to determine how to make the best use of your time. No one has enough time to complete everything; prioritizing will help you make informed decisions.

Priorities
The tasks and activities that you need and want to do, rank-ordered from most important to least important

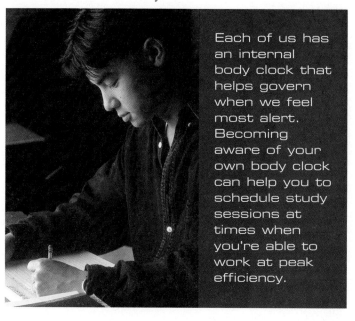

Each of us has an internal body clock that helps govern when we feel most alert. Becoming aware of your own body clock can help you to schedule study sessions at times when you're able to work at peak efficiency.

Set Priorities

Set your priorities for the term. They may include getting to class on time, finishing papers and assignments by their due dates, finding a part-time job that fits your schedule, and reading every assignment before the class for which it is due. Include only items that are important, not everything that you want to do. (For example, if you've always had a yearning to take a martial arts class but never got around to it before, it's reasonable to leave it off your list of priorities.)

To get started, list priorities in any order. Be sure to consider priorities relating to your schoolwork, other work, family, social obligations, and health. After you list them, assign a number to each item indicating its level. Give a "1" to the highest-priority items, a "2" to medium-priority items, and a "3" to the items with the lowest priority.

List of Priorities

Priority	Priority Index

Now redo your list, putting your number 1's first, followed by as many of your number 2's and 3's to which you feel you can reasonably commit.

Final List of Priorities

Priority
1.
2.
3.
4.
5.
6.
7.
8.
9.
10.
11.
12.

What does this list tell you about your greatest priorities? Are they centred around school, friends and family, jobs, or some other aspect of your life? Do you have so many "1" priorities that they will be difficult or impossible to accomplish successfully? How could you go back to your list and trim it down even more? What does this listing of priorities suggest about how successful you'll be during the term?

Identify Your Prime Time Take a look inward. Do you enthusiastically bound out of bed in the morning, ready to start the day and take on the world? Or is the alarm clock a hated and unwelcome sound that jars you out of a pleasant slumber? Are you the kind of person who is zombie-like by 10 at night, or a person who is just beginning to rev up at midnight?

Each of us has our own style based on some inborn body clock. Being aware of the time or times of day when you can accomplish your best work will help you plan and schedule your time most effectively. If you're at your worst in the morning, try to schedule easier, less-involving activities for those earlier hours. If morning is the best time for you, schedule activities that require the greatest concentration at that time.

> "Time moves slowly, but passes quickly."
>
> Alice Walker, *The Color Purple*

But don't be a slave to your internal time clock. Even night people can function effectively in the morning, just as morning people can accomplish quite a bit in the evening. Don't let your concerns become a self-fulfilling prophecy.

rganize: Mastering the Moment

Your time management preparation has brought you to a point where you now know where you've lost time in the past, and your priority list is telling you where you need to be headed in the future.

Now for the present. You've reached the point where you can organize yourself to take control of your time. Here's what you'll need:

- A **master calendar** that shows all the weeks of the term, seven days per week on one page. (See the example of a master calendar on the following page.)

- A **weekly timetable.** The weekly timetable is a master grid with the days of the week across the top and the hours, from 6 A.M. to midnight, along the side.

- A **daily to-do list.** Finally, you'll need a daily to-do list. The to-do list can be written on a small, portable calendar that includes a separate page for each day of the week. Or it can simply be a small notebook, with a separate sheet of paper for every day of the week.

- **Coloured pens or markers** so you can colour-code your schedules. Consider using different colours for classes, assignments, tests, study times, flex time, and so on, so it is immediately obvious how much time you have allotted to each activity.

The basic organizational task you face is filling in these three schedules. You'll need at least an hour to do this, so set the time aside. In addition, there will be some repetition across the three schedules, and the task may seem a bit tedious. But *every minute you invest now in organizing your time will pay off in hours that you will save later.*

Follow these steps in completing your schedule:

1. **Start with the** *master calendar,* **which shows all the weeks of the term on one page.** In most classes, you'll receive a syllabus, a course outline that explains what the course is all about. Traditionally, a syllabus includes course assignments and their due dates, and the schedule for tests that will be given during the term. Write on the master calendar *every* assignment you have, noting it on the date that it is due. If the instructors

Master calendar
A schedule showing the weeks of a longer time period, such as a college or university term, with all assignments and important activities noted on it

Weekly timetable
A schedule showing all regular, prescheduled activities due to occur in the week, together with one-time events and commitments

Daily to-do list
A schedule showing the tasks, activities, and appointments due to occur during the day

Master Calendar Sample

	M	T	W	TH	F	SA	S
	Sept. 1	8	9 Classes start	10	11	12 camping →	13
	14	Add/drop 15 ends	16	English 17 short paper due	18	19	20
	21	22	23	English 24 short paper due	Sociology 25 quiz	26	27
	28	29	30 Psych exam	OCT 1 Music quiz English short paper due	1st Psych 2 paper due	3	4
	5	Music 6 paper due	7	English 8 short paper due	Sociology 9 quiz	10	11
	Holiday! 12 Thanksgiving	13	14	Music quiz 15 English short paper due	16	17	18
	First-yr 19 seminar journal due	20	Psych 21 exam	English 22 short paper due Dad's bd-call	Theatre 23 Midterm	Bartending 24 job	25
	Sociology 26 midterm exam	English 27 midterm exam	28	Eng-short 29 paper due Music quiz	30	31	NOV 1
	2	3	4	English 5 short paper due	Sociology 6 short paper due	1	Darcey's 8 Wedding!
	9	10	11	Eng-short 12 paper due Music quiz	Sociology 13 quiz Psych exam	14	15
	First-yr 16 seminar group project due	17	18 Preregistration for next semester	English 19 short paper due	20	21	22
	23	24	25	26	27	28	29
	30	DEC 1 Music paper due	2	English 3 short paper due	Sociology 4 quiz	5	6
	First-yr 7 seminar final journal due	8	9	Music 10 quiz	Theatre 11 project due Psych exam Last day of class!!	12	13
	English 14 final exam	Theatre 15 final exam Sociology final exam	16	Psych 17 final exam	Music exam 18 MY birthday!	19	20

haven't included due dates, ask; they probably already know, or at least have a general idea of, the week that various assignments will be due. Pencil in tentative assignments on the appropriate date.

Don't only put assignments on the master calendar. Also include important activities from your personal life, drawn from your list of priorities. For instance, if you're involved in a club that is bringing a guest speaker to campus, mark down the date of the event. Finally, schedule some free time—time when you will do something that is just plain fun. Consider these days to be written in stone—promise yourself that you won't use them for anything else except for something enjoyable.

You now have a good idea of what the term has in store for you. In most cases, the first few weeks have few assignments or tests. But as the term rolls on—particularly around the middle and end of the term—things will get more demanding. The message you should take from this: *Use the off-peak periods to get a head start on future assignments.*

Completing a master schedule also may help you head off disaster before it occurs. Suppose, for instance, you find that six weeks in the future you have two papers due and three tests—all in the same week!

After cursing your bad luck, it's time to take action. Begin to think of strategies for managing the situation, such as working on the papers or studying in advance. You might also try to change some due dates. Instructors are far more receptive to requests for extensions on papers if the requests are made well in advance. Similarly, it might be possible to take a test later—or earlier—if you make prior arrangements.

2. **Now move to the *weekly timetable* provided in Figure 2.2.** Fill in the times of all your fixed, prescheduled activities—the times that your classes meet, when you have to be at work, the times you have to pick up your child at daycare, and any other recurring appointments.

Once you've filled in the weekly timetable, as in the one on page 39, you get a bare-bones picture of the average week. You will still need to take into account the specific activities that are required to complete the assignments on the master calendar.

To move from your average week to specific weeks, make photocopies of the weekly timetable that now contains your fixed appointments. Make enough copies for every week of the term. On each copy write the week number of the term and the specific dates it covers.

Using your master calendar, add assignment due dates, tests, and any other activities on the appropriate days of the week. Then pencil in blocks of time necessary to prepare for those events.

How much time should you allocate for schoolwork? One rough guideline holds that every one hour that you spend in class requires, on average, two hours of study outside class to earn a B and three hours of study outside class to earn an A. Do the arithmetic: If you are taking 15 credits (with each credit equivalent to an hour of class per week), you'll need to plan for 30 hours of studying each week to earn a B average—an intimidating amount of time. Of course, the amount of time you must allocate to a specific class will vary from week to week, depending on what is happening in the class.

For example, if you estimate that you'll need five hours of study for a midterm exam in a certain class, pencil in those hours. Don't set up a single block of five hours. People remember best when their studying is spread out over shorter periods rather than attempted in one long block

Figure 2.2

A Weekly Timetable Make a single copy of the blank timetable below. Then fill in your *regular, predictable* time commitments. Next, make as many copies as you need to cover each week of the term. Then, for each week, fill in the date on the left and the number of the week in the term on the right, and add in your *irregular* commitments.

Weekly Timetable

Week of: _____   Week # _____

	Mon	Tues	Wed	Thurs	Fri	Sat	Sun
6–7 A.M.							
7–8 A.M.							
8–9 A.M.							
9–10 A.M.							
10–11 A.M.							
11–12 A.M.							
12 (noon)–1 P.M.							
1–2 P.M.							
2–3 P.M.							
3–4 P.M.							
4–5 P.M.							
5–6 P.M.							
6–7 P.M.							
7–8 P.M.							
8–9 P.M.							
9–10 P.M.							
10–11 P.M.							
11 P.M.–12 (midnight)							

of time. Besides, it will probably be hard to find a block of five straight hours on your weekly calendar.

Similarly, if you need to write a paper that's due on a certain date, you can block out the different stages of the writing process that we'll describe in Chapter 8. You'll need to estimate how much time each stage will take, but you probably have a good idea from previous papers you've written.

Keep in mind that estimates are just that: estimates. Don't think of them as set in stone. Mark them on your weekly calendar in pencil, not pen, so you can adjust them if necessary.

But remember: It's also crucial not to overschedule yourself. You'll still need time to eat, to talk with your friends, to spend time with your family, and to enjoy yourself in general. If you find that your life is completely filled with things that you feel you must do and there is no room

Weekly Timetable

Week of: _9/28_   Week # _3_

	Mon	Tues	Wed	Thurs	Fri	Sat	Sun
6–7 A.M.							
7–8 A.M.							
8–9 A.M.							
9–10 A.M.	9.05 Psych	9.05 Music	9.05 Psych	9.05 Music	9.05 Psych		
10–11 A.M.		↓		↓			
11–12 A.M.		11.15 English		11.15 English			
12 (noon)–1 P.M.	12.20 Theatre	↓	12.20 Theatre	↓	12.20 Theatre		
1–2 P.M.	↓		↓				
2–3 P.M.							
3–4 P.M.	3.00 Sociology		3.00 Sociology		3.00 Sociology		
4–5 P.M.	First-year seminar	Work		Work			
5–6 P.M.	↓						
6–7 P.M.							
7–8 P.M.		↓		↓			
8–9 P.M.							
9–10 P.M.							
10–11 P.M.							
11 P.M.–12 (midnight)							

for fun, then step back and cut out something. Make some time for *your-self* in your daily schedule. Finding time for yourself is as important as carving out time for what others want you to do.

3. **If you've taken each of the previous steps, you're now in a position to work on the final step of organization for successful time management: completing your *daily to-do list*.** Unlike the master calendar and weekly timetable—both of which you develop at the beginning of the term—you shouldn't work on your daily to-do list far in advance. In fact, the best approach is to complete it just one day ahead of time, preferably at the end of the day.

List all the things that you intend to do during the next day. Start with the things you know you must do that have fixed times, such as classes, work schedules, and appointments.

Then add in the other things that you need to accomplish, such as an hour of study for an upcoming test; working on research for an upcoming paper; or finishing up a lab report. Finally, list things that are enjoyable—set aside time for a run or a walk, for example.

The idea is not to schedule every single minute of the day. That would be counterproductive, and you'd end up feeling as if you'd failed if you deviated from your schedule. Instead, think of your daily to-do list as a path through a forest. If you were hiking, you would allow yourself to deviate from the path, occasionally venturing onto side tracks when they looked interesting. But you'd also be keeping tabs on your direction so you would end up where you needed to be at the end and not kilometres away from your car or home.

As in the sample daily to-do list that follows, include a column to check or cross off after you've completed an activity. There's something very satisfying in acknowledging what you have accomplished. As you look at your to-do list with its checkmarks you will also feel a surge of energy, knowing you can get things done.

To-Do List	
for _9/28_ (date)	
Item	✔
Call Chris & get English notes	✓
Meet with Prof. Hernandez	✓
Do laundry	
Work on outline for psych paper	
Return books to library	✓
Call Nettie	
Set up meeting with music group	
Meet Deena	
Review Sociology	✓

Try It! 4

Build a Daily To-Do List

Copy the following blank to-do list as many times as you want or make your own. Then fill in your daily plans and commitments. As you complete them, check them off in the column on the right.

To-Do List	
for_____	
(date)	
Item	**✓**

W ork: Controlling Time

Time management is largely about preparation and organization; the work itself involves completing the activities that you need and want to complete. If you've prepared and organized carefully, you'll be ready to complete your work (see Try It! 4, "Build a Daily To-Do List).

In short, the work of time management is to follow the schedules that you've put together. But that doesn't mean it will be easy. *Our lives are filled with surprises:* Things take longer than we've planned. A friend we haven't spoken to in a while calls to chat, and it seems rude to say that we don't have time to talk. A crisis occurs; buses are late; computers break down; kids get sick.

The difference between effective time management and time management that doesn't work lies in how well you deal with the inevitable surprises.

There are several ways to take control of your days and permit yourself to follow your intended schedule:

- **Just say no.** You don't have to agree to every request and every favour that others ask of you. You're not a bad person if you refuse to do something that will eat up your time and prevent you from accomplishing your goals.

- **Get away from it all.** Go to the library. Lock yourself into your bedroom. Either place can serve to isolate you from everyday distractions and thereby permit you to work on the tasks that you want to complete. Try to adopt a particular spot as your own, such as a corner desk in a secluded nook in the library. If you use it enough, your body and mind will automatically get into study mode as soon as you seat yourself at it.

- **Enjoy the sounds of silence.** Although many students insist they accomplish most while a television, radio, or CD is playing, scientific studies suggest otherwise: We are able to concentrate most when our environment is silent. So even if you're sure you work best with a soundtrack playing, experiment and work in silence for a few days. You may find that you get more done in less time than you would in a more distracting environment.

- **Take control of your communications.** The telephone, e-mail, text-messaging, or instant messenger—who doesn't love to receive messages from others?

  We may not be able to control when communications arrive, but we can control communications until we are ready to receive them. Telephone calls can be stored on answering machines or voice-mail systems, cell phones can be turned off, and e-mail can be read later. If you wait until you have the time to take a message, you'll be able to follow your time management plans far better.

- **Let your fingers do the walking.** As an old advertisement for the Yellow Pages says, "Let your fingers do the walking." Many things can be done over the phone—or via e-mail or voice mail—rather than in person. It is much faster to do banking on the computer than it is to walk over, stand in line, and get waited on, or use the bank machine.

- **Expect the unexpected.** Interruptions and crises, minor and major, can't be eliminated. However, they can be prepared for. By making sure your schedule has some slack in it, you'll have the opportunity to regain time lost to unexpected events.

  Even more important, try to anticipate the unanticipated. How is it possible to plan for surprises? Keep an eye out for patterns. Perhaps one instructor routinely gives surprise assignments that aren't listed on the syllabus. Maybe you're asked to work extra hours on the weekends because someone doesn't show up.

  You'll never be able to escape from unexpected interruptions and surprises that require your attention. But by trying to anticipate them, and thinking about how you'll react to them, you'll be positioning yourself to react more effectively when they do occur.

> "Procrastination has no place if one is trying to reach a goal."
>
> Doug Tettman, Student, Langara College

- **Don't procrastinate.** Procrastination is like a microscopic parasite on your day, invisible to the naked eye, but eating up your time nonetheless.

  It's 10 A.M. You've just come out of your Statistics class. You know that there's going to be a test next week, and you've planned to go over the study notes you made last night. It's right there in your schedule: "10 A.M.—study Statistics." But you're thirsty after sitting in class, so you decide to go and buy yourself something to drink.

  As you head into the snack bar, you pass by the campus store, and you think about how you need to buy a couple of pens. After finding the kind of pen you like, you go to the checkout line. You pass by a rack of magazines, and, after leafing through a few, decide to purchase one. You can read it while you have your drink. You make your way to the cafeteria, buy a coffee, and sip it as you read the magazine.

Suddenly, half an hour has gone by. Because so much time has passed, you decide that it won't be worth it to start studying your Statistics notes. So you spend a little more time reading the magazine and then head off to your next class, which is at 11 A.M.

You can't control interruptions and crises that are foisted upon you by others, but even when no one else is throwing interruptions at us, we make up our own. **Procrastination,** the habit of putting off and delaying tasks that are to be accomplished, is a problem that many of us face. To identify whether you are a procrastinator, use Try It! 5, "Find Your Procrastination Quotient."

If you use the time management techniques that we've been discussing, procrastination should be minimized. But if you find yourself procrastinating, several steps can help you:

Break large tasks into small ones. People often procrastinate because a task they're seeking to accomplish appears overwhelming. If writing a 15-page paper seems nearly impossible, think about writing five three-page papers. If reading a 750-page book seems impossible, think of it as reading several 250-page books.

Start with the easiest and simplest part of a task, and then do the harder parts. Succeeding initially on the easy parts can make the harder parts of a task less daunting—and make you less apt to procrastinate in completing the task.

Work with others. Working with others who must accomplish the same task can help prevent procrastination. Just being in the same physical location with others can motivate you sufficiently to accomplish tasks that you consider unpleasant and on which you might be tempted to procrastinate. For instance, studying vocabulary words can be made easier if you plan a session with a study group. Beware, though—if you spend too much time socializing, you lower the likelihood of success.

Keep the costs of procrastination in mind. Procrastination doesn't just result in delay; it may also make the task harder than it would have been if you hadn't procrastinated. Not only will you ultimately have less time to complete the task, but you may have to do it so quickly that its quality is diminished. In the worst scenario, you won't even be able to finish it.

One antidote to procrastination is working with a study group. You'll be motivated by the presence of others who face the same challenges and assignments that you do.

Balance school and family demands. If you are a full-time student and full-time caregiver for children, time management is especially challenging. Not only do children demand—and deserve—substantial quantities of time, but juggling school and family obligations can prove to be more than a full-time job. Some specific strategies can help, however:

– *Provide activities for your children.* Kids enjoy doing things on their own for part of the day. Plan activities that will keep them happily occupied while you're doing schoolwork.

Find Your Procrastination Quotient

Do you procrastinate?[2] To find out, circle the number that best applies for each question.

1. I invent reasons and look for excuses for not acting on a problem.

    Strongly agree   **4**   **3**   **2**   **1**   **Strongly disagree**

2. It takes pressure to get me to work on difficult assignments.

    Strongly agree   **4**   **3**   **2**   **1**   **Strongly disagree**

3. I take half measures that will avoid or delay unpleasant or difficult tasks.

    Strongly agree   **4**   **3**   **2**   **1**   **Strongly disagree**

4. I face too many interruptions and crises that interfere with accomplishing my major goals.

    Strongly agree   **4**   **3**   **2**   **1**   **Strongly disagree**

5. I sometimes neglect to carry out important tasks.

    Strongly agree   **4**   **3**   **2**   **1**   **Strongly disagree**

6. I schedule big assignments too late to get them done as well as I know I could.

    Strongly agree   **4**   **3**   **2**   **1**   **Strongly disagree**

7. I'm sometimes too tired to do the work I need to do.

    Strongly agree   **4**   **3**   **2**   **1**   **Strongly disagree**

8. I start new tasks before I finish old ones.

    Strongly agree   **4**   **3**   **2**   **1**   **Strongly disagree**

9. When I work in groups, I try to get other people to finish what I don't.

    Strongly agree   **4**   **3**   **2**   **1**   **Strongly disagree**

10. I put off tasks that I really don't want to do but know that I must do.

    Strongly agree   **4**   **3**   **2**   **1**   **Strongly disagree**

Scoring: Total the numbers you have circled. If the score is below 20, you are not a chronic procrastinator and you probably have only an occasional problem. If your score is 21 to 30, you have a minor problem with procrastination. If your score is above 30, you procrastinate quite often and should work on breaking the habit.

If you do procrastinate often, why do you think you do it? Are there particular subjects or classes or kinds of assignments on which you are more likely to procrastinate?

🏃 ***Working in a Group:*** Think about the last time you procrastinated. Describe it as completely as you can. What was the task? What did you do rather than doing what needed to be done? What could you have done to avoid procrastinating in this situation? Ask others what strategy they might suggest for avoiding procrastination.

- *Make spending time with your children a priority.* Carve out "free play" time for your kids. Even 20 minutes of good time devoted to your children will give you and them a lift. No matter how busy you are, you owe it to your children—and yourself—to spend time as a family.

- *Enlist your child's help.* Children love to play "grown up" and, if they're old enough, ask them to help you study. Maybe they can help you clear a space to study. Perhaps you can give them "assignments" that they can work on while you're working on your assignments.

- *Encourage your child to invite friends over to play.* Some children can remain occupied for hours if they have a playmate.

- *Use television appropriately.* Television viewing is not all bad, and some shows and videos can be not just engaging but educational. The trick is to pick and choose what your children watch and not use TV as an all-purpose babysitter. *The Magic Schoolbus, Sesame Street,* and videos of children's classics, for example, can, for an hour or so, be a worthwhile way for children to spend their time while you study.

- *Find the best childcare or babysitters that you can.* The better the care your children are getting, the better you'll be able to concentrate on your schoolwork. You may still feel guilty that you're not with your children as much as you'd like, but accept that guilt. Remember, your attendance of college or university builds a better future for your children.

- *Accept that studying will be harder with kids around.* It may take you longer to study, and your concentration may suffer from the noise that kids make. But remind yourself what that noise represents: the growth and development of someone whom you love. One day your children will be grown, and without a doubt there will be times that you'll miss their high level of energy and activity.

- **Balancing school and work demands.** Juggling school and a job can be exhausting. Not only must you manage your time to complete your schoolwork, but in many cases you'll also face time management demands while you are on the job. Here are some tips to help you keep everything in balance:

  - *Make to-do lists for work, just as you would for your schoolwork.* In fact, all the time management strategies that we've discussed can be applied to on-the-job tasks.

  - *If you have slack time on the job, get some studying done.* Of course, you should never do schoolwork without your employer's permission. If you don't get permission, you may jeopardize your job.

  - *Ask your employer about flextime.* If your job allows it, you may be able to set your own hours, within reason, as long as the work gets done. If this is an option for you, use it. Although it may

Career Connections

Career Planning

There are 180 000 family-owned businesses in Canada, and more than 50 percent of the owners will retire in the next 10 years.[3] In addition, thousands of teachers, civil servants, managers, farmers, politicians, lawyers, nurses, military personnel, engineers, and others are retiring every year as the baby boomers age. Analysts are predicting shortages of skilled workers since not all workplaces are prepared for such massive changes. Studies show that most family businesses have no succession plan, meaning the owners don't have a process in place through which an heir or potential buyer will take over the firm. Early retirement caught the federal government by surprise when more people took buyouts than expected.

Succession planners suggest planning for transitions at least 10 years ahead. If your parents own a family business and you would like to take it over in the future, now is the time to start preparing. If your plans go in another direction, it is still a good thing to plan where you want to be in 10 years and start moving toward that goal.

> Liftking—a custom manufacturer of forklift and other heavy material handling equipment—is a thriving $30 million a year business operating all over the world. Louis Aldrovandi, the founder, wants to ensure that Liftking remains a family business. As a result, the leadership and ownership of Liftking will eventually transfer to his son Mark, the general manager. Mark Aldrovandi has a diploma in business from Ryerson Polytechnical Institute (now Ryerson University) in Toronto. He learned the business from the ground up, starting as a welder and working summers. Over the years, Mark has become familiar with the whole operation.

create more time management challenges for you than would a job with set hours, it also provides you with more flexibility.

– *Accept new responsibilities carefully.* If you've barely been keeping up with the demands of work and school, don't automatically accept new job responsibilities without carefully evaluating how they fit with your long-term priorities. If your job is temporary, you might want to respectfully decline substantial new duties or an increase in the number of hours you work. If you do plan to continue in the job once you're finished school, then accepting new responsibilities may be more reasonable.

– *Always keep in mind why you're working.* If you're working because it's your sole means of support, you're in a very different position from someone who is working to earn a bit of extra money for luxuries. Remember what your priorities are. In some cases, school should always come first; in others, your job may have to come first, at least some of the time. Whatever you decide, make sure it's a thoughtful decision, based on an evaluation of your long-term priorities.

E valuate: Checking Your Time

Evaluating how you use your time is pretty straightforward: You either accomplished what you intended to do in a given period, or you didn't. Did you check off all the items on your daily to-do list? If you go over your list at the end of every day, not only will you know how successful your time management efforts have been, but you will be able to incorporate any activities you missed into the next day's to-do list.

The check-off is important because it provides an objective record of what you have accomplished on a given day. Just as important, it provides you with

Figure 2.3
Building A Career Time Line

	Possible Career	Possible Career	Possible Career	Possible Career	Possible Career
	Child & Youth Worker	*Hotel Management*	*Information Systems Technology*		
Present–six months from now	Complete first term CYW program; pass courses; volunteer in community agency	Complete first term; investigate and apply for summer job in resort	Complete first term; pass courses; take electronics and computer engineering technology		
Six months– one year	Complete first year; complete school field placement; get summer job in kids' camp	Successfully complete first year; get summer job in a resort	Successfully complete first year; get job in computer-related environment		
Two years	Complete second year, and second-year placement; get summer job in field	Complete second year; apply for job in Britain; take Japanese classes	Complete second year; obtain diploma; apply to transfer to bachelor of applied systems technology program		
Three years	Graduate with a diploma in child and youth work	Graduate with diploma in hotel management	Major in network management; secure work experience placement		
Four years	Work in a group home for troubled teens; take courses in assertiveness and anger management	Work for hotel chain: concierge/front desk; apply for international experience: Europe	Graduate with B.A.I.; find job on network administration team		
Five years	Continue taking courses in counselling and family therapy; transfer credits toward B.S.W.	Assistant manager, medium-sized hotel; complete business degree (distance ed)	Take professional development courses as appropriate		
Six years	Apply for senior staff position; qualify to teach anger management courses	Assistant manager, resort hotel in major complex: Caribbean or Mexico	Apply for job as network systems manager; continue upgrading skills especially in area of security		
Seven years	Apply for job as program coordinator	Begin M.B.A.			
Eight years	Graduate with B.S.W.; start supervising students	Continue with international hotel management	Promotion to regional manager, protocol analysis and security		
Nine years	Begin private practice	Graduate with M.B.A.	Apply for national position, network architect		
Ten years		Manager, major hotel chain			

concrete reinforcement for completing the task. As we have noted, there are few things more satisfying than gazing at a to-do list with a significant number of checkmarks.

Of course, you won't always accomplish every item on your to-do list. That's not surprising, nor even particularly bad, especially if you've included some second-level and third-level priorities that you don't absolutely have to accomplish and that you may not really have expected you'd have time for anyway.

Rethink: Reflecting on Your Personal Style of Time Management

At the end of the day, after you've evaluated how well you've followed your time management plan and how much you've accomplished, it's time to rethink where you are. Maybe you've accomplished everything you set out to do, every task for the day is completed, and every item on your to-do list has a checkmark next to it.

Or maybe you have the opposite result. Your day has been a shambles, and you feel as if nothing has been accomplished. Because of a constant series of interruptions and chance events, you've been unable to make headway on your list.

Or—most likely—you find yourself somewhere in between these two extremes. Some tasks got done, while others are still hanging over you. Now is the time to rethink in a broad sense how you manage your time. See Figure 2.3 for building a career time line.

Reconsider Your Personal Style of Time Management We've outlined one method of time management (summarized in the P.O.W.E.R. Plan to the left). Although it works well for most people, it isn't for everyone. Some people just can't bring themselves to be so structured and scheduled. They feel confined by to-do lists.

If you're one of the those people, you don't need to follow the suggestions presented in this chapter exactly. In fact, if you go to any office supply store or your campus bookstore, you'll find lots of other aids to time management. Many publishing companies produce elaborate planners, such as Day-Timer. Similarly, software companies produce computerized time management software, such as Microsoft's Outlook and the Lotus Organizer, and some time management systems are on the World Wide Web (see the Resources section at the end of this chapter or the Online Learning Centre).

Whatever system you choose, the important thing is that you need to pay attention to how you use your time and follow *some* time management strategy. It might consist of jotting down due dates, and then each day looking at them and figuring out what to do that day. It might consist of visualizing yourself completing the tasks you need to and using that visualization to guide your behaviour each day. Or perhaps it might mean working on assignments as soon as you get them. Rather than waiting until the last minute, try to accomplish your work as soon as you know it needs to be done.

Whatever approach to time management you choose, it will work best if it is compatible with your own personal values and strengths. Keep experimenting until you find an approach that works for you.

Consider Doing Less If you keep falling behind, do less. Sometimes we just have so much to do that, even with the best time management

PREPARE
Learn where time is going

ORGANIZE
Use a master calendar, weekly timetable, and daily to-do list

WORK
Follow the schedules you've put together

EVALUATE
Keep track of your short-term and long-term accomplishments

RETHINK
Reflect on your personal style of time management

P.O.W.E.R. Plan

Managing your time effectively will allow you to spend more of it doing the things that are important to you.

skills in the world, we could never accomplish everything. A day has only 24 hours, and we need to sleep for about a third of the time. In the remaining hours, it is simply impossible to carry a full load of classes *and* work full-time *and* care for a child *and* still have some time left to have a normal life.

Consequently, if you consistently fall behind in your work, it may be that you are just doing too much. Reassess your goals and your priorities, and make choices. Determine what is most important to you. It's better to accomplish less, if it is accomplished well, than to accomplish more, but poorly.

Do More If you consistently accomplish everything you want to do and still have time on your hands, do more. Although it is a problem that many of us would envy, some people have too much time on their hands. Their classes may not be demanding, or work commitments may suddenly lessen. Or perhaps a child for whom they are caring begins to attend school full time. In such situations, they may suddenly feel as if their life is proceeding at a more leisurely pace than before.

If this happens to you, there are several responses you might consider. One is to simply relax and enjoy your more unhurried existence. There is much to be said for having time to let your thoughts wander. We need to take time out to enjoy our friends, exercise, or consider the spiritual side of our lives.

"Our costliest expenditure is time."

Theophrastus, quoted in Diogenes Laertius, *Lives and Opinions of Eminent Philosophers*

If you consistently have more time than you know what to do with, rethink how to make use of your time. Reflect on what you want to accomplish with your life, and add some activities that will help you reach your goals. For example, consider becoming involved in an extracurricular activity. Think about volunteering your time to needy individuals and organizations. Consider taking an extra course next term.

But whatever you decide to do, make it a decision. Don't let the time slip away. Once it's gone, it's gone forever. Think of time as a valuable natural resource that should be conserved.

Speaking of Success

Emm Gryner

*Music Industry Arts Diploma,
Fanshawe College, London, Ontario*

Passionate. Creative. Talented. Artistic. Independent. Business-woman. All these words describe Emm Gryner who writes, records, and performs music, as well as runs her own independent label, *Dead Daisy Records*. Emm has released six albums to date and been nominated twice for a Juno award. She was part of the women's music festival, Lilith Fair, and has toured with big-name artists like David Bowie, Jann Arden, Ron Sexsmith, and the Cardigans. However, she has also established a reputation as a musician who is fiercely independent and maintains a strong connection with her fans through an online journal she has written for several years as well as performing in living room shows and smaller venue concerts.

Emm states that being in charge of the business side of the music business is challenging and requires a lot of dedication and responsibility. However, Emm thrives on work, and as president of her own label, she appreciates having artistic control and knows that when something is done, it is done to her liking.

Emm's solid work ethic and do-it-yourself attitude were instilled at an early age by her parents, who run an independent newspaper in

FANSHAWE COLLEGE

Forest, Ontario. A love of music also developed while she lived in Forest. Emm took piano lessons from the age of 5, and by the time she was a teenager she was also playing the bass, writing songs, and recording her own music. After high school, Emm was accepted into Fanshawe College's renowned Music Industry Arts program where she learned more about the production side of the music industry as well as the business side, focusing on topics such as contracts, royalties, copyright, and record marketing and promotion. It was a good background for Emm, who recorded with Mercury Records from 1997–1999, until a corporate takeover ended her deal with the big record company. Since then, with Dead Daisy Records, Emm has been self-directed and self-reliant in her career, saying that she is happy she can create the music she wants without interference from others and so far it's working out well.

How can I manage my time most effectively?

- Decide to take control of your time.

- Become aware of the way you currently use your time.

- Set clear priorities.

- Use such time management tools as a master calendar, a weekly time-table, and a daily to-do list.

How can I better deal with surprises and distractions?

- Deal with surprises by saying no, getting away from it all, working in silence, taking control of communications, using the telephone or computer to conduct transactions, and leaving slack in your schedule to accommodate the unexpected.

- Avoid procrastination by breaking large tasks into smaller ones, starting with the easiest parts of a task first, working with other people, and calculating the true costs of procrastination.

How can I balance competing priorities?

- You *can* balance competing priorities if you begin to see how they co-exist. Manage work time carefully, use slack time on the job to perform school assignments (if permitted), use flextime, accept new responsibilities thoughtfully, and assign the proper priority to work.

P.O.W.E.R. Portfolio

Goal-Setting Models

First, research an occupation of interest to you. Find out as much as you can about what is required academically and personally. Include the employability skills the Conference Board of Canada states are crucial for every employee as well as the skills and training that are specific to the career you are researching.

Second, do a gap analysis. Assess where you stand today and where you want to go. Identify what you need to do to bridge those gaps and set some short-term and long-term goals for yourself. Be sure that your goals are reasonable, attainable, controllable, measurable, and your own.

The models on the following pages are useful for focusing on goal setting. Choose the model that best suits your learning style. Once the model is complete, develop an action plan, and start to put it to work. Be sure to include these activities in your daily planner. By identifying these activities, and writing them down, you create an intention—a commitment to your plan—and begin to work on accomplishing your goals.

Include the model and your action plan in your portfolio as evidence of your project management, time management, goal-setting, and critical thinking skills.

Lateral Bubble Chart
Student: J.C.
Program: Year 1, Business Marketing
Goal: Corporate Communications and Public Relations

J.C.'s long-term goal is to be a corporate communications director for a large sports-affiliated organization. He knows he is in the right program, business marketing, but he also knows there are a limited number of sports-related jobs in Canada. To increase his chances of being hired by an NHL franchise or a major sports venue, J.C. is aware that he needs to work on his marketability. J.C. uses a bubble chart to determine his skills and portfolio inclusions and to set some personal goals. Finally, he prioritizes these goals so he knows which goals to begin working towards right away.

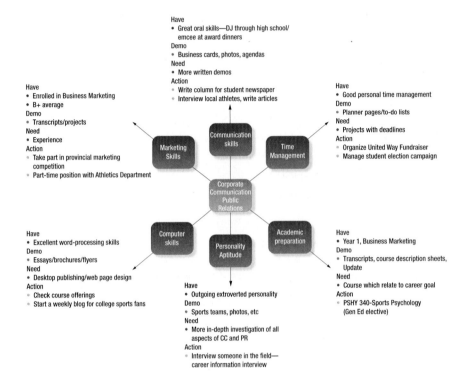

If, when considering your own goals, this approach to goal-setting is helpful, create your own bubble chart and identify your priorities.

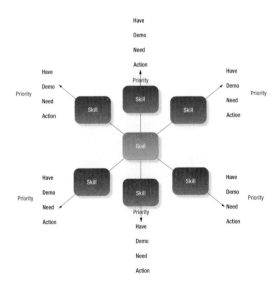

Linear Outline
Student: Quanh
Program: Year 1, Pre-Health Science
Goal: Nursing, Occupational Therapy, or Geriatric Social Worker

Quanh isn't sure what specific field she is going into, but she does know she wants to work with seniors and probably in a health-related field. While she knows that getting high marks is a given, she also knows there will be a lot of nurses retiring in the next few years. Also many facilities will consider her bilingualism (English and Vietnamese) as a real asset. To assess her skills and set some goals, Quanh creates an outline.

Skills	I Have/Proof	Need/Action/To do by
Academic	*Have:* Enrolled in pre-health science *Proof:* Course outlines and transcripts	Need: A's and B's in all subjects Action: Get a physics tutor To do by: Two weeks
Teamwork	*Have:* Sports experience *Proof:* Badminton team photo	Need: Academic team/group experience Action: Join/form study group To do by: End of the week
Communication	*Have:* Good written skills *Proof:* First Psych essay "B"	Need: Stronger oral skills Action: Join Toastmasters To do by: End of semester
Community Service	*Have:* Volunteer work at nursing home *Proof:* Reference letter from volunteer coordinator	Need: Medical setting experience Action: Volunteer at Red Cross To do by: This afternoon

If the linear approach suits you, consider your goals and your skills and strengths and create an outline for yourself.

Skills	I Have/Proof	Need/Action/To do by
	Have: *Proof:*	Need: Action: To do by:
	Have: *Proof:*	Need: Action: To do by:
	Have: *Proof:*	Need: Action: To do by:
	Have: *Proof:*	Need: Action: To do by:

Goal-Setting Chart

Student: Chris
Program: Year 1, Police Foundations
Goal: Police Officer

Chris has wanted to be in law enforcement ever since he met a police officer investigating a break-in at his family's home. While Chris feels confident he is on the right track, he knows there is a lot of competition to get hired. So, Chris uses a graph to see all the aspects of his future career and to see how he measures up. After assessing his employability skills and career specific abilities, Chris has an idea of the goals he needs to set for himself to improve his chances of being hired once he graduates.

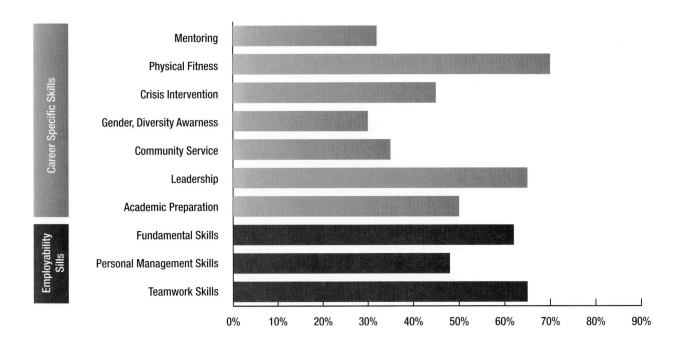

Once Chris completes his assessment, he has a clearer idea of his strengths and his areas of focus. He can identify demonstrations to prove his skills and decide what to include in his portfolio. For example:

Skill:	Have:	Proof for portfolio:	Need:	Goals:	Date to start:

Communication	Excellent oral communication skills	• Telemarketer for Oracle (two years)
		  – two awards for customer service (scan and print awards)
		  – three raises this year (photocopy letters)
			Cross-cultural communication	• Take SOSC255: Cross-Cultural Issues
				• Volunteer as a conversation partner for an international student
					Next semester
					
					As soon as possible

If this approach to goal setting is helpful, use this framework for your own skill assessment and goal-setting exercise:

Student:
Program:
Goal:

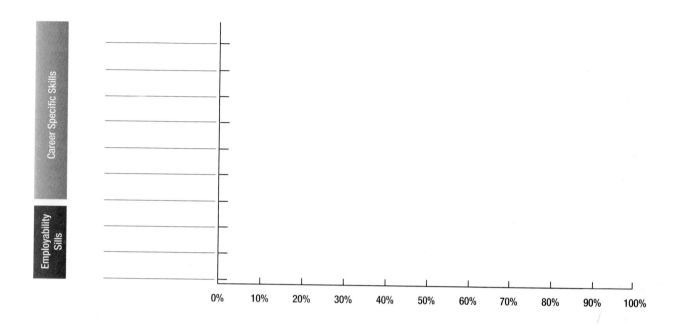

Skill:	Have:	Proof for portfolio:	Need:	Goals:	Date to start:

Resources

On Campus

The official that schedules classes on campus is known as the *registrar*. If you are having difficulty scheduling your classes, the registrar's office can help. In addition, your academic advisor or program coordinator can help you work out problems in enrolling in the classes you want.

If you are having difficulty in managing your time, you can turn to several places. The campus counselling centre will help, as will campus learning centres. Your academic adviser can also be a source of aid.

In Print

Julie Morgenstern's helpful book, *Time Management from the Inside Out* (Owl Books, 2000), emphasizes deciding upon a time management system that fits one's own personal style—whether it be spur-of-the-moment and easily side-tracked or well-organized and efficient.

The Procrastinator's Handbook by Rita Emmett (Walker & Company, 2000) is a great book full of very helpful suggestions and important common sense about human nature, and our collective tendency to be procrastinators.

A helpful resource that offers sound advice on setting and achieving goals is *Goal Setting 101: How to Set and Achieve a Goal* by Gary Ryan Blair (Goalsguy Learning Systems Inc, 2000).

On the Web

The following sites on the World Wide Web provide the opportunity to extend your learning about the material in this chapter. Although the Web addresses were accurate at the time the book was printed, check the P.O.W.E.R. Learning website, <www.mcgrawhill.ca/college/power>, for any changes that may have occurred.

http://csd.mcmaster.ca/student_achievement_series.htm
This is the website of a helpful booklet (one of several on study skills) entitled "Organizing Your Studies and Time," published by McMaster University. The booklet has effective techniques and rationales for attending to time management issues.

www.mindtools.com/page5.html
The focus of this site is how to get the most out of your time. Topics covered include analyzing what time is really worth, prioritizing goals, and planning effective use of the time you actually have.

The Case of . . .

Where Does the Time Go?

As Carl Petersen walked into his apartment, he didn't really have to look at the time—he knew it was too late. He cringed. How could he have spent the entire night with the guys? At first, he had just wanted to play a little basketball with some buddies to burn off some energy. Then they had gone to the Outback Shack for some wings and a couple of games of pool. The next thing he knew, it was after 11 P.M. He and his friends had ended up sharing a few pitchers while watching the game on the big screen TV, and he had nothing to show for the evening.

It was not as if the afternoon had been any better! When he had gotten home from school at 4, he had been dead tired. After eating a bowl of cereal, Carl had taken a nap. When he woke up at 5:30, he checked his e-mail and that had taken an hour. Then, what was supposed to be an hour of hoops had turned into a whole evening shot!

Thinking about his medical terminology test the next day, Carl started to panic. He had to write the test and he had to pass this one. Luckily he had done the chapter exercises and review and was pretty sure he had brought his textbook home. What else was coming up? He clenched his fist as he remembered his logs for last weekend's ride-along shifts with the ambulance crew were now overdue. What else? He was way behind on his reading for anatomy and physiology and he hadn't started reading the book he needed to summarize and critique for next Monday. But he had the weekend to get caught up on everything.

Carl was resolving to change his ways when he suddenly remembered that it was his grandparents' 50th wedding anniversary this weekend and he had promised—promised—his mom he'd be home for the weekend. Carl mentally ran through the labs, assignments, projects, and tests due in the next week. He hadn't started any of them. His heart sank.

As he yawned and wandered into the kitchen to pour some orange juice for himself and begin what he hoped would be a few productive hours before going to bed, he stopped in his tracks. Where was his backpack? After a quick search, he realized it wasn't in his apartment. How was he supposed to study for his test tomorrow? Carl closed his eyes and put his head in his hands—how had he gotten so far behind on everything? He kicked at a pile of dirty clothes in the middle of the floor. His life was coming apart completely. How was he ever going to get it together?

1. What might you tell Carl to help solve his predicament?

2. What could Carl have done to avoid the situation he now faces?

3. What specific time management techniques might Carl have used to prevent these problems from arising?

4. What strategies might Carl use now to take control of his limited time during the coming week?

5. What advice could you give Carl in order to prevent time management problems during the next term?

Recognizing How You Learn, Who You Are, and What You Value

3

Discovering Your Learning Styles

Journal Reflections: How I Learn

Self-Concept: "Who Am I?"

Preparing a Personal Mission Statement

Prepare: Identifying Your Values

Organize: Placing Order on What Motivates You

Work: Creating a Personal Mission Statement

Evaluate: Assessing Your Personal Mission Statement

Rethink: Reconsidering Your Options

Career Connections: Personality Assessments on the Job

To Thine Own Self Be True: No One Is Responsible for Your Life but You

Speaking of Success: Todd Currie

The Case of . . . The Instructor Who Spoke Too Much

The transformation began when Shawn Ahermaa got his first Java project back from his Introductory Software professor. It wasn't so much the grade—which was good—but what the instructor said, almost as an afterthought, as she handed the project back to Shawn: "Nice job. Your design was very creative. Keep it up."

Shawn was pleased. He had always known that he was good at software engineering, and he could write code without making mistakes, but he had never felt very confident in his ability as a designer.

But now something clicked; Shawn's perspective on who he was started to change. Maybe he did have the ability to succeed in a career involving software design. It was a gradual transformation, but after his professor praised his work, Shawn's view of himself began to change.

Through the experiences we have in life, we build a sense of our strengths and weaknesses, what we like and dislike about ourselves. In the process, the sense of who we are also affects the choices we make and the things that we do. So it's not surprising that the accuracy of our understanding of ourselves has an important effect on our success.

In this chapter you will be asked to consider various aspects about yourself. First you'll look at the ways in which you learn and how you can use your personal learning style to study more effectively.

You'll then explore who you are more broadly, considering the various aspects of your personality. You'll see how your self-esteem—the way you perceive your strengths and weaknesses—can lead to success or failure.

Finally, this chapter helps you investigate where you are headed. By identifying your personal values and then creating your own personal mission statement, you'll begin to solidify the knowledge of who you are and where you would be happiest and most productive in the future.

After reading this chapter, you'll be able to answer these questions:

- **What are my learning styles, and how have they affected my academic success?**

- **What is self-concept and how does it affect me?**

- **How does my level of self-esteem affect my behaviour?**

- **What do I value and what motivates me?**

- **How can I determine my needs and make wise personal decisions throughout life?**

Discovering Your Learning Styles

Consider what it would be like to be a member of the Trukese people, a small group of islanders in the South Pacific.

Trukese sailors often sail hundreds of kilometres on the open sea. They manage this feat with none of the navigational equipment used by Western sailors: no compass, no chronometer, no sextant. They don't even sail in a straight line. Instead, they zigzag back and forth, at the mercy of the winds and tides. Yet they make few mistakes. Almost always they are able to reach their destination with precision. How do they do it?

They say it has to do with following the rising and setting of the stars at night. During the day, they take in the appearance, sound, and feel of the waves against the side of the boat. But they don't really have any idea of where they are at any given moment, nor do they care. They just know that ultimately they'll reach their final destination.

It would be foolish to suggest that the Trukese don't have what it takes to be successful sailors. The fact that they don't use traditional Western navigational equipment when they're sailing does not mean that they are any less able than Western navigators. Certainly, if they took a test of Western navigational skills, they would do badly. But their ultimate success cannot be questioned.

What about academic success? Isn't it reasonable to assume that there are different ways to reach academic goals? Wouldn't it be surprising if everyone learned in exactly the same way, without any differences in what worked best for them?

Trukese sailors, who live on a small group of islands in the South Pacific, are able to navigate with considerable accuracy across great expanses of open seas, and they do so without the use of any of the standard navigation tools used by sailors in Western cultures. The navigational achievements of the Trukese sailors illustrate that there are multiple ways to attain our goals and that there is no single route to success.

We don't all learn in the same way. Each of us has preferred ways of learning, approaches that work best for us. And our success is not just dependent on how *well* we learn, but on *how* we learn.

Learning styles reflect our preferred manner of acquiring and using knowledge. These styles are not abilities, but ways of learning.

We don't have just one learning style but a profile of styles. Even though our ability may be equal to someone else's, our learning styles might be quite different.

You probably already know quite a lot about your learning styles. Maybe you do particularly well in your Biology class while struggling with English. Or it may be the other way around. Because biology tends to be about natural processes, teachers present the subject as a series of related facts. English, however, requires you to think more abstractly, analyzing and synthesizing ideas presented in a variety of ways. Whichever subject you prefer, it is almost certain you prefer it because of your learning style.

Though we may have general preferences for fact-based learning or learning that requires more abstract thinking, we all use a variety of learning styles.

Learning style
A person's preferred manner of acquiring, using, and thinking about knowledge

Some involve our preferences regarding the way information is presented to us, some relate to how we think and learn most readily, and some relate to how our personality traits affect our performance. Different approaches to learning overlap one another, and there are few distinct categories. We'll start by considering the preferences we have for how we initially perceive information.

Are You a Primarily Visual, Auditory, or Tactile Learner?

Receptive learning style
How the initial receipt of information relates to learning preferences

One of the most basic aspects of learning styles concerns the way in which we initially receive information from our sense organs—our **receptive learning style.** Some of us have primarily **visual learning styles,** recalling the spelling of a word, for example, or the structure of a chemical compound by reviewing a picture in our head. Or maybe you learn best when you have the opportunity to read about a concept rather than listening to a teacher explain it. Students with visual learning styles find it easier to see things in their "mind's eye"—to visualize a task or concept—than to be lectured about them.

Visual learning style
A style that involves visualizing information in the mind's eye, favouring reading and watching over touching and hearing

Have you ever asked a friend to help you put something together by having her read the directions to you while you worked? If you did, you may have an **auditory learning style.** People with auditory learning styles prefer listening to explanations rather than reading about them. They love class lectures and discussions, because they can easily take in the information that is being talked about.

Auditory learning style
A style that favours listening as the best approach to learning

Students with a **tactile or kinesthetic learning style** prefer to learn by doing—touching, manipulating objects, and doing things. For instance, some people enjoy the act of writing because of the feel of a pencil or a computer keyboard—the tactile equivalent of "thinking out loud" (which would be preferred by someone with an auditory learning style). Or they may find that it helps them to make a three-dimensional model to understand a new idea.

Having a particular receptive learning style simply means that it will be easier to learn material that is presented in that style. It does not mean you cannot learn any other way!

Tactile or kinesthetic learning style
A style that involves learning by touching, manipulating objects, and doing things

You may have a good idea about which learning style suits you best, but Try It! 1, "Learning Style Inventory," will help you further understand your style.

Handling Information: Do You Focus on Pieces or the Whole?

When you are putting a jigsaw puzzle together, do you focus more on the individual pieces and how each one fits together with the one next to it, or is your strategy to concentrate on the whole picture, keeping the finished product in mind?

Analytic learning style
A style that starts with small pieces of information and uses them to build the big picture

The way you approach a jigsaw puzzle provides a clue to the process by which you fit together bits of information. Specifically, the strategy you use suggests which of the following two learning styles you are more comfortable with:

- People with **analytic learning styles** learn most easily if first exposed to the individual components and principles behind a phenomenon or situation. Once they have identified the underlying components involved,

Chapter 3 Recognizing How You Learn, Who You Are, and What You Value

Learning Style Inventory: Are You a Visual, an Auditory, or a Kinesthetic Learner?

Read each statement and select the appropriate number response as it applies to you.[1]

Often (3)   Sometimes (2)   Never (1)

Visual Modality

_____ I remember information better if I write it down.
_____ Looking at the person helps keep me focused.
_____ I need a quiet place to get my work done.
_____ When I take a test, I can see the textbook page in my head.
_____ I need to write down directions, not just take them verbally.
_____ Music or background noise distracts my attention from the task at hand.
_____ I don't always get the meaning of a joke.
_____ I doodle and draw pictures on the margins of my notebook pages.
_____ I have trouble following lectures.
_____ I react very strongly to colours.
_____ **Total**

Auditory Modality

_____ My papers and notebooks always seem messy.
_____ When I read, I need to use my index finger to track my place on the line.
_____ I do not follow written directions well.
_____ If I hear something, I will remember it.
_____ Writing has always been difficult for me.
_____ I often misread words from the text (i.e., "them" for "then").
_____ I would rather listen and learn than read and learn.
_____ I'm not very good at interpreting an individual's body language.
_____ Pages with small print or poor quality copies are difficult for me to read.
_____ My eyes tire quickly, even though my vision check-up is always fine.
_____ **Total**

Kinesthetic/Tactile Modality

_____ I start a project before reading the directions.
_____ I hate to sit at a desk for long periods.
_____ I prefer first to see something done and then to do it myself.
_____ I use the trial and error approach to problem solving.
_____ I like to read my textbook while riding an exercise bike.
_____ I take frequent study breaks.
_____ I have a difficult time giving step-by-step instructions.
_____ I enjoy sports and do well at several different types of sports.
_____ I use my hands when describing things.
_____ I have to rewrite or type my class notes to reinforce the material.
_____ **Total**

(continued on next page)

Try It!

1

Learning Style Inventory—Continued

Total the score for each section. A score of 21 points or more in a modality indicates strength in that area. The highest of the three scores indicates the most efficient method of information intake. The second highest score indicates the modality that boosts the primary strength. For example, a score of 23 in the visual modality indicates a strong visual learner. Such a learner benefits from reading a text, from filmstrips, charts, graphs, and so on. If the second highest score is auditory, then the individual would benefit from audiotapes, lectures, and the like. If you are strong kinesthetically, then taking notes and rewriting class notes will reinforce information.

Learning Styles—Clues and Learning Tips

Clues

Visual learners usually

- Need to see it to know it.
- Have strong sense of colour.
- May have artistic ability.
- Often have difficulty with spoken directions.
- May overreact to sounds.
- May have trouble following lectures.
- Often misinterprets words.

Auditory learners usually

- Prefer to get information by listening; they need to hear it to know it.
- May have difficulty following written directions.
- Have difficulty with reading.
- Have problems with writing.
- Are unable to read body language and facial expressions.

Kinesthetic learners usually

- Prefer hands-on learning.
- Can assemble parts without reading directions.
- Have difficulty sitting still.
- Learn better when physical activity is involved.
- May be very well coordinated and have athletic ability.

Tips

Visual learners should

- Use graphics to reinforce learning: films, slides, illustrations, diagrams, and doodles.
- Colour code to organize notes and possessions.
- Ask for written directions.
- Use flow charts and diagrams for notetaking.
- Visualize spelling of words or facts to memorize them.

Auditory learners should

- Use tapes for reading and for class and lecture notes.
- Learn by interviewing or by participating in discussions.
- Have test questions or directions read aloud or put on tape.

Kinesthetic learners should

- Engage in experiential learning (making models, doing lab work, and roleplaying).
- Take frequent breaks in study periods.
- Trace letters and words to learn spelling and remember facts.
- Use a computer to reinforce learning through the sense of touch.
- Memorize or drill while walking or exercising.
- Express abilities through dance, drama, or gymnastics.

they find it easier to figure out and grasp the broad picture and determine whether particular cases exemplify the principle.

- Those with **relational learning styles** learn most readily if exposed to the full range of material that they are aiming to learn. Rather than focusing on the individual components of a problem, as those with analytic styles prefer to do, people with relational learning styles do best when they are first given the full picture. They can then take this broad view and break it down into its individual components.

For example, consider trying to understand the way that food is converted to energy in a cell. A more analytic learner would approach the task by learning each individual step in the process, first to last. In contrast, a more relational learner would consider the big picture, focusing on the general, overall process and its purpose.

Students who use an analytic style study most effectively by focusing on facts and specific principles, for they excel at organizing information. They often work best on their own, and science and math may come particularly easy to them. Students with a relational style perceive concepts globally, thinking in terms of the big picture. They may be drawn to subject areas that demand the ability to forge a broad overview of material, such as English and history. You probably already have a good idea of whether you have an analytic or relational learning style, but Try It! 2, "Assess Your Analytical and Relational Learning Styles," will help you understand your learning style further.

Multiple Intelligences

The theory of multiple intelligences, developed by Dr. Howard Gardner, proposes that the conventional view of intelligence, based on I.Q. testing, is too narrow. Dr. Gardner asserts that there are eight different approaches to interpreting intelligence, significantly expanding our traditional understanding of the word.

← Enter

Journal Reflections

How I Learn

1. Suppose a friend is teaching you a new and complex procedure (such as a complicated card game or the way to use a piece of computer software). Do you prefer to get the big picture first or the details?

2. Do you think you would ask your friend to slow down while you get the details, or would you be impatient to get started? Would you rather try doing it while your friend talks you through it?

3. Do you tend to picture things while you're learning?

4. When you're in class, what do you do during lectures—try to write down the instructor's exact words, draw pictures, jot down a few big ideas, doodle, tune out?

5. When someone gives you directions to a new place, what do you do?

6. Would you rather read a newspaper, listen to the news on the radio, or watch it on TV? Why do you think you have this preference?

7. When you get a new piece of electronic equipment, do you like to read the instructions or just play with it until you get the hang of it?

Assess Your Analytical and Relational Learning Styles

Consider the following pairs of statements. Place a checkmark next to the statement in each pair that more closely describes your style.

_____1a. Before tackling a complex task that I'm unfamiliar with, I prefer to have detailed instructions on how to do it.

_____1b. I prefer to dive into a new task, trying things out to see what happens and finding my way as I go.

_____2a. I like watching movies a second time because then I know where they're going.

_____2b. I generally don't like watching movies a second time because I know their plots already.

_____3a. I prefer to solve math or science problems using formulas and directions.

_____3b. I prefer to figure out why formulas work.

_____4a. When I read mystery stories, I usually let the author tell the story and reveal the mystery.

_____4b. When I read mystery stories, I like to try figuring out the mystery before the author reveals it.

_____5a. I usually read the instruction booklet before trying out a new piece of software.

_____5b. I never read the instruction booklet before trying out a new piece of software.

_____6a. I prefer to have someone who knows about a subject explain it to me before I try my hand at it.

_____6b. I'm impatient when others try to explain things to me, preferring to get involved in them myself without much explanation.

_____7a. Whenever I see a really amazing special effect in a movie, I like to sit back and enjoy it.

_____7b. Whenever I see a really amazing special effect in a movie, I try to figure out how they did it.

If you tended to prefer the "A" statements in most pairs, you probably have a relational style. If you preferred the "B" statements, you probably have a more analytic style. Remember that no one is purely analytical or purely relational.

Relational learning style
A style that starts with the big picture and breaks it down into its individual components

These intelligences are:

- Verbal/Linguistic ("word smart")
- Logical/Mathematical ("number/reasoning smart")
- Visual/Spatial ("picture smart")

- Bodily/Kinesthetic ("body smart")
- Musical/Rythmic ("music smart")
- Interpersonal ("people smart")
- Intrapersonal ("self smart")
- Naturalist ("nature smart")

By tradition, academic and cultural environments have esteemed linguistic and logical/mathematical intelligence, resulting in our valuing articulate or logical people. However, using multiple intelligence theory, individuals displaying capacity in other intelligences, such as artists, architects, musicians, naturalists, designers, dancers, therapists, entrepreneurs, and others who enrich the world in which we live are also acknowledged, recognized, and esteemed for their gifts.

Research shows that all human beings have elements of these different types of intelligence. Depending on your background and age, some intelligences are more developed than others. Try It! 3, "You and Your Multiple Intelligences," will help you discover what are your strengths. Knowing this, you can work to strengthen the other intelligences that you do not use as often or focus on the intelligences that are well developed.

Personality Styles

Our learning styles are also influenced by our personality. Are you a person who is likely to try out for school productions? Or is the idea of getting on a stage something that is totally lacking in appeal (if not completely terrifying)? Do you relate to the world around you primarily through careful planning or by spontaneously reacting?

According to the rationale of the *Myers-Briggs Type Indicator*, a questionnaire frequently used in business and other organizations, our personality type plays a key role in determining how we react to different kinds of situations. Specifically, the idea is that we work best in situations in which others—both students and instructors—share our preferences and in which our personality preferences are most suited to the particular task on which we are working.

According to studies done on personality, four major dimensions are critical. Although we'll describe the extremes of each dimension, keep in mind that most of us fall somewhere in between each of the endpoints of each dimension.

- **Introverts versus extroverts.** A key difference between introverts and extroverts is whether they enjoy working with others. Independence is a key characteristic of introverted learners. They enjoy working alone and they are less affected by how others think and behave. In contrast, extroverts are outgoing and more affected by the behaviour and thinking of others. They enjoy working with others, and they are energized by having other people around.

"To be fond of learning is to be near to knowledge."

Tze-Sze

- **Intuitors versus sensors.** Intuitors enjoy solving problems and being creative. They get impatient with details, preferring to make leaps of judgment, and they enjoy the challenge of solving problems and taking a big-picture approach. People categorized as sensors prefer a concrete, logical approach in which they can carefully analyze the facts of the situation. Although they are good with details, they sometimes miss the big picture.

You and Your Multiple Intelligences

Read the following statements and check any sentence that accurately describes you. Total your checkmarks and determine if your highest scores are an accurate reflection of you and your multiple intelligences.

Verbal/Linguistic Intelligence

___ I enjoy telling stories and jokes

___ I have a good memory for trivia

___ I enjoy word games (e.g., Scrabble and crossword puzzles)

___ I read books just for fun

___ I am a good speller usually

___ In an argument I tend to use put-downs or sarcasm

___ I like talking and writing about my ideas

___ If I have to memorize something I create a rhyme or saying to help me remember

___ If something breaks and won't work, I read the instruction book first

___ For a group presentation, I prefer to do the writing and library research

Logical/Mathematical Intelligence

___ I really enjoy math class

___ I like logical math puzzles or brain teasers

___ I find solving math problems to be fun

___ If I have to memorize something I tend to place events in a logical order

___ I like to find out how things work

___ I enjoy computer and any math games

___ I love playing chess, checkers, or Monopoly

___ In an argument, I try to find a fair and logical solution

___ If something breaks and won't work, I look at the pieces and try to figure out how it works

___ For a group presentation, I prefer to create the charts and graphs

Visual/Spatial Intelligence

___ I prefer a map to written directions

___ I daydream a lot

___ I enjoy hobbies such as photography

___ I like to draw and create

___ If I have to memorize something I draw a diagram to help me remember

___ I like to doodle on paper whenever I can

___ In a magazine, I prefer looking at the pictures rather than reading the text

___ In an argument I try to keep my distance, keep silent, or visualize some solution

___ If something breaks and won't work I tend to study the diagram of how it works

___ For a group presentation, I prefer to draw all the pictures

Bodily/Kinesthetic Intelligence

___ My favourite class is gym since I like sports

___ I enjoy activities such as woodworking, sewing, and building models

___ When looking at things, I like touching them

___ I have trouble sitting still for any length of time

___ I use a lot of body movements when talking

___ If I have to memorize something I write it out a number of times until I know it

___ I tend to tap my fingers or play with my pencil during class

___ In an argument I tend to strike out and hit or run away

___ If something breaks and won't work I tend to play with the pieces to try to fit them together

___ For a group presentation, I prefer to move the props around, hold things up or build a model

Continued

Musical/Rhythmic Intelligence

___ I enjoy listening to CDs and the radio

___ I tend to hum to myself when working

___ I like to sing

___ I play a musical instrument quite well

___ I like to have music playing when doing homework or studying

___ If I have to memorize something I try to create a rhyme about the event

___ In an argument I tend to shout or punch or move in some sort of rhythm

___ I can remember the melodies of many songs

___ If something breaks and won't work I tend to tap my fingers to a beat while I figure it out

___ For a group presentation, I prefer to put new words to a popular tune or use music

Interpersonal Intelligence

___ I get along well with others

___ I like to belong to clubs and organizations

___ I have several very close friends

___ I like helping teach other students

___ I like working with others in groups

___ Friends ask my advice because I seem to be a natural leader

___ If I have to memorize something I ask someone to quiz me to see if I know it

___ In an argument I tend ask a friend or some person in authority for help

___ If something breaks and won't work I try to find someone who can help me

___ For a group presentation, I like to help organize the group's efforts

Intrapersonal Intelligence

___ I like to work alone without anyone bothering me

___ I like to keep a diary

___ I like myself (most of the time)

___ I don't like crowds

___ I know what I am good at and what I am weak at

___ I find that I am strong-willed, independent, and don't follow the crowd

___ If I have to memorize something I tend to close my eyes and feel the situation

___ In an argument I will usually walk away until I calm down

___ If something breaks and won't work, I wonder if it's worth fixing

___ For a group presentation I like to contribute something that is uniquely mine, often based on how I feel

Naturalist Intelligence

___ I am keenly aware of my surroundings and of what goes on around me

___ I love to go walking in the woods and looking at the trees and flowers

___ I enjoy gardening

___ I like to collect things (e.g., rocks, sports cards, stamps, etc)

___ As an adult, I think I would like to get away from the city and enjoy nature

___ If I have to memorize something, I tend to organize it into categories

___ I enjoy learning the names of living things in our environment, such as flowers and trees

___ In an argument I tend to compare my opponent to someone or something I have read or heard about and react accordingly

___ If something breaks down, I look around me to try and see what I can find to fix the problem

___ For a group presentation, I prefer to organize and classify the information into categories so it makes sense

Continued

You and Your Multiple Intelligences—Continued

TOTAL SCORE

_____Verbal/Linguistic

_____Logical/Mathematical

_____Visual/Spatial

_____Bodily/Kinesthetic

_____Musical/Rhythmic

_____Interpersonal

_____Intrapersonal

_____Naturalist

Eight Styles of Learning

Read the following descriptors and comment on the information; you can utilize the information to power-up your postsecondary learning experience.

Verbal/Linguistic Learner

likes to:	read, write and tell stories.
is good at	memorizing names, places, dates and trivia.
learns best by:	saying, hearing and seeing words; teaching others.
Comments:	_____

Logical/Mathematical Learner

likes to:	do experiments; figure things out; work with numbers; ask questions and explore patterns and relationships.
is good at:	math, reasoning, logic and problem solving.
learns best by:	categorizing; classifying and working with abstract patterns/relationships; organizing information sequentially.
Comments:	_____

Visual/Spatial Learner

likes to:	draw, build, design and create things; daydream; look at pictures/slides; watch movies and play with machines.
is good at:	imagining things; sensing changes; mazes/puzzles and reading maps, charts.
learns best by:	visualizing; dreaming; using the mind's eye and working with colours/pictures.
Comments:	_____

Musical/Rhythmic Learner

likes to:	sing; hum tunes; listen to music; play an instrument and respond to music.
is good at:	picking up sounds; remembering melodies; noticing pitches/rhythms and keeping time.
learns best by:	rhythm, melody and music.
Comments:	_____

Bodily/Kinesthetic Learner

likes to:	move around; touch and talk and use body language.
is good at:	physical activities (sports/dance/acting) and crafts.
learns best by:	touching; moving; interacting with space and processing knowledge through bodily sensations.
Comments:	

Continued

Interpersonal Learner

likes to:	have lots of friends; talk to people and join groups.
is good at:	understanding people; leading others; organizing; communicating; manipulating and mediating conflicts.
learns best by:	sharing, comparing, relating, cooperating, and interviewing.
Comments:	_____

Intrapersonal Learner

likes to:	work alone and pursue own interests.
is good at:	understanding self, focusing inward on feelings/dreams; following instincts; pursuing interests/goals and being original.
learns best by:	working alone; individualized projects; self-paced instruction and having own space.
Comments:	_____

Naturalistic Learner

likes to:	be outside, with animals, geography, and weather; interacting with the surroundings.
is good at:	categorizing; organizing a living area; planning a trip; preservation, and conservation.
learns best by:	studying natural phenomenon, in a natural setting; learning about how things work.
Comments:	_____

- **Thinkers versus feelers.** Thinkers prefer logic over emotion. They reach decisions and solve problems by systematically analyzing a situation. In contrast, feeling types rely more on their personal values when responding. They are aware of others and their feelings, and they are influenced by their emotional responses and attachments to others.

- **Perceivers and judgers.** Before drawing a conclusion, perceivers attempt to gather as much information as they can. Because they are open to multiple perspectives and appreciate all sides of an issue, they sometimes have difficulty completing a task. Judgers, in comparison, are quick and decisive, sometimes making decisions before they have all the available information. They like to set goals, accomplish them, and then move on to the next task.

Each personality type has specific likes and dislikes when it comes to learning preferences. For example, introverts usually enjoy working alone, while extroverts usually enjoy cooperative learning and projects involving many people. Intuitors most enjoy creative problem solving, while sensors flourish with assignments that are concrete and logical. Thinkers prefer to systematically use logic to analyze a problem, and feelers enjoy assignments that involve others and their emotional reactions. Finally, perceivers favour work on which there are multiple sides to an issue, while judgers' preferences are to be decisive, determining goals and sticking to them.

Figure 3.1

Kolb's Experimental
Learning Style

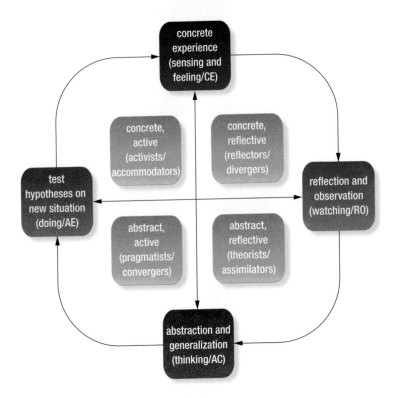

A short, free adaptation of the *Myers-Briggs Type Indicator*, "Personality Pathways: What Is Your Myers-Briggs Personality Type?" can be found at <www.personalitypathways.com/type_inventory.html>. This site has an online Myers-Briggs test as well as descriptors of all 16 types, along with information about careers and personal relationships.

Experiential Learning

Kolb's Learning Style Inventory is based on the idea that learning should be active and grounded in experience. The model has four stages: *watching, thinking, feeling, doing*. Kolb's theory is that learners prefer to start the learning cycle in one of the stages but that we learn from all four stages. The model is often shown in two dimensions, with the horizontal grid focusing on the task, moving from *doing* on the left and *watching* on the right. The vertical dimension focuses on our thought and feeling processes, moving from *feeling* on the top to *thinking* on the bottom. See Figure 3.1.

- *Watching:* Learners who prefer *watching* (RO: reflective observation) use observation to make judgments, preferring lectures, learning logs, or journals to process their learning.

- *Doing:* Learners who prefer *doing* (AE: active experimentation) learn best when they can actively engage in projects, homework, or class discussions.

- *Feeling:* Learners who prefer *feeling* or *sensing* (CE: concrete experience) learn best when they can make feeling-based judgments using specific examples (such as exercises and simulations) in which they can be involved.

- *Thinking:* Learners who prefer *thinking* (AC: abstract conceptualization) learn best when they can apply thinking and analysis to their learning by using case studies or theoretical readings.

Within the quadrants formed by the grids are the learning styles of each person: *theorists* (assimilators), *pragmatists* (convergers), *activists* (accommodators), and *reflectors* (divergers).

- *Assimilators* use abstract conceptualization and reflective observation in their learning process. They ask, "How does this relate to that?" They prefer case studies, reading, and thinking. Their strength is in their ability to create theoretical models. Instructors who lecture and assign papers are effective for learners with this learning style.

- *Convergers* use abstract conceptualization and active experimentation to learn effectively. They ask, "How can I apply this in practice?" They prefer peer feedback and activities that apply skills. Their strength is in their ability to apply skills and ideas. A coach or helper is an ideal instructor for this type of learner.

- *Accommodators* use concrete experience and active experimentation to learn best. They say, "I'm game for anything." They prefer practising the skills, problem solving, small-group discussions, and peer feedback. Experts who model professional practices are effective instructors for these learners.

- *Divergers* like to use reflective observation and concrete experience to learn well. They ask, "What does that mean?" They prefer lectures, with time to think or write about their subject. Their strength lies in their imaginative ability. They like instructors who can provide expert interpretation and set external criteria for evaluation.

Learning styles reflect our preferred manner of acquiring, using, and thinking about knowledge. Tactile learners prefer hands-on learning that comes about through touching, manipulating, and doing things.

To discover where you fit into Kolb's Learning Style Inventory, complete Try It! 4, "Learning Style Indicator."

Facts to Remember about Learning, Personality, Experiential, and Processing Styles

- **You have a variety of styles.** As you can see in Table 3.1 (on page 75) and Try It! 5, "What I Know About My Learning Styles." (on page 76), there are several types of styles. For any given task or challenge, some types of styles may be more relevant than others. Furthermore, success is possible even when there is a mismatch between what you need to accomplish and your own pattern of preferred styles. It may take more work, but learning to deal with situations that require you to use less-preferred styles is important practice for life after college or university.

Try It! 4

Learning Style Indicator

What kind of learner are you? Read each statement carefully. To the left of each statement, write the code that best describes how each statement applies to you.[2]

SECTION 1

Place either an AE or a RO next to the statement below, depending on which part of the statement mostly closely describes you:

_____ (AE): I often produce off-the-cuff ideas that at first might seem silly or half-baked.
(RO): I am thorough and methodical.

_____ (AE): I am normally the one who initiates conversations. (RO): I enjoy watching people.

_____ (AE): I am flexible and open-minded. (RO): I am careful and cautious.

_____ (AE): I like to try new and different things without too much preparation. (RO): I investigate a new topic or process in depth before trying it.

_____ (AE): I am happy to have a go at new things. (RO): I draw up lists of possible courses of actions when starting a new project.

_____ (AE): I like to get involved and to participate. (RO): I like to read and observe.

_____ (AE): I am loud and outgoing. (RO): I am quiet and somewhat shy.

_____ (AE): I make quick and bold decisions. (RO): I make cautious and logical decisions.

_____ (AE): I speak slowly, after thinking. (RO): I speak fast, while thinking.

Total of AEs: _____. Total of ROs: _____. The one that has the larger number is your task preference.

SECTION 2

Place either an AC or a CE next to the statement below, depending on which part of the statement mostly closely describes you:

_____ (AC): I ask probing questions when learning a new subject. (CE): I am good at picking up hints and techniques from other people.

_____ (AC): I am rational and logical. (CE): I am practical and down to earth.

_____ (AC): I plan events down to the last detail. (CE): I like realistic but flexible plans.

_____ (AC): I like to know the right answers before trying something new. (CE): I try things out by practising to see whether they work.

_____ (AC): I analyze reports to find the basic assumptions and inconsistencies. (CE): I rely on others to give me the basic gist of reports.

_____ (AC): I prefer working alone. (CE): I enjoy working with others.

_____ (AC): Others would describe me as serious, reserved, and formal. (CE): Others would describe me as verbal, expressive, and informal.

_____ (AC): I use facts to make decisions. (CE): I use feelings to make decisions.

_____ (AC): I am difficult to get to know. (CE): I am easy to get to know.

Total of ACs: _____. Total of CEs: _____. The one that has the larger number is your thought or emotional preference.

SCORING PROCEDURES

Each preference (high score) from the two above sections is used to determine your learning style. Note that you learn in *all* four styles, but you normally learn best by starting in and using one style the most.

- If you are an AE and a CE then you are a Doer/Accommodator.
- If you are an RO and a CE then you are a Watcher/Diverger.
- If you are an RO and an AC then you are a Thinker/Assimilator.
- If you are an AE and an AC then you are a Feeler/Converger.

Category	Description
Receptive Learning Styles	
Visual	A style that involves visualizing information in the mind, favouring reading and watching over touching and listening.
Auditory	A style in which the learner favours listening as the best approach.
Tactile	A style that involves learning by touching, manipulating objects, and doing things.
Information Processing Styles	
Analytic	A style in which the learner starts with small pieces of information and uses them to build the big picture.
Relational	A style in which the learner starts with the big picture and breaks it down into its individual components.
Personality Styles	
Introvert versus Extrovert	Independence is a key characteristic of introverted learners, who enjoy working alone and are less affected by how others think and behave. In contrast, extroverts are outgoing and more affected by the behaviour and thinking of others. They enjoy working with others.
Intuitor versus Sensor	Intuitors enjoy solving problems and being creative, often taking a big-picture approach to solving problems. Sensors prefer a concrete, logical approach in which they can carefully analyze the facts of the situation.
Thinker versus Feeler	Thinkers prefer logic over emotion, reaching decisions and solving problems by systematically analyzing a situation. In contrast, feelers rely more on their emotional responses and are influenced by their personal values and attachments to others.
Perceiver versus Judger	Before drawing a conclusion, perceivers attempt to gather as much information as they can and are open to multiple perspectives. Judgers, in comparison, are quick and decisive, sometimes making decisions before they have all the available information; they enjoy setting goals and accomplishing them.
Experiential Styles	
Divergers	They prefer to observe or watch others, think, and record thoughts about learning.
Assimilators	They prefer to read or listen to instructions, understand theories, and create theoretical models.
Convergers	They prefer to be coached, learn from an expert, and go step-by-step through a learning process.
Accommodators	They prefer hands-on learning, practising, and working with others.

Table 3.1

Learning, Processing, Personality, and Experiential Styles

- **Your style reflects your preferences regarding which abilities you like to use—*not* the abilities themselves.** Styles are related to our preferences and the mental approaches we like to use. You may prefer to learn tactilely, but that in itself doesn't guarantee that the products that you create tactilely will be good—you still have to work!

- **Your style will change over the course of your life.** You can learn new styles and expand the range of learning experiences in which you feel comfortable. In fact, you can conceive of this book as one long lesson in learning styles because it provides you with strategies for learning more effectively in a variety of ways.

What I Know About My Learning Styles

LEARNING STYLE	I AM BEST DESCRIBED AS:	MY STRENGTHS ARE:	I LEARN BEST BY:	ACTION PLAN
Visual, Auditory, Kinesthetic				
Multiple Intelligence Theory				
Analytic, Relational				
Myers-Briggs Type Indicator				
Kolb's Learning Style Inventory				
Other Things That I Know About Me				
Time				
Responsibilities				
Values				
Other				

Sample: What I Know About My Learning Styles

LEARNING STYLE	I AM BEST DESCRIBED AS:	MY STRENGTHS ARE:	I LEARN BEST BY:	ACTION PLAN
Visual, Auditory, Kinesthetic	a strong visual learner	visualizing, artistic	seeing things— visuals, colours	—I will use colours in my notes and when I am reading my text and diagram some of my notes.
Multiple Intelligence Theory	logical/ mathematic	reasoning, problem-solving	seeing the patterns or relationships	—I will organize my study time using my planner and highlight. —I will try and work by myself or with a study peer.
Analytic, Relational	an analytic learner	focus on facts organizing	starting with the pieces and building up	—I will take a philosophy course and see if I like logic. —I will do the chapter exercises and online quizzes to make sure I know my stuff.
Myers-Briggs Type Indicator	introvert, sensor feeler, perceiver	independence, working logically, values gathering information	working by myself or with one other person	
Kolb's Learning Style Inventory	a converger	apply my skills	step-by-step, coaching	
Other Things That I Know About Me				
Time	prime time— morning	organizing the early part of the day	starting early	—I will use library for early studying and get the hard stuff out of the way.
Responsibilities	part-time job (12 hours per week)	Flexible	staying organized	—I will do some of my reading at work. —I will try and switch Floors in my res—quiet Floor.
Values	value: love, art, freedom	I know what's important to me	having a quiet harmonious environment	—We can study together sometimes instead of just hanging out all the time.
Other	steady relationship	mutually supportive	helping each other	

- **You should work on improving your less-preferred styles.** Although it may be tempting, don't always make choices that increase your exposure to preferred styles and decrease your practice with less-preferred styles. The more you use approaches for which you have less of a preference, the better you'll be at developing the skills associated with those styles.

- **Work cooperatively with others who have different styles.** If your instructor asks you to work cooperatively in groups, seek out classmates who have styles that are different from yours. Not only will your classmates' differing styles help you to achieve collective success, but you can learn from observing others' approaches to tackling the assignment.

Self-Concept: "Who Am I?"

Of course you know who you are: You know your first and last name, you know where and when you were born, and you have no trouble identifying your ethnic background. You may even be able to recite your social insurance number with ease.

"When I discover who I am, I'll be free."

Ralph Ellison, U.S. author

But if this information is all that comes to mind when you think about who you are, you're missing a lot of the picture. What makes you unique and special are your thoughts, your beliefs, your dreams. You have a unique past history, and this set of experiences together with your genetic makeup—the combination of genes you inherited from your parents—is unlike anyone else's.

Self-concept

Your view of yourself that forms over time, comprising three components: the physical self, the social self, and the personal self

Our view of ourselves—our **self-concept**—has three parts:

1. Our *physical self* is both who we are physically—the colour of our eyes or the curliness of our hair—and how we feel about our physical form. We all have our blemishes, protruding stomachs, long noses, or other physical quirks, but we don't all feel the same way about them.

2. Our *social self* is made up of the roles we play in our social interactions with others. As you're reading these words, you're not only a student; you're also a son or daughter, a friend, a citizen, and possibly an employee, a spouse, a lover, or a parent. Each of these roles plays an important part in defining your self-concept.

3. Finally, our self-concept also contains a *personal self*—our inner core, which is that private part of ourselves that no one knows about except us. It consists of the innermost thoughts and experiences that we may or may not choose to share with others.

Self-Concept and Self-Fulfilling Prophecies

The way we view ourselves determines how we interact with others, what challenges we feel ready to take on, and our expectations for future success. If you see yourself as a successful student, you are likely to expect that you'll continue to be a successful student; if you see yourself as an incapable, inept student, your chances for future success are diminished.

In short, our self-concept can act as a self-fulfilling prophecy. A **self-fulfilling prophecy** is the tendency to act in accordance with our expectations and beliefs, thereby increasing the likelihood that events or behaviours consistent with those expectations and beliefs will occur. In other words, believing that something will happen can lead to actions that make it more likely that it actually will happen.

For instance, a person who views herself as a poor student may find herself thinking: "Why bother working hard? I'm no good as a student; that's just the way I am." It's easy to see how such a view could lead to a self-fulfilling prophecy: By not working hard, the student guarantees that the prophecy of poor performance comes true.

On the other hand, self-fulfilling prophecies can have positive effects. A person who sees herself as a good student will probably be motivated to study and will complete assignments enthusiastically. Her view of herself can bring about the expected behaviour—in this case, success.

To get a clearer picture of your own self-concept:

- **Examine the roles you play.** To understand who we are, we need to understand the different roles that we play in life. Consider which of these roles are central to who you are—and who you want to be. Think about the time you spend each day and how much of it is devoted to each of these roles.

- **Identify your strengths and weaknesses.** Look at yourself with a clear and objective eye, and consider what you do particularly well and what you don't do particularly well. If you're honest, you'll come up with several areas in which you need work—and many other areas in which you're already quite strong. Use Table 3.2 to help you organize your thoughts and build an initial inventory of your strengths and weaknesses.

  As you consider your strengths and weaknesses, don't place a value on them. The fact that you procrastinate and put off tasks doesn't make you a bad person, just as the fact that you're a good student doesn't necessarily make you a good person. The point in seeking to identify who you are is to determine your self-concept with accuracy, not to determine how good (or bad) a human being you are.

  Furthermore, be sure you construct your own definition of who you are. Don't let what you believe others think about you determine what *you* know you're good at and bad at. See yourself through your own eyes, not somebody else's.

- **Pull your selves together.** Try to form a coherent view of your self-concept. Seek to understand how the various parts of your self-concept—physical, social, and personal—fit together.

  If you consider your self-concept this way, you'll find that the whole is greater than the sum of the parts. We're not just the bodies we inhabit, the roles we play, and the experiences we have, but something bigger and better.

- **Accept your entire self-concept.** If you're being honest with yourself, you'll find that there are parts of yourself that you like more than others. That's okay. Don't disown the parts you don't like; they're also part of who you are. Instead, accept that some parts of yourself need work, while others are the source of justifiable pride.

Self-fulfilling prophecy
The tendency to act in accordance with our expectations and beliefs, thereby increasing the likelihood that events or behaviours consistent with those expectations and beliefs will occur

Table 3.2

Inventory Your
Strengths and
Weaknesses

Aspects of Self	Strengths	Weaknesses
Physical Self		
Health and fitness		
Sports		
Nutrition and diet		
Appearance		
Other		
Social Self		
Friend		
Son/daughter		
Lover/spouse		
Citizen/community member		
Employee		
Student		
Roommate		
Classmate		
Team or group member (e.g., sports, band, club)		
Other		
Personal Self		
Personal experiences		
Unique traits		
Personality		
Spiritual self		
Habits		
Attitudes/opinions		
Ideas/thoughts		
Other		

Not everything we do belongs in our self-concept. If you once shoplifted when you were a child, that doesn't mean you were a juvenile delinquent then or are a criminal now. Failing a course in high school doesn't make you a failing student.

Make Sure Your Self-Concept Is Yours

Our own perceptions are not the only source of self-fulfilling prophecies. We sometimes permit *others'* views of who we are and their expectations about us to determine our behaviour.

For example, if we think an instructor views us as a particularly hard worker, we may not want to disappoint him by slacking off. If we believe that our boss admires our persistence, we may be motivated to show her our persistence when we're working on a difficult problem.

Responding to others' positive perceptions can be fine, for the results are good. But what happens if someone holds a negative view of who we are? What if we're constantly told that we're not working hard enough, or that we're not as smart as our older brother, or that we are the hard worker but not the creative one?

"A lot of my fellow classmates are younger than me, and therefore concerned with different things."

Kim Ritchie, Student, Lambton College

The results can be devastating. If we consistently hear such messages about who we are, we can come to believe them. Even worse, our behaviour can begin to reflect the negative messages. If we're constantly told that we don't work hard enough, we may in fact *not* work very hard. If we're told we're not as smart as someone else, we may begin to think of ourselves as not very bright. Or if someone tells us we're not creative, we may not try very hard to be creative.

In short, the negative messages that we hear from others can come to act as a prison of others' negative beliefs about who we are and what our capabilities are. It's crucial, then, not to buy into others' negative views of who we are. Instead, we need to create our own self-concept, independent of what we believe others think about us. Our biggest help, and sometimes hinderance, in this effort is self-esteem.

Self-Esteem: Building a Positive View of Yourself

When you think about yourself as a student, you probably don't stop there. Instead, you likely see yourself as a "good" student, a "bad" student, or maybe a "just okay" student. Similarly, when you consider yourself in the role of friend, you may view yourself as a "loyal-to-the-end" friend or maybe, in the opposite case, a "fair-weather" friend. In short, when we look inward at who we are, we don't just stop with a characterization of the different roles that we play in the world. Instead, we place a value on them. We see the various facets of our self-concept not in neutral terms, but as either positive or negative.

Self-esteem is the overall evaluation we give ourselves as individuals. It reflects the degree to which we see ourselves as individuals of worth and determines our general acceptance of ourselves. If we have high self-esteem, we generally feel respect for and acceptance of ourselves. Conversely, if we have low self-esteem, we generally lack respect for ourselves, reject parts of who we are, and judge ourselves negatively.

Self-esteem
The overall evaluation we give ourselves as individuals

To get a sense of your own general level of self-esteem, complete the self-assessment in Try It! 6, "Measure Your Self-Esteem."

Why Self-Esteem Matters

People with high self-esteem are generally happier and better able to cope with adversity. High self-esteem provides a sense of security, because people with high self-esteem feel they are able to deal with problems that may arise.

Try It!
6

Measure Your Self-Esteem

To get an informal estimate of your self-esteem, complete the following scale by placing a check-mark in the appropriate box after each statement.

Statement	Strongly Agree	Agree	Disagree	Strongly Disagree
1. On the whole, I am satisfied with myself.				
2. At times I think I am no good at all.				
3. I feel that I have a number of good qualities.				
4. I am able to do things as well as most other people.				
5. I feel I do not have much to be proud of.				
6. I certainly feel useless at times.				
7. I feel that I'm a person of worth, at least on an equal plane with others.				
8. I wish I could have more respect for myself.				
9. All in all, I am inclined to feel that I am a failure.				
10. I take a positive attitude toward myself.				

Scoring: For statements 1, 3, 4, 7, and 10, score as follows:

Strongly Agree	4 points	Disagree	2 points
Agree	3 points	Strongly Disagree	1 point

For statements 2, 5, 6, 8, and 9, score as follows:

Strongly Agree	1 point	Disagree	3 points
Agree	2 points	Strongly Disagree	4 points

The highest possible score (i.e., an apparently very high level of self-esteem) is 40 points, and the minimum score (i.e., an apparently very low level of self-esteem) is 10. Most people score in the 30-point to 40-point range. A much smaller number of people score in the 20s. A score of 10 to 20 is often found in people who suffer from severe depression. Keep in mind that this is a very rough gauge of self-esteem and that scores will vary depending on many factors, including your mood when you complete the questionnaire.[3]

Do the results of the questionnaire match your own gut feelings about yourself? Do you think your self-esteem has changed? Do you have any ideas as to why?

Self-efficacy
The expectation that you are capable of achieving your goals in many different kinds of situations

They also have a sense of **self-efficacy,** the expectation that they are capable of achieving their goals in many different kinds of situations. High self-esteem can also give people a sense of purpose and the belief that they are productive members of society.

In contrast, individuals lacking in self-esteem are more insecure, and their belief in their ability to reach their goals is weak. They feel less tied to others, and their sense of purpose is not firm. When others are successful, people with low self-esteem may feel jealousy and envy.

Low self-esteem can produce a *cycle of failure* in which low self-esteem leads to low expectations, reduced effort, elevated anxiety, poor performance, and, finally, an affirmation of the low self-esteem that began the cycle in the first place. Such a cycle can be difficult to break (see Figure 3.2).

If a student with low self-esteem begins studying for a test believing that he is likely to do badly, he may put forth relatively little effort. After all, why should he bother, when he sees himself as an incompetent student of little worth? Moreover, because he is virtually sure he is going to do poorly on the test, he may experience extreme anxiety, feeling that (another) failure is lurking just ahead.

Ultimately, the combination of lack of effort and anxiety produced by his low self-esteem do him in, and he actually does do poorly on the test. But the cycle of failure is not yet complete: Rather than telling himself that low effort and elevated anxiety caused his poor test performance, he views it as an affirmation of his inferior ability. In turn, this misperception serves to reinforce his low self-esteem.

Breaking the Cycle of Failure   "Okay," you may be saying to yourself, "I understand that self-esteem is important. But how am I supposed to ignore a lifetime of learning and improve my self-esteem, especially when I have low self-esteem to begin with?"

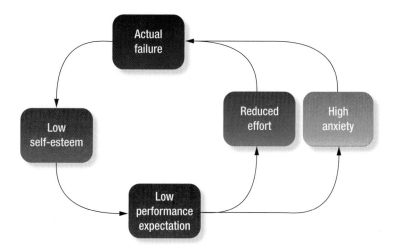

Figure 3.2

The Cycle of Failure

Low self-esteem can lead to low performance expectations. In turn, low performance expectations can produce reduced effort and high anxiety, both of which can lead to failure—and ultimately reinforce the low self-esteem that started the cycle.

Calvin and Hobbes   by Bill Watterson

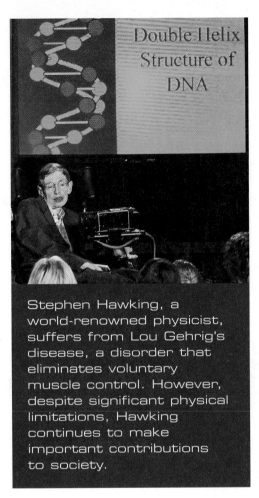

Double Helix Structure of DNA

Stephen Hawking, a world-renowned physicist, suffers from Lou Gehrig's disease, a disorder that eliminates voluntary muscle control. However, despite significant physical limitations, Hawking continues to make important contributions to society.

It's not a simple matter to shed a less-than-ideal view of ourselves and adopt a more positive one. You certainly won't be able to change your basic conception of yourself in the course of a few days.

But you can take some steps to bring yourself closer to an ideal level of self-esteem:

- **Accept yourself, warts and all.** No one is perfect, and becoming a perfect person should not be your goal in life. If it is, you are doomed to failure, because you will never measure up.

  Accept the fact that you're not pleased with certain aspects of yourself and your life. If you didn't realize that some things about yourself need improvement, you are out of touch with who you are.

- **Understand that everyone has value and self-worth.** Every individual has value and self-worth, some unique spark that sets him or her apart from everyone else. Examine yourself and your life, and get a picture of the particulars that make you *you*.

- **Distinguish the different parts of who you are.** No one is all bad, just as no one is all good. Maybe a person who never reached the level of success she wanted to in school turns out to be an excellent employee, the person who always seems to be asked to solve problems or take on challenges no one else can deal with. Another person may not be the kind of husband he wants to be but turns out to be a terrific parent.

Understanding that you have failings in one area of life doesn't mean that you can't be successful in others. It makes no sense to base your self-esteem on what you do worst in life, so don't focus solely on your failings and minimize your successes.

- **Don't just rely on—or wait for—others' praise.** Your self-esteem should not be solely dependent on the praise you get from others. Use your own judgment to evaluate the level of success you've achieved on a given task.

  For instance, you know when you've done your best in writing a paper. If you feel proud of it, celebrate your accomplishment and take pride in it. Instead of waiting for your instructor's feedback, permit yourself to feel good about what you've done. Your self-esteem should be based on your own assessment of your accomplishments, not only on others' assessments.

- **Understand that building self-esteem is a lifelong undertaking.** It's taken a lifetime to develop whatever level of self-esteem you currently have. Your self-esteem is not going to change overnight.

  Rebuilding self-esteem isn't easy. It's particularly hard to do at a time when you face a major life transition, such as the beginning of your postsecondary experience. Your oldest friends and your family may not be nearby, and the level of academic work you encounter presents new challenges. But starting college or university presents a special opportunity to grow and develop. It's a new environment, giving you the opportunity to unlearn old patterns of behaviour that have held you back and master new ones that will permit you to have a more positive view of yourself. Don't let low self-esteem keep you from becoming what you can be.

Preparing a Personal Mission Statement

The life that is unexamined is not worth living.

Twenty-five-hundred years later, Plato's words are still true. If you never consider what you want out of life, what your dreams and aspirations are, and where you're heading, you're in danger of missing out on the most fundamental and meaningful parts of life. The day-to-day details of life will use up all your time, and you won't know exactly where it has gone.

One way to get a clearer picture of your life is to create a formal statement of what you actually hope to achieve during your lifetime. The P.O.W.E.R. framework provides a series of steps that can help you look inward and determine how you want to carry out your life.

P repare: Identifying Your Values

The first step toward understanding yourself is to assess your underlying values systematically. To do this, work through the following steps:

1. Choose the five values that you hold most dear. Here are some examples, but don't restrict yourself to these: a comfortable life, an exciting life, a sense of accomplishment, world peace, beauty, equality, security, freedom, happiness, inner harmony, love, pleasure, religion, self-respect, fame, friendship, wisdom, work, financial security, risk taking, being challenged.

2. For each value, answer each of these questions: *Why* is it important to you? *Who* taught it to you? *How* has it affected your behaviour in the past? *In what ways* can you affirm it through your future behaviour?

   Value #1 _____

   Why it is important:

   Who taught it to you:

   How it has affected your past behaviour:

   In what ways you can affirm it through future behaviour:

   Value #2 _____

   Why it is important:

   Who taught it to you:

   How it has affected your past behaviour:

   In what ways you can affirm it through future behaviour:

Value #3 _____

    Why it is important:

    Who taught it to you:

    How it has affected your past behaviour:

    In what ways you can affirm it through future behaviour:

Value #4 _____

    Why it is important:

    Who taught it to you:

    How it has affected your past behaviour:

    In what ways you can affirm it through future behaviour:

Value #5 _____

    Why it is important:

    Who taught it to you:

    How it has affected your past behaviour:

    In what ways you can affirm it through future behaviour:

rganize: Placing Order on What Motivates You

Self-actualization
A state of self-fulfillment in which people realize their highest potential in their own unique way

Lester B. Pearson, Michael J. Fox, Marc Garneau: What is the common link among these three people? According to psychologist Abraham Maslow, each of them achieved or has achieved **self-actualization,** a state of self-fulfillment in which people realize their highest potential in their own unique way.[4]

According to Maslow, self-actualization is the highest of the various needs that motivate our behaviour. As you can see in Figure 3.3, our underlying needs form a pyramid. At the bottom of the pyramid are our most basic needs, the biological needs that drive our behaviour, including food, water, sleep, and sex. The basic needs are not much different from those that drive the behaviour of nonhuman animals. The needs on the next higher level of the pyramid are safety needs; we need a safe, secure environment in which to function effectively.

Because humans are able to meet their more basic survival needs, they have a chance to move to levels of need that relate to more-advanced qualities, such as the need for love. As the pyramid indicates, our love and belongingness needs come next: our need to form relationships with others and to look outside ourselves. We seek to give affection and to be contributing members of groups within society.

After these needs are fulfilled, we strive for the esteem of others. Esteem relates to the desire to develop a sense of self-worth. We want others to be aware of our competence and worth and to acknowledge our value in the world.

Only after we meet these physiological, safety, love and belongingness, and esteem needs can we strive for self-actualization. Although early views of self-actualization restricted this quality to a few well-known individuals, self-actualization is now generally regarded as a concept that can apply to any of us.

Figure 3.3
Pyramid of Motivational Needs

Self-actualization

Esteem

Love and belongingness

Safety needs

Biological needs

For instance, a parent with excellent nurturing skills who raises a family, an inventor whose product benefits others, and an artist who realizes her creative potential might all be self-actualized individuals.

The crucial characteristic of self-actualization is that we feel at ease with ourselves and satisfied that we are using our talents to the fullest. Achieving self-actualization produces a relaxation of the striving and yearning for greater fulfillment that mark many people's lives. People who are self-actualized can find satisfaction in their current state of affairs.

> "Authentic values are those by which a life can be lived."
>
> Allan Bloom

The pyramid shown in Figure 3.3 can help you to understand yourself more accurately. Use Try It! 7, "Organize Your Needs," to discover the structure of your own motivational needs.

W ork: Creating a Personal Mission Statement

- *To be the first choice for Canadians in Automotive, Sports and Leisure, and Home products, providing total customer value through customer-driven service, focused assortments and competitive operations.*

You may have already guessed the name of the company that would make the statement reproduced above: The Canadian Tire Corporation. Like almost every other major organization, Canadian Tire has a *mission statement*, a statement about what the organization does and the principles that guide its corporate life.

What's good for Canadian Tire is good for you. Each of us should set out a *personal mission statement*, a description encompassing our own personal objectives, long-term goals, and guiding philosophy. It's a kind of personal constitution that sets out broad principles of how we want to conduct our lives. It

Organize Your Needs

Consider the motivational needs illustrated by the pyramid in Figure 3.3 (biological needs, safety needs, love and belongingness, esteem, and self-actualization). Using the blank pyramid below, fill in your own particular needs in the order that best illustrates your personal hierarchy of needs. Don't feel constrained by the ordering in Figure 3.3; each of us has a unique pattern of needs that defines who we are. For example, you might feel that love and belongingness are more-fundamental needs and therefore should be closer to the bottom of the pyramid. Remember, there are no wrong answers.

Answer the following questions about your personal hierarchy of needs:

1. What similarities are there between your order and that suggested by the pyramid in Figure 3.3?

2. What differences are there in your ordering and those suggested by the pyramid in Figure 3.3? What accounts for the differences?

3. How do the values you pinpointed earlier (see "Prepare: Identifying Your Values") relate to the needs you've described in the pyramid? Can you relate your key values to your motivational needs?

is a guideline that allows us to adapt our behaviour to the changing conditions of life without straying from our overall direction and purpose.

If we don't have a mission statement, or at least think about the components of one, we risk drifting aimlessly through life. Constructing a mission statement permits us to make the choices we need to make based on our own personal philosophy. It helps us to move from our abstract values and motivational needs to something concrete.

For example, consider the following mission statement created by one student:

My mission is to use my personal abilities fully to become an engineer who will work on projects that will help others improve the quality of their lives. In addition, I hope to form meaningful relationships with others and to marry and raise children who will make their own contributions to society. Finally, I want to participate in bettering the world by volunteering in organizations that will enhance the quality of my own community.

This mission statement reflects several underlying values and needs: the desire to use work to improve others' lives, the desire to form relationships with others, and the desire to make the world a better place. In some respects it is fairly specific (such as the desire to become an engineer and to marry and have children), while in others it is fairly vague (such as the desire to participate in organizations that can improve community life). The key point is that it provides a general framework, a way of evaluating whether any particular choice fits into this individual's overall personal mission.

To create your own personal mission statement, follow these three preliminary steps:

1. **Summarize your most important values and motivational needs.** You've already assessed your values and motivational needs. Try to distill them into several key principles that will guide your life.

2. **Consider what you want your major product to be.** Canadian Tire sells products for cars, camping, sports, and the home. What do you want to be known and remembered for? your work? your family? your good deeds? your relationships with others? something you've created—art, photos, writing?

3. **Reflect on the kind of person you want to be.** Do you want to be kind, friendly, helpful, assertive, powerful, wealthy, altruistic?

Once you've completed these three steps, you're in a position to create your own mission statement. Use Try It! 8, "Write a Mission Statement."

 valuate: Assessing Your Personal Mission Statement

After you've written a personal mission statement, consider whether it accurately captures what you are looking for in life. Would a friend who knows you well see it as a valid reflection of who you are? Does the mission statement take a long-term view, reflecting not just where you are now, but where you want to be in the future? Is it general enough to fit the many different circumstances in which you will find yourself?

Only you can determine the ability of your personal mission statement to capture what is important to you. If you feel it doesn't, rewrite it. Eventually you'll come up with a statement that illustrates what you feel makes you special.

Try It! 8

Write a Mission Statement

1. What are your most important values (e.g., comfort, environmental awareness, kindness to others, inner harmony, challenge)?

2. What are your motivational needs (e.g., love and belonging, esteem, self-actualization)?

3. In what general area or career do you want to work?

4. What will be your most important "product," for which you want to be known and remembered (e.g., good deeds, wealth, power, prestige, artistic creations, business acumen)?

5. What kind of person do you want to be (e.g., helpful, kind, solitary, powerful, wealthy)?

6. In what sort of community do you want to live (e.g., large city, small city, small town, suburbs, country, woods, farm)?

7. With whom do you want to live (e.g., spouse, friends, children)?

8. What words describe your ideal lifestyle (e.g., sophisticated, woodsy, agricultural, down-home, laid-back, ambitious)?

Now write a one-paragraph mission statement below. You might, for example, state how you plan to achieve your motivational needs and realize your values through your chosen career. Next you might describe the sort of person you want to be and the "product" you plan to contribute to the world. Finally, you might describe your intended lifestyle, including the type of community you would like to live in and the nature of your ideal family. Once completed, include an edited copy of your mission statement in your portfolio.

Personal Mission Statement:

Rethink: Reconsidering Your Options

Personal mission statements are not set in stone; they should be considered living documents that you can change as you become clearer about what you want for yourself.

That's why it's important to periodically revisit your personal mission statement. When you do, ask yourself whether it still represents your values and motivational needs. Consider whether it should be amended to reflect changes that have occurred in your life.

Even if you don't modify it, periodically reading your personal mission

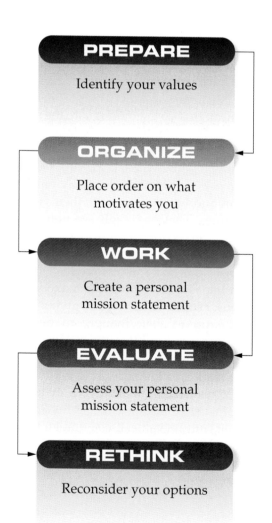

PREPARE

Identify your values

ORGANIZE

Place order on what motivates you

WORK

Create a personal mission statement

EVALUATE

Assess your personal mission statement

RETHINK

Reconsider your options

P.O.W.E.R. Plan

Career Connections

Personality Assessments on the Job

For many reasons, such as improving workplace communication, increasing productivity and efficiency, creating well balanced teams, or even ensuring corporate security, Canadian workplaces increasingly use personality testing as part of their hiring or orientation process. Employers sometimes use certain tests to help judge an applicant's suitability for a particular kind of job or level of responsibility, in other words, to match people to the jobs for which they are best suited. Tests may also measure specific aptitudes such as mechanical skills or sales abilities, or characteristics such as trustworthiness.

In an ideal situation, a person would do the job that best matches her personality, but that is not always possible. However, mismatching a personality to a job can frequently lead to poor performance and employee dissatisfaction. Employers want to know about employees' personalities to reduce conflict and maximize and coordinate staff abilities. Once an individual is on the job, personality testing can be used to identify a person's management or executive abilities in order to promote from within the organization or to do succession planning.

After completing the assessments in this book and at the Online Learning Centre, you should have a good idea of yourself, your strengths, weaknesses, interests, values, and motivations—strategic preparation for the world of work!

Enterprise Rent-A-Car suggests interested applicants consider their emotional intelligence (or EQ) when considering a career with E-Car. EQ describes a set of characteristics that influence a person's ability to be successful in everything from relationships to the workplace, that is, persistence, optimism, self-awareness, and social skills. Enterprise Rent-A-Car is particularly interested in hiring entrepreneurial individuals, feeling that entrepreneurs are happiest when running a business. Take the EQ test at Enterprise Rent-a-Car's website: <www.erac.com/recruit/EQ.htm>.

statement is important. It will remind you of who you are and what you are trying to get from the one life you have. (For a summary of the steps involved in creating a personal mission statement, see the P.O.W.E.R. Plan on the preceding page.)

To Thine Own Self Be True: No One Is Responsible for Your Life but You

"Don't take too many English courses; they're a waste of time because they won't help you get a decent job." "How about going to med school? You'd make a great doctor." "You owe it to your family to be a business major so you can join the family business when you graduate."

Sound familiar? Many of us have heard suggestions like these proposed by parents or others close to us. Such comments are almost always well-intentioned, and often they sound quite reasonable.

Why, then, should suggestions like these be taken with great caution? The reason is they relate to decisions that you, and only you, should make. You are the one who must live with their consequences. You are the one who must live with yourself.

One of the worst reasons to follow a particular path in life is that other people want you to. Decisions that affect your life should be your decisions—decisions you make after you've considered various alternatives and chosen the path that suits you best.

Making your own decisions does not mean that you should ignore the suggestions of others. For instance, your parents do have their own unique experiences that may make their advice helpful, and they sometimes may know you better, in certain respects, than you know yourself: Having participated in a great deal of your personal history, they may have a clear view of your strengths and weaknesses. Still, their views are not necessarily accurate. They may still see you as a child, in need of care and protection. Or they may see only your strengths. Or, in some unfortunate cases, they may focus on only your flaws and shortcomings.

The bottom line is that you need to make your own decisions. People will always be giving you advice. It's up to you, though, to decide whether or not to heed the advice. You need to determine the course of your life and the way you want it to unfold.

It's important to realize that making your own decisions may have costs. For instance, in some cultures loyalty to family and family wishes is a dominant cultural value. If you don't follow your family's suggestions, you may be seen as rebellious and uncaring. Ultimately, though, you have to make your own judgments about what's right for you, following your head—and your heart.

Speaking of Success

Todd Currie

Golf Course Technician Diploma
Seneca College

Todd Currie's job at West Haven Golf and Country Club means 12-hour workdays during peak season and zero chance of a summer vacation, but he loves his work. Todd is Superintendent of Maintenance at West Haven, a private facility in Hyde Park, Ontario. His responsibilities are many; he supervises a staff that fluctuates from six during the winter to over 20 during the summer. He and his staff do everything from looking after the golf course and gardens to maintaining and repairing all the equipment to investigating and ordering materials.

Todd was attending university, studying to be a physical education teacher when he realized it was taking education graduates years to get teaching jobs. As someone who loved golf and had worked at golf courses in the summer to earn tuition, he enrolled in Seneca College's Golf Course Technician Program and hasn't looked back since. Todd, who loves to work outdoors, was very happy with the Golf Course Technician Program, as the learning was very hands-on and focused on getting a job in the golf industry.

Todd continues to take courses in subjects such as pesticide and herbicide use, business administration, communication skills, resource management, and environmental

Seneca

awareness so he can provide the best product possible for the members of the golf and country club. He attends industry conferences as well to keep up with the latest innovations and practices in his field.

Todd says there are many false impressions about careers in the golf industry. Two key misconceptions are that golf courses are major polluters and irrigate constantly in order to keep grass green. Todd says golf courses use the minimum amount of herbicide and pesticide possible, as it is important to keep costs down, but also the health and safety of wildlife, staff, and patrons is paramount. Todd, who is a member of the Oxbow Creek Watershed Project, a committee affiliated with the Upper Thames River Conservation Authority, is also concerned with water use. He states that new varieties of grass make irrigating less necessary and in fact, the drier the greens are the better, as far as golf is concerned.

Todd reiterates that anyone considering a career as a golf course technician must be flexible, as the job entails long hours and lots of variety, but that for people who want to work outdoors, it is a wonderful career.

What are my learning styles, and how have they affected my academic success?

- People have diverse patterns of learning styles—characteristic ways of acquiring and using knowledge.

- Learning styles include visual, auditory, and tactile styles (the receptive learning styles), and analytic and relational styles (information processing styles).

- Personality styles that influence learning are classified along dimensions of introversion/extroversion, intuition/sensing, thinking/feeling, and perceiving/judging.

- Experiential learning styles are reflected in Kolb's Inventory of divergers, assimilators, convergers, and accommodators.

What is self-concept and how does it affect me?

- Self-concept is the understanding of the self that a person forms over time. Its major components are the physical, social, and personal self.

- Self-concept is important because of the effects it has on people's attitudes and behaviour. Self-concept can act as a self-fulfilling prophecy, in that people act in accordance with their self-concepts.

How does my level of self-esteem affect my behaviour?

- Self-esteem is the overall evaluation we give ourselves as individuals.

- High self-esteem can lead to greater happiness, an enhanced ability to cope with adversity, a sense of security and confidence, and self-efficacy.

- Low self-esteem can lead to insecurity, low self-efficacy, and a cycle of failure.

How can I determine my needs and make wise personal decisions throughout life?

- A personal mission statement can be used to determine important values and to state the principles by which we intend to lead our lives.

- People's needs can be organized into a hierarchy in which the most basic and fundamental needs form the base of a pyramid and higher orders of needs sit atop the basic needs.

- Although we should take into account the ideas and opinions of others, we must make our own decisions and choose our own path.

P.O.W.E.R. Portfolio

Self-Improvement

Look back at Table 3.2. Choose several of your major strengths and consider how you can demonstrate these qualities. Identify two or three of your weaknesses and turn them into challenges or goals. For example, "My preference is to work independently, but this semester I will improve my teamwork skills by participating in a study group and volunteering for the foot patrol squad at school." Once you have elaborated on your strengths and weaknesses, put the final copy in your portfolio.

Resources

On Campus

If you are interested in learning more about your pattern of learning styles, visit your campus counselling centre or career centre, where you may be able to take special assessment tests that can pinpoint your learning preferences and offer study strategies based on those preferences.

When dealing with the uncertainties of life and establishing your own sense of direction, it may help to speak to someone who has perspective and experience with college or university students. Here, too, a good place to start on campus is either a general counselling centre or one that is designed to help students choose career paths. Mental health offices can also be helpful in putting you in touch with a therapist with whom you can explore issues revolving around your self-concept and self-esteem. Don't hesitate to get help; you are doing it for yourself.

In Print

Please Understand Me II: Temperament, Character, Intelligence by David Keirsey (Prometheus Nemesis Book Co Inc, 1998) is a helpful book that states that differing styles and temperaments are to be expected and embraced.

Don't Sweat the Small Stuff . . . and It's All Small Stuff (Hyperion, 1997), written by Richard Carlson, is a down-to-earth guide that is meant to help you sort out what is—and is not—important in your life.

On the Web

The following sites on the World Wide Web provide the opportunity to extend your learning about the material in this chapter. Although the Web addresses were accurate at the time the book was printed, check the P.O.W.E.R. Learning website <www.mcgrawhill.ca/college/power>, for any changes that may have occurred.

http://career.missouri.edu
This site has an online version of the *Career Interests Game*, designed to help you match your interests and skills with careers. It can help you begin thinking about how your personality will fit in with specific work environments and careers.

www.keirsey.com/
The Keirsey site provides two online personality questionnaires. The inventories are based on Myers-Briggs, but Keirsey groups personality types according to temperaments.

www.cdm.uwaterloo.ca/step1_3.asp
This site offers an online values exercise that might be helpful in writing your personal mission statement.

The Case of . . .

The Instructor Who Spoke Too Much

Lana Carlson, a 26-year-old woman living in Calgary, Alberta, was at her wits' end. The instructor in her Diagnostic Procedures class spent each 50-minute lecture talking nonstop. He barely paused to acknowledge students' questions, and his only goal seemed to be to present as much material as possible. He even gave assignments in the same fast, nasal tone that he used throughout class.

If it weren't for her friend Darren Rubbell, who was in the same class and patiently explained material after class was over, Lana would never have managed to figure out how to complete the homework assignments. The strange thing was that Darren didn't seem to have much trouble with the professor's endless talking. In fact, he claimed to enjoy the class a lot. He had no trouble following the lectures and understanding the assignments, seeming to absorb like a sponge the information the instructor was spouting.

1. Based on what you know about learning styles, what might be the source of Lana's difficulties?

2. What learning style does the instructor apparently assume all students have? Do you think this is one of Lana's learning styles? Why or why not?

3. How might the instructor change his presentation to accommodate diverse learning styles?

4. Why does Lana's friend Darren have so little trouble with the instructor's lectures?

5. Why do you think Lana has less trouble understanding Darren after class than she has understanding her instructor?

6. If you were Lana, what might you do to improve your situation?

Using Technology for Information Management

4

You and Computers

Journal Reflections:
How I Feel about
Computers

Using E-Mail Effectively

Distance Learning:
Classes Without Walls

*Prepare: Identifying Distance
Learning Course Possibilities*

*Organize: Obtaining Access to
Technology*

*Work: Participating in a Distance
Learning Class*

*Evaluate: Considering Your
"Classroom" Performance*

*Rethink: Reflecting on What and
How You Have Learned*

Locating the
Information You Need

Career Connections:
Researching Careers
on the Web

Speaking of Success:
Shawn Thomson

The Case of . . . The
Unsuspecting
Plagiarist?

Brian Sullivan had never really gotten into computers. Unlike most of his friends, he didn't even use e-mail much, preferring to keep in touch by phone.

So when his psychology instructor announced on the first day of class that her course required extensive use of the Internet, Brian was not very enthusiastic. He was even less enthusiastic when the instructor said the class was going to be paperless. Assignments would be provided on the class website, and papers had to be "handed in" electronically.

For the first month, Brian had a hard time seeing the point to the system. Then, in the middle of the term, his grandfather was in a serious car accident. Brian rushed home to see him; his grandpa was in pretty bad shape. Brian wanted to stick around for a while, but he worried that if he did, he would fall behind in his classes.

Then he found out that the hospital offered visitors Internet access. Though he was hundreds of miles away, Brian could get his psychology and other assignments and e-mail his responses back to the instructors.

The Internet probably saved his academic career that semester.

Looking
Ahead

The technology that permitted Brian to keep up with his classes didn't even exist a dozen years ago. Education is changing, as it takes increasing advantage of "virtual" resources—e-mail, the Internet, and other evolving technologies. In fact, at some point, you might be taking a course entirely on the Web, never setting foot in the same room as your instructor or your classmates.

Technology is making a profound difference in how we are taught, the ways we study and carry out our work, and how we communicate with our professors and other students. It is changing the way you can access the vast quantities of information published each year—tens of thousands of books, journals, and other print materials, and literally millions of Web pages.

In this chapter we discuss how technological advances increase your opportunities to achieve success in college or university. We'll consider the ways in which computers can be used to manipulate data and present it. We'll also talk about distance learning, an approach to education that involves studying with an instructor who may be thousands of miles away. Finally, we'll consider how you can use technology for information management—locating and using both the information traditionally held in libraries and information created for and in the virtual world of cyberspace.

In short, after reading this chapter, you'll be able to answer these questions:

- **What is available on the Internet?**

- **What is distance learning?**

- **What are the basic sources of information?**

- **What do I need to keep in mind as I use the Web to gather information?**

You and Computers

They are an amazing time-saver. They're a great tool that can help you achieve success in your classes. They're the remarkable equivalent of a typewriter, archive, printing press, calculator, and proofreader, all rolled into one.

They can also, at times, be extremely frustrating, annoying, and maddening.

"They," of course, are computers. And you'll need to be able to use them to maximize your success in college or university. These days it's as much a necessity to learn to use a computer as it was for you to learn to use a calculator earlier in your schooling. No one facing the job market in the twenty-first century will want to leave college without basic computer skills.

If you are not yet at ease with computers, relax. No one is born with computer skills. With sufficient practice, however, using a computer will become second nature.

(To explore your feelings about computers, complete the Journal Reflections.)

Word-Processing Programs:
Spreading the Word

A **word-processing program** turns a computer into a smart typewriter—a very smart typewriter. With a word-processing program, everything you write can be stored in a computer's memory, and you can check the spelling of the words you type, automatically keep track of your footnotes, and "cut and paste" material with incredible ease. Most important, word processors take much of the drudgery out of revision. You can quickly delete words and sentences that you don't want, substitute new material in place of what you deleted, and rearrange words, sentences, and entire paragraphs.

Some of the most important things you can do with a word-processing program include:

Journal Reflections

How I Feel about Computers

1. If you had to characterize your general reactions when you hear the words "computer" and "the Internet," what would you say?

2. Do you use e-mail? Do you use the Internet much? Do you use a computer for other things? If so, what have your experiences been like?

3. How satisfied do you feel with your level of expertise in using computers/the Internet? Do you intend to take any steps to increase it?

4. How do you feel about people who are expert in using computers? Do you ever use the term "computer geek" to describe them? If so, what do you mean by it? What do you think others mean by it?

5. Do you think it is harder for older adults to learn about computers? Why or why not?

Word-processing program
Application software that turns a computer into a very smart typewriter

Express Yourself

Type the following sentences on a computer. Use word-processing software to make the appearance of each sentence match the message it conveys (i.e., by using different fonts, different sizes, punctuation marks, symbols, etc.).

No rain, no rainbows.

Life is not a dress rehearsal

Where there's a will, there's a way.

Be prepared.

What goes around, comes around.

The best things in life aren't things.

If you can read this, you're too close.

Step right up and see the Amazing Shrinking Man.

Keep off the grass. This means you.

Question authority.

Danger. Explosives.

After you've completed this exercise, share your results with others in your class or with your study group. Is there a particular approach that works most effectively?

To Try It! online, go to **<www.mcgrawhill.ca/college/power>**.

- *Inserting and deleting text.*
- *Moving and copying text.*
- *Changing the appearance of text.*

     Obviously, before you use an exotic-looking or extra-large or extra-small font size for a paper, consider your instructor's requirements. (And don't expect font size to rescue a paper that's too short: instructors are likely to notice if you use an oversized font to extend the page count of a paper!) Probably the most common font—primarily because it is so easy to read—is Times New Roman at 12-point.

(Reveal yourself typographically in Try It! 1, "Express Yourself.")

- *Adding footnotes or endnotes.*
- *Spell checking of every word.*
- *Checking for basic grammatical errors.*
- *Saving what you write.*

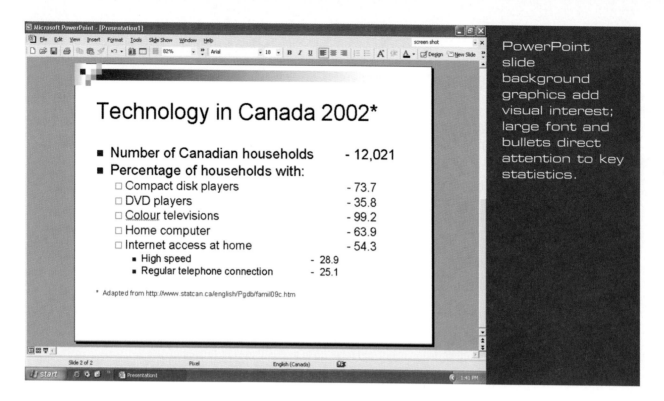

Presentation Programs: Looking Good

Sometimes how you present material is as important as what you're presenting. **Presentation programs** such as PowerPoint help you put your best foot forward by allowing you to create impressive, professional-looking visual materials, including charts, maps, animations, and other graphical elements. The resulting output can be printed onto paper, made into overhead transparencies or slides, run as a "slide show" from your computer, or projected directly from your computer onto a screen through a projector.

There are several keys to developing an effective presentation:

- **Include graphics.** Most presentation programs have an array of graphics that can be added to a slide. A globe, a cap-and-gown, a shooting star, or other objects can add visual spice to your presentation.

- **Remember: Less is more.** Don't try to cram too much information on a particular slide. Avoid putting too many words on a line or using too many colours. Just because you *can* do all sorts of cool things with graphics doesn't mean that you *should*—at least not all at the same time.

- **Unify your presentation.** Individual slides or other presentation materials should have a similar look. Using similar fonts and font sizes unifies your presentation.

- **Check for spelling errors.** Most presentation programs have built-in spell checks. Use them! It's embarrassing to have a 1-metre-high spelling mistake projected onto a screen.

- **Use *animation* if you are using a projector that connects directly to a computer.** Animation allows you to add movement to your presentation. Graphics, sentences, words, or even letters can be made to slide in from the left or right of the screen, or appear (or disappear) as you choose.

To test out using a presentation program, complete Try It! 2, "Presenting. . . ."

Presentation programs
Computer application software that helps you create impressive, professional-looking visual materials that include words, charts, maps, and other graphical elements

Presenting . . .

Type the following key points about using presentation programs into a presentation program, one per page (or "slide"). Use the features of the presentation program to make the points more striking. Work with others in your study group.

Key points:

Include graphics

Remember: less is more

Standardize

Avoid errors

Use animation

How satisfied are you with your presentation? How easy was it to accomplish what you wanted to do? What other things might you have done in creating your presentation?

To Try It! online, go to <**www.mcgrawhill.ca/college/power**>.

Spreadsheet Programs:
Crunching the Numbers

Spreadsheet programs

Application programs that help with budgeting and financial projections and are necessary for business, accounting, and engineering courses

Whether you love or hate math, you're going to like spreadsheet programs, for they take the drudgery out of crunching numbers. **Spreadsheet programs** like Excel help you with budgeting and financial projections and are necessary for accounting and engineering courses. They allow you to perform calculations with complete accuracy.

Spreadsheet programs contain files that are divided into *cells*, which is where you input information. Each cell has an "address" that pinpoints its location by column (designated by a letter) and row (designated by a number).

File Edit View Insert Format Tools Data Window Help																		
	C	D	E	F	G	H	I	J	K	L	M	N	O	P	Q	R	S
1				**Expense Report**							Phone Number 847-555-1000						
2																	
3	**Name** Samuel Spader			**Dept. Name** Information Technologies						**Location** 1 Center					**Period Ending**		1-Jan-0
4																	
5	CAR EXPENSE											Explain Meals, Ent. & Misc	on Reverse Side				Tota
6																	
7	(1)Gas/Oil	Maint.	Plne, Train Limo, Taxi	Car Rental	Tolls Parking	Exhibit Fees	Office Supplies	Printing	Phone	Postage	Hotel & Lodging	Business Meals	Meals Alone	Entertain-ment	Misc.		Expen
8																	$ 1,07
9			356.29			250.00			12.35		375.29	85.37					$
10																	$
11																	$
30																	$
31																	$
32																	$
33																	$
34																	$
35				380.00	36.00						181.27	95.45					$ 69
36																	$
37																	$
38																	$
39																	
40	0.00	0.00	356.29	380.00	36.00	250.00	0.00	0.00	12.35	0.00	556.56	180.82	0.00	0.00	0.00		$ 1,772

Expense report generated by Excel spreadsheet software. Numerical calculations are embedded as formulas in the spreadsheet, simplifying the task of figuring totals.

After you input data, you can instruct the program to perform an amazing array of calculations with a simple formula or command. For example, you can have the program add up a range of cells; subtract the value of one cell from a second cell; or find the square roots of the numbers in three cells and add the results together. Revisions are easy with spreadsheets. Change a number in any cell, and a revised result will be displayed.

Spreadsheet programs also offer easy ways of creating graphs. By entering the appropriate information, you can create a variety of graphs, ranging from bar graphs to pie charts.

Using E-Mail Effectively

What's the first thing you do when you turn on a computer? If you're like most people, you check first for new e-mail messages.

E-mail has become the preferred means of written communication for many of us. Quick, efficient, and (usually) reliable, e-mail is the most widely used feature of the Internet.

Every person using e-mail has at least one address, consisting of these elements:

- **Mailbox name.** The mailbox name—the name assigned to your account on an e-mail system—is often some variant of your own name (e.g., ben_mulroney), though it may also be totally fictitious (e.g., goleafs9).

- **@.** The *at* sign.

- **Domain name.** The domain name is the name of the organization that hosts the e-mail "post office" to which the user subscribes—often an institution (e.g., fanshawec.ca or mcgrawhill.ca), an Internet service provider (e.g., aol.com or earthlink.net), or a multifaceted system such as yahoo.com or hotmail.com.

Writing and Responding to E-mail

Writing e-mail messages is simple. First, type the address of the person to whom you are writing (or, if you've gotten that far already, select it from your e-mail address book). If you are directly e-mailing a professor or instructor, make sure you include your name and course number in the subject line. Just because you know who you are, your prof may not know who "neo@yahoo.ca" is and there may be as many as 12 students named "Jen" in various courses. Always include a brief description of the message in the subject line as well. Always use the subject line; it allows recipients to get a preview of what the message is about and to easily distinguish that message later from other messages that they may have received from you.

Finally, write the message itself. E-mail messages have several features that are not part of more traditional, formal "snail-mail" letters. For instance, writers frequently include abbreviations. Some common ones are IMO ("in my opinion"), BTW ("by the way"), CYA ("see ya"), OIC ("oh, I see"), and WTG ("way to go").

One of the ways that e-mail quickens the pace of communication is the ease with which you can respond to a message you've received. To respond you simply click an on-screen button marked "reply." A new message window appears on screen, and you type in your reply and send off the message.

You can also *forward* messages that you've received to another person who was not an original recipient of the message.

E-mail messages can also contain *attachments,* files that do not appear in the body of the message but that can be opened separately. Attachments can take the form of word-processing documents, audio files, digital photographs, and video clips.

You can use attachments to submit a paper to an instructor. A paper sent as an attachment will be an exact copy of the original file that you produced using a word processor. (Of course, make sure that your instructor accepts assignments via e-mail before you send it.)

Not every message deserves a response. For example, you may receive *spam,* which is the equivalent of junk mail. Spam may range from get-rich-quick schemes to advertisements for body enhancements or pornography. Spam is more than a nuisance; it takes up valuable transmission resources ("bandwidth"), disk space, and computer time. Some e-mail systems allow users to apply a *filter* that uses a few simple rules to separate the wheat (e-mail you actually want to read) from the chaff (spam). Unfortunately, these systems are not perfect: they sometimes let junk through and can even at times dispose of messages you want. The only absolutely reliable way to deal with spam is to delete it yourself as quickly as possible.

Finally, *never* open an attachment from someone you don't know. Computer viruses, which can ruin everything on your hard drive, are often spread through e-mail attachments.

Netiquette: Showing Civility in E-Mail

Although e-mail communication is usually less formal than a letter, you still need to maintain civility. This is especially important, when considering how much workplace communication takes place via e-mail. Here are some rules:

- **Don't write anything in an e-mail message that you'll regret seeing on the front page of the campus newspaper.** Yes, e-mail is usually private; but the private message you write can easily be forwarded by the recipient to another person or even scores of other people. Worse yet, it's fairly easy to hit "reply [to] all" when you mean simply to "reply": in this case, you might think that you are responding to an individual, when in fact the e-mail will go to everyone who received the message along with you.

- **Be careful of the tone you convey.** It is harder on e-mail to convey the same kind of personality, and often the same degree of subtlety, that our voice, our handwriting, or even our stationery can add to other forms of communication. This means that attempts at humour and especially sarcasm can backfire.

- **Don't use all capital letters.** Using all caps MAKES IT LOOK AS IF YOU'RE SHOUTING.

- **Never send an e-mail when you are angry.** No matter how annoyed you are about something someone has written in a message, don't respond in kind—or at least wait until you've cooled down. Take a deep breath, and wait for your anger to pass.

Distance Learning: Classes Without Walls

Do you find that your schedule changes so much from one day to the next that it's hard to fit in a course that meets at a regularly scheduled time? Interested in an unusual course topic that your own school doesn't offer? Want to take a class during the summer, but find yourself summering too far from a postsecondary campus?

The solution to your problem may be to enroll in a distance learning course. **Distance learning** is a form of education in which students participate via the World Wide Web or other kinds of technology. Although most distance learning courses are taught via the Web, some use teleconferencing, fax, and/or express mail.

Distance learning
A form of education in which students participate via the World Wide Web or other kinds of technology

The key feature of distance learning courses is the mediated interaction between instructor and students. Rather than meeting in a traditional classroom, where the instructor, you, and the other students are physically present, distance learning classes are most often virtual. Although some schools are experimenting with "Webcasts" of lectures and with virtual discussion rooms, many students in distance learning courses will never sit through a lecture or even participate in a real-time conversation with students in the class. They may never even know what their instructor or classmates look like or hear their voices.

Typically, if you take a distance learning course today, you may read lecture notes posted on the Web, search and browse websites, write papers, post replies to discussion topics on a *message board*, and take online quizzes and exams. You will see your instructor's and classmates' responses through comments they post on the Web. You may be expected to read a textbook entirely on your own.

Distance learning is not for everyone. Whether you're a good candidate for it or not depends on your preferred style of course-taking. Complete Try It! 3, "Assess Your Course-Taking Style," to see whether you are suited to learn at a distance.

Distance learning classes have both advantages and disadvantages. On the plus side, distance learning courses offer the following:

- **You can take a Web-based distance learning course anywhere that you have access to the Web.** You can be at home, at the school library, or on vacation at the cottage and still participate.

- **Distance learning classes are more flexible than traditional classes.** You can participate in a course any time of the day or night. You set your own schedule.

- **Distance learning classes are self-paced.** You may be able to spread out your work over the course of a week, or you may do the work in a concentrated manner on one day.

Personal Styles: Assess Your Course-Taking Style

Your preferred course-taking style—how you participate in classes, work with your classmates, interact with your teachers, and complete your assignments—may make you more or less suitable for distance learning. Read the following statements and indicate whether you agree or disagree with them to see whether you have what it takes to be a distance learner.

	Agree	Neutral	Disagree
1. I need the stimulation of other students to learn well.			
2. I need to see my teacher's face, expressions, and body language to interpret what is being said.			
3. I participate a lot in class discussions.			
4. I prefer to hear information presented orally rather than reading it in a book or article.			
5. I'm not very good at keeping up with reading assignments.			
6. I'm basically pretty easily distracted.			
7. I'm not very well organized.			
8. Keeping track of time and holding to schedules is NOT a strength of mine.			
9. I need a lot of "hand-holding" while I work on long assignments.			
10. I need a close social network to share my feelings, ideas, and complaints with.			
11. I'm not very good at writing.			
12. Basically, I'm not very patient.			

The more you disagree with these statements, the more your course-taking style is suited to distance learning. Interpret your style according to this informal scale:

Disagreed with 10–12 statements = Excellent candidate for distance learning

Disagreed with 7–9 statements = Good candidate for distance learning

Agreed with 6–9 statements = Probably better taking classes on campus

Agreed with 10–12 statements = Avoid distance learning

To Try It! online, go to <**www.mcgrawhill.ca/college/power**>.

- **You may have more contact with your instructor than you do with a traditional class.** Even though you may not have face-to-face contact, you may have greater access to your instructor, via e-mail and the Web, than in traditional classes. You can leave messages for your instructor any time of the night or day; most instructors of distance learning classes respond in a timely way.

- **Shy students may find it easier to "speak up" in a distance learning class.** You can think through your responses to make sure you are communicating just what you wish to say. You don't have to worry about speaking in front of other people. For many people, distance learning is liberating.

- **You can become a better reader and writer.** Because distance learning usually involves more reading and writing than traditional courses, you receive more practice reading and writing—and more feedback—than in traditional classes.

On the other hand, distance learning has disadvantages that you should keep in mind. You won't have direct, face-to-face contact with your instructor or other students. It may feel isolating to be alone at your computer, and you can feel lost in cyberspace.

In addition, you won't always get *immediate* feedback. In a distance learning class, it may be hours, or sometimes days, before you receive feedback on what you have posted to a message board, depending on how well the pace of other students matches your own. However, to alleviate the isolation and allow for real-time feedback, some online courses do require certain check-in times, regular chats, or group work to encourage the social learning that is so important for some learners. In addition, online tests and exams usually must be written at specific times.

Finally, distance learning classes require significant personal responsibility and time management skills. You won't have a set time to attend class as you do in traditional courses. You must carve out the time yourself. Although instructors provide a schedule when things are due, *you* have to work out the timing of getting them done.

Despite these potential drawbacks to distance learning courses, they are becoming increasingly popular. More and more colleges and universities are offering them. Many companies encourage employees with crowded schedules to take distance learning as a way of providing continuing education.

If you are considering taking a distance education course, follow these steps, which are summarized in the P.O.W.E.R. Plan at the right.

P repare: Identifying Distance Learning Course Possibilities

How do you find a distance learning course? In some cases, your own college or university may offer courses on the Web and list them in your course catalogue. In other cases, you'll have to find courses on your own.

The best place to look is on the Web itself. By searching the Web, you can find distance learning courses ranging from agronomy to zoology. Don't be deterred by the physical location of the institution that offers the course; it doesn't matter where the college is located, because you'll never have to go to the campus itself.

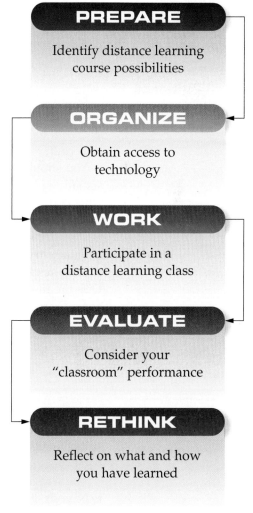

PREPARE

Identify distance learning course possibilities

ORGANIZE

Obtain access to technology

WORK

Participate in a distance learning class

EVALUATE

Consider your "classroom" performance

RETHINK

Reflect on what and how you have learned

P.O.W.E.R. Plan

Working in a Group: Get Some Distance on the Problem

There are over 2700 courses offered online by Canadian colleges and universities. Working by yourself initially, see if you can find distance learning courses of interest to you: start by checking your school's course catalogue to see what might be offered there. If you're already comfortable online, you might also try the following:

- Browse Industry Canada's Campus Connection database for courses by subject area at **<www.campusconnection.ca/index.html>**.

- Take a look at what is being offered by the Canadian Virtual University, a partnership of universities across Canada, committed to delivering university-level programs that can be completed from anywhere in the country or beyond at **<www.cvu-uvc.ca/english.html>**.

- Do a search for online courses being offered in Australia, New Zealand, Scotland, or any other English-speaking country that interests you.

Try to find five courses you would be interested in. After you have completed your list, share your list with others in a group. How diverse were the courses you were able to find? Were particular subject areas better represented than others? Why?

To Try It! online, go to **<www.mcgrawhill.ca/college/power>**.

But before you sign up for a potential course that you would like to count toward your degree, *make sure that your own postsecondary institution will give you credit for it.* Check with your coordinator, advisor, and registrar's office to be certain.

You should also find out what the requirements of a course are before you actually sign up for it. Check the syllabus carefully and see how it meshes with your schedule. If it is a summer course and you are going to be away from your computer for a week, you may not be able to make up the work you miss.

Finally, try to talk with someone who has taken the course before. Was the instructor responsive, providing feedback rapidly? If necessary, could you speak with the instructor by phone? Was the course load reasonable? (Try It! 4, "Get Some Distance on the Problem," will help you to work through the process.)

Organize: Obtaining Access to Technology

Although you don't need to be a computer expert, you will need some minimal e-mail and Web skills to take a distance learning course. If you don't have sufficient technological expertise, beef up your computer skills by taking a computer course or workshop *before* you actually sign up for the course.

You'll also need access to a computer connected to the Internet. It doesn't have to be your own computer, but you will certainly need regular and convenient access to one. Make sure that the computer you plan to use has sufficient internal resources to quickly connect to the Internet; a very slow connection is frustrating.

Be sure to make all your arrangements for computer access prior to the start of a course. It can take several weeks to set up Internet service on a home computer if you don't have it already. In addition, make sure you have compatible software so you can open attachments, read .pdf files, listen to audio selections, view video clips, etc.

W ork: Participating in a Distance Learning Class

Successfully participating in a distance learning course involves several skills that are distinct from those needed for traditional classes. To get the most out of a distance learning course, you'll need to do the following:

- **Manage your time carefully.** You won't have the luxury of a regular schedule of class lectures, so you'll have to manage your time carefully. No one is going to remind you that you need to sit down at a computer and work.

- **Check in frequently.** Instructors may make crucial changes in the course requirements. Make sure to check for any changes in due dates or class expectations.

- **Find a cyberbuddy.** At the start of the semester, try to make personal contact with at least one other student in the class. You can do this by e-mailing, phoning, or actually meeting the student if he or she is geographically nearby. You can share study strategies, form a study group, and share notes. Connecting with another student can help you avoid feelings of isolation that may interfere with your success.

- **Make copies of everything.** Don't assume everything will go well in cyberspace. Make a printed copy of everything you submit, or alternatively have a backup stored on another computer.

- **Have a technology backup plan.** Computers crash, your connection to the Internet may go down, or an e-mailed assignment may be mysteriously delayed or sent back to you. Don't wait until the last minute to work on and submit assignments, and have a plan in place if your primary computer is unavailable.

E valuate: Considering Your "Classroom" Performance

As with any class, you'll be receiving feedback from your instructor. But unlike many courses, in which almost all the feedback comes from the instructor, much of the feedback in a distance learning course may come from your fellow students. What can you learn from their comments?

At the same time you'll be receiving feedback, you will likely be providing feedback to your classmates. Consider the nature of feedback you provide, and be sure that you use the basic principles of classroom civility.

R ethink: Reflecting on What and How You Have Learned

Distance learning is not for everyone. If your preferred learning style involves extensive, face-to-face interaction with others, you may find that your experience is less than satisfying. On the other hand, if you are at ease with computers and enjoy working on your own, you may find distance learning highly effective.

As you reflect on your distance learning experience, go beyond the technology and think about the learning outcomes. Ask yourself whether you learned as much as you would have in a traditional class. You should also consider ways that the experience could have been more effective for you. And think about whether you were so absorbed by the technology that you lost sight of the real goal of the course: learning new material.

Most educational experts believe that distance learning will play an increasingly important role in higher education. Furthermore, because it offers an efficient way of educating people in far-flung locales, it is a natural means of promoting lifelong learning experiences. In short, the first distance learning class you take is likely not to be your last.

One of the greatest advances brought about by developments in information management is in the area of research. We'll now consider some ways in which you can search the two primary repositories of knowledge for any student. One you can walk or drive to—the library. The other—the Internet—doesn't have a physical location. But both are indispensable in anyone's quest for information.

Locating the Information You Need

Becoming Acquainted with Information Sources

In general, you'll find information stored in two distinct kinds of places—libraries and computer information networks.

Libraries No matter how humble or imposing its physical appearance, whether it contains only a few volumes or hundreds of thousands, the library is one good place to focus your efforts as you seek out and gather information.

Although every library is different, all share two key elements: the material they hold—their basic collections—and the tools to help you *locate* the material you need.

What Can Be Found in a Library's Basic Collections? Libraries obviously contain books, but they typically have a lot more than that. In addition to the fiction and nonfiction books on their shelves, libraries usually have some or all of the following:

Microform
A means of storing greatly reduced photographs of printed pages, which can be read using special microform readers; the two main types of microform are microfiche and microfilm

- **Periodicals.** *Periodicals* are popular magazines published for general audiences, specialized journals for professionals in a field, and newspapers. Magazines and journals are often bound and stored by year; newspapers are usually kept in **microform,** in which documents that have been photographed and greatly reduced in size are stored on either microfilm (reels of film) or microfiche (plastic sheets), which can be read with special microform readers.

- **Indexes to Periodicals and Other Information Sources.** How can you learn what articles have been published in magazines, newspapers, and journals? Indexes provide the information.

  An index provides a listing of journal articles by subject area and author. Some indexes also provide a short summary, or **abstract,** of the contents of each article.

  Many kinds of indexes can be found. Some are general, such as the *Reader's Guide to Periodical Literature,* and cover a variety of general circulation magazines of the type you'd find at a decent newsstand, such as *Newsweek, Maclean's,* and *Rolling Stone.* Others are more specialized and concentrate on a particular field. For instance, the *Music Index* is an index of articles about music, and the *Business Periodicals Index* provides information on articles about business.

  Indexes come in both book and computerized form. Although some people prefer to use indexes in book form, computerized indexes such as CD-ROM, web-based or electronic data bases, are considerably easier and quicker to use. Furthermore, you can often download the results of computerized searches at a library onto your own floppy disks, which you can later load into your computer.

Abstract

A short summary of the contents of a journal article

- **Encyclopedias.** Encyclopedias provide a broad overview of knowledge. Some encyclopedias, such as the *Encyclopaedia Britannica* or *World Book Encyclopedia,* attempt to cover the entire range of knowledge, and they may take up many volumes. Others are more specialized, covering only a particular field, such as the *Encyclopedia of Human Behavior* or *The Canadian Encyclopedia.* Most are printed as multivolume sets of books, although an increasing number come in CD-ROM computerized versions. Encyclopedias provide a good general view of a topic, raising key issues that can lead you to more specific and current sources, and as such are a good resource at the earliest stage of your information gathering. Although some encyclopedias lack depth, subject-specific encyclopedias, such as the *Encyclopedia of Sociology*, are comprehensive references with articles written by leading scholars and edited by advisory groups comprised of the top academics in their fields.

> "Knowledge is of two kinds: we know a subject ourselves, or we know where we can find information upon it."
>
> Samuel Johnson

- **Dictionaries.** The reference section of most libraries has a wide range of dictionaries, including specialized dictionaries, such as French–English or manufacturing dictionaries.

- **Government documents.**

- **Musical scores.**

- **Reserve collections.** Reserve collections hold heavily used items that instructors assign for a class. Sometimes reserve material can be checked out for only an hour or two and used in the same room; in other cases the material can be used overnight or for a few days.

  Most libraries offer information sheets describing all the different kinds of materials they have available and how you can find them. Find one of these sheets (often they are at the main desk closest to the entrance) and you have the key to the library.

Using Catalogues
Catalogues contain a listing of all materials that are held in the library. Because they list where the information is physically stored, they also help you find what you're looking for.

Traditionally, catalogues consisted of paper cards that were filed in trays. In large libraries, the card catalogue sometimes extended across several huge rooms. Today, however, the catalogues of an increasing number of libraries are computerized. Rather than physically sorting through cards, users conduct a catalogue search on a computer. In fact, you may be able to access your school's catalogue from home as well as from computers housed in the library itself.

Other libraries use microform media (microfiche or microfilm) for their catalogues. And many libraries are in transition, using a combination of forms.

Although traditional card catalogues (consisting of records of information on actual cards) and computer catalogues (consisting of electronic records) are physically very different, the basic information each contains is the same. Information is usually sorted by title, author name, and subject, which means that each book (or other library holding) actually can be found in three different ways: searching for its author (*author listing*), its title (*title listing*), or its subject (*subject listing*). Individual entries generally include additional information, such as the publisher, date of publication, and similar information pertaining to the item.

Say, for example, you're writing a paper on David Suzuki. To find his books in an electronic catalogue, you enter his name, searching the catalogue for author entries. You may be presented with the following listing:

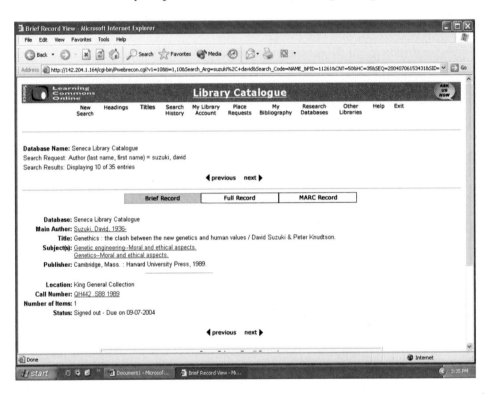

Call number

A unique classification number assigned to every book (or other resource) in a library, which provides a key to locating it

The key piece of information is the book's call number. The **call number** is a classification unique to a book that tells you exactly where to find it. Most postsecondary libraries use the Library of Congress classification system for call numbers, a combination of letters and numbers. The first letter indicates a general topical area, and the numbers provide further classification information. But you don't need to know the system; all that's really important is that it pinpoints the book's location in the library.

Because the record illustrated above is from an electronic search, it contains further helpful information. The words "IN LIBRARY" under "STATUS" tell you that the book has not been checked out by another patron and should be sitting

Try It! 5

Test Drive the Library Catalogue

Go to your college library catalogue (card or electronic) and practise your research skills by looking up information on five of the following topics:

Gandhi's tactics of nonviolent demonstration

the destruction of the Berlin Wall

the origins of rock and roll

Karen Kain's career

the importance of the Lewis and Clark expedition

Anne of Green Gables

the Riel rebellion

cold fusion

job hunting

PC versus Mac computers

professional lacrosse

Some topics are easier to find information about than others. Which topics among those you selected were the most difficult ones? Why do you think that the topics differ in terms of the ease of finding information? If some of the topics produced an overwhelming amount of information, how did you decide where to go first? (Later in the chapter you'll learn some tricks for choosing where to go first for information.)

on the shelf. You'll need to familiarize yourself with your library's particular system to know what specific commands are available to you. Chances are there's a handout or posted set of instructions nearby. Use Try It! 5, "Test Drive the Library Catalogue," to get the hang of your school or community library's system.

Locating Information   Once you have identified the information you're seeking by using the catalogue, you need to actually locate the work. In all but the biggest libraries, you can simply go into the **stacks,** the place containing shelves where the books and other materials are kept, and—using the call number—find what you're looking for. In some cases, however, you won't be permitted to enter the stacks. In libraries with closed stacks, you must fill out a form with the call numbers of the books you want. A library aide will find and deliver the material to a central location.

Stacks
The shelves on which books and other materials are stored in a library

What if you go to the location in the stacks where the material is supposed to be and you can't find it? The most likely explanation is that the material is checked out or is in use by someone else at that time. It may also be incorrectly shelved or simply lost. Whatever the reason, don't give up. If the material is checked out to another user, ask a librarian if you can **recall** the material, a process by which the library contacts whoever has the book and asks him or her to return it because someone else needs to use it.

Recall
A way to request library materials from another user who has them

If the librarian informs you that the material is not checked out to someone else, wait a few days and see whether it appears on the shelf. Someone

Searching for materials in the library stacks can be frustrating if they are not on the shelves. However, you may unexpectedly find relevant and interesting material.

Interlibrary loan

A system by which libraries share resources, making them available to patrons of different libraries

World Wide Web

A graphical interface that permits users to transmit and receive text and pictorial, video, and audio information

Browser

A program that provides a way of navigating the World Wide Web

URL (uniform resource locator)[1]

The address that defines the route to a file on the Web or any other Internet facility

Web page

A location (or site) on the World Wide Web housing information from a single source, and (typically) links to other pages

may have been using it while you were looking for it and then left it to be reshelved. If it was misshelved, the librarian may be able to find it. If the material is truly lost, you may be able to get it from another library through **interlibrary loan,** a system by which libraries share resources, making them available to patrons of different libraries. Ask the librarian for help; an interlibrary loan will take some time—between a few days and several weeks—but eventually you'll be able to get the material.

Finally, even if you do find exactly what you were looking for, take a moment to scan the shelves for related material. Because books and other materials are generally grouped by topic on library shelves, you may find other useful titles in the same place. One of the pleasures of libraries is the possibility of finding on the shelves an unexpected treasure—material that your catalogue search did not initially identify but that may provide you with exactly the kind of information you need.

The World Wide Web   Want to know how to order flowers for your girlfriend in Ottawa? find a long-lost friend? the latest bulletin from Health Canada? biographical information on Jarome Iginla?

There is one place where you can look for all this information—and stand a good chance of finding it: the **World Wide Web**. The Web is a computer resource that links a vast array of information to the user's computer terminal. The information may be text, photos, graphs, or video or audio clips.

Like a library, the Web involves several essential components. They include a browser, Web pages, links, and search engines.

- **Browsers.** To use the World Wide Web, your computer has to have a browser. A **browser,** as its name implies, is a program that provides a way of moving around the Web. Among the major browsers are Netscape's Navigator and Microsoft's Internet Explorer.

   To use a browser, you indicate the location of the information that you're seeking by typing in an address. Web addresses are odd combinations of letters and symbols. They typically start off with "http://www" and then go on from there. The address identifies a unique location on the Web, known as a *Web page* (or sometimes *website*), that you are directing your browser to find. Another term for an Internet address is **URL (uniform resource locator)**.

- **Web pages.** Also known as websites, Web pages are the heart of the World Wide Web. A **Web page** is a location on the World Wide Web that presents you with information. The information may appear as text on the screen, to be read like a book (or more accurately, like a scroll). Or it might be a video clip, an audio clip, a photo, a portrait, a graph, or a figure. It may be a news service photo of the prime minister of Canada or a backyard snapshot of someone's family reunion.

- **Links** (short for hyperlinks). Websites typically provide you with **links**—a means of automatically jumping—to other Web pages or to other places on that website. Just as an encyclopedia article on forests might say at the end, "See also *Trees*," Web pages often provide a means of reaching other sites on the Web—you just have to click on the link with your mouse and you are there.

- **Search engines.** A **search engine** is simply a computerized index to information on the Web. Among the most popular are Yahoo!, Google, AltaVista, and Excite! In fact, Google has become such a popular search engine that it is now a verb, as in "I googled my basketball coach and found out all about his career!"

"First, they do an on-line search."

Search engines themselves are located on the Web, so you have to know their addresses. After you reach the specific Web address of a search engine, you enter the topic of the search. The search engine then provides a list of websites that may contain information relevant to your search.

Keep in mind that search engines cannot search subscription services such as ProQuest, EBSCO, or other scholarly, registered databases that might be available in your school's library—onsite or online.

Some search engines, such as Yahoo.ca, specialize in identifying general directories of information, such as sites from which to search for information on different dog breeds, the Islamic religion, and car repair. Using this type of search engine is analogous to searching for reference books devoted to general topics in a library, rather than searching for the specific facts contained in the reference books.

Other search engines, such as Google or AltaVista, are more useful when you are looking for specific pieces of information, such as who signed the *Canadian Charter of Rights and Freedoms*, what Viagra is, and who Ralph Klein is. This category of search engine identifies pages containing specific keywords, drawn from millions of individual Web pages.

Finally, a third type of search engine is exemplified by Ask Jeeves! and Dogpile. Known as *metasearch tools*, these sites send your search commands to other search engines, compiling the results into a single, unified list.

No single search engine works best. In fact, most people develop their own preferences. The best advice: Try out several of them

Link
A means of jumping automatically from one Web page to another

Search engine
A computerized index to information on the World Wide Web

It is becoming increasingly easy for anyone to put material on the World Wide Web, and many students are creating their own personal Web page containing information and photos about their lives.

Information, Please!

Try to find the answers to the following questions, using at least three of the search engines described in the text.

1. What was the French Revolution and when did it occur?

2. What is the title of a recent biography of Wayne Gretzky?

3. What are the words of Dr. Martin Luther King, Jr.'s "I Have a Dream" speech?

4. Is the birthrate in Quebec higher or lower than that in British Columbia?

5. What is the ecu?

Were some questions particularly easy or hard to answer? Why? Were there differences in the ease of use of the different search engines? Which did you prefer, and why?

and see which works best for you. To get started, use Try It! 6, "Information, Please!"

The Far Reaches of the Web As its name implies, the Web is vast—sometimes frustratingly so.

Although search engines permit you to locate specific information, they do not provide a complete record of everything that is housed in cyberspace. In fact, no one knows how much material exists. Not only is more information added to the Web every day, but the information resides on thousands of individual computers. Anyone with a computer can set up a personal website.

The fact that anyone can put information on the Web is both the biggest asset and greatest disadvantage of using the Web as an information source.

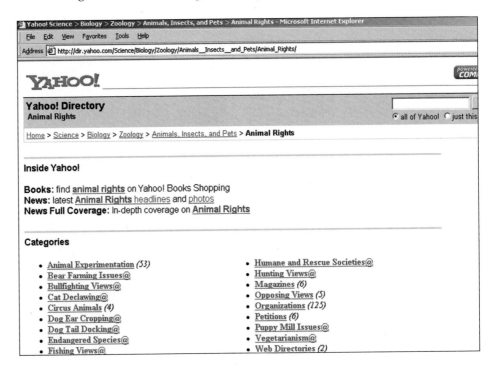

Try It! 7

Work the Web

Use the World Wide Web to locate information about the Canadian women's suffrage movement of the mid-nineteenth and early twentieth centuries. If you are doing it right, you should come across information about The Famous Five (Nellie McClung, Emily Murphy, Irene Parlby, Louise McKinney, and Henrietta Edwards), the Toronto Literary Club, Emily Stowe, the Women's Christian Temperance Movement, Agnes Campbell Macphail, the Persons Case of 1929, the dates women in each province gained the right to vote, and a chronology of the women's suffrage movement in Canada.

Print out or write down what you find, including source documents, bibliographies, interesting links, and dead ends (you are sure to find some strange things out there!).

Evaluate your overall satisfaction with using the World Wide Web for research on this topic. What are the advantages and disadvantages of using the Web compared with traditional, noncomputerized research methods?

Because computer skill is the only expertise a person needs to set up a Web page, there may be as much *mis*information on the Web as there is information. Consequently, keep the usual consumer rule in mind: Buyer beware. Unless the website has been established and is maintained by a reliable organization, the information it contains may not be accurate. (We'll talk more about how to determine the trustworthiness of information on the Web when we discuss evaluating information sources later in the chapter.)

Searching the World Wide Web Using the World Wide Web to find information couldn't be easier—or more difficult. The ease of navigation around the Web makes finding information quite simple. At the same time, though, the mass of information that is tied into the Web can make finding *appropriate* information very tricky. See Try It! 7, "Work the Web."

Using the list of sites generated by a search is simple. With a computer mouse, click on the site address of the relevant document, and the home page of the site will (eventually) appear on your computer screen. You can then take notes on the material, in the same way you'd take notes on material in a book.

The simplicity by which you can navigate great "distances" through the Web also can make it difficult to find exactly the material that will be most helpful. Most of what you will come across may well be of little use. In fact, it's easy to end up in a virtual dead end, in which the information you have found is only minimally related to the topic you're researching. In that case, use the "Back" command on the browser, which will allow you to retrace the route that led to the site on which you currently find yourself.

> "Usually, when doing research, I refer to all forms of information! I do this so that I can cross reference my information and rid my research of any bias, or opinionated info. A wide range of materials and references allows for a broader view on whatever you are trying to locate information for."
>
> Jessica Boffo, Student, Capilano College

Career Connections

Researching Careers on the Web

Gathering and using information is a key skill area in the Conference Board of Canada's Employability Skills 2000+. As far as careers are concerned, the Internet is becoming increasingly important for searching out data on careers, posting résumés, and getting advice on job applications and human resource issues. As well, most Canadian workplaces will now accept job applications by fax or e-mail. In addition, the computer expertise you develop as you research companies, write and revise résumés and cover letters, and apply for jobs online will show potential employers you have the technological skills they are looking for.

Workopolis.com is Canada's biggest job site, with about 30 000 job postings daily. Canadians have enthusiastically embraced this type of career research and application system since its launch in 2000, conducting an estimated 7 million job searches a month. Users can create profiles, save résumés, track job applications, and create job lists.

Workopolis is a partnership of two Canadian media companies, Globe Interactive and Toronto Star Newspapers Ltd. In addition, it contains all career listings from *The Globe and Mail*, the *Toronto Star*, the *Kitchener-Waterloo Record*, and the *Hamilton Spectator*.

Check out the Workopolis site at <www.workopolis.com/index.html>.

The other danger with Web searches is that you may come across information that is so fascinating that you stray off track and lose sight of what you should be doing. It's important, then, to keep in mind what you're supposed to be doing and resist the temptations that the Web offers.

You and Computers: A Word to the Cyber-wary To make use of the Internet and the World Wide Web, you'll need to be familiar with computers—devices about which most of us have strong reactions.

If you are not yet at ease with computers, relax. With sufficient practice, using a computer will become second nature. No one is born with computer skills. Those computer wizards we're all familiar with, fearlessly sitting at a keyboard and tapping away, they, too, at some point knew nothing about computers. But they learned, and so can you. In fact, it's as much a necessity to learn to use a computer as it was for you to learn to use a calculator earlier in your schooling. No one facing the job market in the twenty-first century will want to leave school without basic computer skills.

Using Computers to Present and Gather Information What can computers do for you, aside from providing the gateway to library catalogues, e-mail, and the World Wide Web? Probably the most common use of computers by students is for writing. *Word-processing programs* turn a computer into a smart typewriter—a *very* smart typewriter. With a word-processing program, you can check the spelling of words you type, but beware! Canadian spellcheckers are not always available or reliable; keep your spellchecker on but use it with caution. You must proofread your work closely to make sure the spelling is correct. No spellchecker can replace a good read-through.

If you aren't yet at ease with computers, consider taking a workshop or class on the topic, offered by almost every college or university. In just a few hours, you'll be able to learn word processing and other basic computing skills. It doesn't take long to become proficient, and your mastery of basic computer skills is a prerequisite for achieving postsecondary—and, ultimately, occupational—success.

Narrowing Your Search

Finding information is not the biggest information management task most of us face. After taking advantage of the library and Web, we typically have just the opposite problem: too much information.

How you select and organize what you've found often makes the difference between success and failure. Keep in mind these tips for organizing information effectively:

- **Determine what you're looking for.** Suppose you have to write a paper for your biology class, and, because you have a good friend with AIDS, you decide to write about the disease. You go to the library card catalogue and find that your school has dozens of books about AIDS. You take a look at the World Wide Web and the situation is even worse, with literally thousands of references to AIDS. What do you do next?

  You need to refine your topic, transforming it from a broad, open-ended domain to something more restricted and manageable. Look at a few of the sources you've found and consider the major issues surrounding AIDS. Perhaps some of the books have chapters on particular subtopics, such as research into cures for the disease or its effects on the population in Africa. Because these topics are narrower, they make a more manageable topic for a paper.

- **Identify the key sources of information.** Every field has experts, and you need to make sure that you consider what they have said about your topic. How do you identify the experts? One way is to read through several books and see whose names keep popping up. Another way is to use an encyclopedia to get an overview of your topic. Encyclopedia articles often end with suggested readings; these can guide you to the appropriate sources of information.

- **Keep in mind what you're going to do with the information.** As you begin to do your research, keep your goal in mind. Are you writing a short, two-page paper giving your opinion? a longer term paper? a speech? a worksheet? Knowing what you need to do with the information will help you to organize your information search appropriately.

- **Learn the key issues and controversies.** Every field has key issues and certain controversies that remain unresolved. For example, in psychology, one key issue is whether human nature is the product of biology in the form of genes and biochemical processes or the result of the influence of environment—the culture, religion, and historical events of a particular time and place. Identifying these sorts of issues and controversies in the earliest stages of your research will ensure that you cover what is most important. They can also make the assignment you're seeking to complete—whether it's a paper, a speech, or a report—far more interesting than a mere recitation of facts. For instance, a paper on the treatment of cancer could focus on the use of herbal remedies and other nontraditional treatments that arouse great disagreement among physicians.

- **Use librarians effectively.** The stereotype of a librarian as someone whose main job is to stop people from talking in the library is dead. Librarians today are masters of information management—people who can help you find your way through a huge range of data sources and steer you to the right material.

Make use of librarians—but do it properly. Start by looking for the information yourself. Then, if you're having trouble sorting through what you've found (or can't find material in the first place), ask for help.

The better the question, the better the answer. Ask a precise question, such as, "I'm writing a paper on the environmental effects of using nuclear power to generate electricity. I've found two books, but they're not quite right. I wonder if you have any ideas about where I might find additional material?"

Don't be afraid to ask. Think of librarians as highly trained guides who can save you hours of aimless wandering in an increasingly dense forest of information.

Using the Information You Find

You've found the information that you've been seeking, and you've selected and organized it, focusing on the topic of your research. Now what?

Although we'll be concentrating in future chapters on how to prepare written and oral reports using the sources you have located, it's important to begin the process of putting the information you've gathered into a form that you can use in the future. One time-honoured technique is using file folders and note cards.

Assembling Information Folders   After you have gathered information, break it down into subtopics by placing the raw information you've located (photocopies, computer printouts, and computer disks) into different-coloured file folders, one folder for each subtopic. Label each folder with a stick-on label or note, which will permit you to easily modify the topic of the folder if necessary in the future. This initial sorting will permit you to take the next step in information management: creating note cards.

Note Cards: The Researcher's Basic Tool   Making notes on index cards is the best way of transforming information into a form that can easily be used. They may be low-tech, but they are the best way to note, and later recall, what your research has uncovered. Best of all, they can be sorted an endless number of ways. As you narrow your topic, all you have to do is sort them differently. Note cards have other advantages, too. Even though you gathered your information from six different books, three magazine articles, and a couple of websites, you can place all note cards containing information about the same subtopic together in a stack, even though they came from different sources.

The key is to place no more than one major idea on each card. Sometimes that major idea will take a few words; other times it will consist of several sentences. If you avoid including more than one major idea on a card, you will later find it easy to arrange them and to place related pieces of information together. It often helps to put, in the top corner of the card, the subtopic (such as "Early Influences" or "Husband" or "Customer Service") that the idea fits into; this way you can see it easily.

One other important point about note cards: Make sure every note card contains information that clearly identifies its source. It is extremely important that you know where the idea on the note card came from so you can credit this source later when you write your paper and use the idea. This will also save you a lot of trouble if you need to return to the source of the idea.

Although you don't need to include complete biographical information on every note card, you should keep a master list—either on a separate set of note cards or in a computer file—with the full citation.

Finally, you *must* write the ideas you place on the note cards in your own words. Unless you find some particularly compelling phrases that you think you might want to include in the final paper—which you should set off with quotation marks—always use your own words on note cards. Using your own words will prevent you from accidentally copying others' words and passing them off as your own—which, as we'll discuss next, is the gravest of academic sins. Using your own words also helps ensure that you really understand a concept yourself.

You also can use a word-processing program to take notes. Instead of note cards, place each idea in a separate paragraph, which can then be sorted and shifted around. In fact, some word-processing programs have built-in features to help you organize your research.

Citing Sources   Although there are numerous citation systems for documenting and citing reference materials, the most commonly used style guides are those of the APA (American Psychological Association), MLA (Modern Languages Association), CBE (Council of Biology Editors) and CS (Chicago or Turabian Style). Because of the vast amount of research material on the Internet, all style guides have been adapted to cover citation of electronic sources.

Psychology and social science papers are written in *APA style*. Reference citations are used to document the source of ideas, paraphrases, and direct quotes. Parenthetical references within the text are used and allow the reader to locate the source of information in a reference section at the end of the paper. Footnotes are not used and there is no bibliography.

English and humanities students use *MLA style*. Documenting sources means telling the reader where research sources are located, whether facts, opinions, or quotations. A list of works cited and parenthetical references within the text compose the two parts of documentation.

Natural science writing is frequently referenced or documented using *CBE style*.

The *Chicago or Turabian Style* is used for writing humanities papers and computer papers and articles, and for business writing. To mark citations throughout an essay or article, a writer using the *Chicago Manual's* note-bibliography style inserts a superscript number after each quotation, paraphrase, or summary. Each citation corresponds to a numbered note containing publication information about the source cited. Such notes are called footnotes when printed at the foot of a page and endnotes when printed at the end of an essay, chapter, or book.

Find out what format your instructor wants you to use. If no particular style is required, choose one and apply it consistently. You'll find an excellent online reference with detailed information about these four styles at <www.bedfordstmartins.com/online/shrttoc.html>.

Acknowledging Others' Ideas   As you gather information you will begin to appreciate just how valuable ideas are. In fact, ideas are so valuable that there's no greater sin in the world of academics than **plagiarism,** taking credit for someone else's words, thoughts, or ideas. In the academic world, plagiarism is about the equivalent of stealing a car. Even if you just mean to "borrow" a passage, passing another person's work off as your own is entirely unacceptable.

Plagiarism
Using another author's ideas or words without proper documentation; representing someone else's creative work (ideas, words, images, etc.) as one's own, whether intentional or not.

Furthermore, if you do plagiarize and get caught, the penalty can be severe: In many schools, plagiarism results in dismissal. You could even face legal charges, because almost all published material is copyrighted, which means that it is someone's intellectual property. If an author learns that you have used his or her writing as your own, the author has the right to take you to court and sue for damages.

The best way to avoid plagiarism is to be scrupulous while doing your research. Make sure you put everything you write down into your own words, except for direct quotes. And when you quote directly from someone's work, use quotation marks. In addition, always include complete information about your source. This information should include the author, title, publisher, year of publication, and page numbers.

Be careful when you put ideas into your own words. It's not just a matter of rearranging the words and choosing synonyms for them. For instance, consider the following passage from the book *Canadian Heritage:*[2]

> For over a century, Portuguese have been migrating from their homeland in search of work. Three epochs of migration are discernible for Portuguese men and women. Over one million people left Portugal for Brazil between 1886 and 1950. It was not until the Canadian and Portuguese governments signed labour contract agreements to supply railway construction and agricultural workers after World War II that Canada became a popular option for Portuguese immigrants for the first three decades following the war. The third epoch saw large numbers choose migration targets closer to home in Western Europe.

Here's one way of rephrasing the passage, but one that is so close to the original that it amounts to plagiarism:

> For over a hundred years, Portuguese have been emigrating from their native land to look for employment. Three eras of Portuguese emigration can be seen. More than a million people immigrated to Brazil from 1886 to 1950. For thirty years following the Second World War, after Canada and Portugal agreed on labour contracts supplying workers for railways and farms, thousands of Portuguese immigrated to Canada. The third wave of immigration was to Western European countries nearer to Portugal.

A more appropriate rewording of the original passage would be the following, which more clearly rephrases the authors' ideas:

> In Portugal, three distinct patterns of immigration can be identified over the past century, driven by Portuguese workers seeking employment abroad. First, from 1886 to 1950, more than a million Portuguese emigrated to Brazil. Second, for three decades after the Second World War, thousands of Portuguese settled in Canada, after labour agreements allowing Portuguese workers access to jobs in the railroad and agricultural sectors were signed. Third, the prospect of jobs in Western Europe resulted in emigration to countries nearer Portugal.

Even in this case, it is still necessary to cite the source of the facts or ideas that you are rephrasing by adding a footnote reference to the original work. The keys to avoiding plagiarism are to use your own words and, if you use the words, ideas, or thoughts of others, to be sure to cite the source. However, it is not necessary to have a citation after every sentence. Some facts are so basic ("Japan and Germany were Canada's enemies in World War II") that no source is necessary.

Keep in mind, too, that you must cite material that you find on the World Wide Web. Just because the material may appear on your home computer screen, it still was produced by someone else, and the author must be given credit. Al-

Try It! 8

👥 **Working in a Group:** Summarize, Don't Plagiarize

First, try to capture in your own words the overall meaning of the following quoted passage, without copying or plagiarizing it in any way. Assume that you intend to reflect the main points in a paper of your own. Decide whether you would cite the work in a footnote or other reference within your paper. Try to make your summary 10 to 15 percent of the original length.

1. Excerpted from Granatstein, J. L. (1998, July 1). Mackenzie King. *Maclean's, 111*, pp. 24–25, on William Lyon Mackenzie King's political career:

    > [William Lyon Mackenzie] King was the first "expert" to become prime minister, a genuine student of labour conditions and the need to reconcile the conflict between, as the title of his unreadable 1918 book put it, Industry and Humanity. He took over the reins of government in 1921 when the farmers of Canada were united in revolt against the old party system and its dominance by eastern interests. Within five or six years, he had almost completely absorbed them back into his Liberal party.
    >
    > In his first term, he found the British government trying to whipsaw him into unconditional military support for London's interests in the Middle East, but he evaded the attempt skilfully and lost no support in doing so. In the 1926 King-Byng constitutional crisis—provoked when Lord Byng, the governor general, refused King's request to dissolve Parliament—King was likely in the wrong in seeking to cling to office and in resigning so precipitously that he left Canada briefly without a government. But he succeeded in clipping the wings of the British-appointed governor general. Canadian autonomy—and King—benefited.
    >
    > During the Great Depression, when he was out of office for five years, he dabbled in spiritualism so much that we might think him addled. But when he was re-elected in 1935, his first act was to conclude a major trade agreement with the United States, a step of huge importance. And through skilful practice of his "on the one hand, on the other hand" policies, he brought Canada united into the Second World War in 1939, a feat that seemed unimaginable in 1937. Addled? Hardly.
    >
    > This most pacific of men surprisingly proved himself a great war leader. Under his direction, a strong cabinet mobilized a gigantic war effort. Canada's military was a million strong with the First Canadian Army overseas, a navy of 100 000 and the British Commonwealth Air Training Plan. Astonishingly, this mobilization was accomplished without a huge and divisive split over manpower, although overseas conscription was imposed for a few thousand infantry in November 1944. At the same time, the agricultural and industrial resources of the nation poured forth in unprecedented quantities. Canada became rich during the war, one of the very few beneficiaries of a global tragedy.
    >
    > After peace had come, King, by now over 70 years old, hung on. He took his nation into the discussion that led to NATO, and he ensured a smooth transition to his chosen successor, Louis Saint-Laurent. For 27 years, King dominated Canada.

👥 After you summarize the passage on your own, compare your answers with those of other classmates in a group. What are the different approaches taken by others in your group in attempting to restate the main points in their own words? Is there one best way to capture the main points of the author?

though the rules for how to cite material found on the Web are still developing, it is still necessary to provide the source of anything you come across on the Web. At the very least include the site name, Web address, and author. (Complete Try It! 8, "Summarize, Don't Plagiarize," on page 123 to get some practice in the art of gathering information and ideas without stealing them.)

Copy-and-Paste Plagiarism or Cyber-Cheating   Using the Internet has made researching papers and essays easier and more convenient, but it has also led to an increase in plagiarism and cheating. For students who are short of time or who haven't researched their topics thoroughly, it may be tempting to copy and paste online articles or to download essays posted on sites such as "School Sucks." However, these tactics are counterproductive and very risky. Not only are these students *not* reading, thinking, analyzing, writing, or learning about their topics; cheating is an intellectually dishonest activity and subject to harsh academic penalties. It is just not worth it to cheat.

Professors are becoming more attuned to copy-and-paste plagiarism; it is usually easy to detect differences in writing styles or essays that do not match the topic given. Wayne Petrozzi, who teaches political science at Ryerson University, suspects approximately 8 to 12 percent of student papers he receives have elements of academic dishonesty. Petrozzi doesn't believe the majority of student researchers are wilfully cheating; rather they ". . . just don't know how to write an academic paper."[3] Many instructors routinely inspect student-cheating sites to detect what essays are available (for free or for money). Remember, there is no quality control in cyber-cheating—many online essays are riddled with mistakes!

Aside from plagiarism, some students are using new technologies, such as PDAs (personal digital assistants), graphing calculators, and cell phones with text-messaging features to their advantage by using them as tools to cheat on exams. These tools are the electronic form of note passing. Cheaters using high-tech methods face the same consequences as ever: an inferior academic record, possible suspension or expulsion, and an unproductive learning experience in higher education.

10 + 1 Ways You Can Avoid Plagiarizing

1. Be aware of what plagiarism is, so you can prevent it.

2. Recognize, admit, and accept that plagiarism is dishonest and that it is wrong to lie, steal, and cheat.

3. Acknowledge that academic work takes time and effort. Make a commitment to your studies.

4. Understand what your essay assignment is asking you to do. The clearer you are on your topic, the easier it will be to do a good job without plagiarizing.

5. Begin your assignment in time to finish it without panicking (or plagiarizing).

6. Learn to research properly . . . ask your school librarian, your professors, or peer tutors for help. Or check the Internet.

7. Go to your school's writing centre or learning centre for help if you are not confident of your writing skills.

8. Understand that there is a difference between plagiarism and incorrectly citing your sources. Check and recheck your citations.

9. Put other people's exact words in quotations. There is nothing wrong in using other people's thoughts or words if you acknowledge them!

10. Work with others in a study or writing group and peer edit your work.

11. Learn to **paraphrase**!

Remembering That Not All Sources of Information Are Equal

Paraphrase
Use the ideas in the original passage but put them in your own words, often because you want them to be clearer to your readers.

You have gathered and organized a great deal of information, and as you begin to work it into your final product, you must use your critical thinking skills to evaluate that information. Some of the important critical thinking questions you must address before you can feel confident about what you've found include the following:

- **How authoritative is the information?** It is absolutely essential to consider the source of the material. Approach every piece of information with a critical eye, trying to determine what the author's biases might be. The best approach is to use multiple sources of information. If one source is divergent from the others, you may reasonably question the reliability of that source.

  Another approach is to consider the publisher of the material. For instance, books published by well-established publishers are carefully reviewed before publication to ensure their accuracy.

  Be especially critical of information you find on the World Wide Web. It's important to keep in mind that the Web is completely unregulated and that *anyone* can put *anything* on the Web.

  One way of evaluating Web information is to consider a site's sponsor. Commercial Web pages (whose address includes the letters *.com*, short for commercial) often include the least objective material. Addresses including letters such as *.gc.ca* (Canadian government) or *.bc.ca* (site from British Columbia) generally include information that is more objective. Still, each site must be evaluated on its own merits. Note that much information on the Internet is American and may not be relevant to your research.

- **How current is the information?** No matter what the discipline, information is changing at a rapid rate. Even a field like Chaucerian English, which concentrates on poetry written in the fourteenth century, advances significantly year by year as scholars make new discoveries, come to new insights, and reach new conclusions.

  Consequently, don't assume that, because you're researching a historically old topic, old sources will suffice. Consider whether what you've found is the most recent and up-to-date approach. Compare older sources to newer ones to identify changes in the ways in which the topic is considered.

- **Is anything missing?** One of the hardest questions to answer is whether your research is complete. Have you found all the relevant sources? Have you missed anything that is important?

  Although there is no way to answer these questions definitively, you can do a couple of things. The best way to ensure that you haven't missed anything important is to check out the sources that you have found. Many will have bibliographies and lists of suggested additional readings. By carefully considering this information, you'll be able to get a good sense of the important work in your topic area and to verify that you haven't overlooked some critical source.

You can also talk to your course instructor, describing generally what you've found. Librarians can also be extremely helpful; they may be acquainted with the general topic and know the most definitive sources in the field, including online and electronic sources.

Placing Information in Context

The Information Age presents us with great promise and opportunity. Through the use of media such as e-mail and the World Wide Web, we have at our fingertips the ability to communicate with others around the world. The computer keyboard truly can be said to contain "keys"—to the entire earth and its peoples.

At the same time, the world of information can be overwhelming. It's important, then, to revisit our information-seeking strategies by taking the following points into account:

- **Consider alternative types of information.** Information comes in many forms, and you should make sure that you have exhausted every potential source on your topic. For example, libraries sometimes house graphics and audiovisual material, such as videotapes, audiotapes, and CD-ROMs. Television, which includes both daily news programs and newsmagazines such as *CBC Newsworld* and *The Fifth Estate*, can provide useful information. Finally, once you identify experts in a field, you might try to contact them via letter, phone, or e-mail if you have a specific question. They won't always have the time to respond in a detailed fashion, but it's worth a try.

> "Knowledge, in truth, is the great sun in the firmament. Life and power are scattered with all its beams."
>
> Daniel Webster

- **Gather information from more than one point of view.** Don't settle for one viewpoint. Even if consensus exists on an issue, some dissenters from the predominant view are sure to exist. Seek them out and try to figure out why they hold the views they do. This can help you to better understand the dominant view and may even spur you to reconsider your own opinion or to express it in a new way.

- **Identify your own biases and assumptions about a topic.** We are not empty-headed vessels into which information simply flows, like coffee into a cup. Instead, we consider information in terms of the considerable amount of knowledge we already have. Ask yourself whether your prior knowledge is affecting the way you view the new information to which you're exposed. Have you looked at it as objectively as possible? Do you know what your own biases are? Are you open to new information that might contradict your existing beliefs and feelings?

- **Use information to improve your own life.** Finally, don't get so caught up in gathering material for course assignments that you neglect thinking about how you can use information on a personal level. Wander around the stacks of the library and find a book you want to read. Surf the Web and see what you come across. Taking a break from the serious business of higher education will help you to concentrate more when you do go back to work.

Speaking of Success

Shawn Thomson

General Arts and Science Diploma, Cambrian College, Sudbury, Ontario

It is not often that a 27-year-old is declared a hero and has his hometown proclaim a day in his honour, but it happened to Shawn Thomson on May 20, 2004, as he completed a 18-day, 740-kilometre bike ride from Ottawa to Goderich, Ontario. What made this remarkable feat all the more exceptional is that Shawn, who has cerebral palsy and normally uses an electric wheelchair, rode a bike specially equipped with hand pedals. Shawn made the trip to raise attention and money for the group Mothers Against Drunk Driving (MADD). Shawn spent five years dreaming about the project and six months planning the "Shawn 'MADD Man' Thomson Bike Tour." So the trip, while difficult and exhausting, was the achievement of a very important goal.

Due to a lack of balance, Shawn, whose disability is incurable, cannot walk by himself. However, he refuses to let cerebral palsy keep him from reaching his goals. He credits his parents with instilling him with the motivation to set goals and not to give up. One of his key objectives was to graduate from college.

When investigating postsecondary institutions, Shawn discovered that Cambrian College in Sudbury, Ontario, Canada, through its Glenn Crombie Centre for disability services, provided support for students with disabilities, especially in the

CAMBRIAN COLLEGE

Sudbury • Ontario
www.cambrianc.on.ca

area of adaptive technology. He took advantage of a special needs grant to purchase equipment to make attending college easier. Because Shawn has difficulty controlling and coordinating movement and is subjected to frequent involuntary movements in all four limbs, he used the services of a notetaker who typed notes into a computer and then e-mailed them to

him. In addition, Shawn was able to e-mail some of his assignments to his professors, which allowed him to be more independent in his academic work.

Since graduating from Cambrian, Shawn, like many other people with physical disabilities, has had a hard time finding a job. Shawn is hoping that technology might again help him achieve his goal of a satisfying career. He is currently taking courses in entrepreneurship to develop an online business on eBay. If his business plan is viable, he will have some assistance to get started. If successful, Shawn hopes to teach other people with disabilities how to do business online. Shawn, a self-described "people person," has a great desire to help others and refuses to believe cerebral palsy should prevent him from aiding other people who need assistance.

Why is knowing how to find information important?

- The availability of information has increased so dramatically and continues to increase so rapidly that information management—the ability to find, focus, and use information—has become an essential survival skill.

What are the basic sources for finding and gathering information?

- Information in libraries is available in paper form and in several electronic forms, including microfilm, microfiche, computer disks, and the World Wide Web.

- The World Wide Web is a computer resource that links a vast array of electronic information to users' computer terminals. Web users access Web "pages" (or sites) by using a browser, and may move from site to site by following links on each Web page.

What are the most effective ways to use information sources?

- After gathering information, users need to break it down into subtopics. One way to do this is to put the raw information—photocopies, computer printouts, and computer disks—on each subtopic into separate file folders.

- The easiest procedure for translating raw information into a usable form is to take notes on index cards. Computers may also be used as a replacement for actual cards.

What do I need to keep in mind as I use information from reference resources?

- It is crucial to avoid plagiarism—passing off someone else's words or ideas as your own.

- An important step in using information for research is evaluating the worth of the information that has been gathered by considering how authoritative the source is, whether the author has any potential biases, how recent the information is, and whether anything important is missing from the research.

- As you gather new information, think how it fits with your prior knowledge, and try to identify personal preconceptions or biases that may interfere with your ability to take in the new ideas.

P.O.W.E.R. Portfolio

High-Tech Skills

Information technology (IT) and knowledge management (KM) skills have become crucial in academic and work settings. Consider including a section on IT or KM in your portfolio. An essay in which you have used several methods of gathering information and paraphrased or quoted accurately would be an ideal submission. Or consider developing an intensive bibliography of print and online sources on a particular topic. Or include a critique of a particular website; the critique allows you to summarize the contents and the source objectively. In your observations, be sure to indicate why you chose the selection, what skills, talents, or experiences it demonstrates, and what you learned.

Resources

On Campus

The librarians at your college or university library are the people to whom you should turn first if you need help in locating information. In recent years, librarians—most of whom hold advanced degrees—have significantly changed what they do, and most are now equally at home using traditional print material and searching electronic information storehouses.

If you are having difficulty gaining access to the World Wide Web, you may also find help at your school's computer centre. Most campuses have consultants who can help you with the technical aspects of computer usage.

In Print

Robert Berkman's *Find It Fast: How to Uncover Expert Information on Any Subject Online or in Print* (HarperResource, 5th edition, 2000) provides a step-by-step guide to locating information of all sorts.

The ABCs of e-Learning: Reaping the Benefits and Avoiding the Pitfalls (Pfeiffer, 2002) by Brooke Broadbent offers background information needed to be successful in an e-learning situation. It compares the four basic types of e-learning and gives suggestions for getting started on e-learning.

Finally, *DDC Learning Microsoft Office 2003* (Pearson Education, Bk&CD-ROM edition, 2004) offers very straightforward and easy-to-follow instructions on the features of the whole suite of Microsoft Office programs.

On the Web

The following sites on the World Wide Web provide the opportunity to extend your learning about the material in this chapter. Although the Web addresses were accurate at the time the book was printed, check the P.O.W.E.R. Learning website, <www.mcgrawhill.ca/college/power>, for any changes that may have occurred.

http://wombat.doc.ic.ac.uk/foldoc/index.html
You'll find a free online dictionary of computing at this site. Topics are listed alphabetically, and a search engine helps locate specific information.

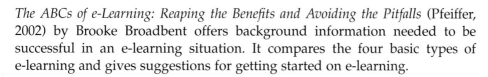

www.ipl.org
This is the first Internet Public Library. Its mission is to discover and organize high-quality information resources. It offers an online text collection of more than 7000 titles, with a search engine to help you find what you're looking for, plus guides to periodicals and newspapers.

www.hamilton.edu/academics/resource/wc/AvoidingPlagiarism.html
A very thorough and informative site illustrates how to recognize and avoid plagiarism.

www.sosig.ac.uk/desire/internet-detective.html
The Internet Detective is a hands-on tutorial to evaluating websites. It includes interactive exercises and tests.

http://library.queensu.ca./inforef/guides/evalchart.htm
This site from Queen's University is a checklist for evaluating Web resources.

www.sc.edu/beaufort/library/pages/bones/bones.shtml
"Bare Bones 101: A Basic Tutorial on Searching the Web" is a primer that helps a new Internet user manage search engines, create search strategies, and practise searching on the main search engines. Includes links to sites helpful for more complex searching.

www.thecanadianencyclopedia.com
The Canadian Encyclopedia Online contains the full text of the printed volumes and junior edition articles, as well.

The Case of . . .

The Unsuspecting Plagiarist

Trisha Cunningham's heart started to beat harder and she blinked back tears when she read her Business Communication teacher's comments scrawled at the bottom of her informal report, *No mark given. Please see me during office hours about this paper.* What could the problem be? This report, a corporate history of Sony Music, was worth 25 percent of her course mark! When she had sent the report by e-mail the previous week, she had felt she had done a good job.

When Trisha met with her professor the next day, she was shocked to learn that large portions of her report were highlighted by *turnitin.com*, an online service teachers at her college regularly used to detect "cut and paste" plagiarism. Trisha had consulted lots of websites during the research stage of her project and she had kept a pretty accurate list of her sources, which she had included in her "Works Cited" list, but it was really hard to know what she could or couldn't use.

Trisha knew she was in trouble when her professor seemed totally unsympathetic about her ignorance of how to include, document, and cite Internet sources in the report. Plagiarism had been covered in class—no excuses!

1. What are some potential consequences of Trisha's plagiarism? Do you agree with the penalties? Why or why not?

2. What do you think Trisha should do about this situation? What are her options? Is there any possibility of a positive ending to this case?

3. Where can Trisha go for help so this will never happen again? How could teachers help students avoid charges of plagiarism?

4. Should online plagiarism (like Trisha's case) be treated the same or differently from cases involving purchased or downloaded essays and research papers? Why or why not?

5. How have cases of plagiarism in the newspaper industry been handled recently? Why are workplace penalties so severe? Or are they severe enough?

Taking Notes

5

Taking Notes in Class
Prepare: Considering Your Goals

Organize: Getting Your Notetaking Tools Together

Journal Reflections: How Do I Take Notes?
Work: Processing—Not Copying—Information

Evaluate: Thinking Critically about Your Notes

Rethink: Activating Your Memory

Taking Notes: Multimedia Technology

Taking Notes as You Study

Speaking of Success: Kofi Boateng

Career Connections: Notetaking on the Job: Taking Minutes

The Case of . . . A Clean Sweep

For Michael Wong, the realization that something fundamental had changed came when he went to his first class in the second term of university. Instead of taking a seat in the back row of class—as he had done in high school and at the start of his first university term—he sat down in the first row.

The change had come as a result of a workshop on notetaking he had attended last semester after getting Cs on three midterms. He had done every assignment and even reviewed extensively, but it turned out that what he had reviewed—his notes—was the problem. In the workshop, he'd learned ways of making sure he got the important information down as he listened to lectures or read assignments. He tried them out, and—a bit to his surprise—found they helped. By the end of the semester, he'd pulled his grades up.

At the same time, Michael's improved notetaking skills led him to pay more attention in class, something he found easier to do sitting closer to the front. As a result, he had become considerably more engaged and interested in what his instructors were saying and ended up with some of the best grades of his scholastic career so far.

Looking
Ahead

Michael Wong's move from the back to the front of the classroom was both a source and a symbol of his academic success. Michael's ability to take good notes is also likely to pay future dividends, because notetaking skills not only help produce academic success in university but also contribute to career success.

In this chapter we discuss effective strategies for taking notes during class lectures, during other kinds of oral presentations, and from written sources such as textbooks. There's a lot more to good notetaking than you probably think—and a lot less if you view notetaking as essentially "getting everything down on paper." As we consider notetaking, we'll pause along the way to discuss the tools of the notetaking trade, how to think your way to good notes, and how to deal with disorganized instructors.

After reading this chapter, you'll be able to answer these questions:

- **What is effective notetaking?**

- **How can I take good notes in class?**

- **What techniques apply to taking notes from written materials?**

Taking Notes in Class

In Canadian colleges and universities, good notetaking is not just a matter of trying to write down everything your instructor says. Students may be enrolled in a class of 30 with an interactive format. Or a large lecture hall with 80 or 800 students trying to make sense of their professor while following a PowerPoint slide show on a big screen. Or a seminar of 12 students having an in-depth discussion. Or a lab where problem-based learning is the norm. Or an online course where students must post response papers to an instructor's query.

All of these learning environments require notetaking but one style of notetaking—writing down everything that the teacher says—is no longer always appropriate. What is important is knowing how to develop an effective approach, adapt it depending on your situation and learning style, and apply it consistently. The P.O.W.E.R. Plan for notetaking can help.

Prepare: Considering Your Goals

As with other academic activities, preparation is a critical component of notetaking. The following steps will prepare you for action:

- **Identify the instructor's—and your—goals for the course.** On the first day of class, most instructors discuss what they'll be covering that term. They talk about their objectives, what they hope you'll get out of the class, and what you'll know when it's over. Most restate the information on the class syllabus, the written document that explains the assignments for the semester. For example, they may say that they want you to "develop an appreciation for the ways that statistics are used in everyday life."

  The information you get during that first session and through the syllabus is critical, because it allows you to calculate the basic direction the instructor plans to take during the course. And even if the instructor's goals aren't stated explicitly, you should attempt to figure them out. But don't just stop with the instructor's goals for the course. In addition to those "external" goals, you should have your own goals. What is it you want to learn from the course? What is it you hope to accomplish? How will the information from the course help you to enhance your knowledge, achieve your dreams, improve yourself as a person? Use Try It! 1, "Identify Course Goals."

- **Complete assignments before coming to class.** Your instructor enthusiastically describes the structure of the neuron, recounting excitedly how neurons don't physically touch one another and how electrons flow across neurons, changing their electrical charge. One problem: You have only the vaguest idea what a neuron is. And the reason you don't know is that you haven't read the assignment.

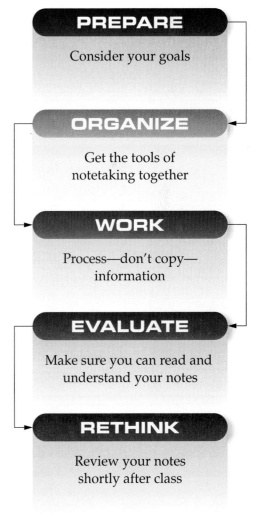

PREPARE
Consider your goals

ORGANIZE
Get the tools of notetaking together

WORK
Process—don't copy—information

EVALUATE
Make sure you can read and understand your notes

RETHINK
Review your notes shortly after class

P.O.W.E.R Plan

Identify Course Goals

What are your goals for each of your courses? What seem to be your instructors' goals for these courses? Use the form below to jot down both your own and your instructors' goals for your courses this term.

Course	My Goals	Instructor's Goals
1.		
2.		
3.		
4.		
5.		
6.		

What are the major differences among your instructors' goals for your various courses this term? Are there common threads among the instructors' course goals? How about your own goals—are they specific to various courses, or are there some common themes? Are you satisfied that your short-term goals for the courses you are taking are consistent with your long-term goals?

Chances are you have found yourself in this situation at least a few times, so you know firsthand that sinking feeling as you become increasingly confused. Because you can't follow the discussion, you can't get interested either, so the class seems boring. But really it is you who are lost. Not only have you begun to fall behind in your course work, you have now wasted an entire class session, simply because you didn't complete the reading you were supposed to before class.

Always go to class prepared: Do all your assignments beforehand. Instructors assume that their students have done what they've assigned,

An engaging lecturer can make even the most complex material come alive in the classroom, whereas an instructor who is unorganized or dull can make coming to class sheer drudgery. No matter what the lecturer's style, however, you need to be prepared to take effective notes.

and their lectures are based on that assumption. It's virtually impossible to get the gist of a lecture if you haven't completed the assignments.

- **Accept the instructor, warts and all.** Not every instructor is a brilliant lecturer. Accept the fact that, just as there are differences in skills among students, some instructors are more adept at lecturing than others.

  Don't let a lousy lecture style—or the fact that the instructor has a bad haircut or badly wrinkled clothing—get in the way of your education. You're going to notice these things, but don't let them interfere with your goals. Good notetaking requires being prepared to listen to the material.

- **Perform a preclass warm-up.** No, this doesn't mean doing jumping jacks just before each class. As you head to class or settle into your seat, review your notes from the previous lecture, looking over what the instructor said and where that lecture left off. You should also briefly review any reading you've been assigned.

  Just read the main headings or summary section. The warm-up doesn't have to be long. The goal is simply to refresh yourself, to get yourself into the right frame of mind for the class. In the same way that a five-minute warm-up before a run can prevent muscle spasms in your legs, a five-minute mental warm-up can prevent cramped and strained brain muscles.

> "We have to keep putting education as a priority; use your opportunity to instill a love of learning."
>
> Roberta Bondar

- **Sit as close to the teacher as possible.** Be sure that you can clearly see the chalkboard or screen if there are overheads, a Power Point presentation, or a computer screen. If you are easily distracted, sit away from your friends and try and maintain eye contact with your teacher.

rganize: Getting Your Notetaking Tools Together

Do you have a favourite pen? a preferred type of notebook? Although taking your favourite kind of notebook and pen to class will not make you a better notetaker, not having them certainly will interfere with your getting the most out of class. Yes, you probably will be able to borrow pen and paper from another student, but having to do so sends a message to both your instructor and yourself. To your instructor it says that you're unorganized and unprepared. The message to yourself is that, as a student, you're neither serious nor particularly concerned with success.

Cornell Notetaking
A notetaking technique that involves splitting the page to include notes, main points, and summary sections

What kind of writing instrument and paper will work best? First, using a pen is generally better than using a pencil. Compared with pencil, ink is less likely to smudge, it generally requires less effort to complete the physical act of writing, and what you produce with ink is usually brighter and clearer—and therefore easier to use when studying. On the other hand, for math and science classes, where you may be copying down formulas in class, a pencil might be better, because it's easier to erase if you make a mistake when copying detailed, complex information.

Figure 5.1

Cornell Notetaking In this example of a student's notes on a lecture about memory, she has written the material in the larger right column during class. Later, when reviewing her notes, she wrote down key pieces of information in the left column.

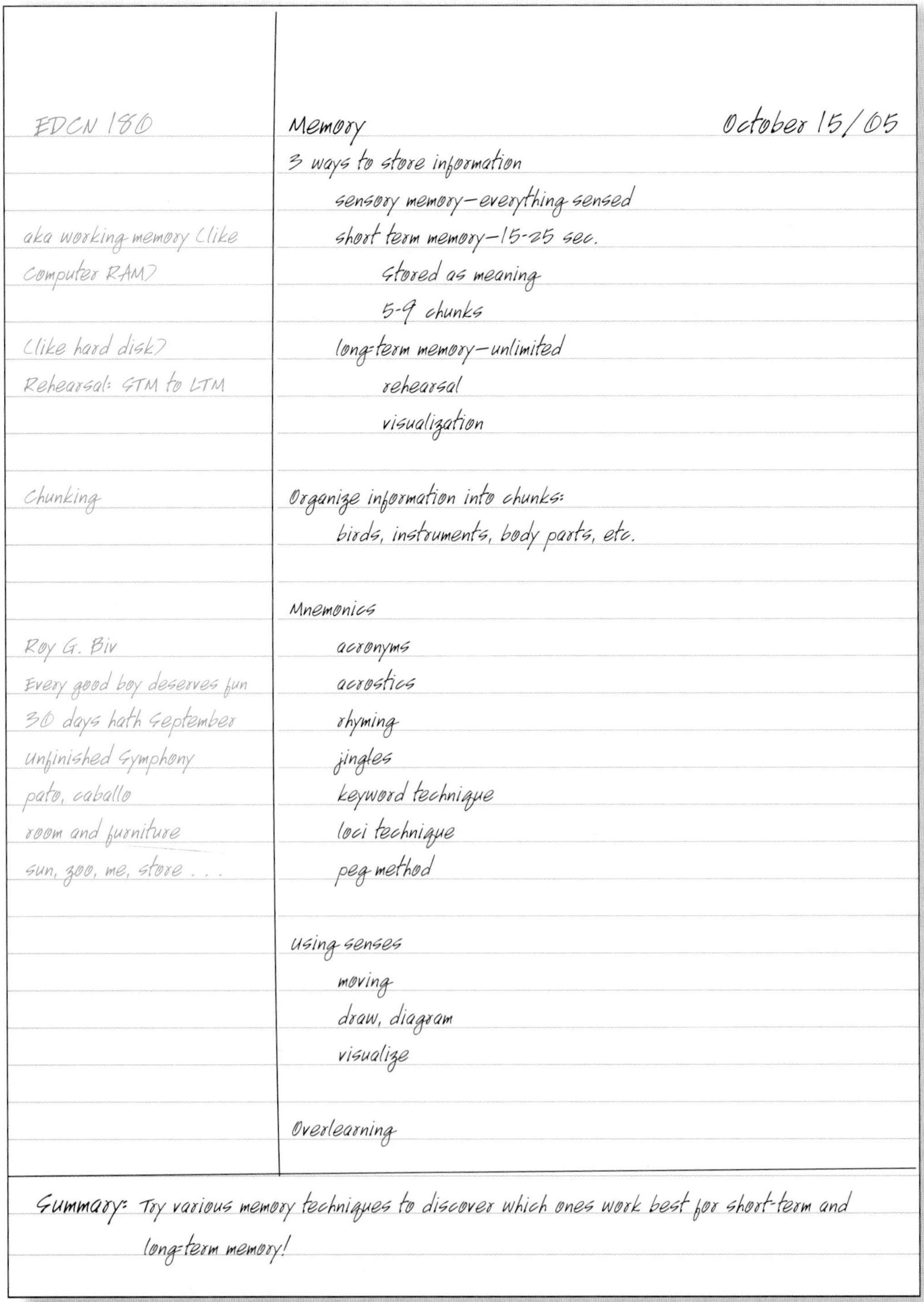

EDCN 180	Memory — October 15/05
	3 ways to store information
	sensory memory—everything sensed
aka working memory (like	short term memory—15-25 sec.
Computer RAM)	stored as meaning
	5-9 chunks
(like hard disk)	long-term memory—unlimited
Rehearsal: STM to LTM	rehearsal
	visualization
Chunking	Organize information into chunks:
	birds, instruments, body parts, etc.
	Mnemonics
Roy G. Biv	acronyms
Every good boy deserves fun	acrostics
30 days hath September	rhyming
Unfinished Symphony	jingles
pato, caballo	keyword technique
room and furniture	loci technique
sun, zoo, me, store . . .	peg method
	Using senses
	moving
	draw, diagram
	visualize
	Overlearning

Summary: Try various memory techniques to discover which ones work best for short-term and long-term memory!

In some cases you might use several different colours. One colour—such as red—might signify important information that the instructor mentions will be on the test. Another colour might be reserved for definitions or material that is copied from the board. A third might be used for notes on what your instructor says.

You also have a choice of many kinds of notebooks. Loose-leaf notebooks are particularly good because they permit you to go back later and change the order of the pages or add additional material in the appropriate spot. But whatever kind of notebook you use, *only use one side of the page for writing; keep one side free of notes.* If you're studying and you want to spread out your notes in front of you, it's much easier if the back of the pages are blank.

In your notebook or binder, have a section for notes and another for assignments, projects, or tests. Make sure that you get a notebook or binder with pockets so that you can put loose-leaf paper in it and also use it to store handouts from the teacher. Or consider using plastic sheet protectors to organize handouts and important notices, such as syllabi, project descriptions, and essay requirements.

It is very important to date all sections every time you write in your notebook. As you complete items in the homework section, check them off or cross them out to show that these are done. If you miss a class, borrow or copy notes from a classmate as soon as possible, and make sure you understand what went on in the class if the notes don't make sense to you.

You should configure notebook pages spatially to optimize later review. According to educator Walter Pauk[1] from Cornell University, the best way to do this is to draw a line down the left side of your notebook page, about 6.5 cm from the left margin and another line 4 cm from the bottom of the page (illustrated in Figure 5.1). Keep the notes you write in class to the right of the line. Indent major supporting details beneath each main idea, trying to use no more than one line for each item, and leave space between topics to add information. When it comes time to review your notes later, you'll be able to jot down a key word, phrase, or major idea on the left side of the page. Or, you could write test questions related to your notes in this margin. Use the bottom section to summarize main ideas.

Some disciplines, such as nursing or paramedicine, may require a different kind of notetaking. Any new style will require some getting used to, but noting and organizing reported information is most effective when you have a systematic approach.

Using Notebook Computers to Take Notes If you're quite comfortable with computers and have a laptop or notebook computer, you might want to consider using it to take notes. There are several advantages: Legibility problems are avoided, and it's easy to go back and revise after you've taken the notes. It's also simple to add material later. Some students with disabilities depend on notebook computers if writing is difficult for them. Printing or e-mailing notes to a classmate absent from class is both helpful and efficient.

Despite their pluses, laptops also have minuses. For one thing, it's hard to make notes in the margins, copy graphical material that the instructor may present in class, reproduce formulas, or circle key ideas. Furthermore, the clattering of the keyboard may be annoying to your fellow students.

A Word of Caution Using notebook computers in the classroom can be distracting in other ways, as well. Students need self-discipline, focus, and commitment to their goals and the goals of the course while using laptops in the classroom in order to avoid temptations such as playing computer games, working on other assignments, surfing the Web, checking e-mail, or instant messaging. Despite a growing tendency to multi-task while on computers, students need to remember that notebook computers are tools to assist in notetaking and should be used responsibly.

Despite concerns, notebook computers in the classroom are here becoming more commonplace. Laptop programs are being instituted in several campuses across Canada. Every student in these programs has a notebook computer and brings it to all classes, where lectures and notetaking are being radically changed. For further information about laptop programs, read about Acadia University's program at <www.acadiau.ca/advantage/> or Sheridan College's program at <www.sheridanc.on.ca/academic/mobile/>.

W ork: Processing—Not Copying— Information

With pen poised, you're ready to begin the work of notetaking. The instructor begins to speak, and you start to write as quickly as you can, taking down as many of the instructor's words as possible.

> "My notes have become briefer, more succinct. I try to pay attention to what is going on rather than try to get every little word down."
>
> Markian Hlynka, Student, University of Alberta

Stop! You've made your first mistake. The central act in taking notes is not writing. Notetaking involves *listening* and *thinking* far more than writing. The key to effective notetaking is to write down the right amount of information—not too much, and not too little. To see how this is true, consider the following recommendations for taking notes:

- **Listen for the key ideas.** Not every sentence in a lecture is equally important, and one of the most useful skills you can develop is separating the key ideas from supporting information. Good lecturers strive to make just a few main points. The rest of what they say consists of explanation, examples, and other supportive material that expands on the key ideas.

  Your job, then, is to distinguish the key ideas from those that are of less importance. To do this, you need to be alert and always searching for the meta-message of your instructor's words. The **meta-message** consists of the underlying main ideas that a speaker is seeking to convey—the meaning behind the overt message you hear.

  How can you discern the meta-message? One way is to *listen for key words*.

  For instance, listen for clues about the importance of material. All phrases like "don't forget . . . ," "be sure to remember that . . . ," "you need to know . . . ," "the most important thing to consider . . . ," "there are four problems with this approach . . . ," and—a big one—"this will be on the test . . . " should cause you to sit up and take notice. Another good sign of importance is repetition. If an instructor says the same thing in several ways, it's a clear sign that the material being discussed is important.

  Be on the lookout for nonverbal signals too. When instructors pause, raise their eyes, glance at their notes, or otherwise change their demeanour, these behaviours are a signal that what they're about to say is important.

Using a laptop computer to take class notes ensures that they will be legible and that it will be easy to revise them after class. However, it's difficult to input graphical material, such as complex formulas, and there's also a danger that you'll be tempted to take too many notes.

Meta-message
The underlying main ideas that a speaker wants to convey; the meaning behind the overt message

- **Use short, abbreviated phrases—not full sentences.** Forget everything you've ever heard about always writing in full sentences. If you try to write notes in complete sentences, you'll soon become bogged down, paying more attention to your notes than to your instructor. In fact, if you use full sentences, you'll be tempted to try transcribing every word the instructor utters, which, as you now know, is not a good idea at all.

  Instead, write in phrases, using only key words or terms. Save full sentences for definitions or quotes that your instructor clearly wants you to know word for word. For example, consider the following excerpt from a lecture:

  > There are two kinds of job analyses: job- or task-oriented analyses, and worker- or employee-oriented analyses. Job analyses just describe the tasks that need to be accomplished by a worker. Employee-oriented job descriptions need to describe knowledge, skills, and abilities the employee must have in order to get the job done. Most job analyses include elements of both job-oriented and employee-oriented types.

Figure 5.2

A Sample Outline

I. Difficulties faced by students seeking affordable housing
   A. Students are subjected to high rents for housing close to campus
      1. Forced to share apartments
      2. Sometimes must live far from campus
   B. Made to sign leases with strict provisions
II. Possible solutions
   A. School offers subsidized housing
      1. Advantage is that housing costs can be lowered
      2. Potential problems
         a. school becomes students' landlord
         b. school uses funds for housing that could be otherwise invested in education
   B. Rent control
      1. Advantage: Rent control can provide reasonably priced rents
      2. Disadvantages
         a. Creates a permanent, expensive rent-control bureaucracy
         b. Landlords may neglect rent-control property
         c. The present shortage of apartments would worsen, because little incentive for owners to increase the number of rental units
         d. Competition for units would dramatically increase
III. Summary
   A. There are advantages and disadvantages to both solutions
   B. May need new, creative solutions

If you were taking notes, you might produce the following:

2 kinds job analyses:
(1) job-oriented (= task-oriented): what worker must do to get job done
(2) worker-oriented (= employee-oriented): describe knowledge, skills, abilities needed
most analyses include both

Note that the lecturer used 67 words, while the notes used only 29 words—fewer than half.

- **Use abbreviations.** One way to speed up the notetaking process is through the use of abbreviations. Among the most common are the following:

and & or +	with w/	without w/o
care of c/o	leads to; resulting in →	as a result of ←
percent %	change △	number #
that is i.e.	for example e.g.	and so forth etc.
no good n.g.	question ?	compared with c/w
page p.	important! !!	less than <
more than >	equals, same as =	versus vs. or v.

- **Take notes in outline form.** It's often useful to take notes in the form of an outline. An *outline* summarizes ideas in short phrases and indicates the relationship among concepts through the use of indentations.

  When outlining, it's best to be formal about it, using roman numerals, regular numbers, and capital and small letters (see the example in Figure 5.2). Or, if you prefer, you can also simply use outlining indentations without assigning numbers and letters.

🏃 Working in a Group: Outline a Lecture

Working with others in a group, take turns slowly reading several paragraphs of the following lecture to each other.[2] As the paragraphs are being read, outline the main arguments on a sheet of paper.

Nunavut became Canada's newest province in 1999. This eastern Arctic territory is home to 24,000 people, mostly Inuit. Though Nunavut lacks heavy industries, it receives a lot of their toxic fallout. The Inuit people of Canada live 1000 kilometres from any significant source of pollution, yet studies have shown that somehow they carry in their bodies twice the amount of *dioxin* as Canadians living near areas where it is produced. The breast milk of Inuit women in Nunavut, for example, contains twice the average concentration of dioxin found in the milk of women in southern Quebec.

Dioxin is the name for closely related chemicals produced in burning, chiefly the incineration of waste. In high doses, it is very toxic, causing skin diseases in humans and cancer in animals.

According to a study initiated by the Commission for Environmental Cooperation (CEC) to test the feasibility of tracking dioxins from source to receptor, of 44,000 different cement kilns, incinerators, and other dioxin producers, most of Nunavut's dioxin comes from industrial combustion in United States. Some even originates as far away as Mexico. The major polluters had the most favourable weather patterns for quickly transporting pollution north and included sources in Iowa, Pennsylvania, and California.

Dioxin released from a smokestack moves with the weather, depositing a light dusting as it travels. Humans take in dioxin by eating. Sometimes, it is deposited on grass, where cows take it up during grazing and their bodies absorb it into the fat cells, where it gradually accumulates. The dioxin then makes its way into meat and milk. At other times, when the dioxin falls on water, it is picked up by algae, which in turn are consumed by crustaceans and fish, and then by the marine mammals that eat them.

In Nunavut, it is the caribou that eat lichens and the seals that eat fish that are the bridge from airborne dioxin to the Inuit table. The Inuit eat both caribou and seal, and because their traditional diet is heavy with animal fats—the repositories of dioxin—they find themselves with unusually high amounts of dioxin in their bodies.

Only 19 of 44,000 sources accounted for more than a third of the dioxin in Nunavut. And only about 600 sources accounted for more than 75 percent of the dioxin. Because the study releases the names of polluters, the Inuit in Nunavut have a way to take their concerns to the source of their problems. The data the people of Nunavut now have offers policy makers and communities a tool for understanding the global impacts of persistent organic chemicals. Many, such as dioxin, are slated for elimination. Environmentalists and scientists, as well as residents of Nunavut hope the data prompt efforts to reduce toxic chemicals at their sources.

🏃 After you have outlined the passage, compare your outline with that of others who took notes on the same passage. What were the main ideas of each passage? How do your notes differ from theirs, and what are the similarities? How might you improve your notes to better capture the main points? Would a different topic produce more or fewer difficulties? Collectively, produce what you believe is the ideal outline, and compare it with those produced by other groups.

Take Notes During Discussions

Try It! 3

Take notes on the following business class discussion about job satisfaction. Use cues from the instructor about the importance and accuracy of each point, and record in your notes only the key points that shed light on the topic.

Instructor: According to a recent survey, 90 percent of Canadians have a positive overall attitude to their jobs. Why might the interpretation of these results be inaccurate? Alicia?

Alicia: Um ...well, I think a lot of people lie on surveys—you know, they might be afraid what they say will get back to their employers.

Instructor: Hmmm, well we can question the validity of survey statistics in general, but there is more to it than just not telling the truth. Anyone else? Kamal?

Kamal: Yeah, I read an article that said that workers are reluctant to admit they made a mistake and so they put an optimistic spin on the situation. I can't remember where I read it.

Instructor: Good point, Kamal. A 1996 Angus Reid poll indicated that although 90 percent of workers reported overall job satisfaction, other factors such as employee recognition, pay, job security, and career advancement had much lower rates. What else?

Emily: Well, job satisfaction is also expressed in work behaviour—last year it seemed as though every time you opened a newspaper or watched the news on TV, people in every part of the country were going on strike or holding protests. I think that indicates that many employees in Canada aren't too happy.

Instructor: Right. These behaviours are indicative of dissatisfaction—particularly related to pay. How else do workers express dissatisfaction?

Mark: What about things like violence in the workplace or industrial sabotage? We keep hearing those stories about disgruntled employees going postal and killing their bosses and coworkers.

Nalani: Get real, Mark. That only happens in the States.

Instructor: Okay, you've hit on some extreme examples, but unfortunately some of them have occurred in Canada, like the Fabrikant murders at Concordia University. Other more common behaviours you might want to consider are employee theft, absentee rates, employee retention, and mental or physical health claims, particularly related to stress or workplace injury. Any other comments?

Outlining serves several functions. It forces you to try constantly to determine the structure of the lecture to which you're listening. Organizing the key points and noting the connections among them helps you to remember the material better because you have processed it more. Outlining also keeps your mind from drifting away from the lecture. The effort involved in seeking out the structure of the lecture will help keep you focused on the material being discussed. Use Try It! 2, "Outline a Lecture," on page 143 to practise your outlining skills.

- **Copy information written on the board or projected from overheads.** If your instructor takes the time to write something out to be displayed in class, you should take the time to copy it. Definitions, quotes, phrases, and formulas—if you see them in writing, they're quite likely important enough to include in your notes. In fact, material displayed prominently

Patty: What about performance? Isn't job performance correlated to satisfaction?

Ron: Not necessarily, Patty. When I was researching my project on job performance, I found out there wasn't a link.

Instructor: Yes and no, Ron. While studies haven't found a strong correlation, there is research that indicates that employees with high job satisfaction provide better customer service and engage in more organizational citizenship activities, such as extending beyond normal duties when necessary, avoiding conflict, or occasionally tolerating minor impositions.

Good discussion, folks. Just to bring this to a end, although Canadians may not be quite as satisfied with their jobs as some surveys suggest, 76 percent would recommend their place of employment to a friend, compared with 66 percent of Americans. In addition, in a recent *Globe and Mail* article, Canadians reported the highest job satisfaction rate of 13 countries—so it may be true that Canadians have a better working life than people in many other countries.

Write your notes here:

Were you able to identify the information that was most important? How would actually seeing the instructor's nonverbal reactions to the students' comments be helpful?

Working in a group, compare your notes on the discussion with those of your classmates. As a group, try to create an optimal set of notes that capture the most important points.

has "test item" written all over it. You might want to highlight such material in some way in your notes.

- **Use different notetaking techniques for class discussions.** Not every course is structured as a lecture. Classes that are based less on lectures and more on class discussion pose greater challenges for notetaking. (Use Try It! 3, "Take Notes During Discussions," on page 144.)

For example, a discussion of the use of tax support of private schools in a sociology class may raise a variety of issues. As students in the class provide their ideas about the meaning of the work, how much—and what—should you place in your notes?

In such situations, the best approach is to take your cue from the course instructor. Often the instructor will pose some questions to get the discussion rolling. Note those questions—they're an important indicator

Figure 5.3

Notes on a Lecture

Here is an instructor's introductory lecture on Margaret Laurence's *The Stone Angel*. At the bottom of the page are two students' notes. Which student—A or B—did a better job of capturing the important points in the lecture?

In today's class, we'll discuss Margaret Laurence's *The Stone Angel*. As I'm sure you all know, Laurence is one of the most important and beloved literary figures in Canada. Born Jean Margaret Wemyss, in Neepawa, Manitoba, in 1926, Laurence wrote some of the most insightful works of Canadian fiction. She received two Governor General's Awards for Fiction and numerous honorary degrees, and she was named Companion of the Order of Canada. Laurence died in 1987.

The Stone Angel was a seminal work for Laurence and for Canadian literature. The first of five "Manawaka" novels, it is a narrative of the memories of Hagar Currie Shipley, who relives her long life as she battles to come to terms with herself and her life before she dies.

Hagar is a unique and complex character whose stubbornness and fierce pride deprive her of knowing love or joy and render her rigid, critical, and unyielding. Despite raging against her impending death, Hagar views her choices and failures unsentimentally, although in the end she does recognize her great losses.

The narrative structure, the weaving of past and present, and themes of motherhood, family heritage, and women's empowerment will be the primary focus of our discussion. I am particularly interested in your views on the roles of identity and loss in this book. Is Hagar's life, in the end, a failure? What resolution and self-understanding, if any, does Hagar achieve?

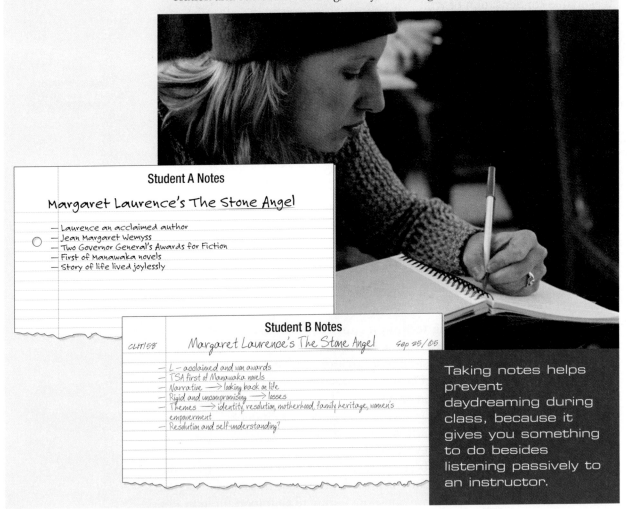

Student A Notes

Margaret Laurence's The Stone Angel

- Laurence an acclaimed author
- Jean Margaret Wemyss
- Two Governor General's Awards for Fiction
- First of Manawaka novels
- Story of life lived joylessly

Student B Notes

CLIT158   Margaret Laurence's The Stone Angel   Sep 25/05

- L — acclaimed and won awards
- TSA first of Manawaka novels
- Narrative ⟶ looking back on life
- Rigid and uncompromising ⟶ losses
- Themes ⟶ identity, resolution, motherhood, family heritage, women's empowerment
- Resolution and self-understanding?

Taking notes helps prevent daydreaming during class, because it gives you something to do besides listening passively to an instructor.

of what the instructor is interested in. The instructor's reaction to particular comments is another clue. Listen to his responses. If he responds enthusiastically to a particular point, highlight it in your notes.

- **Pay particular attention to the points raised by instructors at the end of discussion and lecture classes.** Instructors often provide a summary of the discussion, which is worthy of inclusion in your notes.

Use Special Techniques for "Problem Instructors" As we all know from painful experience, some instructors' lectures are impossible to outline. How do you take notes when the instructor starts talking about one topic and then rambles off onto another one without warning and never seems to get back to the original point? Or if the instructor speaks very quickly and covers too much material too fast for you to follow?

The fact is that all you can do is make the best of a bad situation and adapt your notetaking strategy to it. If no clear message or logical sequence is present in the lecture material, you may be unable to take notes in outline form. In such cases, focus more on creating a summary of what is being said, rather than trying to tease out its underlying structure. Write short "paragraphs" that focus on the major ideas being presented. Although the paragraphs certainly shouldn't consist of full sentences, they should provide a reasonable condensation of what the instructor said.

When you're writing in paragraph form, be sure to leave space after each paragraph. By leaving space, you'll make it easier to go back later and re-structure the material at a point when its underlying meaning is clearer.

You might be able to get a better sense of what the instructor is trying to convey by using your textbook to clarify obscure points. It also may be helpful to pool your notes with those of other students in the class. When the instructor's train of thought is all over the place, two—or more—heads are better than one!

Finally, don't hesitate to ask instructors to clarify what they are saying. In some cases, they simply may not realize how far off track they have gotten. You'll be doing them—and certainly your fellow classmates—a favour by asking for clarification.

Keep a Balance between Too Many Notes and Too Few Notes The key to effective notetaking is to keep a balance between too many and too few notes.

The best way to achieve this balance is by paying close attention in class. By being alert, engaged, and involved in class, you'll be able to make the most of the techniques we've discussed. The result: notes that capture the most important points raised in class and that will optimize your recall and mastery of the course subject matter. (See a sample of two students' notes in Figure 5.3.)

Evaluate: Thinking Critically about Your Notes

Toward the end of class, look over your notes. Now's the time—before the class has ended—to evaluate what you've written.

Try It! 4

Evaluate Your Class Notes

Take a set of notes you made recently during one of your classes and evaluate it on the following criteria.

Statement	Not Even Slightly	Slightly	Moderately	Pretty Well	Very Well
1. I can read my notes (i.e., they are legible).					
2. Someone else can read my notes.					
3. My notes are complete; I missed nothing important.					
4. My notes represent the key points that were covered in class.					
5. My notes reflect the instructor's emphases.					
6. The instructor's key points are clear and understandable.					
7. The notes contain only important points, with no extraneous material.					
8. I understand not only the notes but the class content they reflect.					
9. Using only the notes, I will be able to reconstruct the essential content of the class in three months.					

What do your answers tell you about the effectiveness of your notetaking skills? What might you do differently the next time you take notes?

In a group, evaluate and compare the notes you took during the previous 20 minutes of the class you are in now. How do your notes compare to those of the other members of your group?

After being sure you can answer "yes" to the most basic question—can I read what I've written?—ask yourself these questions:

- Do my notes do a good job of representing what was covered in class?
- Do they reflect the emphases of the instructor?
- Are there any key points that are not entirely clear?
- Do I need help clarifying any of the points my instructor made?

Evaluating your notes is a critical part of the notetaking process. You can get a sense of how effective your notetaking has been while you still have a chance to ask your instructor to clarify anything that is still not clear.

Perhaps, for example, you've left out a key word in a definition. Maybe you don't understand a concept fully, even though you've written about it in your notes. Possibly you've left out the third step in a list of six steps necessary to accomplish something.

If you look over your notes while you're still in class, you have time to ask your instructor for clarification. Or you can wait till the end of class and then go up and raise your question. Most instructors will be happy to answer questions from students who have obviously been actively listening. Just make sure that you add what they tell you to your notes so you'll be able to refer to them later. (To practise evaluating your notes, complete Try It! 4, "Evaluate Your Class Notes," on page 148.)

R ethink: Activating Your Memory

The lecture has ended and class is over. You put the top on your pen, close your notebook, stash everything in your backpack, and head out for a cup of coffee before your next class.

Wait! Before you close up your notebook, finish the P.O.W.E.R. process. Rethink what you've heard. Spending 5 or 10 minutes reconsidering what you've written right now can save you *hours* of work later. The reason: Rethinking promotes the transfer of information into long-term memory (something discussed more in Chapter 9). As you link the new information you've taken down to what you already know and then integrate it, you essentially plug this information into your memory in a much more meaningful way, which means you can remember it better and more easily.

If you looked over your notes to clarify and evaluate the information in them in class, you've already begun the process. Once class is over, you need to review the material more formally. Here's how to do it:

- **Rethink as soon as possible.** Time is of the essence! The rethinking phase of notetaking doesn't have to take long; 5 to 10 minutes is usually sufficient. The more critical issue is *when* you do it. The longer you wait before reviewing your notes, the less effective the process will be.

  There's no doubt that the best approach is to review the material just after the class has ended. As everyone else is leaving, just stay seated and go over your notes. This works fine for classes late in the day, when no other class is scheduled in the room. But what if you must vacate the room immediately after class? The next best thing is to find a quiet space somewhere nearby and do your rethinking there.

  "It is not enough to have a good mind; the main thing is to use it well."

  René Descartes

  Even if you have another class immediately afterwards, you can do your rethinking before that class if you get there early enough. However you do it, the same rule holds: Sooner is better.

  In any case, don't let the day end without examining your notes. In fact, reconsidering material just before sleep is thought to be particularly effective. After rethinking, it may be a good idea to rewrite or copy your notes on a computer. Rewriting notes and adding additional material is a good way to transfer information to your long-term memory.

- **Make rethinking an active process.** Some people feel the notes they take in class are akin to historical documents in a museum, with Do Not Touch! signs hanging on them. You should think of your notes as a construction project and yourself as the person in charge of the project.

  When you review your notes, do so with an eye to improving them. If any information is not entirely clear, change the wording in your notes, adding to or amending what's there. If certain words are hard to read, fix them; it won't be any easier to read them the night before a test—in fact, chances are you'll have even more trouble.

If, on rethinking the material, you just don't understand something, ask your instructor or a friend to clarify it. And when you receive an explanation, add it to your notes so you won't forget it. (You might want to use a different-coloured pen for additions to your notes, so you'll know they came later.)

- **Take the broad view.** When you rethink your notes, don't think of them only in terms of a single lecture or a single class. Instead, take a longer

Figure 5.4

A Concept Map of Margaret Laurence's *The Stone Angel*

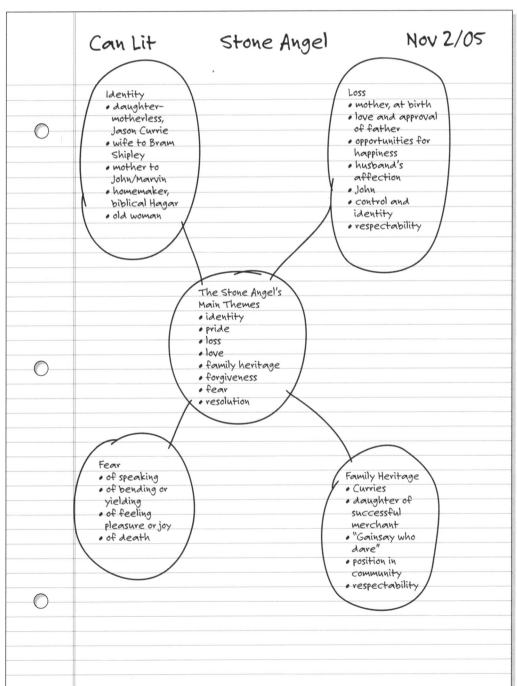

Practise Your Notetaking Skills

Try It! 5

Practise your notetaking skills, using any techniques you find helpful, in one of the classes in which you are enrolled this term. Bring your notes to the class in which you are using this book, and answer these questions:

1. Which specific techniques did I use in taking notes?

_____

_____

2. Which of the notetaking techniques detailed in this chapter was I unable to use, and why?

_____

_____

_____

3. Could I take the notes I made in class and redo them, using one of the techniques in this chapter such as a concept map? _____

After you have taken notes, use the techniques discussed in this chapter to evaluate and rethink them. Creating a concept map on a separate sheet of paper may be particularly helpful.

---

view. Ask yourself how they fit into the broader themes of the class and the goals that you and the instructor have for the semester. How will the information be useful to you? Why did the instructor emphasize a particular point?

If you've configured your notes by leaving a 6.5-cm column on the left-hand side of the page, now is the time to make use of that blank column. Write down key words, significant points, major concepts, controversies, and questions. The process of adding this information will not only help you to rethink the material now, it will also provide guideposts when you study before a test.

- **Create concept maps. Concept mapping** is a method of structuring written material by graphically grouping and connecting key ideas and themes. In contrast to an outline, a concept map visually illustrates how related ideas fit together. The pictorial summary gives you another handle to store the information in memory, and it focuses your thinking on the key ideas from the lecture.

  In a concept map, each key idea is placed in a different part of the map, and related ideas are placed near it—above, below, or beside it. What emerges does not have the rigid structure of an outline. Instead, a "finished" concept map looks something like a map of the solar system, with the largest and most central idea in the centre (the "sun" position), and related ideas surrounding it at various distances. It has also been compared to a large tree, with numerous branches and sub-branches radiating out from a central trunk. (Figure 5.4 presents a sample concept map.)

  Building a concept map has several advantages. It forces you to rethink the material in your notes in a new style—particularly important if

Concept mapping
A method of structuring written material by graphically grouping and connecting key ideas and themes

you used traditional outlining while taking the notes. In addition, it helps you to tie together the material for a given class session. Finally, it will help you to build a master concept map later, when you're studying the material for a final exam. (To practise the techniques we've been discussing, see Try It! 5, "Practise Your Notetaking Skills," on page 151.)

Taking Notes: Multimedia Technology

Many instructors use multimedia technology, such as PowerPoint and video or audio clips, to improve their lectures. Multimedia technology can deepen your understanding of a lecture, but it also makes notetaking more challenging. Often the classroom's lights are dimmed and it may be difficult to take legible notes. It may be more difficult to follow the message of multimedia presentations than a "chalk and talk" lecture. A PowerPoint slideshow likely includes just the main points in a lecture so don't be content with copying points from the slides . . . listen carefully to the content presented by your instructor and expand upon it in your notes.

Some professors post PowerPoint lectures on a course website before the start of class. If this is a feature of your course, consider printing out a copy of the lecture, and bring it to class to take notes on. However, this may be a very expensive way to take notes, as most computer labs in schools charge for printing and even printing off material at home adds up, compared with the cost of loose-leaf paper or notebooks. It may be more beneficial, as well as cheaper, to copy the notes manually. You will be more actively involved in the notetaking process, rather than just printing the notes off. Or save paper and download the notes and expand upon them on your notebook or desk computer.

Taking Notes as You Study

Weighing as much as 2.5 kg, bulky and awkward, and filled with tonnes of information, it's the meat-and-potatoes of postsecondary life: your course textbook. You might feel intimidated by its size; you might be annoyed at its cost; you might think you'll never be able to read it, let alone understand, learn, and recall the material in it. How will you manage?

Study notes
Notes taken for the purpose of reviewing material

The answer involves taking **study notes,** notes taken for the purpose of reviewing material. They are the kind of notes that you take now to study from later. (We'll consider *research notes,* notes that you take to write a paper or prepare a report, in Chapter 8 when we discuss writing papers.)

Several strategies are useful for taking study notes from material such as magazines, books, journals, and Web pages. Which approach works best depends on whether you can write on the material you want to take notes on.

Speaking of Success

Kofi Boateng

*Law and Security Diploma,
Niagara College*

A graduate of the Law and Security Program at Niagara College, Kofi Boateng works as a child and youth worker. He works with teenagers who cannot live at home for a variety of reasons. As a member of a shift team that must work together in a very supportive and collegial manner, Kofi learned and refined many of these teamwork skills while at college.

Kofi was a member of the varsity basketball team at Niagara. Playing basketball required a huge time commitment, due to practices, games, and out-of-town tournaments, and at times Kofi worried about keeping up with his schoolwork. He found that professors would postpone assignments, or tests due to his athletic obligations, but generally Monday was the day teachers wanted him to catch up, which was difficult after an exhausting weekend playing away-games. Kofi and other teammates used their time on the bus heading to and from matches to read and study so they didn't fall behind in their work. This was a good use of travelling time, and it also allowed the basketball players to remain in good academic standing, which ensured they could keep on playing for the team.

In addition, Kofi and several other classmates from Law and Security would informally gather to study

course material in preparation for tests and assignments. Kofi, an associative learner, listens to lectures and links new points with ideas or concepts already discussed. As a result, his notes were not always complete, so working with others was a great way to fill in any blanks.

Kofi could then use his recall of the group discussion and relate it to class lectures, discussion, and reading when studying.

Kofi's favourite class was psychology, but he found it difficult to listen to detailed lectures, full of new concepts, theories, and specialized vocabulary and take notes as well. Kofi noticed other classmates taping their professor's lectures and he also started to tape the lectures and write his notes after class. Not only did this strategy allow him to pay full attention to class discussions, but also allowed him to review course material as he worked on his notes.

At Niagara, working in teams—athletic or academic—helped Kofi prepare for employment in the group home; it also helped him realize the value of everyone's contribution to a common effort, a crucial skill he passes on to the at-risk youth he counsels.

Career Connections

Notetaking on the Job: Taking Minutes

Meetings are becoming increasingly important, especially in industries where product development and marketing programs rely heavily on teamwork across departments. Survey results show that executives on average spend 40 to 50 percent of their working hours in meetings.

The most important reason to create a record of meetings is to create a shared group memory. Individuals selectively perceive, retain, and recall their own experiences. Therefore, meeting participants will each remember a meeting quite differently. It is important that minutes accurately reflect what occurred in the meeting, the decisions that were made, and the things that individuals are committed to doing because of the meeting.

If you are assigned to take the minutes of a meeting, your notetaking skills will come in handy. Even if you are just an attendee, it is a good idea to take notes, to keep track of what you need to follow-up.

3M has a template of three basic steps that can simplify minute-taking:[3]

1. *Action items.* Action items are to-dos assigned to attendees at the meeting. Record the task, the person responsible, and the date agreed on to complete the task.
2. *Decisions.* All decisions that may affect future choices of the group should be recorded.
3. *Open issues.* New issues raised at the meeting but not resolved there should be recorded so they can be carried over to a future meeting.

Using a digital whiteboard allows meeting participants to see the minutes as they are compiled and have input into their creation. In addition, the digital whiteboard allows virtual meetings to occur, with attendees from various centres participating in the meeting and seeing the minutes produced in real-time. Rather than having the minutes reproduced on paper, they can be e-mailed to participants or placed on an Intranet.

Taking Notes on Material You Can Write On

Here are some suggestions for creating study notes for material on which you can annotate the text directly by underlining, highlighting, or writing in the margins:

- **Integrate your text notes into your study notes.** If you want to create study notes from written material on which you can write, start by annotating the pages as you normally would. Use the techniques that work best for you: highlighting, underlining, circling, making marginal notes—whatever you generally use. These techniques are discussed in detail in Chapter 7; you may want to look ahead to that discussion.

  After you've finished reading and annotating the material, it's time to create study notes. While it's still fresh in your mind, go back over the material and your text annotations, and create your study notes.

  The study notes should provide a summary of the key points. They might be in outline form or in the form of concept maps. They should supplement and summarize the annotations you've made on the text.

  Furthermore, any notes you take should stand on their own. For instance, they should include enough information to be useful whether or not you have the book or article on hand.

- **Use flash cards.** If you feel confident that the annotations you've written in the book are sufficiently comprehensive, you might consider taking notes on flash cards. **Flash cards** are simply index cards that contain key pieces of information that you need to remember.

Flash cards are particularly useful in subjects that present many small bits of information to remember, such as foreign language vocabulary words or scientific formulas. When you need to learn a list of foreign words, for instance, you can write a foreign word on one side of a card and its English meaning on the other side.

One of the greatest virtues of flash cards is their portability. Because they are small, they can fit into your pocket or handbag, and you can look at them at odd times when you have a spare moment.

Flash cards
Note cards that contain key pieces of information to be remembered

Taking Study Notes on Material You Can't Write On

Taking notes on material that can't be written on is a different story. Library books, magazines, journal articles, and materials on library reserve that are shared with others require a different approach.

- **Approach the written material as you would a class lecture.** The techniques we discussed earlier for taking notes in class can all be adapted for taking notes from written material. In fact, the task is often easier, because you'll be able to refer back to what was said earlier —it's in black and white in front of you.

- **Laptop computers can be especially helpful in creating study notes.** Because it's often easier and quicker to take notes using a word-processing program (if you're a good typist), computers can help you take more-detailed notes from written material on which you can't write. If your typing skills are below par, consider taking a word-processing course or use a typing tutorial software program to increase your speed and accuracy. Keyboard skills are now essential in the classroom and in the workplace.

- **Use all the tricks of the trade we discussed earlier for taking notes from a class lecture.** Look for the key ideas, definitions, quotes, and formulas, and include them in your notes. Use the headings that are included in the text, such as chapter and section titles. Bold or italic type is also a clue that an important point is being made. Graphs and charts often provide critical information.

- **Use the same form of notetaking that you use in class lectures.** If you take notes in class using the two-column method (in which you reserve a 6.5-cm column on the left side of your paper for adding comments during later review of the notes), use that technique here as well. If you write your notes in outline form, create an outline based on the written material. If you often create graphics such as concept maps, create them now. The point is to produce notes that are consistent with those you take during class lectures.

What is effective notetaking?

- The central feature of good notetaking is listening and distilling important information—not writing down everything that is said.

How can I take good notes in class?

- Prepare for taking notes by identifying the instructor's and your own goals for the course, completing all assignments before arriving in class, and warming up for class by reviewing the notes and assignments from the previous class.

- Sit as close to the teacher as possible. Be sure that you can clearly see the chalkboard or screen if there are overheads, a Power Point presentation, or a computer screen. If you are easily distracted, sit away from your friends and try and maintain eye contact with your teacher.

- Before writing notes, listen and think, processing the information that the instructor is attempting to deliver.

- Notes should be brief phrases rather than full sentences and, if possible, be in outline form to reveal the structure of the lecture. Material written on the board should usually be copied word for word.

- Before leaving class, evaluate your notes, verifying that they are complete and understandable while there is still time to correct them. As soon as possible after class, actively rethink your notes.

What techniques apply to taking notes from written materials?

- Taking good study notes from written materials involves many of the principles that apply to taking good notes from oral presentations, although the source material can be consulted repeatedly, making it easier to get the information down accurately.

- Concept maps and flash cards can be helpful tools for notetaking from textbooks.

P.O.W.E.R. Portfolio

Take Note

Consider including a set or example of study notes in your section on knowledge management. Or perhaps you could include notes you took at a meeting you attended, or an interview you did for your school's paper. Reflect on what skills or abilities are demonstrated in your submissions, as well as their importance to you as a learner.

Resources

On Campus

If you are having difficulty taking class notes effectively, talk with your course instructor. Bring your notes with you soon after a class has ended, and let the instructor assess what you are doing correctly and what could stand improvement.

    If your problems persist, and you have great difficulty translating the spoken word into notes, then there's a small possibility that you suffer from an auditory learning disability. Be tested by your school's learning disabilities office or counselling office to address this or rule it out.

In Print

Take Notes (Career Press, 1994), by Ron Fry, provides an overall view of how to take good notes in classes.

Another approach can be found in James Roberts's *Bud's Easy Note Taking System* (Lawrence House, 1995), which offers many useful suggestions.

Finally, *Noteworthy: Listening and Notetaking Skills* (2nd ed.), by Phyllis Lim and William Smalzer (William S. Hein & Co., 1995) provides a fine overview of strategies for increasing your listening and notetaking expertise.

On the Web

The following sites on the World Wide Web provide the opportunity to extend your learning about the material in this chapter. Although the Web addresses were accurate at the time the book was printed, check the P.O.W.E.R. Learning website, <www.mcgrawhill.ca/college/power>, for any changes that may have occurred.

www.yorku.ca/cdc/lsp/notesonline/note4.htm
York University's Counselling and Development Centre has an example of the Cornell system. One advantage of this system is that it allows you to make use of your existing strengths as a notetaker.

www.coun.uvic.ca/learn/program/hndouts/class1.html
An effective method for organizing complicated information is through concept mapping. This site has a tutorial that presents information in passage form and then asks you to create a concept map. The concept map created by the authors is only a click away.

The Case of . . .

A Clean Sweep

Sunhee Park came home from school feeling pretty good about her semester. She attended all her classes, kept up with her assignments, and had gotten decent marks on two quizzes. Despite living on her own and working 12 to 15 hours a week at a local video store, Sunhee was confident that everything was under control.

However, mid-terms were two weeks away and it was time to get organized. Two hours later and her room was a total disaster . . . handouts, PowerPoint printouts, and folded pieces of paper with notes on them were all over her desk, bed, and chair. Her notebook was a jumble of all her course notes, and her textbooks were filled with notations, highlighted sections, folded-over pages, and scraps of paper. As she dumped her backpack out on the floor, pens, highlighters, two floppy disks, and two illegible Post-It notes fell out.

Sunhee looked at the piles of stuff that represented her semester so far and wished she could have a "Clean Sweep" crew come and organize her life.

1. On a scale of 1 to 10, with 1 being terrible and 10 being wonderful, how would you rank Sunhee's dilemma? Why? Can she turn her situation around?

2. What stage of the P.O.W.E.R. process is Sunhee stuck in? What does she need to do to get back on track?

3. Why do you think Sunhee has managed to do so well up to this point in the semester?

4. What advice would you give to Sunhee on notetaking?

5. If a "Clean Sweep" crew took a look at your notes (from classes, online studies, and reading) what would its verdict be? Why? What kind of action will you take regarding your notetaking?

Taking Tests

6

Getting Ready

Journal Reflections:
How I Feel about Tests

Prepare: Readying Your Test-
Taking Strategies

Organize: Facing the Day of the
Test

Taking the Test

Work: Tackling the Test

Career Connections:
Professional Tests:
More Exams and Tests

Evaluate: Taking Your Own
Final Examination

Rethink: Reflecting on the Real
Test of Learning

Speaking of Success:
Asta Kovanen

The Case of . . .
Too Many Questions,
Too Little Time

inette Berger looked at her trembling hands and told herself to breathe in . . . one, two, three . . . and out . . . one, two, three . . . . In high school Ginette used to get stomach aches and shortness of breath around exam time. Her guidance counsellor suggested she might have test anxiety and so she learned some relaxation techniques. When Ginette started her interior design program, she was so excited. She loved her program, but postsecondary was a lot harder than high school. As a familiar sense of dread came over her, Ginette reminded herself to breathe . . .

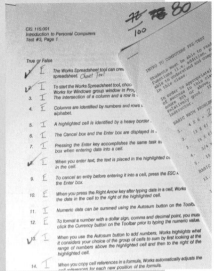

Ginette is not alone in her dread of exams. For many students, tests represent the most anxiety-producing events in their postsecondary careers.

They needn't be *so* bad. There are strategies and techniques you can learn to reduce the fearsomeness of tests. In fact, in some ways learning *how* to take tests is as important as learning the content that they cover. Taking tests effectively is an acquired skill. It does not just involve mastering a body of information; it also requires mastering specific test-taking skills.

It is those skills we consider in this chapter. One of the first steps is to demystify tests. You will learn about the different types of tests and strategies that you can apply before you even take a test. You will become familiar with various types of test questions and learn a strategy that matches each type of question.

We will also explore two aspects of test taking that may affect your performance: test anxiety and cramming for a test. You will learn ways to deal with anxiety, keep your cramming to a minimum, and make the most of cramming if you *do* have to resort to it.

The chapter ends with suggestions for evaluating your performance toward the end of a test session and for using your test results to improve your performance the next time you take a test.

After reading this chapter, you'll be able to answer these questions:

- **What kinds of tests will I encounter in college or university?**

- **What are the best ways to prepare for and take various kinds of tests?**

- **What are the best strategies for answering specific kinds of test questions?**

Getting Ready

Although tests are a fact of academic life, there are aspects of them that those who give tests—as well as those who take them—don't like very much.

Students hate tests because they produce fear, anxiety, apprehension about being evaluated, and a focus on grades instead of learning for learning's sake. Instructors hate tests because they produce fear, anxiety, apprehension about being evaluated, and a focus on grades instead of learning for learning's sake. That's right: Students and instructors dislike tests for the very same reasons.

However, tests are also valuable. A well-constructed test identifies what you know (and don't know) and where the gaps in your knowledge are. They help you see how your performance compares to that of others. Knowing that you'll be tested on a body of material is likely to motivate you to learn material more thoroughly.

But there's another reason why you may dislike tests: You may assume that tests have the power to define your worth as a person. However, *tests are not a measure of your value as an individual—just how well (and how much) you studied and how well you learned the material.*

If you do badly on a test, you may be tempted to believe that you've received some fundamental information about yourself from the professor and the college or university, information that says you're a failure in some significant way.

This is a dangerous—and wrongheaded—assumption. If you do poorly on a test, it doesn't mean you're a bad person, or stupid, or that you'll never do better again and that your life is ruined. If you don't do well on a test, you're the same person you were before you took the test—no better, no worse. You just did poorly on a test, period.

Tests are tools; they are indirect and imperfect measures of what we know. Someone with a great deal of knowledge can do poorly on a test; perhaps anxiety made her blank out or she went too slowly early on and was unable to complete the test.

How I Feel about Tests

1. What general feelings do you have about tests?

2. What are your first memories of being in a testing situation? What were your feelings, and why?

3. What uses do you think tests serve?

4. Do you think tests are ever misused? In what ways?

5. In general, what makes a test "good" from your perspective?

6. What *specific* characteristics does a good test have?

7. In general, what makes a test "bad" from your perspective?

8. What *specific* characteristics does a bad test have?

9. What factors contribute to your success or failure on a particular exam? Which of these factors are under your control?

Another person may know considerably less and still do better on the test simply because he may have learned some test-taking skills along the way.

How much we reap the benefits of a test depends on several considerations: the kind of test it is, the subject matter involved, and above all how well we prepare for it. Let's turn, then, to the first step in test taking: preparation. (The five steps are summarized in the P.O.W.E.R. Plan below.)

P repare: Readying Your Test-Taking Strategies

Preparation for tests requires several strategies (see Try It! 1, "Complete a Test-Preparation Checklist"). Among the most important are the following:

Remember Everything You Do in a Course Is Preparation for a Test Completing a reading assignment, writing a paper, filling out a worksheet—everything you do during a course helps to prepare you for a test. There is no surer way to get good grades on tests than to attend class faithfully, to take good notes, and to complete all class assignments seriously and on time.

Preparing for tests is a long-term proposition. It's not a matter of giving your all the night before the test. Instead, it's a matter of giving your all to every aspect of the course.

Know What You Are Preparing For Determine as much as you can about the test before you begin to prepare for it. The more you know about a test, the better you'll be able to get ready.

To find out about an upcoming test, ask these questions:

- Is the test called a "test," "exam," "quiz," or something else? As you can see in Table 6.1, the names imply different things. For simplicity's sake, we'll use the term test throughout this chapter, but know that these distinctions exist and they should affect the way you prepare.

- What material will the test cover?

- How many questions will be on it?

- How much time is it expected to take? a full class period? only part of a period?

- What kinds of questions will be on the test?

- How will it be graded?

- Will sample questions be provided?

- Are tests from previous terms available?

Review Your Notes If you have regularly taken and reviewed your notes for your courses, you have a great start on preparing for your test. The rationale for Chapter 5's notetaking strategies is now obvious: the reason you worked so hard to understand the coursework earlier in the year was so that you would be well prepared for tests and exams.

PREPARE
Review your work regularly

ORGANIZE
Bring the right tools to the test; follow directions carefully

WORK
Tackle the test

EVALUATE
Save time to check your work; know when to stop

RETHINK
Reflect on what you've learned when you get a test back

P.O.W.E.R. Plan

Try It! 1

Complete a Test-Preparation Checklist

Before taking your next test, complete the following test-preparation checklist.

Test-Preparation Checklist

- ☐ I checked whether it's a quiz, test, or exam.
- ☐ I began preparation long before the test (e.g., by taking notes in class).
- ☐ I understand what material will be covered.
- ☐ I have reviewed my textbook and have completed the review questions at the end of the chapter.
- ☐ I have done sample tests on the textbook's CD-ROM or website.
- ☐ I know how long it will take.
- ☐ I know what kinds of questions will be on the test.
- ☐ I know how it will be graded.
- ☐ I obtained sample questions or previous tests, if available.
- ☐ I formed or participated in a study group.
- ☐ I studied with my study group more than once.
- ☐ I used different and appropriate preparation strategies for each type of question.
- ☐ I read my class notes.
- ☐ I composed some essay questions.
- ☐ I answered essay questions aloud.
- ☐ I actively memorized facts and details.
- ☐ I made and used note cards.
- ☐ I created and used a test like the real test.

Table 6.1

Quizzes, Tests, Exams . . .
What's in a Name?

Although they may vary from one instructor to another, the following definitions are the ones most frequently used:

Quizzes. A **quiz** is a brief assessment, usually covering a relatively small amount of material. Some quizzes cover as little as one class's worth of reading. Although a single quiz usually doesn't count very much, instructors often add quiz scores together, and collectively they can become a significant part of your final course grade.

Tests. A **test** is a more extensive, more heavily weighted assessment than a quiz, covering more material. A test may come every few weeks of the term, often after each third or quarter of the term has passed, but this varies with the instructor and the course.

Exams. An **exam** is the most substantial kind of assessment. In many classes, just one exam is given—a *final exam* at the end of the term. Sometimes there are two exams, one at the midpoint of the term (called, of course, a midterm) and the other at the end. Exams are usually weighted quite heavily because they are meant to assess your knowledge of all the course material up to that point.

Study groups, made up of a few students who study together for a test, can help organize material, provide new perspectives, and motivate members to do their best.

Form a Study Group

Study groups are small, informal groups of students who work together to learn the course material and study for a test. Forming such a group can be an excellent way to prepare. Some study groups are formed for particular tests, while others meet regularly throughout the term.

The typical study group meets a week or two before a test and plans a strategy for studying. Members share their understanding of what will be on the test, based on their own perceptions of what an instructor has said in class about the upcoming test. Together, they develop a list of review questions to guide their individual study. The group breaks up, and the members study on their own.

A few days before the test, members of the study group meet again. They discuss answers to the review questions, go over the material, and share any new information they may have about the test. They may also quiz one another about the material to identify any weaknesses or gaps in their knowledge.

Study groups

Small, informal groups of students whose purpose is to help members study for a test

Study groups can be extremely powerful because they help accomplish several things:

- They help members to organize and structure the material, which forces members to approach the material in a systematic and logical way.

- They aid in the sharing of different perspectives on the material.

- They help prevent students from overlooking any potentially important information.

- They force their members to rethink the course material, explaining it in words that they and the other group members will understand. As we will discuss in Chapter 9, this helps both understanding and recall of the information when it is needed on the test.

- They help motivate members to do their best. When you're part of a study group, you're no longer working just for yourself; your studying also benefits the other study-group members. Not wanting to let down your classmates in a study group may sometimes give more of a push to your study habits than you get from working only for yourself.

There are some some potential drawbacks to keep in mind. Study groups don't always work well for students with certain kinds of learning styles who prefer to work independently. In addition, "problem" members who don't pull their weight, may cause difficulties for the group. In general, though, the advantages of study groups usually far outweigh their possible disadvantages.

Review Your Textbook and Do Sample Tests

Most textbooks come with sample test questions at the end of every chapter and many have accompanying CD-ROMs or online learning centres with sample tests. These resources are tremendously helpful in determining what you need to study—as well as where you don't need to focus your attention.

Match Test Preparation to Question Types

Match Test Preparation to Question Types   Test questions come in different types (see Table 6.2), and each requires a somewhat different style of preparation.

- **Essay questions.** Essay questions are meant to see whether you have a broad knowledge of the material being tested. You'll need to know not just a series of facts but also the connections between them, and you will have to be able to discuss these ideas in an organized and logical way. Essay exams focus on the ways in which the various pieces of information on a topic fit together.

   The best approach to studying for an essay exam involves four steps:

   1. Carefully read your class notes and any notes you've made on assigned readings that will be covered on the upcoming exam. Also go through the readings themselves, reviewing underlined or highlighted material and marginal notes.

   2. Play professor: Think of likely exam questions. To do this, you can use the keywords, phrases, concepts, and questions you've earlier created in your notes. In addition, your class instructor may have given you a list of possible essay topics.

   3. Without looking at your notes or your readings, answer each potential essay question—aloud. Don't feel embarrassed about doing this. Talking aloud is often more useful than answering the question silently in your head.

      You can also write down the main points that any answer should cover. Don't write out complete and full answers to the questions, because your time is probably better spent learning the material you'll be tested on. The one exception is if your instructor tells you exactly what essay question is going to be on the exam. In that case, it pays to write out the answer.

Table 6.2

Types of Test Questions

Essay

Requires a fairly extensive, on-the-spot composition about some topic. An essay question may call on you to describe some person, process, or event, or it may ask you to compare or contrast two separate sets of material.

Multiple-choice

Usually contains a question or statement, followed by a number of (usually four or five) response choices. You are supposed to choose the most correct response from the possible response choices that are offered.

True–false

Presents statements about a topic that are either accurate or inaccurate. You are to indicate whether each statement is accurate (true) or inaccurate (false).

Matching

Presents two lists of related information, arranged in column form. Typically you are asked to pair terms, concepts, and definitions with one another.

Short-answer

Requires brief responses (at most a few sentences) in a kind of mini-essay.

Fill-in

Requires you to add one or more missing words to a sentence or series of sentences.

4. After you've answered the questions, check yourself by looking at the notes and readings once again. If you feel confident that you've answered particular questions adequately, check them off. You can go back later for a quick review.

   If there are questions that you had trouble with, review that material immediately. Then repeat the third step above, answering the questions again.

- **Multiple-choice, true–false,** and **matching questions.** While the focus of review for essay questions should be on major issues and controversies, and on integration of the material—more of a big picture focus—studying for multiple-choice, true–false, and matching questions requires more attention to the details.

   Almost anything is fair game for multiple-choice, true–false, and matching questions, and so you can't afford to overlook anything when studying. This means that your studying needs to be detail-oriented. And it means that you must put your memory into high gear and master a great many facts.

   It's a particularly good idea to write down important facts on index cards like those below. Remember the advantages of these cards: They're portable and available all the time, and the act of creating them helps drive the material into your memory. Furthermore, you can shuffle them and test yourself repeatedly until you know you've mastered the material.

- **Short-answer** and **fill-in questions.** Short-answer and fill-in questions are similar to essays in that they require you to recall key pieces of information; that is, you have to dredge the information up from your memory rather than, as is the case with multiple-choice, true–false, and matching questions, finding it on the page in front of you. However, short-answer and fill-in questions—unlike essay questions—typically don't demand that you integrate or compare different types of information. Consequently, the focus of your study should be on the recall of specific, detailed information.

Test Yourself Once you feel you've mastered the material, test yourself on it. There are several ways to do this. One is to create a complete test for yourself, in writing, making its form as close as possible to what you expect the actual test to be. For instance, if your instructor has told you the classroom test will be primarily made up of short-answer questions, your test should be too. One bonus: Constructing a test is actually an excellent way of studying the material and cementing it into memory.

Avro Arrow—CF-105 (1949)
–advanced, supersonic, twin-engine, all-weather interceptor jet aircraft
–2 prototype airframes—$2 million apiece
–engine/fire-control & missile systems costs rose— $12.5 million per aircraft
–test flights indicated plane could be world's fastest & most advanced
–project cancelled on 20 February 1959—all plans and prototypes destroyed

Endoplasmic reticulum (ER):
Smooth ER—makes fats (lipids)
Rough ER—has ribosomes, which make proteins
Together, they make membranes for whole cell (for plasma membrane, mitochondrion, etc.). Also make more of themselves.

You might also construct a test and administer it to a classmate or a member of your study group. In turn, you could take a test that someone else has constructed. The combined experience of making and taking a test on the same general subject matter is among the very best ways to prepare for the real thing.

Deal with Test Anxiety What does the anticipation of a test do to you? Do you feel shaky or frantic, as though there's not enough time to get it all done? Do you feel as if there's a knot in your stomach? Do you grit your teeth?

Fortunately, **test anxiety** is a temporary condition characterized by fears and concerns about test taking. Almost everyone experiences it to some degree; but if it is too great, it can make it harder for you to study and do your best on a test.

You'll never eliminate test anxiety completely, nor do you want to. A little bit of nervousness can energize us, making us more attentive and vigilant. Like any competitive event, testing can motivate us to do our best. So think of test anxiety as a desire to perform at your peak—an ally at test time.

For many people, however, anxiety can spiral into the kind of paralyzing fear that makes your mind go blank. So you definitely want to keep it in its place. There are several ways to do this:

1. *Prepare thoroughly.* The more you prepare, the less test anxiety you'll feel. Good preparation can give you a sense of control and mastery, and it will prevent test anxiety from overwhelming you.

2. *Take a realistic view of the test.* Remember that no single test determines how you'll do for the rest of your life. Your future success does not hinge on your performance on any single exam.

3. *Learn relaxation techniques.* You can learn to reduce or even eliminate the jittery physical symptoms of test anxiety by using relaxation techniques. These techniques are covered in Chapter 14, but the basic process is straightforward: You want to breathe evenly, gently inhaling and exhaling. Focus your mind on a pleasant, relaxing scene such as a beautiful forest or a peaceful spread of farmland, or on a sound such as ocean waves.

4. *Visualize success.* Think of an image of your instructor handing back your test, on which you've received an A. Or imagine your instructor congratulating you on your fine performance the moment you walk into your classroom on the day after the test. Positive visualizations such as these, which highlight your potential success, can help replace negative images of failure that may be fuelling your test anxiety.

5. *Set up a special testing arrangement.* If your test anxiety is severe, visit the counselling or student learning centre at your school. You may be able to set up a special testing arrangement that can accommodate your test anxiety.

Cramming: You Shouldn't, But . . . You know, of course, that **cramming,** hurried, last-minute studying, is not the way to go. You know that you're likely to forget the material the moment the test is over because long-term retention is nearly impossible without thoughtful study. But . . .

. . . it's been one of those weeks where everything went wrong.

. . . the instructor sprang the test on you at the last minute.

. . . you forgot about the test until the night before it was scheduled.

Test anxiety
A temporary condition characterized by fears and concerns about test taking

Cramming
Hurried, last-minute studying

Have you ever crammed for a test? If so, you know how exhausting it can be, and how easy it is to overlook crucial material. However, time pressures sometimes make cramming your only option. When that happens, there are strategies you can use to help you make the best use of limited time.

Whatever the reason, there may be times when you can't study properly. What do you do if you have to cram for an exam?

The first thing to do is choose what you really need to study. You won't be able to learn everything, so you have to make choices. Figure out the main focus of the course, and concentrate on it. Don't spend a lot of time on what you're unable to do. Beating yourself up about your failings as a student will only hinder your efforts.

Instead, admit you're human and fallible like everyone else. Then spend a few minutes developing a plan for what you can accomplish in the limited time you've got.

Once you have a strategy, prepare a one-page summary sheet with hard-to-remember information. Just writing the material down will help you remember it, and you can refer to the summary sheet frequently over the limited time you do have to study.

Next, read through your class notes, concentrating on the material you've underlined and the key concepts and ideas that you've already noted. Forget about reading all the material in the books and articles you're being tested on. Instead, only read the passages that you've underlined and the notes you've taken on the readings. Finally, maximize your study time. Using your notes, note cards, and concept maps, go over the information. Read it. Say it aloud. Say it aloud again. Think about it and the way it relates to other information. In short, use all the techniques we've talked about for learning and recalling information.

Just remember: When the exam is over, material that you have crammed into your head is destined to leave your mind as quickly as it entered. If you've crammed for a midterm, don't assume that the information will still be there when you study for the final. In the end, cramming often ends up taking more time for worse results than does studying with more appropriate techniques.

Organize: Facing the Day of the Test

You've studied a lot, and you're happy with your level of mastery. Or perhaps you have the nagging feeling that there's something you haven't quite gotten to. Or maybe you know you haven't had enough time to study as much as you would have liked, and you're expecting a disaster.

Whatever your frame of mind, it will help to organize your plan of attack on the day of the test. What's included on the test is out of your hands, but what you bring to it, you can control.

For starters, bring the right tools to the test. Have at least two pens and two pencils with you. It's usually best to write in pen because, in general, writing tends to be easier to read in pen than pencil. But you also might want to have pencils ready. Sometimes instructors will use machine-scorable tests, which require the use of pencil. Or there may be test questions that involve computations, and solving them may entail frequent reworking of calculations.

You should also be sure to bring a watch to the test, even if there will be a clock on the wall of the classroom. You will want to be able to pace yourself properly during the test. Having your own watch will help you feel more in control of your time during the test.

Sometimes instructors permit you to use notes and books during the test. If you haven't brought them with you, they're not going to be of much help. So make sure you bring them if you are allowed. Even for closed-book tests, having such material available before the test actually starts may allow you a few minutes of review after you arrive in the classroom.

On the day of a test, avoid the temptation to compare notes with your friends about how much they've studied. Yes, you might end up feeling good because many of your fellow classmates studied less than you. But chances are you'll find others who sound like they have spent significantly *more* time studying than you, and this will do little to encourage you.

> "A gem cannot be polished without friction, nor a person perfected without trials."
>
> Chinese Proverb

Plan on panicking. Although it sounds like the worst possible approach, permitting yourself the option of spending a minute feeling panicky will help you to recover from your initial fears.

Finally, listen carefully to what an instructor says before the test is handed out. The instructor may tell you about a question that is optional or worth more points or inform you of a typographical error on the test. Whatever the instructor says just before the test, you can be sure it's information that you don't want to ignore.

Taking the Test

ork: Tackling the Test

Take a deep breath—literally.

There's no better way to start work on a test than by taking a deep breath, followed by several more. The deep breaths will help you to overcome any initial panic and anxiety you may be experiencing. It's okay to give yourself over for a moment to panic and anxiety, but, to work at your best, use the relaxation techniques that we spoke about earlier to displace those initial feelings. Tell yourself, "It's okay. I am going to do my best on this." Don't let your mind get sidetracked by panicky thoughts.

Read the test instructions and *then skim through the entire exam.* Look at the kinds of questions that are asked and pay attention to the way they will be scored. If the point weighting of the various parts of the exam is not clear, ask the instructor to clarify it. Your goal is to know how to allocate your time. You don't want to spend 90 percent of your time on an essay that's worth only 10 percent of the marks, and you want to be sure to leave time at the end of the test to check your answers. An initial read-through also helps you verify that you have every page of the exam and that there is no other physical problem with it, such as badly copied pages or ink marks that partially obscure some of the questions.

If there are any lists, formulas, or other key facts that you're concerned you may forget, jot them down now on the back of a test page. You may want to refer to this material later during the test.

Once this background work is out of the way, you'll be ready to proceed to actually answering the questions. These principles will help you to do your best on the test:

- **Answer the easiest questions first.** By initially getting the questions out of the way that are easiest for you, you accomplish several important things. First, you'll be leaving yourself more time to think about the tougher questions later. In addition, moving through a series of questions without a struggle will build your confidence. Finally, working through several questions will build a base of points that may be enough to earn you at least a passing grade.

- **Write legibly on one side of the paper.** If an instructor can't read what you've written, you're not going to get credit for it, no matter how brilliant your answer. So be sure to keep your handwriting or printing legible.

  It's also a good idea to write your answers to essay questions on only one side of a page. This will allow you to go back later and add or revise information.

- **Master machine-scored tests.** Tests will sometimes be scored, in part, by computer. In such cases, you'll usually have to indicate your answers by filling in—with a pencil—circles or squares on a computer answer sheet.

  Be careful! A stray mark or smudge can cause the computer scanner to misread your answer sheet, producing errors in grading. Be sure to bring a good eraser in addition to a pencil; the biggest source of mistakes in machine grading is incomplete erasing on a test.

  It's best to write your answers not only on the answer sheet but also on the test itself (if the test is not intended for future reuse). That way you can go back and check your answers easily— a step you should take frequently.

> "The biggest problem I have with tests is the course gives you a lot of general info, but the exam has very specific questions. I keep reviewing, cram as much in my head as possible, and make educated guesses as to what the exam question will be."
>
> Scott Acorn, Student, Capilano College

Use Strategies Targeted to Answering Specific Types of Test Items Every type of item requires a particular approach. Use these strategies to tailor your approach to specific kinds of questions:

- **Essay Questions.** Essay questions, with their emphasis on description and analysis, often present challenges because they are relatively unstructured. Unless you're careful, it's easy to wander off and begin to answer questions that were never asked. To prevent that problem, the first thing to do is read the question carefully, noting what specifically is being asked. If your essay will be lengthy, you might even want to write a short outline.

Pay attention to key words that indicate what, specifically, the instructor is looking for in an answer. Certain action words are commonly used in essays, and you should understand them fully. For instance, knowing the distinction between "compare" and "contrast" can spell the difference between success and failure. Table 6.3 defines common action words. Also refer to Try It! 2, "Understand Action Verbs in Essay Questions."

Use the right language in essays. Be brief and to the point in your essay. Avoid flowery introductory language. Compare the two sentences that follow:

> "In our study of Canadian engineering triumphs, it may be useful to ponder how the completion of the Canadian Pacific Railway came to represent such an important milestone in the field, and it will be seen that there are several critical reasons why it did have such an impact."

> "The completion of the Canadian Pacific Railway was momentous for several reasons."

This second sentence says the same thing much more effectively and economically.

Essays are improved when they include examples and point out differences. Your response should follow a logical sequence, moving from major points to minor ones, or following a time sequence. Above all,

Table 6.3

Action Words for Essays

These words are commonly used in essay questions. Learning the distinctions among them will help you during tests.

Analyze: Examine and break into component parts.

Clarify: Explain with significant detail.

Compare: Describe similarities and differences.

Compare and contrast: Describe and distinguish similarities and differences.

Contrast: Explain and distinguish differences.

Critique: Judge and analyze, explaining what is wrong—and right—about a concept.

Define: Provide the meaning.

Discuss: Explain, review, and consider.

Enumerate: Provide a listing of ideas, concepts, reasons, items, etc.

Evaluate: Provide pros and cons of something; provide an opinion, and justify it.

Explain: Give reasons why or how; clarify, justify, and illustrate.

Illustrate: Provide examples; show instances.

Interpret: Explain the meaning of something.

Justify: Explain why a concept can be supported, typically by using examples and other types of support.

Outline: Provide a framework or explanation—usually in narrative form—of a concept, idea, event, or phenomenon.

Prove: Using evidence and arguments, convince the reader of a particular point.

Relate: Show how things fit together; provide analogies.

Review: Describe or summarize, often with an evaluation.

State: Assert or explain.

Summarize: Provide a condensed, precise list or narrative.

Trace: Track or sketch out how events or circumstances have evolved; provide a history or time line.

Understand Action Verbs in Essay Questions

Answer the following questions about Section 2 of the *Canadian Charter of Rights and Freedoms* by outlining your responses, paying attention to the various action verbs that introduce the questions.

Section 2 of the *Canadian Charter of Rights and Freedoms* states:

Everyone has the following fundamental freedoms:

1. freedom of conscience and religion
2. freedom of thought, belief, opinion, and expression, including freedom of the press and other media of communication
3. freedom of peaceful assembly
4. freedom of association

1. Summarize Section 2 of the *Canadian Charter of Rights and Freedoms.*

2. Interpret Section 2 of the *Canadian Charter of Rights and Freedoms.*

your answer should address every aspect of the question posed on the test. Because essays often contain several different, embedded questions, you have to be certain that you have answered every part to receive full credit.

- **Multiple-Choice Questions.** If you've ever looked at a multiple-choice question and said to yourself, "But every choice seems right," you understand what can be tricky about this type of question. However, there are some simple strategies that can help you deal with multiple-choice questions.

   First, read the instructions carefully to determine whether only one response choice will be correct, or whether more than one of the choices may be correct. In some cases, the most correct answer is the right choice. Almost always only one choice is right, but in some cases instructors may permit you to check off more than one answer.

3. Evaluate Section 2 of the *Canadian Charter of Rights and Freedoms*.

4. Discuss Section 2 of the *Canadian Charter of Rights and Freedoms*.

5. Analyze Section 2 of the *Canadian Charter of Rights and Freedoms*.

How do your answers differ for each question? Which of the questions provoked the lengthiest response? Which of the questions could you answer best?

Turn to the first question and read the question part—the part before the response choices. *Before you look at the choices, try to answer the question in your head.* This can help you avoid being confused by inappropriate choices.

Next, *carefully read through every choice.* Even if you come to one that you think is right, keep reading—there may be a subsequent answer that is better.

Look for absolutes like "every," "always," "only," "none," and "never." Choices that contain such absolute words are rarely correct. Less absolute words, such as "generally," "usually," "often," "rarely," "seldom," and "typically" may indicate a correct response.

Be especially on guard for the word "not," which negates the sentence ("The one key concept that is not embodied in the Canadian Charter of Rights and Freedoms is . . . "). It's easy to gloss over "not," and if you have the misfortune of doing so, it will be nearly impossible to answer the item correctly.

If you're having trouble understanding a question, underline key words or phrases, or try to break the question into different short sections. Sometimes it is helpful to work backward and look at the response choices first to see whether you can find one that is clearly accurate or clearly inaccurate.

*Use an **educated guessing** strategy*—which is very different from wild or random guessing. Unless you are penalized for wrong answers (a scoring rule by which wrong answers are deducted from the points you have earned on other questions, rather than merely not counting at all toward your score), it always pays to guess.

The first step in educated guessing is to eliminate any obviously false answers. The next step is to examine the remaining choices closely. Does one response choice include a qualifier that makes it unlikely ("the probability of war always increases when a South Asian leader is facing political difficulties")? Does one choice include a subtle factual error ("Prime Minister Pierre Trudeau imposed the *War Measures Act* in 1970 after the FLQ murdered a British diplomat")? In such cases, you may be able to figure out the correct response by eliminating the others.

- **True–False Questions.** Although most of the principles we've already discussed apply equally well to true–false questions, a few additional tricks of the trade may help you with this question type.

  Begin a set of true–false questions by marking the items you're sure you know the answer to. But don't rush; it's important to read every part of a true–false question, because key words such as "never," "always," and "sometimes" often determine the appropriate response.

  If you don't have a clue about whether a statement is true or false, here's another last-resort principle: Choose "true," if you won't be penalized for guessing. In general, more statements on a true–false test are likely to be true than false.

- **Matching Questions.** Matching questions typically present you with two columns of related information, which you must link using a process of elimination. For example, a list of terms or concepts may be presented in one column, along with a list of corresponding definitions or explanations in the second column. The best strategy is to reduce the size of both columns by matching the items you're most confident about first; this will leave a short list in each column, and the final matching may become apparent.

- **Short-Answer and Fill-In Questions.** Short-answer and fill-in questions basically require you to *generate and supply* specific information in your own words. Unlike essays, which are more free-form and may have several possible answers, short-answer and fill-in questions are quite specific. There is usually only one answer, which you must come up with on your own. Responding to them requires that you pay special attention to what, in particular, you are being asked.

  Use both the instructions for the questions and the questions themselves to determine the level of specificity that is needed in an answer. Try not to provide too much or too little information. Usually, brevity is best.

About Academic Honesty Perhaps it's a tempting thought: A glance at a classmate's test may provide the one piece of information that you just can't remember.

Educated guessing

The practice of eliminating obviously false multiple-choice answers and selecting the most likely answer from the remaining choices

Academic honesty

Completing and turning in only your own work under your own name

You owe it to yourself not to do it. **Academic honesty**—completing and turning in only your own work under your own name—is the foundation of postsecondary life and your personal life. Copying from a classmate's paper is no different from reaching over and stealing that classmate's calculator or watch.

Cheating can take several forms. It may involve copying another's work, using a calculator when it's not allowed, discussing the answer to a question, copying a computer file when it's unauthorized, taking an exam for another person, or stealing an exam. Whatever the form, academic dishonesty is wrong. It diminishes the academic community, it makes the grading system unfair, and it ultimately reduces the meaning of your grade. It certainly damages academic and personal growth. It can't help but reduce self-esteem, and it robs the cheater of self-respect. Finally, getting caught leads to many unpleasant scenarios: failing the exam on which the cheating has taken place, failing the entire course, being brought before an academic honesty or review committee, having a note placed in your academic file, being placed on academic probation, or even being thrown out of school. Cheating is simply not worth it.

E valuate: Taking Your Own Final Examination

The last few minutes of a test may feel like the final moments of a marathon. You need to focus your energy and push forward harder. It can be make-or-break time.

Save some time at the end of a test so you can check your work. You should have been keeping track of your time all along, so plan on stopping a few minutes before the end of the test period to review what you've done. It's a critical step, and it can make the difference between a terrific grade and a mediocre one. It's a rare person who can work uninterrupted on a test and commit absolutely no errors—even if he or she knows the material backward and forward. Consequently, checking what you've done is crucial.

Career Connections

Professional Tests: More Exams and Tests

Accreditation Exams
Careers in paramedicine, nursing, business, computers, and technology have standardized tests you must pass to be accredited in your field. Furthermore, many professions require practitioners to regularly pass similar exams. Accreditation exams may be paper or computer and they may involve a practical demonstration.

Competency Assessments
Many companies now assess employees on competencies, which are the knowledge, skills, and abilities that demonstrate successful performance in the workplace. Competency testing can occur in many ways, but two common methods are testing employees at an assessment centre and 360-degree feedback.

At an assessment centre, employees are evaluated based on the behaviours demonstrated in situational tests or scenarios. There is a high correlation between assessment centre scores on high-performance competencies and actual performance in jobs. This 360-degree feedback (a process where feedback is elicited from a person's manager, the person's peers, staff reporting to that person, and the person) is commonly used for developmental purposes in an organization.

As can be seen from the Toyota model below, your portfolio (where you always link knowledge, skills, and ability to demonstration) can be helpful preparation for workplace assessments:

At Toyota, competencies are linked to performance and business strategy. Skills necessary in cultivating the behaviours that support business objectives are targeted and encouraged to grow. Toyota appraises as its core competencies (knowledge, skills, and abilities that are critical to an organization) customer satisfaction, teamwork, problem solving, efficiency, quality, and quantity of work. Pay increases are available to those willing to learn new skills, as opposed to just those with seniority or experience.

Academic honesty is the bedrock of post-secondary life. The risks of cheating—getting caught and causing damage to your sense of self-worth—far outweigh any momentary benefits.

Start evaluating your test by looking for obvious mistakes. Make sure you've answered every question and haven't skipped any parts of questions. If there is a separate answer sheet, check to see that all your answers have been recorded on the answer sheet and in the right spot.

If the test has included essay and short-answer questions, proofread your responses. Check for obvious errors—misspellings, missing words, and repetitions. Make sure you've responded to every part of each question and that each essay, as a whole, makes sense.

Check your responses to multiple-choice, true–false, and matching questions. If there are some items that you haven't yet answered because you couldn't remember the necessary information, now is the time to take a stab at them. As we discussed earlier, it usually pays to guess, even randomly if you must. On most tests, no answer and a wrong answer are worth the same amount—nothing! Only occasionally will instructors deduct points for wrong answers, and you will know in advance if that is their policy.

What about items that you initially were genuinely unsure about and for which you guessed at the answer? Unless you have a good reason to change your original answer—such as a new insight or a sudden recollection of some key information—your first guess is likely your best guess.

Know When to Stop After evaluating and checking your answers, you may reach a point when there is still some time left. What to do? If you're satisfied with your responses, it's simply time to tell yourself, *Let it go.*

Permit yourself the luxury of knowing that you've done your best and it's time to hand the test to your instructor. Just because there is time remaining in the class period and some of your classmates are still working on their tests, you don't have to continue reviewing your work over and over. In fact, such behaviour is often counterproductive, because it may lead you to start overinterpreting test items and reading things into questions that really aren't there.

Disaster! I've run out of time! It's a nightmarish feeling: The clock is ticking relentlessly, and it's clear that you don't have enough time to finish the test. What should you do?

Stop work! Although this advice may sound foolish, the most important thing you can do is to take a minute to calm yourself. Take some deep breaths to replace the feelings of panic that are likely welling up inside you. Collect your thoughts, and plan a strategy for the last moments of the test.

If there are essays that remain undone, consider how you'd answer them if you had more time. Then write an outline of each answer. If you don't have time even for that, write a few keywords. Writing anything is better than handing in a blank page, and you may get at least some credit for your response. The key principle here: Something is better than nothing, and even one point is worth more than zero points.

The same principle holds for other types of questions. Even wild guesses are almost always better than not responding at all to an item. So rather than telling yourself you've certainly failed and giving up, do as much as you can in the remaining moments of the exam.

Refer to Try It! 3, "Take a Test-Taking Test," and think of the strategies discussed so far in this chapter.

Try It! 3

Take a Test-Taking Test

Take the following test on test-taking skills, which illustrates every question type discussed in this chapter. Answers to all questions except short-answer and essay questions are provided at the end of the test.

Before taking the test, think of the test-taking strategies we've discussed in the chapter, and try to employ as many of them as possible.

Multiple-choice section

1. Tests are useful tools for which of the following purposes?
   a. determining people's likely level of future career success
   b. indicating strengths and gaps in people's knowledge
   c. defining people's fundamental abilities and potentials
   d. evaluating people's individual worth and contributions

2. One of the main advantages of study groups is that
   a. every individual must contribute equally to the group.
   b. group members can help each other during the test.
   c. each member has to memorize only a fraction of the material.
   d. groups motivate their members to do good work.

3. Which of the following is a good way to deal with test anxiety?
   a. visualizing success on the test
   b. drinking coffee or other stimulants
   c. telling yourself to stop worrying
   d. focusing on the importance of the test

4. Which of the following is likely to be the most effective cramming technique?
   a. preparing a one-page summary of the most important information
   b. quickly reading all articles and textbook chapters covered on the test
   c. neatly recopying all class notes and note cards while reading them aloud
   d. underlining or highlighting key information in the textbook and other resources

Matching section

___ 1. Essay question

___ 2. Quiz

___ 3. Multiple-choice question

___ 4. Matching question

___ 5. True–false question

___ 6. Fill-in question

A. A question in which the student supplies brief missing information to complete a statement

B. Hurried, last-minute studying

C. An informed attempt to select an answer by eliminating clearly incorrect answers

D. A question in which the student must link information in two columns

E. A brief test

F. A question requiring a lengthy response in the student's own words

(continued on next page)

Take a Test-Taking Test—Continued

___ 7. Short-answer question

G. Deduction of points for incorrect responses

___ 8. Guessing penalty

H. Representing another's work as one's own

___ 9. Test anxiety

I. A question requiring a brief response in the student's own words

___ 10. Cramming

J. A question that requires selection from several response options

___ 11. Academic dishonesty

K. A feeling of fear induced by testing

___ 12. Educated guess

L. A question requiring students to distinguish accurate and inaccurate statements

Fill-in section

1. Fear of testing that can interfere with test performance is called _____.

2. Last-minute studying is called _____.

3. The primary source of error on machine-scored tests is incomplete _____.

4. After inspecting the test and identifying areas that will be easy and those that will be hard, a reasonable test-taking strategy is to answer the _____ questions first.

True–false section

1. The best way to prepare for an essay test is to review detailed factual information about the topic. T ____ F ____

2. True–false questions require students to determine whether given statements are accurate or inaccurate. T ____ F ____

3. You should never permit yourself to feel panicky during a test. T ____ F ____

4. A good evaluation strategy toward the end of a test is to redo as many questions as time permits. T ____ F ____

5. For short-answer questions, students must select brief responses from response choices listed on the test form. T ____ F ____

6. In responding to essay questions, you should answer briefly and use plain language. T ____ F ____

7. In a multiple-choice question, the words "always" and "never" usually signal the correct response. T ____ F ____

8. It is usually unwise to guess on a multiple-choice test. T ____ F ____

9. If you run out of time at the end of a test, it is best to write brief notes and ideas down in response to essay questions, rather than leave them completely blank. T ____ F ____

10. Students' comments on the amount of studying they have done before a test are generally accurate. T _____ F _____

Short-answer section

1. What are five things you should find out about a test before you take it?

2. What is academic honesty?

Essay section (write your answers on a separate sheet of paper)

1. Explain how tests can be useful to students and teachers.

2. Discuss the advantages of using a study group to prepare for an examination.

3. Why is academic honesty important?

Answers. Multiple-choice: 1B, 2D, 3A, 4A; Matching: 1F, 2E, 3J, 4D, 5L, 6A, 7I, 8G, 9K, 10B, 11H, 12C; Fill-in: test anxiety, cramming, erasing, easy; True–False: 1F, 2T, 3F, 4F, 5F, 6T, 7F, 8F, 9T, 10F; Short-answer: See page 162 and pages 174 and 175.

After you have completed the test, consider these questions: Did you learn anything from taking the test that you might not have learned if you hadn't been tested on the material? How effective were the test-taking strategies you employed? Were any types of strategies easier for you to employ than others, and were any types of questions easier for you to use them on than others? Exchange your essay responses with a classmate, and critique the essays. How do the responses of your partner compare to your own?

R ethink: Reflecting on the Real Test of Learning

Your instructor is about to hand the graded exams back. All sorts of thoughts run through your head: How did I do? Did I perform as well as my class-mates? Will I be pleased with my results? Will the results reflect the amount of effort I put into studying? Will I be embarrassed by my grade?

Most of us focus on the evaluative aspects of tests. We look at the grade we've received on a test and take it to be a measure of something important. It's a natural reaction.

There is another way to look at test results: They can help guide us toward future success. By looking at what we've learned (and haven't learned) about a given subject, we'll be in a better position to know what to focus on when we

Analyze Returned Tests

You can help yourself to perform better on tests by evaluating your strengths and weaknesses as a test-taker. Complete the chart and follow the directions to analyze the information about a test you didn't do as well on as you'd expected.

Directions

1. Complete the top portion of the form. Be as specific and honest as possible in describing the way you studied (or didn't study).

2. Under questions missed, write in the numbers of the actual test questions that were incorrect on your test. If you missed questions 5, 8, 13, and 29, those are the numbers you should write in that column.

3. Now go across the rows of the chart. For example, if you got question 5 wrong, determine:
   - How many points were taken off?
   - What kind of question or problem was it?
   - What do you think was the reason that you got it wrong?

4. Look for patterns. Ask:
   - What kinds of questions did you have the most difficulty with?
   - Which questions were worth the most points?
   - What can you do to improve yourself on your next test?

5. Ask yourself what you still don't understand about the test or test question(s) that you answered incorrectly.
   - Did you have difficulty understanding the instructor's comments?
   - Write down any questions that you need to ask your instructor.
   - If you have questions for the professor, or want to clarify how you can improve in your next test, make an appointment to discuss these issues.

6. Make a list of the things you need to do to be more successful on your next test. Ask questions like:
   - How can I make sure I understand the material?
   - Do I need to manage my time better so I can spend more time studying?
   - How can I determine what is important to study?

7. Look at tests from other courses and see if there is a pattern. What can you learn from your successes and failures?

take future exams. Furthermore, by examining the kinds of mistakes we make, it's more likely that we can do better in the future. Use Try It! 4, "Analyze Returned Tests," to evaluate your strengths and weaknesses as a test-taker.

When you get your test back, you have the opportunity to reflect on what you've learned and to consider your performance. Begin by looking at your mistakes. Chances are they'll jump out at you since they will be marked incorrect. Did you misunderstand or misapply some principle? Was there a certain aspect of the material covered on the test that you missed? Were there particular kinds of information that you didn't realize you needed to know? Or did you lose some points because of your test-taking skills? Did you make careless

Course: _____   Date of exam:_____

Predicted grade: _____   Actual grade: _____   % of total grade: _____

Relevant details of the study process: (# of days/time spent studying, special methods used, etc.)

_____

_____

_____

Question Profile			Reason that Answer was Incorrect			
Question Missed	Points Lost	Type of Question*	Carelessness	Material Unfamiliar	Mis-interpreted	Not Complete

* MC = multiple choice   T/F = True/False   COM = completion
  MA = Matching   ESS = Essay

You may want to use other categories, i.e., for math: calculation, word problem, formula, etc.

errors, such as forgetting to fill in a question or misreading the directions? Was your handwriting so sloppy that your instructor had trouble reading it?

Once you have a good idea of what material you didn't fully understand or remember, get the correct answers to the items you missed—from your instructor, fellow classmates, or your book. If it's a math exam, rework problems you've missed. Finally, summarize—in writing—the material you had trouble with. This will help you study for future exams that cover the same material.

Finally, if you're dissatisfied with your performance, talk to your instructor—not to complain but to seek help. Instructors don't like to give bad grades, and they may be able to point out problems in your test that you can address readily so you can do better in the future. Demonstrate to your instructor that you want to do better and are willing to put in the work to get there. The worst thing to do is crumple up the test and quickly leave the class in embarrassment. Remember, you're not the first person to get a bad grade, and the power to improve your test-taking performance lies within you.

What If You Fail?

If you have put forth your best effort in preparing for a test or exam—you have consistently attended class, taken good notes and reviewed them, kept up with the reading, asked questions in class, and participated in a study group—and you failed, approach your instructor and ask for some feedback and advice on how to improve your results for the next test or exam. If you feel out of your depth, let your instructor know—he may be able to advise you on your options. In addition, approach your academic advisor *early* if your first batch of test scores are poor or below your usual level. Your college or university undoubtedly has resources, ranging from peer mentors to learning resource centres, that can help those motivated to help themselves.

If those resources don't help, ask what the date is for withdrawing from the course without academic penalty. It is better to drop a course than to fail it. However, withdrawing from a course may affect your full-time status or student loan, so be sure you know the consequences.

If you have not put forth the effort needed to succeed in college or university, you should reflect on your behaviour. Has the transition to postsecondary life been more difficult than you expected? Are you preoccupied with your social life? Are you having roommate or family problems that interfere with your ability to concentrate? Are you emotionally, mentally, and physically ready for college or university? For some students, taking a year off to work, travel, and mature is the best way to ready themselves for higher education. Some students and their parents may resist putting off school, knowing graduation is delayed by a year, but in the end, it could save a lot of money (for lost tuition, books, living expenses) and prevent your ending up with a poor academic record. Students who are unmotivated to succeed should seek academic counselling early to help make the best decisions for their futures.

Students who have experienced academic failure in the past may become academically frustrated or defeated, which in turn, can lead to lack of confidence or unrealistic academic expectations. If you give up easily or approach assignments and tests with low expectations of success, your campus counselling centre may be able to help you with techniques and coping strategies. However, it is up to you to recognize that you need assistance and seek it.

Looking *Back*

What kinds of tests will I encounter in college or university?

- Although tests are an unpopular fact of academic life, they can provide useful evaluative information about your level of knowledge and understanding about a subject.

Speaking of Success

Asta Kovanen

The Okanogan Valley College of Massage Therapy

Working with people and travelling are two of Asta Kovanen's passions and she believes she will be able to pursue both of those interests after completing her studies at The Okanogan Valley College of Massage Therapy, in Vernon, British Columbia.

The OVCMT is Asta's third post-secondary school. After graduation from high school, she entered college because "that was what you were supposed to do," but without a clear direction and too much partying, she left. She realized she wasn't committed and didn't love what she was doing—she felt she was wasting her time.

After some time away from school, including spending a year volunteering in Mexico and Honduras, she developed a different perspective. Asta realized how many resources are to be had for students in Canada and decided she was ready to take advantage of the educational opportunities available to her.

Asta then began to study international relations at a large university, but the huge impersonal classes and big city didn't appeal to her—she

realized a largely theoretical approach to education would not give her the people contact she wanted and she realized she was unhappy in what she calls the "bubble world" of academics.

Asta now feels she is in a perfect place for her; massage therapists both work with people and have the

opportunity to travel the world. In addition, she loves that her program at OVCMT is extremely practical—after the first year she is qualified to work in a spa; after the second year, she is eligible to work in most provinces; and after year three she can be a registered massage therapist in British Columbia. This career will allow her to work almost anyplace in the world.

Asta says she has to work extremely hard to stay on top of all the

work expected in her intensive program, especially tests and exams. Oral, practical, and conventional academic evaluations are given on a frequent basis. She and others in her courses have formed study groups and work collaboratively to reinforce the large quantities of material associated with anatomy, physiology, and the musculoskeletal system. With likeminded classmates who want the same level of experience as she does, Asta focuses on being super-prepared, but she is aware that stress can take a toll on students in her program, so she insists on being well-rested for tests and exams.

While Asta is fully committed to being a successful student, she recognizes that her whole identity is much more than that, so she makes time for friends, family, other activities and especially fun and laughter, both of which are great stress busters.

- There are several types of tests, including brief, informal quizzes; more substantial tests; and even more weighty exams, which tend to be administered at the midpoint and end of a course.

What are the best ways to prepare for and take various kinds of tests?

- Good test preparation begins with completing the course assignments, attending class regularly, and paying attention in class. It also helps to find out as much as possible about a test beforehand and to form a study group to review material.

- If cramming becomes necessary, focus on summarizing factual information broadly, identifying key concepts and ideas, and rehearsing information orally.

- When you first receive the test, skim it to see what kinds of questions are being asked; figure out how the different questions and sections will be weighted; and jot down complex factual information that is likely to be needed for the test.

- Answer the easiest questions first, write legibly, use only one side of each sheet of paper, mark answer sheets carefully, and record answers in the test book as well as the answer sheet.

What are the best strategies for answering specific kinds of test questions?

- For essay questions, be sure to understand each question and each of its parts, interpret action words correctly, write concisely, organize the essay logically, and include examples.

- For multiple-choice questions, read the question very carefully and then read all response choices. Educated guessing based on eliminating incorrect response choices is usually a reasonable strategy.

- For true–false and matching questions, quickly answer all the items that you are sure of and then go back to the remaining items.

- The best strategy for short-answer and fill-in questions is to be very sure about what is being asked. Keep answers complete but brief.

P.O.W.E.R. Portfolio

Put It to the Test

Consider including in a portfolio a successful test from your current semester along with a reflection on what skill set or competency it relates to. *For example, a dental assistant student could put in a test from his dental records course, indicating the ways in which it relates to development of a professional-level dental vocabulary, communication skills, teamwork, or accuracy and detail.* Or put two tests in your portfolio, indicating why you may have done better on the second test and how you improved your test-taking strategy.

Resources

On Campus

Colleges and universities often provide a variety of resources for students having difficulties with test taking. Some offer general workshops for students, reviewing test-taking strategies.

If you find that you are experiencing significant test anxiety when taking a test or in the days leading up to it, talk to someone at your campus counselling centre or health centre. They can help you learn relaxation techniques and can provide psychological counselling to help make your anxiety manageable.

In Print

Test Taking Strategies & Study Skills for the Utterly Confused by Laurie Rozakis (McGraw-Hill; 1st edition, 2002) is a useful book that includes chapters about taking specific kinds of tests such as true-false, multiple choice, fill-in-the-blank, matching, and math tests.

A book specifically designed for adults who need work-related training or a certificate/degree to become more successful in their careers but who are held back by poor study habits is *The Secrets Of Taking Any Test: Learn the Techniques Successful Test-Takers Know* by Judith Meyers, published by Learning Express (2000). Other postsecondary students can also use the author's simple 20-step program to discover their own style. This book contains information about how to make your own learning style work for you.

On the Web

The following sites on the World Wide Web provide the opportunity to extend your learning about the material in this chapter. Although the Web addresses were accurate at the time the book was printed, check the P.O.W.E.R. Learning website, <www.mcgrawhill.ca/college/power>, for any changes that may have occurred.

www.coun.uvic.ca/learn/program/hndouts/simple.html
This page gives examples of question words that are often found in essay assignments or in essay questions on exams. Possible plans of action for each question type are outlined. These outlines are useful as a starting point for understanding how to approach essay questions.

www.iss.stthomas.edu/studyguides/tstprp1.htm
This website from St. Thomas University gives helpful tips on how to prepare for tests; a companion page at <www.iss.stthomas.edu/studyguides/tsttak1.htm> gives hints on how to take tests.

www.mentalhealthscreening.org/college/
This anonymous online screening test from Virginia Tech gives students an idea of whether they should contact a counsellor for assistance with anxiety, depression, alcohol, or eating disorders. To do this test, click on the link "Take a Sample Test."

The Case of . . .

Too Many Questions, Too Little Time

There was no reason to panic, said Mia Varela to herself at the start of the test. The exam, a midterm in her computer programming course, contained 50 multiple-choice questions (each worth 1 point) and two case studies (worth a total of 50 points). And she did have 75 minutes to complete the test.

"Let's see," she said to herself. "At 1½ minutes per multiple-choice question, that would take 75 minutes. Hmm . . . that's no good. How about a minute for each one? Fifty minutes for the multiple-choice questions, leaving 25 minutes for the case studies. That ought to work. I'll get the multiple-choice questions out of the way first."

But things didn't work out the way she planned. After an hour she had completed only 40 of the multiple-choice questions and hadn't even started on the case studies. With only 15 minutes left, panic began to set in. She had trouble thinking. She began to feel certain that she'd fail the test. She thought about how she hadn't studied enough. If only she'd worked harder. How could she explain this failure to her friends . . . to her parents . . . to herself. The thoughts kept coming, and time kept ticking away.

1. Is there evidence that Mia didn't study effectively for this type of test?

2. What was right about Mia's initial approach to the test?

3. What should Mia have done differently in calculating the amount of time to devote to each portion of the test? Why?

4. What should Mia have done to be aware of and address her timing problem sooner?

5. How should Mia have dealt with her panic? Were her thoughts productive or counterproductive? Why?

6. If you were in Mia's shoes, what would you do now, with only 15 minutes left in the test?

Building Your Reading and Listening Skills

7

Sharpen Your Reading Skills

Journal Reflections: How I Read

Prepare: Approaching the Written Word

Organize: Gathering the Tools of the Trade

Work: Getting the Most Out of Your Reading

Evaluate: Considering What It Means and What You Know

Rethink: Getting It the Second Time

Dealing with Learning Disabilities

Building Listening Skills

Career Connections: Active Listening in the Workplace: A Matter of Life and Death

Speaking of Success: Rachel Trail

The Case of . . . What's Wrong with this Picture?

"**R**ead the first two chapters in your accounting textbook by next Thursday." "I've put three marketing articles on reserve in the library, and you'll need to have them read by our next class." "Take a look at the first three problems in your economics book, and see if you can solve them."

For purchasing student Chris O'Hara, these reading assignments—handed down by different instructors on the same day in early October—felt like nails in his coffin. How was he supposed to finish all this reading in the next two days, in addition to studying for a computer test, writing a paper for communications, and putting in eight hours at his part-time job?

Although the papers and tests were hard enough to deal with, it was the constant reading that was proving the most difficult challenge for Chris during his first term of college. He was a conscientious student who attempted to get everything done, but no matter how hard he tried, he just couldn't get everything read on time. When he pushed himself to read quicker and absorb more, he actually read and retained *less.* Thoughts about how he needed to read more quickly crowded out the meaning of whatever he was reading, and he had to go back over the material all over again, slowing him down even more as the reading assignments kept piling up.

For many students like Chris O'Hara, reading assignments are the biggest challenge in college or university. The amount of required reading is often enormous. Even skilled readers are likely to find themselves wishing for a way to read more quickly and effectively.

Fortunately, you can improve your reading skills. In this chapter, we'll go over several strategies that will help you to read more effectively. You can assess your attention span, consider what you should do before you even start reading an assignment, and discover some ways of getting the most out of your reading.

Then we shift gears, moving from the written word to the spoken word. We'll look at ways of listening effectively and actively. We'll consider how you should listen and what you should be listening *for.* We'll also talk about "problem" instructors, whose lectures . . . well, let's just say they leave something to be desired. After reading this chapter, you'll be able to answer the following questions:

- **How do my reading style and attention span affect my reading?**

- **How can I improve my concentration and read more effectively?**

- **What is active listening, and what is the difference between hearing and listening?**

- **How can I improve my listening skills?**

Sharpen Your Reading Skills

What kind of reader are you? Do you plod through reading assignments, novels, and magazines and, like Chris, end up feeling that you're taking far too long? Or maybe you whip through chapters, devour books, and fly through the daily newspaper but then find you can't recall the information as precisely as you'd like or remember where you saw the data on television violence that you need for your sociology paper?

Before going any further, think about your own *reading style*—your characteristic way of approaching reading tasks—by completing the Journal Reflections.

Read for Retention, Not Speed

You may have seen advertisements promoting reading systems that promise to teach you to read so quickly that you'll be reading entire books in an hour or so.

Forget it: It's not going to happen. For one thing, certain biological aspects relating to the eye movements involved in reading simply prevent people from reading (and ultimately comprehending) so rapidly.

The act of reading is designed to increase our knowledge and open up new ways of thinking. It can help us achieve new levels of understanding and get us thinking more broadly about the world and its peoples. In the end, then, it ultimately doesn't matter how fast we can read. The key to good reading is understanding—not speed.

Common Reading Problems . . . or Are They? If you get headaches, become easily fatigued, or experience blurred vision when reading, your trouble might not be a reading problem . . . it could be related to your vision. Be sure to get an eye exam—if your difficulties are physiological in nature, you might need glasses or contact lenses.

Journal Reflections

How I Read

Think about how you read by answering these questions.

1. When you open a textbook you have never seen before, what do you tend to look at first? Do you read any of the materials in the front or back of the book? Do you check out the table of contents?

2. When you start a new textbook chapter, what do you do first?

3. Are your reading habits the same or different for pleasure reading versus assignment reading?

4. What is the most difficult book you are reading this semester? Why is it difficult?

5. What is the easiest book you are reading this semester? Why is it easy?

6. How do college or university reading assignments differ from high-school reading assignments?

7. What do you do when something you're reading makes absolutely no sense to you?

8. Do your reading habits differ depending on the subject you're reading about?

On the other hand, if you get bored quickly while reading, procrastinate on your reading assignments, or are easily distracted, you may need to clarify your goals, work on time management, or organize your reading space so it is easier to concentrate.

In describing how the principles of P.O.W.E.R. Learning can be used to become a better reader, we'll focus on the type of reading that is typically called for in academic pursuits—text chapters, original texts, worksheets, and the like. However, the same principles will help you get more benefit and enjoyment out of your recreational reading as well.

Advance organizers
Broad, general ideas related to material that is to be read or heard that pave the way for subsequent learning

Frontmatter
The preface, introduction, and table of contents of a book

P repare: Approaching the Written Word

Preparation to begin reading isn't hard, and it won't take very long, but it's a crucial first step in applying P.O.W.E.R. Learning (summarized in the P.O.W.E.R. Plan below). Your aim in preparation is to become familiar with any advance organizers provided in your text or other reading material or to create a set of advance organizers regarding the material you're planning to read. **Advance organizers** are broad, general ideas related to new material that pave the way for subsequent learning. Ultimately they can help us recall material better after we've read it. (To prove the value of advance organizers, look at Try It! 1, "Discover How Advance Organizers Help.")

What's the Point of the Reading Assignment? Before you begin an assignment, think about what your goal is. Will you be reading a basic textbook, on which you'll be thoroughly tested? Is your reading supposed to provide background information that will serve as a context for future learning but that isn't essential to your success in the course? Is the material going to be useful to you personally? Realistically, how much time can you devote to the reading assignment?

The way you answer questions about your goal for reading will help you determine the reading strategy to adopt. You aren't expected to read everything with the same degree of intensity. Some material you may feel comfortable skimming; for other material you'll want to put in the maximum effort.

Understand the Point of View of the Material Itself Is what you are reading a textbook or an essay or article? If it is an essay or article, why was it written? to prove a point? to give information? to express the author's personal feelings? Knowing the basic purpose behind what you are reading (even if its specific point and message aren't yet clear) can really help as you read because it gives you a sense of why the writer wrote the piece.

Start with the Frontmatter If you'll be using a text or other book extensively throughout the term, start by reading the preface and introduction and scanning the table of contents—what publishers call the **frontmatter.** Instructors often don't formally assign the frontmatter, but

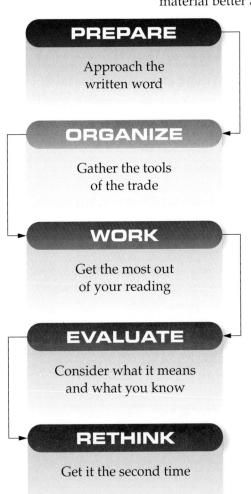

PREPARE
Approach the written word

ORGANIZE
Gather the tools of the trade

WORK
Get the most out of your reading

EVALUATE
Consider what it means and what you know

RETHINK
Get it the second time

P.O.W.E.R. Plan

Try It!

1

Discover How Advance Organizers Help

Read this passage. What do you think it means?

The procedure is actually quite simple. First you arrange items into different groups. Of course, one pile may be sufficient, depending on how much there is to do. If you have to go somewhere else due to lack of facilities, that is the next step; otherwise, you are pretty well set. It is important not to overdo things. That is, it is better to do too few things at once than too many. In the short run this may not seem important but complications can easily arise. A mistake can be expensive as well. At first, the whole procedure will seem complicated. Soon, however, it will become just another facet of life. It is difficult to foresee any end to the necessity for this task in the immediate future, but then one can never tell. After the procedure is completed, one arranges the materials into different groups again. Then they can be put into their appropriate places. Eventually, they will be used once more and the whole cycle will then have to be repeated. However, this is a part of life.[1]

If you're like most people, you don't have a clue about what this all means. But suppose you had been given some context in advance and you knew before reading it that the description had to do with washing laundry. Now does it all fall into place? Read the passage once more, and see how having an advance organizer helps.

reading it can be a big help because it is there that the author has a chance to step forward and explain, often more personally than elsewhere in a scholarly book, what he or she considers important. Knowing this will give you a sense of what to expect as you read.

By reading the frontmatter, you can get inside the author's head, obtaining insight into the author's goals, values, and strategies in writing the book. You also might find information about the author's background, and perhaps even a photo. Use this material to "personalize" the author, to gain some insight into the kind of person he or she is. The information you obtain from the frontmatter will provide a mental hook on which you can hang the new ideas to which you'll be exposed. (For practice with frontmatter, do Try It! 2, "Read the Frontmatter.")

Create Advance Organizers To create advance organizers, skim through the table of contents, which provides the main headings of what you will be reading. Textbooks often have chapter outlines, listing the key topics to be covered, and these also can provide a way of previewing the chapter content. As you read the outline, thoughts about what you already know about the topic are likely to come to mind, and you can begin to consider how the new material in the book may relate both to what you know as well as to your goals for the reading assignment itself and your more long-term goals.

Texts also often have end-of-chapter summaries, and many articles include a final section in which the author states his conclusions. Take a look at these ending sections as well. Even though you haven't read the material yet and the summary probably won't make complete sense to you, by reading the summary, you'll get an idea of what the author covers and what he considers important in the chapter.

You can also get a sense of advance organizers from what your course instructor says about the chapter or its topic. Sometimes instructors will mention

Try It! 2

Read the Frontmatter

Have you read the frontmatter of *this* book? Go there now. If you've already read it, review it. If you haven't, read it now. Then answer the following questions:

What are the goals of this book? _____

_____

_____

_____

Who are the authors, and what qualifies them to write this book? _____

_____

_____

Do you think the authors have an understanding of students? _____

Do you think the authors have an understanding of what students should do to become successful in their studies? _____

Is there anything in the frontmatter that made you curious? Does anything seem particularly interesting? _____

_____

_____

After reading the frontmatter, do you feel confident that you can learn what the authors want to teach? Do you feel that you *want* to learn it? _____

things to pay particular attention to or to look for, such as "When you read Will Kymlicka's *Citizenship and Identity in Canada,* notice how he lays out his argument and what his key points are." Sometimes instructors will say why they assigned a reading. Such information provides clues that can help you develop a mental list of the key ideas relating to the chapter.

Whatever you use to construct them, the crucial feature of advance organizers is to provide a framework and context for what you'll be reading. And having a framework and context can spell the difference between fully comprehending what you read and misunderstanding it.

Try It! 3, "Create an Advance Organizer," illustrates how to put all this practice to good use.

rganize: Gathering the Tools of the Trade

It's obvious that the primary item you'll need to complete a reading assignment is the material that you're reading. But there are other essential tools you should gather to organize yourself, potentially including the following:

Create an Advance Organizer

Use any information you have available to create an advance organizer for this chapter. Feel free to return to the frontmatter, skim the section headings, read the "Looking Back" chapter summary, or recall anything your instructor said about the chapter. (If you come across words, phrases, or ideas that seem unfamiliar or incomprehensible, it may be helpful to think of several questions you would ask if you had the opportunity.)

Complete the following statements to prepare your organizer:

The key topics that will be covered in the rest of this chapter are . . .

_____   _____

_____   _____

_____   _____

_____   _____

I think I will be most interested in . . .

_____

_____

_____

_____

I think I will be least interested in . . .

_____

_____

_____

_____

I hope the chapter covers this topic: _____

Words, phrases, and ideas that are unfamiliar to me include . . .

_____

_____

_____

If the authors were here, I would ask . . .

_____

_____

_____

Note: You may want to use this Try It! as a starting point for advance organizers for each chapter in this book.

- A pencil or pen to write notes in the margin.

- A highlighter to indicate key passages in the text.

- A copy of the assignment, so you'll be sure to read the right material.

- A pad of paper or index cards for notetaking if the material is particularly complex. If you routinely use a word processor to take notes, get it ready.

- A dictionary. You never know what new words you'll encounter while you're reading, and a dictionary is the reference tool of choice. If you don't have a dictionary handy, you'll be tempted to skip over unfamiliar words—a decision that may come back to haunt you. Avoid the temptation to say "I'll do it later" by keeping a dictionary close by.

Give Yourself Time   There's one more thing you need to prepare successfully for a reading assignment: enough time to complete it. The length of reading assignments is almost never ambiguous. You will typically be given a specific page range, so you will know just how much material you will need to cover.

Now get a watch and time yourself as you read the first three pages of your assignment, being sure to pay attention to the material, not the time! Timing how long it takes to read a representative chunk of material gives you a rough measure of your reading speed for the material—although it will vary even within a single reading assignment depending on the complexity of the material.

You'll also need to consider your current reading **attention span**—the length of time that you usually sustain attention. You can get a general sense of this by using Try It! 4, "Discover Your Attention Span."

Use the three pieces of information you now have—the length of the assignment, your per-page reading speed at full attention, and your typical attention span—to estimate roughly how long it will take you to complete the reading assignment. In addition to distractions, you may need to interrupt your reading to look up words in the dictionary, get a drink, stretch, answer the phone, or do a number of other things. You may also decide to break your reading into several sessions, in which case your total reading time may be greater since you will have to get reacquainted with the reading assignment each time you sit down again. Finally, as you begin to use the techniques in this chapter regularly, your reading attention span should increase, which will change your calculation.

Attention span
The length of time that attention is typically sustained

W ork: Getting the Most Out of Your Reading

Finally, it's time to get down to work and start reading.

Obviously—because it's what you're doing at this very moment—you know how to read. But what's important is what you do *while* you're reading. Here are several things that will help you get the most out of the process of reading.

Try It! 4

Discover Your Attention Span

To get an idea of the length of your current attention span for reading, perform this exercise over the next few days.

1. Choose one of the textbooks that you've been assigned to read this semester.

2. Start reading a chapter, without any preparation, noting in the chart below the time that you start reading.

3. As soon as your mind begins to wander and think about other subjects, stop reading and note the time on the chart below.

4. Using the same textbook, repeat this process four more times over the course of a few days, entering the data on the chart below.

5. To find your reading attention span, find the average number of minutes across the five trials.

Trial #1:   Starting time: _____   Ending time: _____
Number of minutes between start and end times: _____

Trial #2:   Starting time: _____   Ending time: _____
Number of minutes between start and end times: _____

Trial #3:   Starting time: _____   Ending time: _____
Number of minutes between start and end times: _____

Trial #4:   Starting time: _____   Ending time: _____
Number of minutes between start and end times: _____

Trial #5:   Starting time: _____   Ending time: _____
Number of minutes between start and end times: _____

Reading attention span (the average of the number of minutes in the last column, found by adding up the five numbers and dividing by five) = _____ minutes

---

Ask yourself these questions about your reading attention span.

1. Are you surprised by the length of your reading attention span? In what way?

2. Does any number in the set of trials stand out from the other numbers? For instance, is any number much higher or lower than the average? If so, can you account for this? For example, what time of day was it?

3. Do the numbers in your trials show any trend? For instance, did your attention span tend to increase slightly over the course of the trials, did it decrease, or did it stay about the same? Can you explain any trend you may have noted?

4. Do you think your attention span figures would be very different if you had chosen a different textbook? Why?

Despite the throngs of students walking by on the campus of Dalhousie University in Halifax, the student seated on the bench seems to have no trouble concentrating on what she's reading. On the other hand, if you are easily distracted, choosing an isolated location to read is a wise strategy.

Stay focused The TV show you watched last night, your boyfriend forgetting to meet you at the bus stop, your father's heart attack, your grumbling stomach—there are a million and one possible distractions that can invade your thoughts as you read. Your job is to keep distracting thoughts at bay and focus on the material you are supposed to be reading. It's not easy, but there are things you can do to help yourself stay focused:

- **Read in small bites.** If you think it is going to take you four hours to read an entire chapter, break up the four hours into more manageable time periods. Promise yourself that you'll read for one hour in the afternoon, another hour in the evening, and the next two hours the following day. One hour of reading is far more manageable than a four-hour block.

- **Take a break.** Actually, plan to take several breaks to reward yourself while you're reading. During your break, do something enjoyable—eat a snack, watch a bit of a ball game on television, play a video game, or the like.

  Just try not to get drawn into your break activity to the point that it takes over your reading time.

- **Deal with distractions.** Sometimes problems have a way of popping into our minds and repeatedly distracting us. If a particular problem keeps interrupting your concentration—such as a difficulty you're having on the job—try to think of an action-oriented strategy to deal with it. You might even write your proposed solution down on a piece of paper. That can move the problem out of the mental realm of your head and put it into concrete form on paper, potentially making it less intrusive.

Write While You Read Writing is one of the most important aspects of reading. If you haven't underlined, jotted notes to yourself, placed checkmarks on the page, drawn arrows, constructed diagrams, and otherwise defaced and disfigured your book while you're reading, you're not doing your job as a P.O.W.E.R. reader.

"What is reading but silent conversation?"

Walter Savage Landor, *Imaginary Conversations*

The idea of writing on a book page may go against everything you've been taught in the past. (And of course you should never write on a library book or one that you've borrowed from a friend.) If your practice has been to "save" your textbooks, either because you want to keep them untarnished for your old age or because they will fetch a higher price if you sell them back to the bookstore, rethink your strategy. The greater success you'll experience by writing extensively in your book while you're reading is a far better tactic in the long run.

What should you be writing while you are reading? There are several things you should write down:

- **Rephrase key points.** Make notes to yourself, in your own words, about what the author is trying to get across. Don't just copy what's been said. Think about the material, and rewrite it in your own words.

  Writing notes to yourself in your own words has several consequences, all good. First, you make the material yours; it becomes something you now understand and part of your own personal knowledge base.

  Second, trying to summarize a key point in your own words will make it very clear whether you truly understand it. It's easy to be fooled into thinking we understand something as we're reading along. But the true test is whether we can explain it to ourselves (or someone else) on our own, without referring to the book or article.

  Third, the very act of writing engages an additional type of perception, involving the tactile sense of moving a pen or pressing a keyboard. Engagement of an additional perceptual system will help you learn the material in a more active way.

  Finally, writing notes and phrases will help you study the material later. Not only will the key points be highlighted, but your notes will also quickly bring you up to speed with your initial thoughts.

- **Highlight or underline key points.** Very often the first or last sentence in a paragraph, or the first or last paragraph in a section, will present a key point. (Remember those lessons about "topic sentences" you had in high-school English classes? Writers really use them.)

  Before you highlight anything, though, read the whole paragraph. Then you'll be sure that what you highlight is, in fact, the key information. Topic sentences do not always fall at the beginning of a paragraph.

  Be selective in your highlighting and underlining. A page covered in yellow highlighter may be artistically appealing, but it won't help you understand the material any better. Highlight only the key information. It may be that only one or two sentences or phrases are highlighted on a page. That's fine. What is important is that when you go back to study the material, your memory will be jogged. *In highlighting and underlining, less is more.* One rule of thumb is that no more than 10 percent of the material should be highlighted or underlined.

- **Use arrows, diagrams, outlines, tables, time lines, charts, and other visuals to help you understand and later recall what you are reading.** If there are three examples given for an assertion, number them. If a paragraph discusses a situation in which an earlier point does not hold, link the original point to the exception by an arrow. If a sequence of steps is presented, number each step.

  For example, after you have annotated *this* page, it might look something like what is shown on the next page:

the bookstore, rethink your strategy. The greater success you'll experience by writing extensively in your book while you're reading is a far better tactic in the long run.

What should you be writing while you are reading? There are several things you should write down:

Put key points into my own words.

- **Rephrase key points.** Make notes to yourself, in your own words, about what the author is trying to get across. Don't just copy what's been said. Think about the material, and rewrite it in your own words.

    Writing notes to yourself in your own words has several consequences, all good. First, you make the material yours; it becomes something you now understand and part of your own personal knowledge base. ✓✓

    Second, trying to summarize a key point in your own words will make it very clear whether you truly understand it. It's easy to be fooled into thinking we understand something as we're reading along. But the true test is whether we can explain it to ourselves (or someone else) on our own, without referring to the book or article.

    Third, the very act of writing engages an additional type of perception, involving the tactile sense of moving a pen or pressing a keyboard. Engagement of an additional perceptual system will help you learn the material in a more active way.

    Finally, writing notes and phrases will help you study the material later. Not only will the key points be highlighted, but your notes will also quickly bring you up to speed with your initial thoughts.

Use highlighter – but less is more not more than 10% highlighted.

- **Highlight or underline key points.** Very often the first or last sentence in a paragraph, or the first or last paragraph in a section, will present a key point. (Remember those lessons about "topic sentences" you had in high-school English classes? Writers really use them.) ← *topic sentence*

    Before you highlight anything, though, read the whole paragraph. Then you'll be sure that what you highlight is, in fact, the key information. Topic sentences do not always fall at the beginning of a paragraph.

    Be selective in your highlighting and underlining. A page covered in yellow highlighter may be artistically appealing, but it won't help you understand the material any better. Highlight only the key information. It may be that only one or two sentences or phrases are highlighted on a page. That's fine. What is important is that when you go back to study the material, your memory will be jogged. *In highlighting and underlining, less is more.* One rule of thumb is that no more than 10 percent of the material should be highlighted or underlined.

Use visuals

- **Use arrows, diagrams, outlines, tables, time lines, charts, and other visuals to help you understand and later recall what you are reading.** If there are three examples given for an assertion, number them. If a paragraph discusses a situation in which an earlier point does not hold, link the original point to the exception by an arrow. If a sequence of steps is presented, number each step.

    For example, after you have annotated *this* page, it might look something like what is shown on the next page:

Particularly if your learning style is a visual one, representing the material graphically will get you thinking about it—and the connections and points in it—in new and different ways. Rather than considering the material solely in verbal terms, you now add visual images. The act of creating visual annotations will not only help you to understand the material better but it will also ease its later recall as well. See Try It! 5, "Mark up a Book Page."

- **Look up unfamiliar words in a dictionary.** Even though you may be able to figure out the meaning of an unfamiliar word from its context, use a dictionary to ensure that what you think it means is correct. A dictionary will also tell you what the word sounds like, which may be important if your instructor uses the word in class.

Try It! 5

Working in a Group:
Mark up a Book Page

First, working alone, read the following excerpt and use the techniques we've discussed for marking up a page to highlight its key points.

The more parents speak to their children, the better their children's language skills.

Understanding Language Acquisition:
Identifying the Roots of Language

Anyone who spends even a little time with children will notice the enormous strides that they make in language development throughout childhood. However, the reasons for this rapid growth are far from obvious. Two major explanations have been offered: one based on learning theory and the other on innate processes.

The **learning-theory approach** suggests that language acquisition follows the principles of reinforcement and conditioning discussed in Chapter 6. For example, a child who utters the word "mama" is hugged and praised by her mother, which reinforces the behavior and makes its repetition more likely. This view suggests that children first learn to speak by being rewarded for making sounds that approximate speech. Ultimately, through a process of shaping, language becomes more and more like adult speech (Skinner, 1957).

The learning theory approach is supported by research that shows that the more parents speak to their young children, the more proficient the children become in language usage (see Figure 8-11). In addition, higher levels of linguistic sophistication in parents' speech to their young children are related to a greater rate of vocabulary growth, vocabulary usage, and even general intellectual achievement by the time the children are 3 years of age (Hart & Risley, 1997).

On the other hand, the learning theory approach is less successful when it comes to explaining the acquisition of language rules. Children are reinforced not only when they use proper language, but also when they respond incorrectly. For example, parents answer the child's "Why the dog won't eat?" as readily as they do the correctly phrased question "Why won't the dog eat?" Both sentences are understood equally well. Learning theory, then, has difficulty in providing the full explanation for language acquisition.

Pointing to such problems with learning theory approaches to language acquisition, Noam Chomsky (1968, 1978, 1991), a linguist, provided a ground-breaking alternative. Chomsky argued that humans are born with an innate linguistic capability that emerges primarily as a function of maturation. According to his analysis, all the world's languages share a similar underlying structure called a **universal grammar.** Chomsky suggests that the human brain has a neural system, the **language-acquisition device,** that both permits the understanding of the structure of language and provides strategies and techniques for learning the unique characteristics of a given native language.

learning-theory approach: The theory suggesting that language acquisition follows the principles of reinforcement and conditioning

universal grammar: Noam Chomsky's theory that all the world's languages share a similar underlying structure

language-acquisition device: A neural system of the brain hypothesized to permit understanding of language

Working in a group, compare and contrast your annotations with those of some classmates. How do their annotations differ from yours? Why did they use the annotations they did? Which annotation techniques worked best? Which were easiest to use? How might these annotations help you to remember what is important? If there were different sorts of material presented on the page, such as mathematical formulas, would you use different kinds of annotations?

Evaluate: Considering What It Means and What You Know

Evaluation is a crucial step in reading. You need to be able to answer the seemingly simple question: "What does all this mean?"

But there's another aspect to evaluation. You need to evaluate, truthfully and honestly, your own level of understanding. What do you know as a result of your reading? Evaluation, then, consists of the following steps:

- **Identify the main ideas and themes and their value *to you personally.*** Try to determine the take-home message of the material you've read. For example, the take-home message of a chapter in a recreation management textbook might be, "Future challenges involve meeting the needs of diverse populations, marketing in a fiscally responsible and entrepreneurial manner, involving partners from all sectors, and using technology for efficiency and improved customer service."

  Sometimes the main ideas and themes are spelled out, and at other times you will have to deduce them for yourself. Evaluate the main ideas and themes in terms of their usefulness to your own understanding of the topic.

- **Prioritize the ideas.** Of all the information that is presented, which is the most crucial to the main message and which is the least crucial? Make a list of the main topics covered and try to rank them in order of importance.

- **Think critically about the arguments presented in the reading.** Do they seem to make sense? Are the author's assertions reasonable? Are there any flaws in the arguments? Would authors with a different point of view dispute what is being said? What other perspectives might the author have taken?

- **Talk out loud! Pretend you are explaining the material to a fellow classmate who missed the assignment.** This is one time when talking out loud when no one is around is not only normal but also beneficial. Summarize the material aloud, as if you were talking to another person.

  Talking out loud does two things. First, it helps you identify weak spots in your understanding. Talking to yourself will help you nail down concepts that are still not clear in your mind. Second, and equally important, because you are transforming the written word into the spoken word, you are thinking about the information in an additional way, which will help you remember it better.

- **Be honest with yourself.** Most of us are able to read with our minds on cruise control. But the net result is not much different from not reading the passage at all. If you have drifted off while you've been reading, go back and reread the passage.

- **Pat yourself on the back.** Just as you've done during each of your reading breaks, reward yourself for completing the reading passage. But keep in mind there's one more step before you can really relax, and it's a crucial one: rethinking what you've read.

R ethink: Getting It the Second Time

You're human, so—like the rest of us—when you finish a reading assignment you'd probably like nothing more than to heave a sigh of relief and put the book and what you've read away.

By now you know that there's a crucial step you should take that will assist you in cementing what you've learned into memory: rethinking what you've read. If you do it within 24 hours of first reading the assignment, it can save you hours of work later.

The best way to rethink an assignment is to reread it, along with any notes you've taken. "Yeah, right," you're probably thinking. "Like I have time for that." The benefits of rereading can't be overstated. Rereading transfers material from your short-term memory to your long-term memory. It solidifies information so that it will be remembered far better over time.

> "I can always stop reading a book or magazine if I am not enjoying it, but I have to plough through a dull textbook."
>
> Keely Robinson, Student, Niagara College

Rereading will take *far* less time than the first read-through did. In fact, it isn't necessary to read word for word. You already know what's important and what's not important, so you can skim some of the less important material. But it is wise to reread the more difficult and important material carefully, making sure that you fully understand what is being discussed and why.

Rethinking should be the central activity as you reread the passage and your notes. You need to be sure that your understanding is complete and that you're able to answer any questions that you had earlier about the material.

The Concept Map As a Rethinking Tool As we saw in Chapter 5, **concept mapping** is a method of structuring written material by graphically grouping and connecting key ideas and themes. Each key idea is placed in a different part of the map, and related ideas are placed near it— above, below, or beside it. A concept map looks similar to a graphic of the solar system, with the central idea in the middle, surrounded by related concepts.

Concept mapping
A method of structuring written material by graphically grouping and connecting key ideas and themes

Concept maps help you to rethink material you've read, especially if you used a more traditional outline earlier. Furthermore, once you have developed a concept map for a particular aspect of the material, you can create additional, expanded concept maps involving related information.

Concept maps are particularly useful for people with learning styles that have particular strengths involving spatial relationships. Furthermore, students with certain kinds of learning disabilities—a topic to which we turn in the next section—can also benefit from the use of concept maps.

An example of a concept map involving the material we've discussed so far is illustrated at the top of the next page. Note how it summarizes the material and shows how it is related to the central topic of "Reading with Understanding." Also, see Try It! 6, "Make a Concept Map," on page 203.

This concept map illustrates the key ideas of reading with understanding.

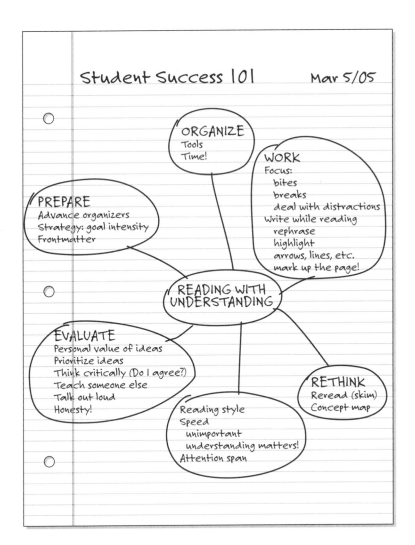

Student Success 101   Mar 5/05

ORGANIZE
Tools
Time!

WORK
Focus:
  bites
  breaks
  deal with distractions
Write while reading
  rephrase
  highlight
  arrows, lines, etc.
  mark up the page!

PREPARE
Advance organizers
Strategy: goal intensity
Frontmatter

READING WITH UNDERSTANDING

EVALUATE
Personal value of ideas
Prioritize ideas
Think critically (Do I agree?)
Teach someone else
Talk out loud
Honesty!

Reading style
Speed
unimportant
understanding matters!
Attention span

RETHINK
Reread (skim)
Concept map

Dealing with Learning Disabilities

Approximately 1 in every 10 Canadians, or about three million people across the country, are affected by a learning disability, and they come from all age, ethnic, and social groups.[2] **Learning disabilities** are characterized by difficulties in processing information when listening, speaking, reading, or writing, in which there is a discrepancy between learning potential and actual academic achievement.

One of the most common kinds of learning disabilities is dyslexia, a reading disability that produces the misperception of letters during reading and writing, unusual difficulty in sounding out letters, spelling difficulties, and confusion between right and left. Although its causes are not yet completely understood, one likely explanation is a problem in the part of the brain responsible for breaking words into the sound elements that make up language.

People with learning disabilities are sometimes viewed as unintelligent. Not so! There is no relationship between learning disabilities and IQ. For instance, dozens of well-known and highly accomplished individuals suffered from dyslexia, including physicist Albert Einstein, poet William Butler Yeats, Walt Disney, and Cher.

By the time they reach a postsecondary school, most people with learning disabilities have already been diagnosed. If you do have a diagnosed learning

Learning disabilities
Difficulties in processing information when listening, speaking, reading, or writing, characterized by a discrepancy between learning potential and actual academic achievement

Make a Concept Map

Here's a chance to create a concept map. Using the space provided below, map out the "Building Listening Skills" section of this chapter. Place the main topic ("Tips for Active Listening . . .") in the centre and group other related concepts together. Feel free to link concepts with lines or add any other marks that will help you structure the content and make sense of the section when you return to it for rethinking and review.

disability, it is important to disclose your situation to your instructors and other school officials if you need special services.

In some cases, students with learning disabilities have not been appropriately evaluated before college or university. If you have difficulties such as mixing up and reversing letters frequently and suspect that you have a learning disability, someplace on campus can provide you with guidance. One place to start: your school's counselling or student services centre.

However, just because you are having trouble with reading assignments doesn't automatically mean that you have a learning disability. Not only is the kind of reading you do in college or university more difficult than what you did in high school, there's more of it. It's only when reading represents a persistent, long-term problem—one that won't go away no matter how much work you do—that a learning disability becomes a possible explanation.

Consider these basic two facts: Most of us talk at a rate of around 125 words a minute, but the average listener can comprehend close to 700 words per minute.

Then why is it so hard to listen closely to what someone is saying? Why do our minds wander, and why do we often recall so little about a class when it is over?

The answer rests on the difference between *hearing* and *listening*. Although our sensory capabilities permit us to *hear* far more words than are produced in a given minute by the average speaker, that doesn't mean we actively *listen* to speech. **Hearing** is the involuntary act of sensing sounds. The annoying drip of a faucet or the grating sound of a roommate's voice speaking on the phone in the next room are two examples of how hearing is both involuntary and often meaningless.

In contrast, **listening** is the voluntary act of focusing on what is being said, making sense of it, and thinking about it in a way that permits it to be recalled accurately. Listening involves concentration, and it requires shutting out competing thoughts, such as what we need to pick up at the grocery store or why our date last night was so terrific.

Active listening is an essential component of success, not only in school but also in the broader world. For animals, recognizing the warning cry of another member of the same species can literally mean the difference between life and death. For people, effective listening permits us to know that even though our friend says it's fine if we postpone our hiking trip, she is really disappointed; it enables us to hear the sound of a horn warning us not to walk into a car's path, allows us to respond emotionally to the lyrics of a song, and helps us decide whether a defendant in a trial is telling the truth.

Hearing
The involuntary act of sensing sounds

Listening
The voluntary act of focusing on sounds and making sense of them

"I'm glad I understand that while language is a gift, listening is a responsibility."

Nikki Giovanni, *Racism 101*

When you are in class, it's essential that you listen and understand. Active listening will help you understand class presentations better. It will aid you in mastering material, permit you to participate more in class, and help you work with your classmates more effectively.

Tips for Active Listening: Listen Up!

You already know many of the techniques of effective listening from the chapter on notetaking. In fact, if you are taking good notes, chances are you are an active listener already. What follows is a list of the most important techniques of active listening and some tips for listening even when the speaker is making it difficult to stay interested.

- **Choose a seat that will promote active listening.** You should certainly choose a seat that will permit you to see and hear clearly, but there's more to your choice than that. Picking the right seat in a classroom can make a big difference.

Where is the best place to sit? Usually it's near the front centre of the classroom. Instructors make more eye contact with the people near them, and they sometimes believe that the best, most-engaged students sit closest. Conversely, they may assume that students who sit as far toward the back of the room as they can get are less involved. (There's a certain reality to that assumption: Research shows that more questions are asked by students sitting close to instructors than by those farther back.)

Furthermore, sitting in the back of the class may make you feel disengaged and out of touch with what is happening at the front of the room. In turn, this may make it easier for your mind to wander.

Everyone needs to make a personal choice about what works best. If you feel as if you're on display in the front of the class and sitting there inhibits your asking questions, then choose a different seat.

- **Focus on what is being said.** Active listening involves listening not just to a speaker's individual sentences, but also to the overall message. Ask yourself what the speaker's overall theme is. As you saw in the chapter on taking notes, compared with the written word, which provides thematic clues such as titles, headings, and paragraphs, the spoken word is less concrete. Consequently, you have to work to figure out the structure of the speaker's message. Good lecturers have a series of broad ideas that they want to convey. It's your job, as an active listener, to unearth them while not losing track of the details of the message.

In essence, successful listening involves paying attention to two kinds of messages: the actual message and what's called the meta-message. The actual message consists of the verbatim transcript; it is what the speaker actually says, on a surface level. But all

Career Connections

Active Listening in the Workplace: A Matter of Life and Death

Effective listening is required across all sectors and all types of jobs. Many organizations specifically train call centre staff or customer service reps in effective listening skills; similarly, managers also frequently receive training to improve communication, including listening skills. So, honing your listening skills now will pay big dividends when you enter the world of work. All jobs involve listening, to some extent, but for employees in careers like law enforcement, emergency services, medicine, social work, air traffic control, or crisis intervention, the quality of their listening skills could be a matter of life and death.

Situations that involve people who are ill, injured, distressed, difficult to deal with, or in danger usually require clarification and sometimes negotiation, both of which require advanced listening skills.

The RCMP considers effective listening a functional competency and trains and tests cadets on their listening skills. See <www.rcmp-learning.org/fr-welc.htm> for the RCMP Online University information on listening. Numerous other police departments across Canada train officers to use active listening to defuse potentially dangerous situations, such as domestic disputes. In some situations, such as are often found in community policing, negotiating or mediating alternative resolutions to disputes can reduce the trauma and long-term effects that traditional policing can sometimes produce.

speakers also have a **meta-message,** the underlying main ideas that they want to convey through the spoken message.

Sometimes a speaker will explicitly state the meta-message. For example, an instructor might say at the start of a class, "Today I'll be trying to give you a feel for the ways that social protest informed the national consciousness in the 1960s." In other cases, though, the meta-message may not be so obviously stated, and listeners will have to figure out the underlying themes. Some strategies for doing so follow.

- **Pay attention to the nonverbal messages that accompany the verbal message.** Does an instructor get excited about a particular topic? Does she get agitated? Does the speaker seem unenthusiastic when talking about something? Use nonverbal cues to gauge the importance of a particular part of a message relative to other things being said. Being able to "hear" nonverbal messages can also help you pick up the unspoken messages people give. (See *Career Connections* on the previous page for a discussion of the importance of listening in a professional context.)

- **Listen for what is *not* being said.** Sometimes silence is not just golden, but informative as well. By noting what topics are *not* being covered in class, or are presented only minimally, you can gauge the relative importance of ideas in comparison with one another.

  This is where preparation comes in. The only way to know what's not being discussed is to have done the assigned readings in advance. This information is important. It will help you get a good sense of an instructor's priorities and help you later when the time comes to study for exams.

- **Take notes.** As you no doubt know from experience, no one's memory is infallible. Unless you take careful and accurate notes, you're likely to end up with little or even no recollection of the details of a speaker's message, as we discussed in Chapter 5. Furthermore, taking notes will aid active listening by helping you to focus on the speaker's message.

- **Adopt a questioning attitude, in which your goal is not passive acceptance of the instructor's message but active evaluation.** Do you agree with the speaker? Do you understand the reasoning behind the speaker's arguments? Are the arguments logical? Is this information consistent with other material that's been presented earlier?

- **Ask questions.** One of the most important things you can do during a class is to ask questions. Raising questions will help you evaluate, clarify, and ultimately better understand what your instructor is saying. Even beyond these critical goals, questions serve several other purposes.

  For one thing, raising questions will help you to personalize the material being covered, permitting you to draw it more closely into your own framework and perspective. Furthermore, when you ask a question and it is answered satisfactorily, you become personally engaged in what the instructor is saying.

  Questioning also increases your involvement in the class as a whole. If you sit back and never raise questions in class, you are much less likely to feel a real part of the class. Becoming an active questioner will rightly make you feel like you have contributed something to the class. Remember, if you are unclear about some point, it is likely that others share your lack of clarity.

  Finally, by asking questions in class, you serve as a role model for other students. Your questions may help break the ice in a class, making it easier for others to raise issues that they have about the material. And ultimately the answers that the instructor provides to *others'* questions may help *you* to better understand and evaluate your understanding of the material.

Breaking the Ice: Tips for Getting over Stage Fright and Asking Questions in Class

Raising your hand in class can be intimidating. You may be afraid that you'll say something dumb, making it clear to the whole class just how out of it you are; or that everyone will be staring at you; or that your instructor and fellow classmates will resent your wasting valuable class time with your own trivial questions.

Although it may not be possible to fully banish such self-defeating thoughts, you can follow three strategies to make it easier to raise questions.

1. **Sit in the front of the room.** Sitting close to the instructor will make it easier to ask questions. Moreover, if you sit in the back of the room and ask a question, the students in front of you will likely swivel around and look at you. In that case, if you already feel intimidated, your feelings of anxiety may rise off the charts.

2. **Write down your question.** If you anticipate that you'll stumble or forget what you want to say, write down your question before raising your hand. The idea is not to read it word for word, or even refer to it at all when you actually ask your question. But writing it will help you quickly organize your thoughts, and having it handy in written form will reduce your anxiety because you know you have a safety net.

3. **Be one of the first students to ask a question.** One reason people sometimes give for not having asked questions is that others have already asked so many questions that there's no time. Or that others have already addressed the issue. Or that others' questions were so good that they make yours look silly. To avoid this difficulty, be among the first to ask questions. Don't wait for others to break the ice; go for it.

Asking questions in class does more than just provide you with the opportunity to clarify points you don't understand. It often will make you feel more a part of the class, and it will encourage other students to participate.

The Problem Instructor

He talks too fast . . . she mumbles . . . he puts down people when they ask a question . . . she rambles and goes off on boring tangents . . . she explains things in a way that doesn't make much sense.

In the real world of the college or university classroom, not every instructor comes to class with a finely honed lecture that is clear, compelling, and interesting and presents it beautifully. As we first discussed when we considered strategies for taking notes in Chapter 5, we have all suffered through instruction that is deficient in one or more ways. What should you do when you find yourself in such a situation?

1. *Remember that this too shall pass.* First, keep in mind that this is a temporary condition; your experience usually won't last more than one term. Most instructors are conscientious and well prepared, and unless you have enormously bad luck, the unpleasant experience you're having now will not be routine.

2. *Ask questions about the material.* Even if you have no idea what is going on in class—or *especially* if you have no idea—ask questions. You are not the only one struggling with the instructor's shortcomings. You will be doing everyone in the class a favour if you admit you're not following what an instructor is saying and ask for clarification.

3. *Ask—privately—for the instructor to change her behaviour.* It is not bad classroom etiquette to ask an instructor to speak a little slower. Instructors sometimes get carried away with enthusiasm and begin speaking faster and faster without even being aware of it. Very often a reality check from a student will be welcome. But don't couch your comment in way that makes the instructor feel inept ("Could you slow down; you're going too fast and losing me"). Instead, keep the comment neutral, without placing blame. For instance, you might simply say, "I'm having trouble keeping up with you; would it be possible for you to speak a little more slowly?"

4. *Pool your resources.* Get together with other students in the class and work out a strategy for dealing with the situation. If an instructor speaks too fast and you just can't keep up with the flow of information, meet with your fellow students and compare what you've gleaned from the class. They may have understood or noted material that you missed, and vice versa. Together, you may be able to put the pieces of the puzzle together and get a fuller understanding of the material.

5. *Listen to the lecture again.* You might bring a tape recorder to class (but request the instructor's permission first!). Then, after class, you can play back the tape at your leisure.

   There's another option: Many instructors teach multiple sections of the same course. If this is the case, you might, schedule permitting, sit in on an additional section of the course. The second time around the information may become much clearer.

If you've ever been totally lost following a lecture, you may have discovered that speaking with your instructor immediately after class was helpful. Most instructors are very happy to go over and clarify key points that they've covered during class. They also appreciate your initiative and interest.

6. *Talk with the instructor after class.* If you feel totally lost after a lecture, or even if you've missed only a few points, speak with the instructor after class. Ask for clarification and get her to re-explain points that you missed. Such a dialogue will help you to understand the material better. But it will also do something more: help build your relationship with your instructor.

Speaking of Success

Rachel Trail

University of King's College

Rachel Trail attends one of the oldest and smallest universities in Canada—The University of King's College in Halifax. However, the diversity of the people at King's and their range of interests and reasons for attending university fascinate her. She finds greater freedom and increased autonomy to be major appeals associated with the postsecondary experience. She especially values how classes are organized time wise and work wise, and while there is additional responsibility related to going to university, Rachel appreciates the control she has in choosing what to do and when to do it.

Rachel loves to read but the reading list associated with the study of western thought in the Foundation Year Program at The University of King's College in Halifax is formidable—over 30 classic texts by Plato, Kant, Darwin, Freud, and Shakespeare to name just a few authors. In addition, most of the texts are difficult, so Rachel has developed a few strategies to help with the level and volume of reading she is required to do.

First, she thinks of paragraphs as mini essays with a structure that can help her anticipate the reading's

UNIVERSITY OF
KING'S
COLLEGE•HALIFAX

message and prepare for the ideas and concepts of the material. She looks for the structure as she reads the passage briefly and then reads the piece again one or two more times to capture the main points. This technique is also essential when reading poetry, especially when the imagery doesn't really cohere well.

With so many books to read and understand, the volume of reading can be somewhat overwhelming. Rachel finds that breaking large reading assignments into manageable chunks works well for her. In addition, at King's students focus on developing critical thinking skills by questioning, contemplating, and evaluating topics in a larger context and from several perspectives. So, by talking about the assigned works in small discussion groups, the information and learning are reinforced.

As far as future studies are concerned, Rachel Trail is thinking about majoring in Spanish. The development of solid reading skills early on in her academic career will serve her well as she moves on to read classic literature in a foreign language.

How do my reading style and attention span affect my reading?

- The most important aspect of reading is understanding, not speed. People have different reading styles that can be modified to improve their ability to read with understanding.

- One problem people have with reading is a limited attention span. However, attention span can be increased with self-awareness and practice.

How can I improve my concentration and read more effectively?

- Reading should be approached with a clear sense of purpose and goals, which will vary from assignment to assignment. Examining the front-matter of a book and creating advance organizers are also useful activities.

- Maintain focus by breaking down the reading into small chunks, taking breaks as needed, dealing with distractions, and writing while reading. It is also helpful to identify the main ideas, prioritize them, think critically about the arguments, and explain the writer's ideas to someone else.

- Concept maps that structure and relate ideas can aid rethinking.

What is active listening, and what is the difference between hearing and listening?

- Listening is a voluntary act that involves focusing on what is being said, making sense of it, and thinking about it. In contrast, hearing is the involuntary act of sensing sounds.

- Active listening involves paying attention to what is being heard. It permits the mastery of material, facilitates class participation, and enables cooperation with other students.

How can I improve my listening skills?

- Active listening involves focusing on what is being said, including the speaker's meta-message, paying attention to nonverbal messages, listening for what is not being said, and taking notes.

- Asking questions in class clarifies ambiguous information, helps to personalize the material being covered, increases your level of involvement in the class, and makes it easier for other students to ask questions.

- Active listening also involves carefully analyzing the speaker's message, presentation, arguments, and nonverbal behaviour, and examining your own listening behaviour and reactions.

P.O.W.E.R. Portfolio

Reading and Listening

1. Keep an ongoing reading list—books, articles, or magazines you read —for school, work, or pleasure. Create a Top 10 Books to Read list and

start reading! Keep track of new vocabulary words. Consider including your list, along with reflective comments, in your portfolio.

2. Consider becoming a conversation partner with a person whose first language is not English. This experience will demonstrate how difficult and how important the art of listening is. Consider including a log and reflective comments in the "Volunteer" or "Interests" section of your portfolio!

Resources

On Campus

If you are experiencing unusual difficulties in reading and the problem is one you encountered in high school, you may have a learning disability. If you suspect this is the case, take action. Many colleges and universities have offices that deal specifically with learning disabilities. You can also talk to someone at your school's counselling centre who can arrange for you to be tested.

In Print

The third edition of Kathleen McWhorter's book *Academic Reading* (Longman, 5th edition, 2003) provides a complete set of guidelines for reading textbooks and other kinds of writing you will encounter during college or university. Another useful volume is *Breaking Through: College Reading* (Longman Publishing Group, 6th edition, 2001), by Brenda Smith.

Integrating College Study Skills: Reasoning in Reading, Listening, and Writing (Wadsworth Publishing, 6th edition, 2001), by Peter Elias Sotiriou, advises and demonstrates how to use reasoning to connect students' reading, writing, and listening skills. Sotiriou uses a thoughtful, measured approach, with specific strategies for studying, reading, notetaking, and exam-taking.

On the Web

The following sites on the World Wide Web provide the opportunity to extend your learning about the material in this chapter. Although the Web addresses were accurate at the time the book was printed, check the P.O.W.E.R. Learning website, <www.mcgrawhill.ca/college/power>, for any changes that may have occurred.

www.ucc.vt.edu
This site has links to several helpful reading resources, including sections on how to analyze essays, skimming and scanning, how to read a difficult book, and SQ3R, an approach to reading, and retaining, textual material.

www.ldonline.org/ld_indepth/postsecondary/index.html
This site has information to assist students with learning disabilities in the planning and selection process, plus lots of advice on creating a successful postsecondary education experience.

www.ucc.vt.edu/stdysk/addhandbook.html
This site offers a handbook for students with ADHD (attention deficit hyperactivity disorder).

The Case of . . .

What's Wrong with this Picture?

Rahman Ali groaned in frustration as he left his Elements of Design course. He guessed he'd only understood about 50 percent of what the instructor had said. In general, Rahman felt his Photography program was going well, but this course was impossible.

Part of the problem was the size of the class—it was a common course for visual arts students and there were about 150 students in the class. Part of the problem was the type of class—every class was a PowerPoint presentation. And the third part of the problem was sheer volume—their instructor showed at least 30 slides a class, so there wasn't a lot of time for discussion. Rahman felt that he couldn't take up class time asking the teacher to speak a little slower or to re-explain points he didn't understand. It didn't make matters any better when his classmates whose first language was English said they were having trouble understanding their teacher as well.

As Rahman considered his options, no clear answer was obvious. He'd worked for a year after high school to save money for college and he wasn't going to quit. And the design course was compulsory—he couldn't drop it. Rahman tried to consider his options, but he couldn't focus on a clear solution.

1. How would you advise Rahman to prepare for his design course? What could he do in advance of each class?

2. What organizational strategies could Rahman apply to his listening skills for this course? How could he and his classmates help themselves to feel more successful in this course?

3. Why is listening such a hard skill for English-as-a-second-language learners? Is it as difficult for students whose first language is English? Why or why not?

4. A design course has lots of terms borrowed from French, Italian, Latin, or Greek. What other courses or programs have particularly difficult vocabulary?

5. Why is evaluation important for listening? How could Rahman evaluate his listening comprehension?

6. In what ways can Rahman use rethinking techniques to improve his understanding in his Elements of Design course?

Writing
and
Speaking

8

The Writing Process

Prepare: Confronting the Blank
Page

Journal Reflections: How I Feel About Writing

Organize: Constructing a
Scaffold

Work: Writing the Work

Evaluate: Acting as Your Own
Best Critic

Rethink: Reflecting on Your
Accomplishment

Speaking Your Mind

Career Connections: Write Away

Journal Reflections: How I Feel About Public Speaking

Speaking of Success: John Lu

The Case of . . . the Reluctant Speaker

It was 3:23 A.M. Maria Ramos knew the exact time because that's what the numbers on her digital clock radio indicated at the precise moment she bolted awake in a cold sweat. She had been dreaming about the moment in her Landscape Design class, now only a few hours away, when she would have to give an oral presentation.

Maria was nothing less than terrified by the thought. A quiet and shy person by nature, she didn't like to be the centre of attention in groups. The thought of everyone in the class observing her intently and listening to what she had to say filled her with fear.

A few hours later, after failing to get back to sleep, Maria timidly made her way to the front of the classroom, well aware of her thumping heart and sweaty palms.

Then, as she began to speak, something happened. She saw interest on the faces of her classmates and instructor—interest in what she was saying. Maria started to calm down. She realized that she would manage to get through her talk and she actually might do a decent job. She took a deep breath to relax and tried not to talk too fast. "I can do this," she said to herself.

Maria had found her voice and her classmates were listening.

Looking
Ahead

Few activities raise so many concerns as writing and public speaking, yet few are as important to your success, not only in college or university but in the world outside the classroom. Writing and oral presentations are major parts of your postsecondary classes, and you shouldn't be surprised to find them a part of your professional life later. Learning how to write and speak well will not only increase your success in college or university and beyond, but it will also improve your peace of mind!

This chapter focuses on writing and speaking. We begin by considering how to write college- or university-level papers, as well as other kinds of writing. We'll talk about how to get started writing a paper and how you can move from a rough first draft to a final draft of which you can be proud.

The second part of the chapter looks at oral presentations. We'll discuss ways of getting over stage fright and how to engage listeners from the very start of your talk. We'll consider the importance of practising neither too little nor too much.

After reading this chapter, you'll be able to answer these questions:

- **What are the best techniques for getting started and writing a first draft?**

- **How can I move from my first draft to my final draft?**

- **How can I lose my fears of public speaking and make effective oral presentations?**

The Writing Process

What happens when you sit down to write? Does the sight of a blank page or blank screen leave your mind similarly blank? Do your fingers, which move so quickly when you're playing a game on the computer, become sluggish when poised over a keyboard to write a paper?

Writing is not easy, and for many students, writing assignments raise more anxieties than any other academic task. This anxiety has many causes. For one thing, papers often compose a large part of your final course grades, putting pressure on you to do well. Maybe you always do all your writing at the last minute, with a deadline looming. Perhaps you've never really been taught how to write well. Or maybe you believe that there's some sort of special writing gene that you just weren't born with.

Stop! Delete from your memory any negative preconceptions you may have about writing. There is no mystery to writing; it's a skill that can be taught, and a skill that, with practice, anybody can learn. *Writing is not a product you read; it is a thinking and reasoning process that is the means of producing that product,* a skill that can be learned like any other, not a talent you are born with or without.

Using strategies based on P.O.W.E.R. Learning (summarized in the P.O.W.E.R. Plan), you will be able to achieve the goal of writing clearly and competently. These strategies will help you to build on your strengths and maximize your abilities. They will permit you to translate what's inside your head into words that communicate your experience or thoughts directly.

Prepare: Confronting the Blank Page

Nothing is more intimidating than a blank piece of paper or computer screen. That intimidation is something that every writer faces, no matter how proficient. Shakespeare, Jane Austen, Mark Twain, Margaret Laurence, Ralph Ellison, and Mordecai Richler all felt the challenge of having to fill that void with words.

Looked at another way, nothing is more liberating than a blank page. It offers every possibility, and it gives you the freedom to say whatever you want to say. And therein lies the key to good writing: deciding what it is you want to say.

Preparation is a central aspect of successful writing. Writing is a process, and preparation for it encompasses the following steps.

Decide What Your Goal Is To write successfully, you need to think about the end product. Is it a long research paper, based on information you must gather? an essay arguing a particular point of view? a fictional short story? a critique of someone else's work or argument? a book or movie review?

PREPARE
Approach writing as a process

ORGANIZE
Write a flexible outline and construct a thesis statement

WORK
Get it down in the first draft; Refine it in the second draft

EVALUATE
Be your own best critic: finetune your work

RETHINK
Reflect on the writing process: what worked, what didn't?

P.O.W.E.R. Plan

Nothing is more intimidating than a blank piece of paper—or a blank computer screen. On the other hand, it can also be liberating, offering you the freedom and opportunity to say what *you* want to say.

Most often, you'll be working to complete a class assignment that will explain what the goal is. But sometimes the assignment will provide you with several choices; it may even be vague or imprecise. If this is the case, your first step will be to decide just what you'll be doing through your writing.

If there is a choice among different types of writing, decide which will make you most comfortable. If one choice is to prepare an essay and you are creative and enjoy expressing your opinions, choose that option. If you enjoy gathering information and drawing a conclusion from your findings, a research paper might be the best choice.

Choose Your Topic Once you've determined the specific type of writing you are going to do, the next step is to choose a topic. Although instructors usually assign a particular topic, in some cases the choice will be left to you. However, the freedom to choose a topic does not come without a price. In fact, many students find that choosing what to write about is harder than actually writing the paper itself. Here are some things you can do to choose an appropriate topic:

"How do I know what I think 'til I see what I say?"

character in an E.M. Forster novel

- **Use "freewriting."** According to Peter Elbow, a writing expert who has revolutionized the teaching of writing, one of the reasons we find writing so hard is that we have a set of censors inside our heads.[1] At a moment's notice, those censors are ready to spring up and whisper, "That's no good," when we set pen to paper.

    However, you can keep these internal voices at bay using a technique called "freewriting." In **freewriting,** you write continually for a fixed period, such as 5 or 10 minutes. The only rule that governs freewriting is to write continually, without stopping. It doesn't matter whether the product is bad; it doesn't matter whether it's good. The only principle you must follow in freewriting is to get something—anything—down on paper.

    Try it, and you'll see how liberating freewriting can be. Of course, the product will not be perfect, but you'll most likely find that you've written something of value to you.

    Suppose, for example, you are stuck for a topic. Through freewriting you can explore your feelings about the course you are going to be writing for, what you like and don't like, and get some rough ideas down on paper. What's more, you'll probably form an "attitude" toward one or more potential topics, which can be used to add a personal voice and authenticity to your writing.

    Once the freewriting session is completed, you may want to write a single sentence that captures the main point of what you have written—the

Freewriting
A technique involving continual, nonstop writing, without self-criticism, for a fixed time

Brainstorming
A technique for generating ideas by saying out loud as many ideas as can be thought of in a fixed time

"centre of gravity," Elbow calls it. You can then use this sentence as a springboard for further exploration of ideas the next time you write. See Try It! 1, "Set Yourself Free: Freewriting."

- **Use brainstorming.** The oral equivalent of freewriting is brainstorming. While freewriting is done alone, brainstorming is most often done with others. In **brainstorming,** you say out loud as many ideas as you can think of in a fixed time. Although brainstorming works best when you do it in a group, you can do it by yourself. (This is one of those times when talking to yourself has its benefits.) Initially, the goal is simply to produce as many ideas as possible, no matter how implausible, silly, or irrelevant. Jot down the ideas that intrigue you as they come up, so you don't forget them.

  As with freewriting, the idea is to temporarily silence the censors that prevent us from saying whatever comes into our heads. In brainstorming, the initial goal is not to produce high-quality ideas, but a high quantity of ideas. You can revisit and evaluate the ideas later. Refer to Try It! 2, "Get Your Brain Storming: Using Brainstorming to Generate Ideas," on page 219.

Decide Who Your Audience Is

That's easy, you may be thinking; it's my instructor. *Not so fast.* Although the instructor is the most obvious reader for what you write, you should think of your audience in terms of the ultimate purpose of the writing assignment. For example, if you're writing a paper about the dangers of global warming, are you directing it to a layperson who knows little about the issue? Or are you writing it for someone with a good understanding of science, someone who already knows about atmospheric pressure, *El Niño,* and the ozone layer? Clearly, the answer to this question will make a difference in how and what you write.

In short, it's crucial to know—and to keep in mind—the people who may read your paper. What is their level of knowledge about the topic? Are they already predisposed to a particular position? What

Set Yourself Free: Freewriting

Use this space to practise freewriting for five minutes. Optional guidance is offered below, but if you want to go ahead and "just do it," simply start writing. Be sure to keep your hand moving; stop controlling yourself. Write only for yourself; forget about what others might think—be frank.

If you need a little more guidance, you are not alone; most people need help the first time they try it. There are actually two kinds of freewriting: plain vanilla freewriting (like that above) and *focused* freewriting. Focused freewriting gives you a starting point.

Here are some starting points for focused freewriting:

Today I feel . . .   I get sick when . . .

I remember . . .   I know . . .

I don't like . . .   I am . . .

I really like . . .   I am not . . .

Using one of these lead-in phrases as a starting point, return to the blank space and begin your freewriting.

What is the main point of what you wrote? Was freewriting effective in helping you get something down on paper? Was it easy or difficult for you? Can you think of how the process of freewriting might help you when it's time to write a paper?

do you think they would like to take away with them after reading what you've written?

Keeping an audience in mind serves another purpose: It personalizes your writing. Rather than targeting your writing to a nondescript group of individuals ("all the people who might be worried about global warming"), you individualize your audience. Think of the reader as your sister, or a friend, or

Working In a Group: Get Your Brain Storming: Using Brainstorming to Generate Ideas

Your sociology instructor has asked you to come up with 10 ideas for a five-page paper on crime in Canada. Brainstorm in a group and come up with a list of possible topics, assigning one member of the group to record ideas below.

As you brainstorm, keep the length of the paper assigned and the sort of topic suited to sociology generally in mind. Remember, the idea is to produce as many possibilities as you can, without evaluating how realistic or feasible they may be. Think quantity over quality.

After your group has finished brainstorming, go back to your answers and circle each that you think is realistic for a paper topic. Did brainstorming work? Did you surprise yourself with the number of possibilities you generated?

your next-door neighbour. Think of how that individual would feel after reading what you've written, and what you would say to convince him or her. Remember, your writing is a representation of you as an individual. It means something to you, and you want its impact to be felt just as personally by another individual.

Research the Topic To write most papers, you must do research, which can also help you further refine your topic. We discussed methods of doing research in Chapter 4, and you might want to review the process.

Break the Task Down into Pieces If authors planning to write a book sat down at their word processor and thought about the 500 pages that they needed to write to complete the book, they probably would never finish the book. Such thoughts are at best mind numbing and at worst totally unproductive and paralyzing. Instead, professional writers break their task down into smaller, manageable pieces. Maybe they decide that they'll write a certain number of pages in a given time, such as four or five pages a day. Or maybe they plan on writing a chapter each week.

You probably don't have as much time to devote to your writing as a professional writer, so the chunks you break your writing into should be shorter. For instance, if you have to write a 10-page paper, don't think of it as 10 pages. Instead, break it down into chunks of two pages a day, spread out over five days. Or think of it in terms of the major sections: an introduction, a description of the background of an issue, arguments in favour of a position, arguments against a position, and a conclusion. You could then schedule the writing of each section on a different day.

rganize: Constructing a Scaffold

When we read and listen to information, the organization phase is easy: The author or speaker has (we hope) already constructed a framework for presenting the information to us. Our job as readers and listeners is to figure out what that organization is, like detectives following a trail of clues.

When we're writing, however, we're creating something that hasn't existed before. Consequently, it's up to us to come up with the scaffolding on which to place our written product.

Construct an Outline (and Be Ready to Change It)
The fundamental key to organizing an extended piece of writing is the outline. An outline provides a roadmap to follow when we're writing, a set of sequential steps that show us where we are heading and how we are going to get there.

The secret of successful outlining is flexibility. It is essential to keep an open mind about sequencing and to avoid getting locked in too early to a pattern that might later prove unworkable. The best approach is to place possible outline topics, based on your research, on index cards. Then read through all the cards and try to place them in a logical order. Ask yourself how the information represented by the cards builds up into a complete and convincing presentation. Remember your audience and treat your readers courteously. Ask yourself what a reader would have to know already in order to understand a given fact or argument. Try out several sequences, and determine which order works best.

You can do the same thing on a computer screen using a word-processing program. List all your topics and rearrange them to your heart's content. If you use the program's outlining feature, it will even renumber the outline as you make changes.

Develop the Paper's Structure Although sometimes instructors provide a structure for a paper, you may have to construct one yourself. One way to do this is to follow the **ABBCC structure.** "ABBCC" stands for the five parts of a typical research paper: argument, background, body, counterarguments, and conclusion. Each part plays a specific role in the overall paper:

- **Argument.** Just as we introduce ourselves when we meet someone for the first time, a writer needs to introduce a reader to the main argument being put forward in the paper. Every paper should have a main argument or **thesis,** a one- or two-sentence description of the main point or stand that is being taken in the paper. For instance, your thesis might make the argument that "Personal character does not matter in leaders; what matters is their effectiveness in accomplishing the goals for which they were elected."

  A thesis should be stated as a contention ("people are their own worst enemies") or in terms of some action verb ("the technological revolution requires that people receive more education"). An effective thesis statement takes a position on some issue and includes such key words as "should" or "ought." For instance, "Smoking should be banned from restaurants and bars" presents a thesis statement. However, "This paper will discuss smoking in restaurants and bars" is simply stating the topic.

  The argument need not be the first sentence of the paper—it is usually wise to start off with something that grabs readers' attention. Begin with a controversial quote, an illustrative story, or a personal encounter—anything that is likely to make a reader sit up and take notice.

  In addition to presenting the main thesis of the paper, the argument section should lay out the areas that you will cover and the general scope of the paper. You should use this section to present the paper's overall perspective and point of view. However, you shouldn't provide evidence yet for why your arguments are correct; save that for the body of the paper. Refer to Try It! 3, "Make Your Point: Write a Thesis Statement."

- **Background.** You'll need to provide readers with a context in which to place your paper's arguments, and the background section is the place to do it. Provide a brief history of the topic, talking about different approaches that have been taken and different schools of thought. Introduce any unusual terminology you might need to employ. If the topic is highly controversial, trace the controversy, and discuss why people have found the topic so controversial. For example if you are arguing that young offenders are treated too leniently by the court system, you should review major components of the *Youth Justice Act.*

- **Body.** The body makes up the bulk of most papers. In the paper's body, you restate your thesis and provide evidence as to why the thesis is correct.

ABBCC structure
The structure of the typical research paper, consisting of argument, background, body, counterarguments, and conclusion

Thesis
The main point or position being argued in a paper, typically stating the writer's opinion about the paper's topic

Make Your Point: Write a Thesis Statement

Write a thesis statement for each topic below. Remember that the thesis should be a contention or should use an action verb.

global warming and modern technology

drinking and driving

euthanasia

service charges for using bank machines

graduated drivers' licences

sovereignty for Quebec

same-sex marriages

Evaluate each thesis statement that you wrote. Do they all contain a contention or action verb? Is there a relationship between how controversial a topic is and how easy it is to write a thesis statement?

👥 **Working in a Group:** Each group member should generate three potential topics for a paper and compose a thesis statement for each. As a group, evaluate each thesis statement.

This evidence should be presented in a logical order. Exactly what this means depends on your topic. You may need to work chronologically if you are discussing a historical event. In other cases, you will want to start with the least controversial arguments and gradually move into the ones that are the most debatable.

When deciding the order in which to present information, keep your audience firmly in mind. For instance, a paper on the dangers of electromagnetic radiation written for a Community Law class would be very different from one written for a Physics class.

- **Counterarguments.** You will also need to touch on information that runs counter to your own thesis. Acknowledge the counterarguments to your position, and then go on to systematically refute each one. This section need not be long, but it is crucial. By doing this you help reinforce your own position and strengthen your argument, showing that you have arrived at your point of view fully aware of—and unconvinced by—opposing views.

- **Conclusion.** A good ending to a paper is as important as a good beginning. It's where you pull everything together, and it is your last chance to drive home your thesis.

    The conclusion should summarize the thesis and the arguments that you have made regarding it. Do not introduce new information; all information should have been introduced earlier. The conclusion is a recap of the information and ideas in the paper. Close with a flourish. You might cite a quotation, present an anecdote that is linked to one you presented at the start of the paper, or pose a question ("If the government turns its back on welfare recipients, how can we claim to have a just society?"). However you choose to conclude the paper, make sure that it ties the various pieces together.

W ork: Writing the Work

Now comes the moment that so many dread. It's time to face that blank page or screen and actually start writing. However, if you've followed the steps above and carefully prepared and organized, this phase is likely to be easier than you expect. In fact, you should be so well prepared that you know just how to proceed; your outline provides a clear roadmap of where you are headed, and your research note cards will permit you to flesh out the points of your outline. One way to look at your outline is that it provides you with the major headings of your paper. The job of writing the paper then becomes a matter of matching the research to the appropriate outline heading, rather than starting with a blank sheet of paper.

Still, the work of writing is rarely problem-free. The best way to proceed is to divide the actual work of writing into two stages: writing the first draft and revising your draft.

Writing the First Draft Starting a first draft is like diving into a cold lake. You know the initial plunge will be painful because the water is icy cold, but you also know that once you're in the lake it won't be so bad.

It's the same thing with writing a first draft. Getting started is often the hardest part. However, once you've put even a few words on paper, it gets easier.

If you've ever gone white-water rafting, you know that following the water's rhythm permits you to remain afloat. In the same way, on those occasions when you achieve a steady rhythm while writing and the words are coming rapidly, stick with it and go with the flow. Revising can come later.

When you set pen to paper or fingers to keyboard to begin writing, don't feel that you are carving your words in stone. Permit yourself to be less than perfect. Don't worry about word choice, grammar, sentence structure, spelling, or punctuation. That can come later. The first draft is meant to give you something to move on from. The important thing is to fill up that blank space with *something*.

What's the rationale for such an approach? It's considerably easier to work from an existing draft—even one that is far from perfect—than to work from nothing. In most ways, the first draft is the hardest work you'll have to do, and it's important to get the process underway. By liberating yourself from the constraints of getting things perfect the first time, you will make the process—that of translating what's in your head into a final form that others can see—far easier.

There are several strategies you can use to make writing the first draft less painful:

- **Start where you like.** You need not follow the order of the outline when you write. For example, some writers start a paper by writing the conclusion section first. By keeping the end in mind, they know just where they are headed, making the journey a little easier. Similarly, other writers save the beginning of the paper for last, reasoning that they'll be better able to tell their readers where the paper is going after it has actually gotten there.

  What's most important is that you start writing *something*. Write whatever part of the paper you feel most comfortable writing, because just having something on paper is a comforting feeling and will encourage you to write the rest.

- **Turn off your inner critic.** If you're anything like most people, with every word you write, there's probably a voice somewhere in your head that's whispering, "Terrible sentence. Dumb idea. Forget it, you idiot, you'll never finish this paper." That's the voice of your inner critic, and it's a voice that keeps many of us from reaching our potential as good writers.

  Your job is to turn that voice off, at least for now. (You'll want to use it later, when the nagging may come in handy as you revise your work.) While you're working on your first draft, you want to give yourself permission to let your creative processes put words on paper. As long as you write things down, you'll be able to go back, change things, and make your paper better. But you can't revise what isn't there.

- **Go with the flow.** When you're writing your first draft, try to write quickly. Writing often takes on a rhythm, and you should try to write in sync with the flow of that rhythm. If you're on a roll, go with it. Don't stop to edit your work; that will happen later.

If you're having trouble getting into a rhythm and each word is like pulling teeth, take a break. Do something entirely different for a few minutes and then return with a fresh mind.

If you're really having trouble, try rearranging your note cards. You might even shuffle them (after you've first numbered them so you can go back to the original order). Placing them in a random order may provide a fresh way of looking at your topic, and this may in turn free you enough to get your writing started.

- **Don't be afraid to modify your outline.** When you start writing, it's easy to fall into the trap of viewing an outline as a rigid, unbending framework. But this is not what an outline is; your outline is a living document, and you should feel free to rearrange headings and even to deviate from it as you're creating your first draft. You'll have the opportunity later to check that the writing still follows a logical course.

  Many writers find that their outlines need to be revised, and so might yours. The outline you started with may be incomplete, or the topics may have to be presented in a different order. As you're writing your draft, you may uncover gaps in the outline. That's fine; that's why you're writing a first draft and not pretending to start with a final one.

- **Use your own voice.** Just as we all have distinctive speaking voices, each of us has a distinct *writing* voice. That voice represents our own unique style, a reflection of our outlook on life and of our past writing experiences.

  Novice writers sometimes get hung up trying to use a voice that isn't their own. For example, they may use words they would never normally use when speaking to someone else.

  Avoid the temptation to write as if you were someone else. Instead, use your own natural voice and vocabulary, and don't use big words in an effort to impress your audience. If you'd feel foolish saying "heretofore" in a conversation, you shouldn't use it when you're writing a paper. Don't scan the thesaurus in search of unusual words, and don't give in to the temptation that word-processor thesauruses offer of plugging in new and unusual words for simple ones. Just because you *can* do something doesn't mean you should.

Voice
The unique style of a writer, expressing the writer's outlook on life and past writing experiences

"In university-level writing or even reading, you cannot possibly finish it all in one sitting or in the last minute. You have to go through it thoroughly and take certain steps to complete it."

Mary Xavier, Student, University of Windsor

- **Forget about it.** The last step in creating a first draft is the easiest. When you have finished your sketch of the entire paper, from introduction through conclusion, put it aside. To revise your draft effectively—the next step in writing—it's necessary to mentally remove yourself from the situation. Like waiting for tea to steep to reach its full potency, you need to let your mind idle in neutral for a while so that it will be at full strength when you move on to the next phase of writing: revision.

Revising Your Draft Remember that inner critic—that voice in your head—that you tuned out while you were writing the first draft? It's time to tune it back in.

The fact is that most of writing is *re*writing. That's why you should not torture yourself over your first draft too much. The difference between success

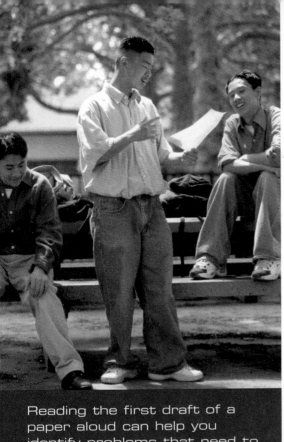

Reading the first draft of a paper aloud can help you identify problems that need to be addressed in a revised draft.

and failure in writing rests in the revision process. Sure, it's possible to hand in a first draft, and sometimes you'll even get a passable grade. But if you want to reach your own potential as a writer, you *must* revise.

Don't feel that revising is something that only students have to do. Professional writers may go through dozens of drafts—and still not be completely satisfied. Virtually no one has the ability to write a first-draft paper that is so lucid and compelling that it stands on its own.

Following several basic rules can make the revision process work smoothly for you:

- **Read the first draft out loud.** Read your paper out loud—to yourself, a friend, or your computer. It doesn't matter who's listening.

  Reading out loud does several things. You'll more easily discover missing words, verbs that don't match the subject of the sentence, shifts in tense, missing transitions, and other things that you might have to fix. The combination of speaking and reading helps make problems more apparent than if you were simply reading the first draft to yourself silently.

  But reading aloud does something more. It slows you down. Speaking takes longer than silent reading, and the slowed pace of oral reading can help you identify things that need revising that you'd otherwise miss.

- **Take the long view.** Start off by taking the broadest perspective possible and asking yourself a series of questions:

  What is the purpose of my paper and has that purpose been fulfilled?

  Have I addressed every aspect of the assignment?

  Does the paper tell its readers everything they need to know?

  Will the audience be able to follow the paper's logic?

  Does the paper make its points clearly?

  Are the transitions between sections clear?

- **Be ruthless.** Remember, writing isn't etched in stone. The tendency is to feel that once we've put words on paper, they are something more than just words. They tend to take on a life of their own—a life that we have created and are often reluctant to change or part with.

  It is natural to feel a bit parental toward our first draft, but it is important to fight this instinct. Now is the time to give full voice to your inner critic. You need to be merciless and unforgiving with passages, paragraphs, phrases, and words that don't sound right or that do not ultimately add to the arguments you're trying to make. Don't tear *yourself* down; however, like a coach demanding the best from his or her players, be demanding of your performance.

  Start pruning at the paragraph level. Assess each paragraph to make sure that it adds to the final message, that it flows from the previous paragraph logically, and that it is consistent with what you are trying to accomplish in the section of the paper in which it is located.

  Then move to the level of sentences and words. Evaluate each sentence, and then each word, to make sure that it adds to the clarity of your message.

By paring down your writing, you let your ideas stay closer to the surface, rather than being obscured by repetition and excess words. If you are extremely fond of a phrase or a group of words that seem to be unnecessary, start by cutting them out and setting them aside. You can ease the pain by saving what you've cut. Write down or print out the sections and phrases of which you're particularly proud, put them into an envelope, and toss the envelope into the top drawer of your dresser. You never know when you might need it. More important, knowing that you can save the cut material may make it easier to do the necessary cutting.

> "Wrestling with words gave me my moments of greatest meaning."
>
> Richard Wright, author

- **Check sequence and logic.** It's now time to reverse course. Whereas before the focus was on cutting extraneous material, you now need to check what's left with a view toward *adding* material.

  For example, because of earlier deletions, it may be necessary to add or modify transitions between sections and paragraphs. Ideas should flow logically, and the reader should be able to understand the structure in which they are set.

  If the logic or the structure of the paper has been lost, restore it by reordering the ideas you've presented. You can reorder sentences within paragraphs, and you can reorder paragraphs within sections.

- **Check punctuation and spelling.** Make sure you've fulfilled the basic requirements of punctuation that have been drummed into you since elementary school. Check for the obvious stuff; sentences should start with capital letters and end with the appropriate punctuation, commas should set off nonrestrictive clauses, and the like. Use a style manual if you're unsure.

  Check spelling carefully. This is one of the areas in which word processors earn their keep best, by checking the spelling of every word. The spellcheck feature not only will identify every misspelled word (that is, every word not in its dictionary), but it will prompt you with alternatives for those words that are misspelled.

  Don't rely completely on the spellchecker, however. Such programs can find only misspellings that do not happen to form actual words; if what you typed forms words, the spellchecker will leave it alone, even if the words you typed were not the ones you wanted to use.

- **Make it pleasing to the eye.** Instructors are human. They can't help but react differently to a paper that is neatly typed compared with one that is handwritten in a difficult-to-read scrawl.

  A neat paper conveys a message: I'm proud of this paper. I've put time and effort into it. This is my best work. A sloppy paper says something different.

  Take the time, then, to make sure your paper looks good. This doesn't mean that you need to invest in a fancy plastic cover, or worry about the alignment of the staples, or spend a lot of time deciding which font to use on your word processor. But it does mean that you should make sure the quality of the essay's appearance matches the quality of the writing.

Evaluate: Acting as Your Own Best Critic

Because you've already put so much work into your paper, you might be tempted to rush through the final stages of the P.O.W.E.R. process. Avoid the temptation. If you've carefully revised your paper, the last stages will not be time-consuming, and they may have a significant effect on your paper's ultimate quality—and your success.

Take these steps to *evaluate* what you've written:

- **Ask yourself whether your paper accomplishes what you set out to do.** The beginning of your paper contains a thesis statement and the argument that you intended to make. Does your paper support the thesis? Are the arguments upheld by the evidence you've reported? Would an impartial reader be convinced by what you've written?

- **Put yourself in your instructor's shoes.** Does the paper precisely fit the assignment requirements? Does it meet the instructor's underlying goals in giving the assignment?

- **Check the mechanical aspects of the paper.** Make certain the paper represents you the way you want to be represented. Not only should the grammar and spelling be correct, but the paper should also look good. If your instructor requires that citations or references be reported in a certain style, make sure you've followed that style. As mentioned in Chapter 4, different disciplines require different referencing systems. The four main styles are MLA (for arts and humanities), APA (for social sciences), CBE (for natural science), and Chicago or Turabian style (for humanities, computer science, health, and business).

If you've revised the paper with care, it will likely pass muster. If it doesn't, though, go back and work on it again. By this point, it should require only minor tinkering to get it into shape.

Rethink: Reflecting on Your Accomplishment

Rethinking is the homestretch of the writing process. It's a moment to savour, because it permits you take a long view of what you've accomplished. You've gone from a blank page to words on paper that tell a story—a story that you've put together. You've turned nothing into something—an achievement in and of itself.

Rethinking occurs on several levels: rethinking the message, mechanics, and method. But don't address them until a little time has passed since you completed the evaluation of the paper. Wait a day or so, and then reread the paper. Then, bringing your critical thinking skills to bear, reflect on the following:

- **Rethink the message.** Be sure that the overall message your paper conveys is appropriate. A paper is like an advertisement. In most papers, you are seeking to communicate information to convince someone of a particular opinion. Make sure that the message is the one you want to communicate, and that ultimately the paper is successful in making the case.

- **Rethink the mechanics.** A television commercial filled with fuzzy images and jerky camera shots would not be very compelling, no matter how good the underlying product. In the same way, a paper with mechanical errors will not impress your readers or persuade them that your arguments are correct. Take another look at your writing style, then, to make sure you are putting your best foot forward. Look at grammar, punctuation, and word usage to make sure the choices you've made are appropriate.

- **Rethink the method.** Every time you finish a paper, you learn something—something about the topic of your writing and something about yourself. Ask yourself what you have learned to help you become a better writer in the future. What might you have done to improve the writing process? What could have gone better? What will you do differently the next time you write? Keep in mind that the P.O.W.E.R. approach represents a general process and that you may choose to emphasize particular stages according to what works best for you.

Above all, remember what you've accomplished. You've transformed what's inside your head—your thoughts, your ideas, your values—into something that can reach and potentially influence other people. Through your writing, you have exercised the ability to move others and get them to think in new ways. You've made a difference. That's the real power of writing. Refer to Try It! 4, "Thinking Critically about Writing."

Speaking Your Mind

Public speaking ranks right at the bottom of most first-year postsecondary students' rankings of their academic abilities.[2] In fact, surveys of the general population find that most people are more afraid of public speaking than of dying! It's not surprising. How often are we so totally exposed to others' scrutiny? Not only do we have to worry about the message we're communicating—just as with our writing—but in addition, each of us has to be concerned about nonverbal behaviour and the impression we are making: *Is my hair sticking up? This sweater was a big mistake. Are they bored? I wish my hands would stop shaking.*

Although you may always be a little nervous about public speaking, it's important to keep several points in mind:

- Audiences are generally sympathetic. They've all been where you are and probably share your fears about public speaking. They're on your side and are rooting for you to succeed.

- Once you start speaking, it will become easier. Anxiety tends to be highest *before* you start talking. Most people find that after they start a talk, their nervousness tends to decline.

- Practice helps. Practice and preparation for the talk will go a long way toward easing your tension.

Keep in mind, too, that in many fundamental ways, speaking is like writing. You need to consider who your audience is, muster your arguments, and decide how to sequence those arguments. Consequently, the P.O.W.E.R. writing framework that we presented earlier in the chapter applies to speaking as well:

- **Prepare** what you will say and how you will say it. Think about your audience and the occasion on which you will speak, and try to be sure your words match both audience and occasion.

Thinking Critically about Writing

Read the following short composition and identify what style of writing the author has used. What were the author's goals for this short essay? What are its strengths and weaknesses? What mechanical errors has the author made (if any)? How would you improve this composition?

A Modest Pride

It's not that I'm a weak guy, just that I had been somewhat self-conscious about my strength early on in my high school career. My gym class didn't help too much, either. Thanks to a demeaning test of strength appropriately dubbed the "Grip Test," once each semester I was provided the opportunity to squeeze a gadget, get a score, and have my teacher announce it out loud, no matter how high or (as in my case) how low it was. No matter how hard I tried, the cruel and callous scale never registered above 40. Almost every other male in the class could boast of a high-40s or mid-50s score. I hated that test with a passion. Until the last one. When my final semester rolled around and I had the gripper placed in my palm, I was prepared for the same old same old. I had been improving slightly from semester to semester, but nothing impressive ever happened. I drew in a deep breath, squeezed, looked at the scale, and almost passed out. Sixty-six! In a way only a teen could appreciate, for an accomplishment only a teen would find meaningful, I thought I was in heaven. My success was even sweeter as I watched jocks pale in comparison when they took the test. Sure, to some people my academic accomplishments seem fairly impressive, and I would agree. Yet the grip test situation was much more personal and represented success in an area I normally don't pay attention to. Plus I learned two things. One: I can pride myself on the smallest triviality. Two: I'm glad we didn't measure strength in our gym classes with the bench press.

- **Organize** your thoughts, using notes to cue you to the main parts of your presentation and making logical connections for your audience to follow.

- **Work** carefully during your presentation by speaking clearly and calmly to your audience and avoiding distracting mannerisms or body language.

- **Evaluate** your performance after you finish your presentation and ask others to evaluate it, too. Take notes on the feedback you receive from yourself and others.

- **Rethink** your entire approach to preparing for and delivering presentations each time you make one. Make the changes you feel will improve your performance.

Meeting the Challenge of Public Speaking

Although speaking and writing are both concerned with communicating your thoughts to others and they share many features, they are not the same. In fact, speaking presents several unique challenges. Among the factors that you need to take into account when you are speaking are these:

- **The first minute counts—a lot.** If you can get your audience's attention, arouse their interest, and engage them in the first few minutes, you're on your way to a successful speech. On the other hand, let them drift off early on and you've lost them—potentially for good.

How do you get them interested? There are several ways:

Begin with an anecdote. *"It was a scientist's dream, experienced as he dozed off in front of a fire, that led to one of the most important biological discoveries of all time."*

Start with a quotation. *" 'I have seen the enemy, and he is us.' But are we really the enemy? I believe . . . "*

Arouse their curiosity. *"I have a secret, one that I've kept hidden for many years—until now."*

Talk about the significance of the topic. *"If you think that global warming is not a problem, take a look at the changes in weather patterns across North America this year."*

Ask a question. *"Have you ever wondered how you could save enough money to buy a new car?"*

Use humour. *"My introduction to gardening was not promising: Seeking to surprise my mother, I 'weeded' her garden so enthusiastically that I pulled up all her flower seedlings."*

See Try It! 5, "Let's Talk."

- **Provide oral transition points.** When we're reading a textbook selection, we usually have the luxury of knowing exactly when a transition point occurs; it's marked by a title, section heading, or new paragraph. These markers help us construct a mental map that permits us to understand the overall structure of the piece we're reading.

Listeners don't have the same advantage. Unless the speaker orally signals that he or she is moving to a new part of a talk, listeners will get lost.

Career Connections

Write Away

The first and most memorable pieces of writing your prospective employer sees from you are a cover letter and your résumé. Remember these three key points:

1. In your cover letter, emphasize what you can do for the employer, not what the employer can do for you.

2. Summarize your qualifications. Learn the core competencies of the job you are applying for and highlight the ones that match your skill set.

3. Request an interview; the purpose of sending a cover letter and résumé is to get an interview.

Instead of ending your résumé with "References available on request," why not let the employer know you have a portfolio by closing with, "Portfolio available for review."

Preparation and confidence are key to any successful interview. Creating a portfolio is an intensive review of your skills and abilities, which ensures you are prepared. When you see all the demonstrations you have compiled, you will feel more confident and capable.

Logistics processes—such as supply chain management, transport, distribution, and inventory control—consume anywhere from 10 to 70 percent of company operating budgets and contribute roughly 10 percent to Canada's gross national product. The Canadian Professional Logistics Institute's unique website at <www.loginstitute.ca/prolog/infokit/> is a forum for logistics professionals and employers to communicate. Logistics professionals can create and maintain their own portfolios online with specialized software, for job searches and for career planning. At the same time, employers can post positions on the site. Based on the information given, the website will match portfolios and postings.

Let's Talk

Devise a one-minute opening to a talk about the thing you know most about in this world: you. The topic can be about one of your experiences or about anything that concerns you or reveals a little bit about your past, your feelings, or your opinions. Use any of the opening strategies that we've considered.

Which strategy are you going to employ? _____

Now write your opening:

_____

_____

_____

_____

_____

_____

_____

_____

_____

_____

_____

Now try it out on a friend or classmate. Remember: Limit what you say to the one-minute opening.

When you're finished, ask yourself these questions: How well do you think your strategy worked? Why? Would another strategy have worked as well or better? What did your audience think of your opening? Why do you think it had the effect it did? Did your opening make your audience want to hear more? Did your opening make you want to write more?

Not only will they be unable to understand the structure of the talk, they won't know where the talk is headed.

However, there are several ways to erect verbal signposts throughout a speech. By using phrases such as the following, you can alert listeners that a twist in the journey lies ahead:

"To understand the problem, we need to consider . . ."

"The problems are clearly daunting. But there are solutions. Let's consider some of them. . . ."

"Now that we've considered the solutions, we need to take a look at their costs. . . ."

"Let's go back for a moment to an earlier point I made. . . ."

"To sum up, the situation offers some unexpected advantages. . . ."

- **Avoid clichés.** "At the end of the day," "the bottom line," and "at this moment in time" are all examples of overused expressions that can irritate listeners and diminish the effectiveness of your presentation. Other sayings to avoid include "like," "24/7," "absolutely," "address the issue," "awesome," "ballpark figure," "basically," "bear with me," "I hear what you're saying," " in terms of," "it's not rocket science," "literally," "prioritize," "pushing the envelope," and "thinking outside the box."[3]

- **Make your notes work for you, not against you.** A speaker is giving a talk, and suddenly she loses her place in her notes. She fumbles around, desperately trying to find her place and figure out what comes next.

    It's a painful situation to watch—and even worse for the person experiencing the problem. How do you avoid finding yourself in such a predicament?

    One way is by thoroughly acquainting yourself both with what you are going to say *and* with your notes. Once again, practice is your best friend, but the type of notes you have also makes a big difference.

    There are as many forms of notes as there are speakers. Some speakers write out their entire talk in advance; others use no notes at all, counting on memorizing their talk. Avoid either extreme. If you write out your complete speech in advance, you'll experience an overwhelming urge to read it to your audience. Nothing could be more deadly. On the other hand, if you memorize your talk and have no notes at all, you'll be susceptible to a memory lapse that can make you feel completely foolish. Even if you can remember your talk successfully, you may end up sounding mechanical, like an amusement park guide who has given the same speech about the "jungle cruise" at least a thousand times.

Journal Reflections

How I Feel About Public Speaking

Just how do you feel about speaking in public? Explore your feelings—both positive and negative—by considering these questions:

1. How, in general, do you feel about public speaking? How much experience have you had speaking to an audience?

2. Do you think other people feel better about speaking in public than you do? Do most people you know like or dislike it?

3. Ask a few of your friends how they feel about public speaking. What was their reaction to the question?

4. What was the best experience you ever had with public speaking? Why was it positive?

5. How do you think your audience felt about your speaking while it was occurring?

6. What was the worst experience you ever had with public speaking? Why was it bad?

7. How do you think your audience felt about your speaking while it was occurring?

8. What is the worst part of public speaking for you: before, during, or after speaking?

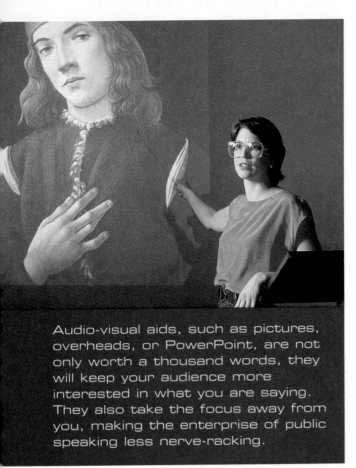

Audio-visual aids, such as pictures, overheads, or PowerPoint, are not only worth a thousand words, they will keep your audience more interested in what you are saying. They also take the focus away from you, making the enterprise of public speaking less nerve-racking.

The best approach is to choose a middle ground. Develop an outline that includes the major points you want to cover, and have this outline in front of you when you speak. It should be written or typed on a sheet of paper, or you might use index cards (number them!). In addition, write out and memorize your opening and closing statements.

By memorizing the opening and closing statements, you'll have the opportunity to look your audience in the eye and engage them nonverbally at two of the most crucial junctures in your talk—the beginning and the end. Using an outline for most of your talk permits you to sound natural as you speak. You'll probably use slightly different words every time you give your talk, which is fine.

- **A picture can save you a thousand words.** Maps, charts, photos, drawings, figures, and other illustrations add another dimension to a presentation, helping to engage listeners. Computer programs, such as PowerPoint, permit you to create graphics relatively painlessly.

  You can even use props. For example, if you are talking about a series of Supreme Court of Canada rulings, you might incorporate a gavel into your talk. Visual aids make abstract concepts more concrete and immediate.

  Visual aids serve another function. They can reduce your anxiety. You can be assured that when an audience is focusing on an illustration or prop, their attention is drawn away from you, at least temporarily. Just knowing this may be enough to lower your anxiety level. (Just resist the temptation to play with your props as you talk!) Refer to Try It! 6, "Prop Yourself Up."

- **Use the right amount and kind of practice.** After you've written your opening and closing statements, constructed an outline, and decided what visual aids to use, it's time to practise. It's not just the amount of practice that is critical. *How* you practise is as important as *how much* you practise.

  Running through your speech mentally will help you to familiarize yourself with your presentation, but you really need to give the speech out loud. Only by hearing yourself speak can you actually get a sense of how the presentation works as an oral presentation.

  Practise in front of a friend or classmate. It is only by actually trying out your talk in front of a warm body that you'll be able to approximate the experience of actually speaking in public, and your audience can provide you with feedback regarding what is working and what is not. Audio-taping or videotaping your talk can also be helpful, but if you tend to be your own worst critic, it is best to use someone else.

  How much practice is enough practice? You've probably done enough when you do a good job giving a talk twice in a row. That's sufficient. You don't want to overpractise. If you practise your talk too many times, you'll become so bored with it that the actual talk will sound canned and unconvincing.

Prop Yourself Up

Think of at least three visual aids or props that could accompany the various presentation ideas listed below:

a speech on the dangers of biological warfare

a three-minute talk on the times when lying is acceptable

a talk about the significance of the use of cell phones while driving

a review of a movie you've seen recently

- **Fight stage fright.** As you know, for many people, the mere thought of speaking in front of others causes a knot of fear to form deep in their gut. Even those who routinely speak in front of others experience some degree of anxiety. (Ask one or two of your course instructors if they ever feel nervous when teaching a class. You may be surprised at the answer you get.)

  Although you won't be able to alleviate your stage fright completely, several techniques can reduce the anxiety that public speaking produces. First, make sure you're wearing clothes that are comfortable and that make you feel pleased with your appearance on the day of a talk. If you feel good about your appearance, you'll be more relaxed.

  Five minutes before you get up to speak, take three slow, deep breaths. Concentrate on the feeling of the air going in and out of your body. If a particular part of your body feels tense, tighten it up even more and then relax it. Do it several times. Finally, visualize yourself giving the speech successfully and the relief that you'll feel afterwards.

- **Monitor your nonverbal behaviour.** Anxiety about public speaking can do strange things to people's bodies. Their hands may shake or feel icy cold. They may pace back and forth like a caged lion. They may sweat profusely. They may stand rigidly while speaking, looking like stiff toy soldiers. Or they may slump over a podium as if they wished they could dissolve into thin air.

  To avoid appearing as if you are scared to death—even if you are—stand up straight and tall. Let your hands fall comfortably at your sides, using them smoothly—not jerkily—when you need to gesture to make a point. Look directly at different members of your audience, shifting your gaze from one person to the next. Eye contact engages audience members, making them feel that your words are directed straight toward them.

If the thought of eye contact scares you, try a trick that some speakers use. Look directly at the *hairline* of different audience members; to your listeners, this is generally indistinguishable from eye contact, and yet it can help you avoid becoming distracted by a facial expression that you may interpret—or misinterpret—negatively: *Is she bored? Is he angry at what I'm saying?*

Speaking Off-the-Cuff:
Extemporaneous Speaking

What do you do when an instructor calls on you in class and asks, "What do you think the point of this poem is?" Just as anxiety producing as giving a prepared talk (and probably a lot more common) is public speaking that is extemporaneous. **Extemporaneous talks** are unprepared presentations that require you to speak on a moment's notice.

Extemporaneous talk

An unprepared, off-the-cuff oral presentation

Extemporaneous speaking happens far more frequently than you may like to think: your professor asks you to explain why organizations are moving to flatter structures; a coworker or classmate asks you to explain how a particular software program works; you visit your landlord to complain about the water heater that keeps breaking, and the landlord asks you for details about the problem. The response you give in each of these situations (and many others) is very much an exercise in extemporaneous speaking. Refer to Try It! 7, "Put Yourself on the Spot."

"PREPing" to Speak Extemporaneously Just because extemporaneous speaking is, by definition, unplanned, it does not have to be totally off the top of your head. There is a simple process that you can use when you're put on the spot. Known as the PREP formula, it consists[4] of breaking down an answer into four parts:

- **Point of view.** Initially provide your point of view, delineating a clear view of where you stand on the issue.

- **Reasons.** Provide the chief reasons why you believe your position is correct.

- **Evidence or examples.** Give specific evidence to support your point of view.

- **Point of view, restated.** Restate your point of view.

Here's an example:

Professor Fiske: Who can tell me whether First Nations land claims are a uniquely Canadian problem? Sylvie, why don't you take a stab at the answer?

Sylvie: I don't believe land claim issues are uniquely Canadian at all [**point of view**]. If we look at other times in history or at other parts of the world today, we find all sorts of land claims issues [**reasons**]. For example, consider the United States and Mexico. Or look at the difficulties that Zimbabwe is having. Or look at Australia or New Zealand [**evidence or examples**]. So, it's hard for me to understand how anyone could contend that land claims are uniquely Canadian. Settling Aboriginal land claims is a complicated issue many nations are now dealing with [**point of view, restated**].

Working in a Group: Put Yourself on the Spot

Each member of a class group should write two questions on separate note cards. Some examples: "Are basketball players paid too much?" "What's the best way to wash dishes?" "How can you get people to exercise more?"

Place the cards, face down, on a table. Have the first group member choose one of the cards at random and immediately answer the question using the PREP system. Every person should take a turn answering a question.

After each person gives an extemporaneous speech, evaluate the responses by answering the following questions as a group: Generally, how effective was the person's response to the question? What were its greatest strengths? What could have been done better?

Although using the PREP system may seem awkward at first, you'll find it easy to learn. And with sufficient practice, it will become automatic, saving you lots of mental scrambling the next time you're called on in class.

Remember: You're Already an Accomplished Public Speaker

Speaking in front of others is something you've done all your life. It may have been in moments of intimacy or friendship with just one other person present. It may have been with a group of friends deciding on what kind of pizza to order, with you arguing against anchovies and your friends arguing in favour. It may have been as an athlete, with you shouting encouragement to your teammates. The point is that you've already spoken in front of others—lots of times.

When you are faced with giving a formal presentation, then, give yourself credit for the times you've already spoken publicly. Let go of your fears and enjoy your moment in the spotlight. You may well find that the ability to impart what you know to others is a satisfying and rewarding experience.

> "If you have an important point to make, don't try to be subtle or clever. Use a pile driver. Hit the point once. Then come back and hit it again. Then hit it a third time—a tremendous whack."
>
> Sir Winston Churchill

Speaking of Success

John Lu

*B.A. Advanced, Economics, University of Manitoba;
Creative Communications Program Diploma, Red River
Community College*

In April 1997, John Lu decided to turn his back on a stable, lucrative career in the financial industry to pursue his love of language. Armed with a B.A. in economics and with almost 11 years of experience working for a major Canadian bank, John enrolled in the Creative Communications program at Winnipeg's Red River College in 1998.

"It's great to dream and when you put that dream into action, it becomes a goal," John says of his dream of starting a career in TV journalism. Ironically, John says he wasn't particularly goal oriented in university, but when he returned to community college, he made the most of his opportunity at RRC. "I have never been more successful in an academic setting than I was in community college."

In his final year at RRC, John had an internship at Winnipeg's CTV affiliate, CKY5, which landed him a part-time job as a news reporter. However, a subsequent internship at The Sports Network (TSN) led to a full-time offer he couldn't refuse. John is a sports fan and plays sports as well, so a job offer with the na-

tionwide sports network was doubly attractive.

In addition to sports reporting, John has now had several stints on the anchor desk, which allows him to develop his skill set into that of a complete broadcaster. Now that he has several years' experience at TSN, John says he has a greater comfort level in his job, but still retains the excitement and enthusiasm he has

always had. John says there is a lot to be said for doing what you enjoy, and that a bad day at TSN is better than most good days at other places!

Every career in journalism, whether print or broadcast, is based on writing. John was used to writing university essays, but in college he practised several different styles of writing, including scripts, poetry, and prose, to improve his skills. As for being in front of the camera, he admits he likes "hamming it up." He credits singing in choirs, being in a

band, emceeing, and taking part in amateur drama productions with his being comfortable in front of people. John says it was an easy adjustment to go from being in front of a live audience to reporting to thousands of sports fans on TV.

John says that while it is important to work hard in college, it is more important to work smart. To that end, he made the most of the intense and interactive program at Red River College, enjoying the sense of camaraderie he developed among his peers. Respect for his classmates has transferred to his coworkers; John's philosophy is to "treat them well." Sports has its share of big egos, but John believes in being humble.

John's career has had many highlights, including covering the 2003 World Series, the 2004 Toronto Maple Leafs training camp in Stockholm, Sweden, and the 2004 World Cup of Hockey. And who knows, perhaps he will be covering the 2008 Olympic Games from Beijing. John is brushing up on his Mandarin just in case.

What are the best techniques for getting started and writing a first draft?

- Freewriting and brainstorming can help you choose a topic.
- Identifying the audience for writing is essential.
- Breaking down large writing tasks into smaller, more-manageable pieces helps pave the way for completing a writing assignment.
- Good organization, which is essential to both writer and reader, often follows the ABBCC structure: argument, background, body, counter-arguments, and conclusion.

How can I move from my first draft to my final draft?

- Use your outline as your roadmap.
- Begin the first draft by plunging in, starting anywhere in the paper.
- Revision is an essential part of writing; most of writing is rewriting.

How can I lose my fears of public speaking and make effective oral presentations?

- Although public speaking can be intimidating, audiences are generally sympathetic, speaking becomes easier once it is underway, and practice leads to success.
- The first minute of the presentation, oral transition points, visual aids, and having enough practice are important.
- Use the PREP system to give extemporaneous (unrehearsed) talks.

P.O.W.E.R. Portfolio

Writing and Speaking

1. Writing samples are frequently included in portfolios to demonstrate competence, skills, and range of experience. Consider including writing samples that closely relate to your academic or career goals. For example, if you were headed toward a health-related career, objective description, accurate summaries, case histories, and daily charts or logs would be appropriate inclusions. If you were considering a career in communication arts, suitable entries would be scripts, articles, stories, press releases, brochures, newsletters, and printouts from Web pages. If your goals are primarily academic, include samples of your best analytical essays, reports, or critiques, and keep adding submissions as your writing skills develop. Remember to include your reasons for including specific writing samples and what they signify about you.

2. Consider including evidence from speeches, oral presentations, panel discussions, or other public speaking venues. You can include programs, scripts, printouts from PowerPoint presentations, photographs, and instructor's grade sheets and comments. So many jobs today require presentation skills that it is essential to prove your mastery in this area. Your reflective comments should indicate what you learned and your goals for the future.

3. Most people have a resume, but now is an ideal time to update or renovate your resume and include it in your portfolio. Consider keeping your resume file on your portfolio disk, so your data stays together. Make sure your document is up to date and error free. Write a cover letter to go with your resume. Again, reflect and comment.

Writing a Resume Although most employers have very specific expectations for what they look for in a resume and what style resume they want, some elements of resumes are quite predictable. Following are some specific points you should include in a resume:

- **Personal Information**
  Name—your full name, typed in capital letters.
  Address—your address, written out in full, without abbreviations.
  Telephone—your home phone number with area code
  E-mail Address—use a neutral or professional-sounding e-mail address.
- **Job Objective** Briefly describe your job objective so the employer knows exactly what type of work you're looking for. Relate your job objective to the position you're applying for.
- **Related Skills** List your skills and abilities associated with the job you're applying for. These can be from paid or unpaid work, volunteer experience, field or cooperative education placements, or hobbies. Consider including employability skills you identified earlier in P.O.W.E.R. Learning.
- **Education** List your education, starting with the most recent degree or diploma program or course and working backwards. This is called reverse chronological order. Include the name and location of postsecondary schools you attended, the type of programs you took, your areas of interest, and the years you completed.
- **Additional or Specialized Education or Training** Certificates or diplomas should also be listed, including those for short courses, such as computer or software courses, first aid or CPR programs; special licences or qualifications; or any other instruction that might be useful to the job you want.
- **Work Experience** List the companies or organizations where you have worked, volunteered, or completed work placements. Include locations (cities and provinces) and dates (year) you worked.
- **Duties** Outline the type of tasks you performed, focusing on duties that took the most time, or involved the most responsibility. Include from three to five duties for each job.
- **Additional Experience** Use this section to include other information, such as additional languages you speak, software programs you know, and other abilities that relate to the job.
- **Interests/Activities** Briefly mention those interests and activities that demonstrate qualities employers may value. For example, bike riding, hiking, and amateur sports may show an interest in health and fitness. Be sure to mention achievements or awards you may have received.
- **References** References are not included in your resume, but you should have them ready if they are requested. Ask permission before including someone on your reference list. You should have the names of three references with their current addresses and telephone numbers.

An example of a student resume is shown on the next page.

Thomas S. Thapa
195 Millfield Drive
Oshawa, Ontario, L5M 1M8

Phone: (903) 555-1316   E-mail: progrmr@yahoo.ca

OBJECTIVE

To obtain a full-time position as a computer programmer analyst in a high-tech organization where I can contribute fully and continue to develop my skills

EDUCATION

Durham College, Oshawa, Ontario
Diploma, Computer Programmer Analyst (2005)
* Graduated with an A average

SKILLS

Computer Software/Programming
* DOS/Windows... Microsoft Visual Basic, Visual C++, XML, ABAP Programming
* Object-oriented development of Windows-based client/server systems
* Reliable systems combining with COM and Internet technologies
* Oracle Database
* Server side programming with PHP
* Interface Design & Web Architecture

Teamwork/Problem-Based Learning
* Team-member studying programming languages, database design/development
* Integrate programs with varieties of network delivery systems including Internet/Intranet systems

COOPERATIVE EDUCATION WORK EXPERIENCE

Web Page Developer   Lawson Technologies, Milton, Ontario   2005
* Publication of client website on the Internet
* Setting up of client hosting, e-mail, and statistics for client websites
* Performing manual and/or electronic search engine registrations for client websites
* Search engine optimization
* Providing technical support for clients

Programmer   Technology in Motion, Oshawa, Ontario   2004
* Computing support and development
* Development of learning tools
* Software and hardware installation and testing
* Development of software templates

ACTIVITIES AND INTERESTS
* Treasurer, International Students' Association
* Hiking, rock climbing, trekking
* Playing guitar

REFERENCES

Available upon request

Resources

On Campus

If you are having difficulties with writing, the first place to turn is to a co-operative classmate. Ask someone to read a draft of a writing assignment. He or she may be able to make enough constructive comments to allow subsequent drafts to come more easily. In addition, some colleges and universities have writing clinics where you can bring a draft of your paper and work with a counsellor or peer tutor. Finally, your instructors may be willing to read preliminary drafts of your work.

In Print

Canadian author Martin M. Antony addresses the anxiety that affects many people when considering public speaking in *10 Simple Solutions To Shyness: How To Overcome Shyness, Social Anxiety & Fear of Public Speaking* (New Harbinger Publications, 2004). This book also deals with social anxiety, a common problem that can affect school and workplace communication.

Hamilton Gregory's book, *Public Speaking for College and Career* (McGraw-Hill, 7th edition, 2005), provides an excellent introduction to public speaking. It is filled with tips for planning and delivering oral presentations.

Michael Harvey's book, *The Nuts and Bolts of College Writing* (Hackett Publishing Company, 2003), provides useful information for postsecondary writers.

On the Web

The following sites on the World Wide Web provide the opportunity to extend your learning about the material in this chapter. Although the Web addresses were accurate at the time the book was printed, check the P.O.W.E.R. Learning website, <www.mcgrawhill.ca/college/power>, for any changes that may have occurred.

www.utoronto.ca/writing/other4.html
The University of Toronto has an excellent online writing support site. A particularly useful Web page is the Online Resources for Students of English as a Second Language, which provides links to many helpful sites.

http://web.uvic.ca/wguide/Pages/MasterToc.html
A very comprehensive site, the University of Victoria's Writer's Guide provides sample essays, a complete list of literary terms, and helpful information on topics such as citing sources, grammar, and spelling.

http://people.hsc.edu/faculty-staff/cdeal/mainsections/student.html
Hampden-Sydney College's Online Speaking Centre is a very instructive site with lots of information on various types of oral presentations, including group presentations. It also includes a section on ethical speaking to help students avoid verbal plagiarism.

The Case of . . .

the Reluctant Speaker

"No one," thought Maggie Ryan to herself, "could hate public speaking more than I do."

Maggie, who already thought of herself as somewhat shy, was horrified at the thought of giving a presentation. Not only did she not like talking in front of others, exposing herself to their scrutiny, but also she was conscious of her strong Newfoundland accent, which her friends at the Western community college she attended teased her about.

Maggie was sure she'd never be able to stand up in front of the class. She made up her mind to ask her instructor whether she could write a paper instead of making the oral presentation. But before she could, one of her friends in the class told her that he had already asked for an alternative assignment for himself and that the instructor had flatly refused. The instructor had merely said that it would be a "good experience" to give the talk.

Maggie was stuck.

1. How would you advise Maggie to prepare and organize for her talk?

2. Maggie expressed a willingness to write a paper instead of giving a talk. Should she prepare the paper and read it for her presentation? Why or why not? How might she use the research for her paper to help with her talk?

3. Maggie is especially nervous about speaking because she believes that her accent interferes with understanding. How might she deal with this particular anxiety? How could friends or classmates help her?

4. Do you think props would be helpful for Maggie? What purpose might they serve?

5. What advice would you give Maggie about what to do during her talk to reduce her anxiety?

6. What tips would you give Maggie to ensure her audience is engaged?

Improving Your Memory

9

The Secret of Memory

Prepare: Determining What You Need to Remember

Organize: Relating New Material to What You Already Know

Work: Using Proven Strategies to Memorize New Material

Journal Reflections: What Sort of Memory Do I Have?

Career Connections: Memory on the Job

Evaluate: Testing Your Recall of New Information

Rethink: Consolidating Memories through Repeated Review

Speaking of Success: Elaine Hudson

The Case of . . . the Group of Seven

The stack of note cards kept getting higher and higher.

And as it grew, so did Jamila Hassan's sense of panic. Jamila had methodically written each new accounting vocabulary word she had encountered over the term onto an index card, just as her instructor had recommended. But as the term wore on and the stack grew higher, Jamila felt she'd never be able to memorize all the words in time for the final exam. There were already so many words, and there were still a few weeks left in the term. How could she ever manage to recall them all?

Jamila decided that desperate measures were called for. She began to take her stack of cards with her everywhere she went. Whenever she had a spare moment, she would shuffle through the cards, trying to memorize the words, one by one. She sometimes felt a little silly, sitting in the laundromat, eating meals, and riding on the bus with her thick stack of cards, but as she spent more time going over the words, she became more confident, and she began to recall more of them each time she reviewed them.

It worked! By the time of the final exam, half of which consisted of defining key terms, Jamila was thrilled to realize that she had succeeded in memorizing most of the words. The exam was easy for her, and she ended the semester with an A in the course.

Looking
Ahead

Most of us have experienced the challenge of memorizing a seemingly insurmountable amount of information, and we tend to focus on our memory failures far more than our successes. But the truth is that our memory capabilities are truly astounding. If you are like the average college or university student, your vocabulary contains some 50 000 words. You know hundreds of mathematical facts, and you can recall detailed images from scenes you saw years ago. In fact, simply cataloguing the memories you already have might well take a lifetime.

In this chapter, you'll learn how you can improve the memory skills you already have. We'll examine what memory is, why it sometimes fails us, and how this can be prevented. You will also become acquainted with specific ways you can learn information that will help you recall it when you need to.

After reading this chapter, you'll be able to answer these questions:

- **What is memory and how does it function?**

- **Why might I have problems with memory, and how can I deal with those problems?**

- **What are some techniques I can use for memorizing information?**

The Secret of Memory

There's one well-kept secret about memory, and you should never forget it: You remember everything.

Sure, sometimes you have trouble recalling information that you know you've learned. Or maybe you don't recall that you learned it, even though you did. But this is not because information has disappeared from your head; the problem is one of *retrieval*. **Retrieval** entails finding information stored in memory and returning it to consciousness for further use. Every piece of information that you've ever learned—if you really learned it at some point in the past—is buried somewhere in your brain. The problem is that you can't always find it.

The proof of this assertion comes from the biology of memory. Consider what happens when you're exposed to some new material. Say your geometry instructor spends a class talking about the Pythagorean formula in geometry, which maintains that the square of the length of the hypotenuse of a right triangle is equal to the sum of the squares of the lengths of the two other sides. (You may recall this formula as $a^2 + b^2 = c^2$.)

When you first learn the formula, the wiring connecting a handful of the 70 trillion or so brain cells in your head is changed—forever. The information on the Pythagorean formula is etched into some tiny part of your brain, and unless that part of the brain is damaged in some way through injury or disease, it will stay there for the remainder of your life. This doesn't mean that you will easily find the information when you need it. But it does mean that that particular piece of information remains patiently in place, potentially retrievable the next time you encounter a geometry problem.

The practical outgrowth of this biological process is straightforward: You already remember everything you need to know, and a lot more. With some effort, you could remember the names of everyone in your third-grade class. You know what you ate when you went to the eighth-grade dance. You remember the name of the body of water that borders Iraq. And you even could have remembered where you left your keys the last time you misplaced them.

> "A retentive memory may be a good thing, but the ability to forget is the true token of greatness."
>
> Elbert Hubbard, *The Note Book*

The key to successful recall is to learn the material initially in a way that will allow you to recall it easily later. If you have trouble remembering material that you've already learned, then the trick is figuring out a way to retrieve that material from memory. In short, we need to devise ways to free the memories that reside within our brains.

As important as memory is, however, forgetting is helpful at times, too.

The Value of Forgetting

Legend has it that the actress Ingrid Bergman once said, "Happiness lies in good health and a bad memory."[1]

Although it's tempting to think of forgetting as the enemy of memory, in fact it's just the opposite. If we never forgot anything, think how cluttered our minds would be. Forgetting permits us to disregard inconsequential details

Retrieval
The process of finding information stored in memory and returning it to consciousness for further use

Remember Details

Read the following story. Pay attention to the details, but don't take notes or make lists.

Demain entered the marketplace slowly, feeling his way. He had never seen such confusion.

Hundreds of wagons, caravans, booths, and carts were drawn up in a broad U-shape, occupying three sides of the enormous town square, their awnings and curtains open and inviting. The colours and odours were a sensual assault; he perceived them not just through his eyes and nose, but as if they were pressing forcibly against his skin. And the sounds! He could scarcely keep himself from bolting back the way he had come, to the safety of the countryside.

A sense of wonder pushed him forward. He walked past gold merchants, with their grey cloaks and watchful eyes, and a potter, her shop filled three shelves high with vases, bottles, and jars of deep blues, reds, and yellows that Demain—accustomed to the brown clay that adorned his mother's kitchen—had never even imagined possible. Cloths were on sale in the booth next to the potter's—shamelessly long bolts of impossibly patterned prints, depicting herons, bulls, schools of fish, a field of wheat, great bowls of fruit, and men and women engaged in the pursuits he knew from stories: They danced in bold colours and graceful postures, harvested vast fields of bounty, fought battles of intricate strategy, and drank and courted in riotous taverns.

Past the dealers in rugs, chairs, hats, shoes, and wagons; past the blacksmith's huge muddy arms beating out rugged tools and fine weapons; past the fortune tellers and musicians, Demain at last came to the vendors of food and drink. Never had he felt so hungry. He was lifted off his feet—he swore he was floating—by the aroma of long lines of sausages, sides of beef, whole lambs, chickens on spits the length of spears, bacon and hams, fried potatoes, great vats of boiling vegetables, stewing tomatoes, and breads—all shapes and sizes of loaves, twisted into braids, curled into circles, flattened, puffed, elongated, pocketed, and glazed.

Demain felt the two coppers in his pocket—his holiday bounty—and hoped they would be enough.

Note: We'll return to the story of Demain later. For now, read on . . .

about people, experiences, and other sources of information that otherwise would burden us.

For example, would it really be useful to know that we dropped our fork in the middle of dinner six weeks ago? Would it be helpful to remember that a professor wore the same stained sweater six classes earlier? Would our lives be any richer if we knew that the subway car we took a day ago had a defaced advertisement for sunscreen? One man—whose memory was so good that he could repeat passages that he'd read 15 years earlier (in a foreign language he didn't even speak!)—was dull and disorganized. He couldn't even read with ease, because virtually every word he came across evoked a tidal wave of memories from his past.

In short, think of forgetting as a friend that permits your memory to operate at peak efficiency. Of course, forgetting shouldn't be your *best* friend. The focus of this chapter will be to figure out how to hold onto memories that we want to keep, using the strategies summarized in the P.O.W.E.R. Plan on the next page.

Prepare: Determining What You Need to Remember

Memorize what you need to memorize. Forget about the rest.

The average textbook chapter has something like 20 000 words. If you had to recall every word of the chapter, it would be nearly impossible. Furthermore, it would be a waste of time. Being able to spew out paragraphs of material is quite different from the more important ability to recall and deeply understand academic material in meaningful ways.

It helps to approach learning the material in a chapter in a different way. You are not going to learn or memorize 20 000 words, but within those words there may be only 20 concepts that you do need to learn. And perhaps there are only 10 keywords that are totally unfamiliar to you. *Those* are the pieces of information that should be the focus of your efforts to memorize.

In short, the first step in building a better memory is to determine just what it is that you want to recall. By extracting what is important from what is less crucial, you'll be able to limit the amount and extent of the material that you need to recall and you'll be able to focus on what you need to remember. See Try It! 1, "Remember Details," on the previous page.

To determine what is important, look at the overall, big picture. Don't get lost in minute details. Instead, prepare yourself by taking a broad overview of the material you need to know and decide what your goal is going to be.

Organize: Relating New Material to What You Already Know

PREPARE

Determine what you need to remember

ORGANIZE

Relate new material to what you already know

WORK

Use proven strategies to memorize new material

EVALUATE

Test your recall of new information

RETHINK

Consolidate memories through repeated review

P.O.W.E.R. Plan

Don't think of memorization as pumping gasoline (new information) into an almost-empty gas tank (your brain). You're not filling something that is empty. On the contrary, you are filling a container that already has a lot of things in it, that is infinitely expandable, and that never empties out.

If you approach each new memorization task as something entirely new and unrelated to your previous knowledge, you'll have enormous difficulty recalling it. However, if you connect it to what you already know, you'll be able to learn it more easily and recall it far better than if you just dump it into your head. The way to get your brain to do this organizational work for you is by thinking about the associations the new material has with the old.

> "Human memory works its own wheel, and stops where it will."
>
> William Saroyan, *Chance Meetings* (1978)

Say, for example, you need to remember information about the consequences of global warming, such as the fact that the level of the oceans is predicted to rise. One way to think about the new material you want to remember is to relate it to information that you already possess.

What would help you remember a person's name after you were introduced for the first time?

For example, you might think about the rising level of the ocean as it relates to your personal memories of visits to the beach. You might think what a visit to the beach would be like with dramatically higher water levels, visualizing a severely reduced shoreline with no room for sitting on the beach. Then, whenever you think about global warming in the future, your mind is likely to associate this fairly abstract concept with its concrete consequences for beaches. The association you made while rehearsing the information makes it personal, long-lasting, and useful.

Memories can also be organized by place. *Where* you learn something makes a difference in how well you can recall it. Memory researchers have found that people actually remember things better in the place where they first studied and learned them. Consequently, one of the ways to jog your memory is to try to recreate the situation in which you first learned what you're trying to remember. If you memorized the colours that litmus paper turns when it is placed in acids and bases while you were lying in bed, it might be helpful during a test to recall the correct colours by imagining yourself lying on your bed thinking about the colours. By mentally recreating your previous study session in bed, you can jog your memory.

Another effective place-related strategy is to introduce new data into your mind in the place that you know you're going to need to recall it at some future moment. For instance, suppose you know that you're going to be tested on certain material in the room in which your class is held. Try to do at least some of your studying in that same room. (The reviewing techniques we covered when discussing notetaking in Chapter 5 will be very helpful in this way as well.) Then, when you take the test, the associations you've formed between the material and the physical location of your studying may aid recall.

W ork: Using Proven Strategies to Memorize New Material

One of the good things about the work of memorization is that you have your choice of literally dozens of techniques. Depending on the kind of material you need to recall and how much you already know about the subject, you can turn to any number of methods. Do the exercise in Try It! 2, "Organize Your Memory," on page 252.

As we sort through the various options, keep in mind that no one strategy works by itself. Choose a combination of strategies that works best for you, and feel free to devise your own strategies or add those that have worked for you in the past.

Review Your Notes After Class Research shows you forget up to 70 to 80 percent of material within 48 hours of class. You can change this simply by taking 10 to 15 minutes within one hour after class to review what

Rehearsal
The process of practising and learning material to transfer it into memory

Mnemonics
Formal techniques used to make material more readily remembered

you have learned. (Students who review in this manner tend to remember 70 to 80 percent of material two days later.)[2]

Rehearsal Think it again: rehearsal. Say it aloud: rehearsal. Think of it in terms of the three syllables that make up the word: re—hear—sal. Okay, one more time—say the word "rehearsal."

If you're scratching your head over the last paragraph, it's to illustrate the point of **rehearsal:** to transfer material that you encounter into memory. If you don't rehearse information in some way, it will end up like most of the information to which we're exposed: on the garbage heap of lost memory.

To test whether you've succeeded in transferring the word "rehearsal" into your memory, put down this book and go away for a few minutes. Do something entirely unrelated to reading this book. Have a snack, catch up on the latest sports scores on TSN, or read the front page of the newspaper.

Are you back? If the word "rehearsal" popped into your head when you picked up this book again, you've passed your first memory test. You can be assured that the word "rehearsal" has been transferred into your memory.

Rehearsal is the key strategy in remembering information. If you don't rehearse material, it will never make it into memory. Repeating the information, summarizing it, associating it with other memories, and above all *thinking about it* when you first come across it will ensure that rehearsal will be effective in pushing the material into memory.

Mnemonics This odd word (pronounced in an equally odd fashion, with the "m" silent—"neh MON ix") describes formal organization techniques used to make material more readily remembered. **Mnemonics** are in fact the tricks-of-the-trade that professional memory experts use, and you too can use them to recall the sort of list items you will often need to recall for tests. See Try It! 3, "Do It Yourself Acronyms and Acrostics," on page 254.

Among the most common mnemonics are the following:

Journal Reflections

What Sort of Memory Do I Have?

1. Overall, what kind of memory would you say you have: excellent, good, average, poor? Why?

2. What kinds of information do you remember best: faces, shapes, colours, smells, names, dates, or facts? Why?

3. What kinds of information do you have the greatest difficulty remembering? Why do you think this type of information is hard for you to remember?

4. Is there any particular source of information about which you can remember exceptional amounts, such as hockey records or movie trivia? Why do you think you remember this information so readily?

5. Think about some of the information from your early school years that you can still easily recall. What factors contributed to this information becoming firmly embedded in your memory?

6. What kinds of memorization techniques do you now use? Have you ever tried any in the past that didn't work? What do you think you can do to improve your memory?

7. Do you ever find yourself recognizing someone's face but being unable to recall the name that goes with it? What do you do? When you're introduced to new people, do you do anything special to remember their names? If so, what?

8. Do you ever feel that information is "on the tip of your tongue" but you just can't seem to retrieve it? Have you ever recalled the information you were seeking just a few minutes too late? What do you do if this happens?

Organize Your Memory

As critical thinking expert Diane Halpern points out, having an organized memory is like having a neat bedroom: Its value is that you know you'll be able to find something when you need it. To prove the point, try this exercise she devised.[3]

Read the following 15 words at a rate of approximately one per second:

girl

heart

robin

purple

finger

flute

blue

organ

man

hawk

green

lung

eagle

child

piano

Now, cover the list, and write down as many of the words as you can on a separate sheet of paper. How many words are on your list? _____

- **Acronyms**

    FACE

    Roy G. Biv

    P.O.W.E.R.

Acronym

A word or phrase formed by the first letters of a series of terms

You're already well acquainted with **acronyms,** words or phrases formed by the first letters of a series of terms. For instance, FACE spells out the names of the notes that appear in the spaces on the treble clef music staff ("F," "A," "C," and "E," starting at the bottom of the staff.) Roy G. Biv is a favourite of physics students who must remember the colours of the spectrum (**r**ed, **o**range, **y**ellow, **g**reen, **b**lue, **i**ndigo, and **vi**olet.) And P.O.W.E.R. stands for—well, by this point in the book, you probably remember.

The benefit of acronyms is that they help us to recall a complete list of steps or items. The drawback, though, is that the acronym itself has to be remembered, and sometimes we may not recall it when we need it. For

After you've done that, read the following list:

green

blue

purple

man

girl

child

piano

flute

organ

heart

lung

finger

eagle

hawk

robin

Now cover this second list and write down as many of the words as you can on the other side of the separate sheet of paper.

How many words did you remember this time? Did you notice that the words on both lists are identical? Did you remember more the second time? (Most people do.) Why do you think most people remember more when the words are arranged as they are in the second list? Does it seem plausible that the organization of the second list makes it easier to remember the words?

Working in a group: Discuss with your classmates ways in which you can organize material from one of your current classes to make it easier to remember.

instance, Roy G. Biv is not exactly the sort of name that readily comes to mind. And if we're unable to remember an acronym, it won't be of much use to us. Even if we do remember Roy G. Biv, we might get stuck trying to recall what a particular letter stands for. (For example, we'd probably prefer not to spend a lot of time during a test trying to remember if the "B" stands for brown, or beige, or blue.)

- **Acrostics.** After learning to use the acronym "FACE" to remember the notes on the spaces of the music staff, many beginning musicians learn that the names of the *lines* on the staff form the acrostic, "Every **G**ood **B**oy **D**eserves **F**udge." **Acrostics** are sentences in which the first letters spell out something that needs to be recalled. The benefits—as well as the drawbacks—of acrostics are similar to those of acronyms.

- **Rhymes and jingles.** "Thirty days hath September, April, June, and November . . . " If you know the rest of the rhyme, you're familiar with one of the most commonly used mnemonic jingles in the English language. Similarly, some of us learned the main theme of Schubert's *Unfinished Symphony* by singing the words "This is the symphony that Schubert wrote and never finished" when the theme first appears. For those who

Acrostic
A sentence in which the first letters of the words correspond to material that is to be remembered

Working in a Group: Do It Yourself Acronyms and Acrostics

In the first part of this Try It!, work individually to create an acronym and an acrostic.

1. Figure out a Great Lakes acronym using the first letters of their names (which are Erie, Huron, Michigan, Ontario, and Superior).

2. Devise an acrostic to help remember the nine planets in order of their average distance from the sun. Their names, in order, are Mercury, Venus, Earth, Mars, Jupiter, Saturn, Uranus, Neptune, and Pluto.

After you've tried to create the acronym and acrostic, meet in a group and discuss these questions: How successful were you in devising effective acronyms and acrostics? Do some of the group members' creations seem to be more effective than others? Why? Is the act of creating them an important component of helping to remember what they represent, or would having them created by someone else be as helpful in recalling them? For your information, a common acronym for the Great Lakes is **HOMES** (**H**uron **O**ntario **M**ichigan **E**rie **S**uperior), and a popular acrostic for the order of the planets is **M**y **V**ery **E**ducated **M**other **J**ust **S**erved **U**s **N**ine **P**izzas.

learned to recognize the symphony by using this mnemonic, it is virtually impossible to hear the symphony without recalling the words.

Although mnemonics are helpful, keep in mind that they have a number of significant shortcomings. First, they don't focus on the meaning of the items being remembered. Instead, mnemonic devices use characteristics such as the letters that make up the words being memorized. Consequently, the information is learned by rote, rather than by considering what it means and thinking critically about its relationship to other material. Because information that is learned in terms of its surface characteristics—such as first letters that form a word—is less likely to be retained than information that is learned in terms of its meaning, mnemonic devices are an imperfect route to memorization.

There's another problem with mnemonics: Sometimes it takes as much effort to create a mnemonic device as it would to memorize the material in the first place. And because the mnemonic itself has no meaning, it can be forgotten.

Despite their drawbacks, mnemonics can be useful. They are particularly helpful when the material being memorized includes a list of items or a series of steps.

The Keyword Technique Learning the vocabulary of a foreign language is often one of the toughest tasks for beginning students. The **keyword technique** can help ease the pain. In the keyword technique, a foreign

Keyword technique
A memory technique in which a foreign word to be learned is linked by an image to an English word with a similar sound

word is paired with a common English word that has a similar sound. The English word is known as the keyword.

For example, suppose you needed to learn the Spanish word for duck, which is *pato*, pronounced "pot-o." The first thing you'd do would be to think of an English word that sounds like "pot-o" and to picture it in your mind. One obvious choice would be a pot, simmering on a stove. This is your keyword.

The next step is to form an image in your mind that relates the meaning of the Spanish word to the image of the keyword. Because *pato* means duck, the desired image will relate a duck and a pot. The clear choice: a duck simmering in a pot on a stove.

Here's another example. The Spanish word for horse is *caballo*, pronounced "cob-eye-yo." In this case, you might link a horse with a corncob and an eye, both of which would be keywords, and come up with an image of a horse with huge, bulging eyes munching on a corncob. Or perhaps you could incorporate all three syllables of *caballo* and form an image of a horse with bulging eyes eating a corn cob and playing with a yo-yo. It's fine that the result is an outlandish image. In fact, the more eccentric the image, the easier it will be to recall.

The Method of Loci and the Peg Method: Special Help for Recalling Sequences and Lists

The ancient Greeks had a way with words. Their orators could deliver speeches that went on for hours, without notes. How did they remember what they wanted to say?

They used a procedure called the **method of loci**. *Loci* is the Latin word for "places," and it helps describe a procedure in which items in a sequence you want to remember—such as the sections of a speech or a series of events—are thought of as "located" in different places in a building.

Consider, for example, a speech that has three major sections: an introduction, a main body, and a conclusion. Imagine further that each of the three sections has various subcomponents that you need to recall.

To use the method of loci, you first visualize the living room, kitchen, and bedroom of a house with which you are familiar. Next, you mentally "place" the introduction of the speech into the living room of the house. You then mentally place each of the *parts* of the introduction on a different piece of furniture, following the way in which the furniture is laid out in the room (for example, you might proceed clockwise from the door). The easy chair might contain the first point of the introduction, the sofa the next point, and an end table the last point. Then you'd move into the kitchen and do the same thing with the body of the paper, laying out your arguments on different pieces of kitchen furniture or appliances. Finally, you'd end up in the bedroom, where you'd "place" the conclusion.

A close cousin of the method of loci is the peg method. The **peg method** uses a series of key words tied to numbers to help in the recall of numeric information. For instance, a set of "pegs" that you could use would link numbers with these words:

One is a sun,

Two is a zoo,

Three is me,

Four is a store,

Five is a dive,

Method of loci
A memory technique in which the elements in a list are visualized as occupying the parts of a familiar place

Peg method
A memory technique in which a series of memorized words is linked by images to a list of items to be remembered

Six are sticks,

Seven is heaven,

Eight is a gate,

Nine is a pine,

Ten is a den.

By thinking of exotic images using the peg words tied to the numbers, you can recall specific numbers that you need to memorize. For instance, suppose you had trouble remembering the value of *pi*, used to calculate the circumference of a circle (3.14, in case you don't remember). Translate the number into the relevant peg words—me (three), sun (one), and store (four)—and imagine an image linking the three. One obvious possibility is an image of yourself wearing sunglasses, heading out to a store on a sunny day. A less obvious and more exotic possibility is an image of yourself bowling a large sun into the front of a store.

The peg system can also be used to memorize ordered lists of items, when the sequence in which they appear is important. In this use, the peg system is very similar to the method of loci. You simply link images of the ordered set of items to the 10 "numbers." The first item is linked with the sun, the second with a zoo, and so on. Refer to Try It! 4, "Peg the Memory."

Involve Multiple Senses   The more senses you can involve when you're trying to learn new material, the better you'll be able to remember. Here's why: Every time we encounter new information, all our senses are potentially at work. For instance, if we witness a car crash, we receive sensory input from the sight of the two cars hitting each other, the sound of the impact, and perhaps the smell of burning rubber. Each piece of sensory information is stored in a separate location in the brain, and yet all the pieces are linked together in extraordinarily intricate ways.

What this means is that when we seek to remember the details of the crash, recalling a memory of one of the sensory experiences—such as what we heard—can trigger recall of the other types of memories. For example, thinking about the *sound* the two cars made when they hit can bring back memories of the way the scene *looked*.

You can make use of the fact that memories are stored in multiple ways by applying the following techniques:

Have you ever wondered how some waitstaff can remember what their customers have ordered without writing anything down? They use the same simple memory strategies that you can use to recall information you'll need to remember for tests.

- **When you learn something, use your body.** Don't sit passively at your desk. Instead, move around. Stand up; sit down. Touch the page. Trace figures with your fingers. Talk to yourself. Think out loud. It may seem strange, but doing this increases the number of ways in which the information is stored. By involving every part of your body, you've increased the number of potential ways to trigger a relevant memory later, when you need to recall it. And when one memory is triggered, other related memories may come tumbling back.

Peg the Memory

After you've learned the "peg" poem, it can come in handy in a variety of areas. Try it. Use the peg system to memorize the organization of the Canadian government in the list below. For instance, for the monarchy, think of an image that links the monarch with the sun (remember "one is the sun" from the poem). Do the same for the rest of the components of the government.

1. Monarchy: Monarch and Governor-General

2. Executive: Prime Minister, Cabinet, Privy Council, and federal departments

3. Legislature: Senate and House of Commons

4. Judiciary: Supreme Court, Federal Court, Tax Court

Now cover up the list. What is number two on the list? What is number four on the list?

How well did the peg method work for you? Do you see its value for other topical areas? If you are taking a foreign language class, can you apply the method? Could you apply it to other kinds of classes? Do you see any drawbacks to its use?

- **Draw and diagram the material.** We've already considered (in Chapter 5) the power of concept maps, the method of structuring written material by graphically grouping and connecting key ideas and themes. When we create a concept map, one of the things we're doing is expanding the modalities in which information can be stored in our minds.

Other types of drawing can be useful in aiding later recall. Creating drawings, sketches, and even cartoons can help us remember better. Your creations don't have to be great art, or detailed, involved illustrations. Even rough sketches are effective, because creating them gets both the visual and tactile senses involved.

- **Visualize. Visualization** is a technique by which images are formed to ensure that material is recalled. For instance, suppose you're told that memory requires three basic steps: the initial recording of information, the storage of that information, and, ultimately, the retrieval of the stored information. As you read the three steps, you probably see them as logical and straightforward processes. But how do you remember them?

You might visualize a computer, with its keyboard, disks, and monitor (as in Figure 9.1). The keyboard represents the initial recording of

Visualization
A memory technique in which images are formed

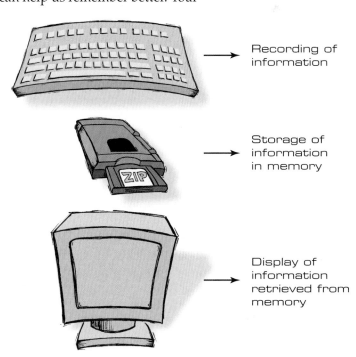

Recording of information

Storage of information in memory

Display of information retrieved from memory

Figure 9.1

information. The disk represents the storage of information. And the monitor represents the display of information that has been retrieved from memory. If you can put these images in your mind, it will help you to remember the three basic memory steps later.

Visualization serves several purposes: it helps make abstract ideas concrete, it engages multiple senses, it permits us to link different bits of information together, and it provides us with a context for storing information.

What kind of visualization works best? There's a simple rule: Weird is good. The more extreme, outlandish, and eccentric the image you create, the more notable it will be and so the easier it will be to remember. And if you can remember the image, you'll probably remember the information that's attached to it. Refer to Try It! 5, "Visualize the Possibilities."

Think Positively   Emotions matter. If you're in a negative frame of mind when you try to memorize something, your negative feelings can become attached to the memory, making you less likely to recall it because you'll automatically tend to avoid those bad feelings. The opposite is also true: If you think positively about the process of memorization, those more-positive feelings will end up being etched into your memory.

Of course, feelings can't be turned off in the same way we're able to turn off a light. If you feel nervous and scared about memorizing all the formulas you need to for your chemistry midterm, you can't just tell yourself it's great fun. But if you recognize your feelings, they lose much of their power to influence you and to block memories.

Overlearning   Think back to when you were learning your basic multiplication facts ($1 \times 1 = 1$; $1 \times 2 = 2$; and so forth). Let's suppose you had put each multiplication problem on a flash card, and you decided to go through your entire set of cards, trying to get every problem right.

> "A pessimist sees the difficulty in every opportunity; an optimist sees the opportunity in every difficulty."
>
> Sir Winston Churchill

The first time you went through the set of cards and answered all the problems correctly, would you stop there? Would you feel as if you'd actually learned and memorized them perfectly and that you'd never again make an error?

Probably not. The prudent assumption would be that you needed a few more instances of flawless performance before you'd be justified in concluding that you had adequately memorized the problems.

If this were your gut feeling—that you needed several instances of perfect performance to be sure you had learned the multiplication facts completely— you'd have stumbled on the principle of overlearning. **Overlearning** consists of studying and rehearsing material past the point of initial mastery. Through overlearning, recall becomes automatic. Rather than searching for a fact, going through mental contortions until perhaps the information surfaces, overlearning permits us to recall the information without even thinking about it.

To put the principle of overlearning to work, don't stop studying at the point when you can say to yourself, "Well, I'll probably pass this test." You may be right, but that's all you'll do—pass. Instead, spend extra time learning the material until it becomes as familiar as an old, comfortable shoe. At that point, overlearning has occurred, and you'll be able to recall the material with ease.

Overlearning
Studying and rehearsing material past the point of initial mastery, to the point at which recall becomes automatic

Visualize the Possibilities

You may have noticed how important visualization is to memory. In fact, many of the techniques we've discussed in this chapter rely in some measure on visualization, especially your visualization of extreme or absurd images.

Test the truth of this statement by drawing a concept map—itself a visual form of organizing material—of the concept of visualization. Using the space below, link as many other memory and mnemonic techniques to the word "Visualization" as you can. You may be surprised at the richness of your map.

Visualization

How well does the concept map reflect what you know about visualization? Is it a useful tool for you? Do you think that the act of creating a concept map itself is helpful in memorizing the material and that using someone else's concept map would be less helpful than creating your own?

Working in a group: Compare your concept map with those of your classmates. What are the major similarities and differences, and why do you think they occurred? Are some of the particular concept maps likely to help recall information about visualization more easily than others?

Career Connections

Memory on the Job

Increasing your memory skills is not important only in college or university; having a good memory will also be important to your career success.

Not all professionals need the same kind of memory skills. TV camera operators must remember lighting combinations, while physicians have to keep track of a host of medical conditions and medicines. But in all professions, memory abilities are crucial.

A particularly important skill is remembering people's names. Remembering the names of coworkers, clients, and contacts is important professionally, and it is also a sign of good manners.

Shannon Smith, founder of Premiere Image International Inc., <www.premiereimageintl.com/>, coaches individuals on improving social skills, self-presentation, image, etiquette, and memory skills. Her clients include CBC, CIBC, Royal Bank, Digital, Upjohn, and the Bank of Montreal.

To remember names, Shannon Smith suggests you follow these six steps:

1. **Listen closely.** Did you hear the name correctly? Ask for the name to be repeated or for the spelling.
2. **Use the name** throughout the conversation.
3. **Anchor the name in your mind** by associating it with something that will come to mind when next you meet. Perhaps something with the same name—or make up a rhyme—Joe White can fight.
4. **Imprint the "image" of the person** in your mind— something always makes someone stand apart. It could be the walk, tilt of head, or the style in which the person is dressed.
5. **Write it down.** Take time after a meeting to jot down the names of the people you met.
6. **Pay attention to the smallest detail!** Be observant and you'll be successful in remembering those names.

The big secret is paying close attention, as if that person were the only one in the room who mattered.

Evaluate: Testing Your Recall of New Information

The memory strategies just described can bring you to a point where you probably feel comfortable in your ability to remember the material you've been learning. Once you've used one or more of them to help you process the material you are learning, it's time to test yourself—to evaluate whether you'll be able to recall the material when you need it. There are several ways to evaluate your memory:

- **Use in-text review questions and tests.** Many textbook chapters end with a quiz or a set of review questions about the material. Some have questions scattered throughout the chapter. Don't avoid them! Not only do such questions indicate what the writer of the book thought was important for you to learn and memorize, but they can also provide an excellent opportunity for evaluating your memory.

  Even if you've answered the review questions earlier—while you were first reading the material (which is always a good idea), answer them again later as you study for the test and then the final exam.

- **Test yourself.** Temporarily transform yourself into your instructor, and prioritize what you're most likely to be tested on. Then create your own test, writing out some questions.

  Later, after as little as a few hours, take the test, and then grade it. How have you done? If you've achieved a "grade" that you're satisfied with, fine. If you've missed some key pieces of information, then you'll want to return to work and spend more time on memorization.

- **Team up with a friend.** When it comes to evaluating your memory, two heads are often better than one.

Working with a classmate can help you test the limits of your memory and assess areas in which you need work.

For instance, you and a friend can take turns testing yourselves, switching back and forth between asking and answering questions. Turn it into a contest: One of you can be Alex Trebek of *Jeopardy!*, and the other, a contestant. You can even work in groups. The important thing is to switch who's asking and who's answering the questions. Even when you're directing questions to others—officially evaluating their memory—you're giving your own memory a workout.

![R] ethink: Consolidating Memories through Repeated Review

Like fine wines, memories need time to age. Psychologists talk about this as the process of **memory consolidation.** What this means is that the physical links between brain cells that represent memory in the brain need time to become fixed and stable. This process explains why information is not suddenly and permanently established in memory the first time we're exposed to it. In fact, the process of consolidation may continue for days and even—in some cases—for years.[4]

Obviously you don't have years to wait. But it does pay to try to memorize material in advance of the time that you'll really need to use it. Then, when you go back to reconsider it, it will become even more well-established in your mind.

The phenomenon of memory consolidation explains why cramming is not a great idea. As we discussed in the chapter on taking tests, cramming is the process of spending the preceding evening or even the hours just before a test trying to memorize as much as possible. The memories that come from cramming simply don't last, because they aren't rehearsed and processed sufficiently. It's far more effective to distribute studying over many shorter sessions, rather than squeezing it into a single, long session just before a test. Fatigue and anxiety prevent long, last-minute practice sessions from being as effective as practice that is spread out.

The best way to ensure good memory is to return to the material even after your personal evaluation tells you that you can recall it easily. Wait several days, if possible, and then review it again. You'll be able to identify the aspects of the material that you know well, and the things that just haven't jelled yet in your memory. Rethinking the material not only permits you to take another look at what's in memory, but it also helps you identify where you need more work. Refer to Try It! 6, "Remember Demain."

Memory consolidation

The process by which the physical links between brain cells that represent memory become fixed and stable over time

The Canadian inventors of *Trivial Pursuit* knew how much fun memory games could be. Players know the value of having a teammate to help remember obscure facts. In the same way, studying with others can help you test and expand your own memory and reveal areas that need more work.

Remember Demain

Remember the passage earlier in this chapter (Try It! 1) about Demain, who found himself in the midst of a colourful, aromatic bazaar of booths and shops? Without turning back to the passage, write down everything you can remember about what Demain experienced in the marketplace—the shops, sights, and foods.

_____

_____

_____

_____

_____

_____

_____

_____

_____

_____

_____

_____

_____

_____

Now reread the passage, trying to remember its details by using one or more techniques from this chapter. You might use the method of loci, the peg method, the method of organizing ideas into chunks, or other techniques. Then answer these questions about the passage:

1. What scenes were depicted on the cloths? _____

_____

_____

2. What were the gold merchants wearing? _____

_____

3. After the cloth shop, what businesses did Demain pass to arrive at the vendors of food and

drink? _____

_____

4. What foods did Demain see and smell at the fair? _____

_____

_____

How would you assess your performance on these questions? Do you think you would have remembered more initially if you had used some of the memory techniques in this chapter? Do you see how you could employ these techniques in your own studying? Did one seem to work better for you than others?

Speaking of Success

Elaine Hudson

*Computer Information Systems—Networking Diploma,
Nova Scotia Community College (Truro)*

Elaine Hudson, who graduated from Nova Scotia Community College's Computer Information Systems—Networking Diploma with an A+ average, says that returning to school "was the best thing I've ever done for myself." As an adult student with high personal expectations and a solid work ethic, Elaine started NSCC with a strong commitment to school and was not satisfied until she did as well as she knew she could. For her academic excellence, Elaine received the prestigious *Alan Murray Award*, Xerox Canada Aboriginal Scholarship's top award.

To reach her academic goals after 20 years of working, Elaine had to work hard and organize herself well. Elaine admits that retention of material was a bit difficult at first due to the large amounts of course material to understand and remember as well as the fact that she was out of practice at studying. It was only after graduating that Elaine was diagnosed with Arteriovenous Malformation, a rare disease characterized by both motor and sensory deficits. Elaine's memory was somewhat affected and she had had to work all the harder to retain information and to excel academically.

Giving back to the community and helping others are very important to Elaine. She contends that compassion helps to extend people's vision,

NSCC
NOVA SCOTIA COMMUNITY COLLEGE
Education that **Works**

stating, "Too often our vision is directed inward to our own little corner of the world. We don't look outward until something happens to impact that. It is important for all of us to look outside ourselves and have some responsibility for the world around us. Many little inputs make a big impact." Elaine is employed doing accounting and computer work at Ulnooweg Development, a corporation that serves the needs of aboriginal small businesses in the Maritimes. She has also been involved in the Davis Inlet Relocation project, where she built a computer program that tracks people, properties, and property maintenance. In addition, Elaine devotes time to environmental and animal rescue issues and serves on the board of the Society for the Prevention of Cruelty to Animals.

Elaine encourages students to persevere and find other avenues if they find roadblocks to achieving their goals, saying, "Just do it! You may feel overwhelmed at times, but it will definitely be worth it!"

What is memory and how does it function?

- Information we actively process is permanently etched into the brain, but it is not always readily available for retrieval. The challenge is to recall information when we need it, and the key to effective recall is learning material in a way that makes recall easy.

- Forgetting is essential to permit us to disregard unimportant details and focus on what is important.

Why might I have problems with memory, and how can I deal with those problems?

- The problems we have with memory are mostly related to the inability to recall or retrieve information when it is needed. However, if information is rehearsed carefully, you can usually recall it more easily.

- Memory can be improved through careful preparation, by selecting in advance the pieces of information that are worthy of memorization and rehearsal.

- Another key to effective memorization is linking new information to information that is already in memory.

What are some techniques I can use for memorizing information?

- Many memory techniques are available to improve memorization. Rehearsal is a primary one, as is the use of mnemonics such as acronyms, acrostics, and rhymes.

- Other memory techniques are the keyword technique, the method of loci, the peg method, visualization, and the use of multiple senses while learning new material.

- Overlearning is a basic principle of memorization.

- Memory takes some time—days or even longer—to reach the point of consolidation, at which the physical links between brain cells that represent memory become stable. The need for consolidation explains why cramming is ineffective for long-term recall.

P.O.W.E.R. Portfolio

Keep It in Mind

Consider your most effective techniques for improving your memory and include examples in your portfolio, along with an assessment of and reflections on your memory skills. For example, a concept map with the skeleton of a major research paper, the acronyms you create for recalling the cranial nerves, or flash cards for remembering geological terminology not only demonstrate your perseverance, but can also indicate your creative problem-solving skills!

Resources

On Campus

If you have considerable difficulty in memorizing material compared with your classmates, it's possible that you might have a learning disability. If you suspect this, visit the campus learning disabilities office or counselling centre.

In Print

Harry Lorayne's and Jerry Lucas's *The Memory Book* (Ballantine, 1996) offers a simple system for improving memory.

Carol Turkington's *12 Steps to a Better Memory* (Pocket Books, 2003) is helpful if you want to have a better memory for lists and other difficult-to-remember material.

Your Memory: How It Works and How to Improve It, by Kenneth L. Higbee (Marlowe & Company, 2nd edition, 2001) deals with numerous memory techniques, such as the link and story, loci, peg, and phonetic mnemonic systems. Detailed and informative, students can learn to remember to-do lists, names and faces, speeches, concrete facts, dates, and numbers.

On the Web

The following sites on the World Wide Web provide the opportunity to extend your learning about the material in this chapter. Although the Web addresses were accurate at the time the book was printed, check the P.O.W.E.R. Learning website, <www.mcgrawhill.ca/college/power>, for any changes that may have occurred.

www.coun.uvic.ca/learn/program/hndouts/map_ho.html
This site aids in concept mapping, an effective memory aid that improves recall by building meaning structures around key concepts.

www.mindtools.com/memory.html
This comprehensive site provides several methods for improving memory. It includes examples of how each technique can be applied to such topics as remembering lists and foreign languages.

The Case of . . .

the Group of Seven

For Jason Marchuk, Canadian art history had always been a hard subject. Although he had no trouble with his studio art classes, he had difficulty keeping names, dates, and places straight.

Consequently, when his Art History instructor, Ms. Teeler, announced that a major exam was coming up, Jason panicked. He hadn't even finished all the assigned reading, and here he was expected to learn what seemed to be virtually everything there was to know about Canadian art history since 1665. Ms. Teeler had said that the test would focus in particular on Tom Thomson and the Group of Seven. When Jason couldn't even recall three members of the Group of Seven, he knew he'd better get started memorizing. But where should he begin?

1. How should Jason prepare for the exam? Should he simply get the art history textbook and start reading? Why or why not?

2. How can Jason prevent the facts of art history from appearing to be a jumble of random words and numbers? How should he use his existing knowledge to structure historical information? Why might this become easier the more often Jason does it?

3. Jason is expected to remember the names of the Group of Seven, names that seem unusual to him and very hard to remember. Which memory technique is likely to be most effective? How would it work?

4. To remember lists of events in the development of the Group of Seven, what technique would you recommend that Jason use? How would it work?

5. How could Jason use multiple senses while learning about Tom Thomson and the Group of Seven?

Making Decisions That Are Right for You

10

Making Good Decisions: A Framework

Prepare: Identifying Your Goals to Help Make Decisions

Organize: Considering and Assessing the Alternatives

Journal Reflections: My Decision Crossroads

Work: Making and Carrying out the Decision

Career Connections: Weighing Career Possibilities

Evaluate: Considering the Outcomes

Rethink: Reconsidering Your Goals and Options

Problem Solving: Applying Critical Thinking to Find Solutions

Don't Fool Yourself: Avoiding Everyday Problems in Critical Thinking

Speaking of Success: Jeff Goplin

The Case of . . . Left Holding the Lease

For Scott Gerofsky, the moment of truth was fast approaching. He had to make up his mind and decide what he was going to do when he graduated.

Throughout his university career, he had intended to go to law school, and he had majored in criminology. He had taken the LSAT, the pre-law standardized test, at the beginning of his fourth year and had done well. He had applied to law schools and been accepted at a decent one. It seemed that his future in law was well in hand.

Except for one thing: He was no longer sure he wanted to be a lawyer.

The reason for his indecision was a job that he had during the summer between his third and fourth years. Although he was just a glorified gofer on the film, *Mean Girls*, which was shot in Toronto, the director caught his attention. Directing looked like terrific fun, and the idea of becoming a film director had taken hold of him. Scott had spoken to the director, who had told him that it was a terrific, although high-stress, job. He also told Scott that the sooner he started working in the film industry, the better.

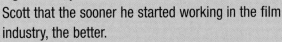

Scott couldn't shake the idea that he might be able to build a career in the movie industry. However, his girlfriend and family were dead set against the idea. His father argued that Scott should consider working in the film industry only after he got his law degree. But Scott was unconvinced; he didn't want to give up the idea of becoming a director in Toronto, Vancouver, or even Hollywood.

As his last semester went by, Scott knew he had to make up his mind. But which decision was the right one?

Looking Ahead

Like Scott, we all face important decisions in our lives at one time or another. How can we make the right decisions and avoid making the wrong ones? The best way is to employ some systematic, basic techniques that can help improve the quality of our decision making.

This chapter will give you a sense of what decision making is and is not and discuss a structured process that can help make your decisions the right ones. We'll also consider the related issue of problem solving. You'll confront a variety of problems as you proceed through college or university, and solving them will often be challenging. We'll look at several proven techniques for approaching and ultimately solving problems.

Of course, making decisions and solving problems is never easy. Sometimes the best decision or solution to a problem is one that doesn't initially occur to us because of the mental blind spots we all have. The best problem solvers and decision makers have learned how to use critical thinking to see around these blind spots. Consequently, we'll examine some common problems that can affect our thinking and discuss several biases that can make us jump too quickly to conclusions.

After reading this chapter you'll be able to answer these questions:

- **How can I improve the quality of my decisions?**

- **What strategies can I use for problem solving?**

- **What are some problems that affect critical thinking, and how can I avoid them?**

Making Good Decisions: A Framework

Making choices is a constant part of everyday life. **Decision making** is the process of deciding among various alternatives. Whether you are trying to decide between buying a Ford or a Honda, between renting an apartment that is close to your job and farther from campus or renting one that is close to campus but farther from work, or simply between having a hamburger or pizza—every one of these choices requires a decision. Some decisions are easily made and have few consequences, but others, such as whether to major in music composition or business administration, can be gut-wrenching and involve the deepest examination of beliefs and values.

Whatever the decision, however, it is possible to map out a strategy for making the decision that is best for you. Even though some decisions require more thought than others, every decision can benefit from systematically thinking through the options involved, based on the P.O.W.E.R. Plan illustrated on the right below.

Decision making
The process of deciding among various alternatives

 repare: Identifying Your Goals

Every decision starts with the end: what you want to accomplish by making the decision. Ask yourself why a decision is necessary and what you want to achieve by making it.

For example, suppose you are trying to decide between two alternative careers: either being a sales representative for a sporting goods manufacturer or working in and eventually running your own sporting goods store.

In such a case, the only way to make an appropriate decision is to know your goals. You need to consider both short- and long-term goals. For instance, becoming a sales representative would provide good benefits, such as health insurance, a company car, and a bonus plan. It would also allow you to meet colleagues with similar goals and interests and provide both opportunities to attend formal training programs and the chance to work your way up the corporate ladder.

On the other hand, although you might have a lower starting salary and fewer benefits working in a sporting goods store, there would probably be more job security. Even more important, it would give you the opportunity to achieve your long-term goal of learning how to run your own business. Both jobs might at first be equally rewarding in terms of satisfaction—new jobs tend to be exciting just because they are new—but one may grow stale, while the rewards of the other might continue to increase over the course of a career. In short, you need to consider both the short term and the long term when identifying your goals.

Thinking about the goals involved in decisions is an important process. Identifying the goals that underlie decisions

PREPARE
Identify your goals to help make decisions

ORGANIZE
Consider and assess the alternatives

WORK
Make and carry out the decision

EVALUATE
Consider the outcomes

RETHINK
Reconsider your goals and options

P.O.W.E.R. Plan

ensures that we make our decisions in the context of our entire lives and not just to provide short-term answers to immediate problems.

Organize: Considering and Assessing the Alternatives

Every decision is based on weighing various alternatives. Determining what those alternatives are, and their possible consequences, is often the most difficult part of decision making. Here's a process to help make sure you've considered all the alternatives.

Develop a List of Flexible Alternatives   It's important not only to think thoroughly about the obvious alternatives, but also to consider alternatives that are less obvious. For instance, if you are trying to obtain additional funds to support your school's theatre group, you might consider the alternatives of raising ticket prices for productions, holding a raffle to raise funds, or asking for sponsorship from a local business. After additional thought, you might reframe the issue as one of how to best place pressure on the school's administration to increase funding for your group.

The way you develop and frame alternatives is critical to the solution that you ultimately reach. The more alternatives you have, and the more ways that you conceptualize those alternatives, the better you will be able to come to a good solution.

How can you be sure that you've considered all the alternatives? You can't. But using the freewriting technique described in Chapter 8 can help you maximize your efforts to develop reasonable alternatives.

We've all been there: facing a mind-boggling array of similar choices. However, by systematically assessing the alternatives, it's possible to make an informed decision that will satisfy us.

Assess Alternatives Once you have generated as extensive a list of alternatives as possible, assess them. You need to follow three key steps when assessing each alternative:

1. *Determine the possible outcomes for each alternative.* Some outcomes are positive, some negative. Consider as many as you can. For example, if you are considering ways for solving transportation problems, one alternative might be to purchase a car. That alternative produces several potential outcomes. For example, you know that it will be easier to get wherever you want to go, and you might even have a better social life—clearly positive outcomes. But it is also true that buying and owning a car will be expensive, or you might get into an accident—both negative outcomes.
2. *Determine the probability that those outcomes will take place.* Some outcomes are far more likely than others. To take this into account, make a rough estimate of the likelihood that an outcome will come to pass, ranging from 100 percent (it is certain that it will occur) to 0 percent (it is certain that it will never occur). For instance, consider these possible outcomes to buying a car:

Alternative: Purchase car

Outcome	Probability
Easier transportation	100%
Greater expense	100%
Greater opportunities for part-time job	50%
Improve social life	30%
Get in accident	5%

Obviously, the probabilities are just guesses, but going through the exercise of estimating them will make the outcomes more real and will permit you to compare the various alternatives against one another more easily.

Journal Reflections

My Decision Crossroads

Have you ever made a decision that proved to be of great importance in terms of the direction your life would take? For example, perhaps you broke off a romantic relationship, or decided to quit a sports team because practice took up too much time, or participated in a deliberate act of civil disobedience during a protest rally. Reflect on that decision by answering these questions:

1. What was an important decision that you made that had significant effects on your life?
2. In what ways did that decision change your life?
3. What have been the main benefits (for yourself and others) that you derived from the decision?
4. What have been the main disadvantages (for yourself and others) of the decision?
5. Considering both the benefits and disadvantages of the decision, how would you judge your decision?
6. To what extent did you anticipate the effects the decision would have on your life?
7. Every decision to do something is also a decision not to do other things. What did your decision keep you from doing?
8. If you had it to do over again, would you make the same choice?

3. *Compare the alternatives, taking into account the potential outcomes of each.* After assessing the potential outcomes for the first alternative you're considering and the probability that it will occur, do the same thing for the next alternative, repeating the process for as many alternatives as you have devised. Finally, systematically compare each of the alternatives. Then ask yourself the key question: Which alternative, on balance, provides the most positive (and most likely) outcomes?

Obviously, not every decision requires such an elaborate process. In fact, most won't. But when it comes to major decisions, ones that potentially will have a major effect on you and your life, it's worthwhile to follow a systematic process.

Take a look at *Career Connections* on the next page for another process that you can follow to help you make a career decision.

W ork: Making and Carrying out the Decision

If all else fails, toss a coin to decide what alternative to follow. Tossing a coin at least brings you to a decision. Then, if you find you're unhappy with the result, you'll have gained important information about how you really feel regarding a particular choice.

Working through the previous steps will lead you to the point of decision: choosing one of the alternatives you've identified. Having carried out the steps will make the actual decision easier, but not necessarily easy.

Choosing among Alternatives The reason that important decisions are difficult is that the alternatives you have to choose from carry both benefits and costs. Choosing one alternative means that you have to accept the costs of that choice as the price for obtaining the benefits. And not choosing other alternatives means that you have to give up the benefits of the other alternatives, even though you have also avoided their costs.

What if, after going through the steps of the process laid out here, you still can't make up your mind? Try these strategies:

- **Give the decision time.** Sometimes waiting helps. Time can be an ally by giving you a chance to think of additional alternatives. Sometimes the situation will change, or you'll have a change in viewpoint. If you are having great difficulty making up your mind about something, decide to give the decision some time.

- **Make a mental movie, acting out the various alternatives.** Many of us have difficulty seeing ourselves in the future and envisioning how various options would play out. One way to get around this difficulty is to cast yourself into a series of "mental movies" that have different endings depending on the decision you make. Working through the different scripts in your head makes potential outcomes far more real and less abstract than they would be if you simply left them as items on a list of various options.

- **Toss a coin.** This isn't always as crazy or escapist as it sounds. If each alternative seems equally positive or negative to you, pull out a coin and assign each of the two alternatives to either side. Then flip it.

Career Connections

Weighing Career Possibilities

Some of the most important decisions you'll ever make concern choosing a career. Here's one method that can help you choose between different possible careers:

- Generate a selection of choices to consider after graduation. Make a list of possibilities—including work possibilities (e.g., computer programming, banking, teaching, health sciences, business, computer software development, etc.), study possibilities (e.g., business school, grad school), and even some dream possibilities (e.g., jazz musician, overseas stint with Crossroads Canada).

- Determine your values—they are most important things to consider when choosing an occupation. If you don't consider your values when planning your career, there's a good chance you'll dislike your work and, therefore, not succeed in it. For example, someone who needs autonomy would not be happy in a job where every action is decided by someone else. Generate a list of factors to use in assessing after-graduation possibilities. For instance, consider how the following factors will affect your career satisfaction:

  - the benefit to society of what you are doing
  - a good income
  - your parents' opinions
  - interaction with people
  - achievement
  - status
  - autonomy
  - job security
  - freedom and spare time
  - the likelihood of success
  - the everyday working conditions

- Determine how well a particular option fulfills each value you consider important. Systematically consider how a potential career fulfills each your values. One easy way to do this is to create a chart like the one in Table 10.1.

- Compare different choices. Using the chart, evaluate which of your possible choices most closely matches your values. Keep in mind that this is just a rough guide and that it's only as accurate as (1) the degree to which you know what is important to you and (2) your understanding of a given choice. Use the results in conjunction with other things you find out about careers—and yourself.

Workplaces have values as well. For Telus, Canada's second-largest telecommunications company, their values "inspire how we act and make decisions with each other as employees, with our customers, suppliers, and competitors, and in our communities." Telus's corporate values include (1) embracing change and initiating opportunity, (2) growth, (3) spirited teamwork, and (4) innovation. When considering a career, it is also important to know whether your values and your employer's values are in harmony.

Table 10.1

Making Career Decisions

Life-Satisfaction Considerations	Possible Choice #1 *Computer programming*	Possible Choice #2	Possible Choice #3	Possible Choice #4
Desire to benefit society	✓			
Good income	✓			
Parents' opinions	✓			
Friends' opinions				
Interest in the activity	✓			
Prestige of job				
Job security				
Good vacations				
A lot of spare time				
Likelihood of success	✓			
Working conditions				
Other:				
Other:				
Other:				
Other:				
Other:				

The real power of the coin-toss strategy is that it sometimes will help you find out your true feelings. It may happen while the coin is in the air or it may be that when you see the result of the coin toss, you won't like the outcome and will say to yourself, "No way." In such a case, you've just found out how you *really* feel about which alternative to choose.

- **Learn to view indecision as a decision.** Sometimes we spend so much time making a decision that our indecision becomes a decision. It works like this: Suppose a friend asks you to help her work on a student government task force that is studying the use of alcohol on campus. You'd like to participate, but, because you'll have to commit to a term-long series of meetings, you're worried about the expenditure of time it will take.

Because the first meeting isn't going to occur for a few weeks, you have some time to make up your mind. But you just can't seem to decide, even though you think about the pros and cons every once in a while. Finally, it's the day of the meeting, and you still don't know what to do.

The truth is, you've made the decision: You don't really want to be on the committee. Your indecision is telling you that you don't have sufficient interest to make the commitment. In some cases, then, viewing your own behaviour gives you the response to your question.

> "Generally, I take life one day at a time. Recently, however, I have become more goal oriented. This comes with age, I'm sure. You realize that life is short, and if you do not plan for your goals, they may not get done."
>
> Marlene Luscombe, Student, Trent University

- **Go with your gut feeling.** Call it what you like—gut feeling, intuition, superstition—but sometimes we need to go with our hearts and not our minds. If you've thought rationally about a decision and have been unable to determine the best course of action but have a gut feeling that one choice is better than another, then follow your feelings.

    Following a gut feeling does not mean that you don't need to consider the pros and cons of a decision rationally and carefully. In fact, generally our "intuitions" are best when informed by the thoughtfulness of a more-rational process.

Carrying out the Decision Ultimately, decisions must move from thought to action—they need to be carried out. Consequently, the final stage in making a decision is to act on it. You need to turn what you've decided on into behaviour.

Evaluate: Considering the Outcomes

Did you make the right decision?

Even if you've spent time and mental effort in thinking through a decision, you still need to consider the results. Even well-considered decisions can end up being wrong, either because you neglected to consider some aspect or alternative or because you or the situation changed.

For instance, suppose you were trying to decide between a major in management or information technology (IT). If you decide to go into management, it means that you'll be taking more courses related to finance and economics than if you had decided on an IT major. As you take these courses, you will be finding out whether you're enjoying them and how comfortable you feel with them. If you find you are consistently unhappy with these courses (and therefore your choice of major), you should allow yourself to re-evaluate your decision and reconsider the alternatives. It's not too late to change your mind about your decision.

> "Nothing is more difficult, and therefore more precious, than to be able to decide."
>
> Napoleon I, *Maxims* 15

In fact, even major decisions are often reversible. That's why it's so important to evaluate your choices. If you chose the wrong alternative, reverse course and reconsider your options.

It's not bad to change your mind. In fact, admitting that a decision was a mistake is often the wisest and most courageous course of action. You don't want to be so rigidly committed to a decision that you're unable to evaluate the consequences objectively. Give yourself permission to be wrong.

Rethink: Reconsidering Your Goals and Options

We can get to most places by multiple routes. There's the fastest and most direct route, which will get us to our destination in the least amount of time. Then there's the longer, more scenic route, where the trip itself provides pleasure. You can "take the long way home," as the song goes.

Is one route better than the other? Often not. Both take us to our destination, so we've succeeded no matter which way we've chosen. However, the experience of reaching our goal will have been very different.

Decisions are similar to travelling down different routes. There's often no single decision that is best for us, just as there's often no single road to a particular place. Consequently, it's important to periodically reconsider the major decisions that we've made about our lives.

Ask yourself these questions:

- Are my decisions still producing the desired consequences?

- Are my decisions still appropriate, given my circumstances and changes in my life?

- Are my decisions consistent with what I want to get out of life?

- Do my decisions fit with my mission statement (a written guiding philosophy of life, discussed in Chapter 3)?

Periodically taking stock like this is the best way to make sure that your decisions are taking you where you want. Taking stock also helps you to be more effective in making future decisions that affect your life.

Problem Solving: Applying Critical Thinking to Find Solutions

Two trains are approaching one another, each moving at 100 kilometres an hour. If the trains continue moving at the same speed, how long will it be before . . .

Problem solving

The process of generating alternatives and finding solutions

If this is what comes to mind when you think of problem solving, think again. **Problem solving** encompasses more than the abstract, often unrealistic situations portrayed in math texts. It involves everyday, commonplace situations: How do we divide the grocery bill so that each person pays a fair share? How do I keep my one-year-old from tumbling down the stairs when there seems to be no way to fasten a gate at the top? How can I stop an annoying classmate from getting on my nerves? How do I manage to study for a test and complete a paper the same evening?

While decision making is most focused on *choosing* among various alternatives, the central issue in problem solving is *generating* alternatives. Since many problems require that decisions be made regarding alternatives, decision making and problem solving are often related.

What's the Problem?

The first step in solving any problem is to be as clear as you can about what the problem is. This may sound easy, but often it isn't. In fact, it may take some time to figure out just what is being asked. The reason is that some problems are big and hard to define, while others are quite precise, such as mathematical equations or the solution to a jigsaw puzzle. Determining how to stop the nuclear arms race between India and Pakistan and finding peace in the Middle East are big, ill-defined problems. Simply determining what information is required to solve such problems can be a major undertaking.

It's also necessary to determine what's important in coming to a solution. To determine what is critical in solving a problem, ask yourself these questions:

1. What is the initial set of facts?

2. What is it that you need to solve?

3. Which parts of the problem appear to be most critical to finding a solution?

4. Is there some information that can be ignored?

As you clarify what the problem is, you may find that you have encountered similar problems before. Your experience with them may suggest the means to the solution of the current problem. For example, consider the problem of the trains rushing toward one another. If you have worked on this kind of problem before and you know how quickly each train is moving and their starting points, there's a fairly simple equation you can write to determine how long it will take before they meet. On the other hand, to solve most of the problems we face in our daily lives, we have to do more than reach into our memories of prior situations. Instead, we need to devise novel approaches. How do you do this? There are several strategies you might use.

Strategies for Working on Life's Messier Problems

- **Trial and error.** Although it's a fairly primitive strategy, trial and error sometimes works. For instance, to invent a workable light bulb, Thomas Edison needed a good filament, the part of the bulb that actually glows. He tried out one material after another for the filament until he finally found one that worked.

- **Break the problem down into smaller, more-manageable pieces.** Break a problem down into a series of subgoals. As you reach each subgoal, you get closer to your overall goal of solving the problem. For example, if your goal were to spend your third year in your school's foreign exchange program in Ecuador, a subgoal would probably be to learn some basic Spanish. By reaching this subgoal, you move closer to reaching your ultimate goal—a year abroad in a country that interests you.

> "Problems are only opportunities in work clothes."
>
> Henry J. Kaiser, *Maxim*

- **Work backward.** Sometimes you know the answer to the problem, but not how to get there. Then it's best to work backward. A **working backward** strategy starts at the desired solution or goal and works backward, moving away from the goal. For example, consider this problem:

  Water lilies on a certain lake double in area every 24 hours. From the time the first water lily appears until the lake is completely covered takes 60 days. On what day is the lake half covered?

  It's impossible to solve this problem by breaking it down into subgoals, but most people solve it almost immediately if they work backwards. Here's a hint: If the pond is fully covered on day 60, how much is it covered the day before? Because the water lilies double each day, there had to be half as many the day before day 60. The answer, then, is that half the lake is covered on day 59. Only by moving backward could you see the solution clearly.

Working backward

The strategy of starting at the desired solution or goal and working toward the starting point of the problem

Table 10.2
The Truth Table

	Monday	Tuesday	Wednesday	Thursday	Friday	Saturday	Sunday
Sally lies			X	X	X	X	X
John lies	X	X					X

- **Use a graph, chart, or drawing to redefine the problem.** Transforming words into pictures can often help us to devise solutions that otherwise would elude us. One good example is this problem:

  Sally lies on Wednesday, Thursday, Friday, Saturday, and Sunday, but tells the truth on all other days. John lies on Sunday, Monday, and Tuesday, but tells the truth on all other days. One day Sally and John had lunch together. One exclaimed: "I lied yesterday." The other replied: "Me too."

  Question: On which day did they have lunch together?

  Hint: Use a table (see Table 10.2 above).

  Answer: Wednesday—John lied on Tuesday and is telling her the truth, because he tells the truth on Wednesdays. Sally is lying to John as she lies on Wednesday, but told the truth on Tuesday.

- **Consider the opposite.** Problems can sometimes be solved by considering the opposite of the problem you're seeking to solve. For example, to define "good mental health" you might try to define "poor mental health."

- **Use analogies.** Some problems can be solved through the use of **analogies,** comparisons between concepts or objects that are alike in some respects, but dissimilar in most others. For instance, if you liken a disastrous experience attending summer camp to a voyage on the *Titanic,* you're using an analogy.

  Analogies may help us gain additional insight into the problem at hand, and they may provide an alternative framework for interpreting the information that is provided. For instance, manufacturers of Pringles potato chips found that they could cut packaging costs if they slightly moistened the chips before packaging them—an idea that came when researchers noticed that dry tree leaves, which normally crumble easily, could be packed together tightly if they were wet.

- **Take another's perspective.** By viewing a problem from another person's point of view, it is often possible to obtain a new perspective on the problem that will make it easier to solve.

- **Forget about it.** Just as with decision making, sometimes it's best simply to walk away from a problem for a while. Just a few hours or days away from a problem may give us enough of a break to jar some hidden solutions from the recesses of our minds. The idea of "sleeping on it" also sometimes works; we may wake up refreshed and filled with new ideas.

Solve the problems in Try It! 1, "Exercise Your Problem-Solving Skills," on page 280.

Assessing Your Potential Solutions

If a problem clearly has only one answer, such as a math problem, this step in problem solving is relatively easy. You should be able to work the problem and figure out whether you've been successful. In contrast, messier problems have several possible solutions, some of which may be more involved and costly than others. In these cases, it's necessary to compare alternative solutions and choose the best one. For example, suppose you want to surprise your best friend on her birthday. She is working in Lethbridge, about 145 kilometres from you, and you need to find a way to get there. Perhaps you could rent a car, take a bus, or find some other way. Money is an issue. You will want to figure out how much each alternative costs before choosing one as your solution to the problem. Since every penny you spend getting there is a penny less that you will have to celebrate, you will want to weigh the options carefully.

Finally, spend a bit of time seeing where you can refine the solution. Is the solution you've devised adequate? Does it address all aspects of the problem? Are there alternative approaches that might be superior? Answering these questions, and refining your solution to address them, can give you confidence that the solution you've come up with is the best one. For example, if you're trying to get to Lethbridge, you might decide to try to find a ride with someone going to Lethbridge that day, using the ride board at your school. Maybe your friend's family is going to be driving in and could pick you up. Maybe someone could lend you a car for the trip.

Reflect on the Process of Problem Solving

It's natural to step back and bask in the satisfaction of solving a tough problem. That's fine—but take a moment to consider your success. Each time we solve a problem, we end up a couple steps ahead the next time around, but only if we've thought about the process we went through to solve it.

Go back and consider what it took to solve the problem and your emotional reactions along the way. Can the means you used to come up with your solution be applied to more complex kinds of problems? If you arrived at a solution by drawing a chart, would this work on similar problems in the future? Taking a moment to rethink your solution can provide you with an opportunity to become an expert problem solver and, more generally, to improve your critical thinking skills. Don't let the opportunity slip away.

Don't Fool Yourself: Avoiding Everyday Problems in Critical Thinking

As you have probably noticed already, the quality of the thinking you do regarding problems and decisions plays a crucial role in determining how successful you are. Being able to think clearly and without bias is the basis for critical thinking.

Working in a Group: Exercise Your Problem-Solving Skills

Working in a group, try to solve these problems.[1] To help you devise solutions, a hint regarding the best strategy to use is included after each problem.

1. One cold, dark, and rainy night, a motorist has a flat tire on a deserted stretch of country road. He pulls onto the shoulder to change it. After removing the four lug nuts and placing them into the hub cap, he removes the flat tire and takes his spare out of the trunk. As he is moving the spare tire into position, his hand slips and he upsets the hub cap with the lug nuts, which tumble off into the night where he can't find them. What should he do? (*Hint:* Instead of asking how he might find the *scattered* lug nuts, reframe the problem and ask where else he might find other lug nuts.)

2. A worker paving a walk needs to add water quickly to the concrete she has just poured. She reaches for her pail to get water from a spigot in the front of the house, but suddenly realizes the pail has a large rust hole in it and cannot be used. As the concrete dries prematurely, she fumbles through her toolbox for tools and materials with which to repair the pail. She finds many tools, but nothing that would serve to patch the pail. The house is locked and no one is home. What should she do? (*Hint:* When is a pail not a pail?)

3. What day follows the day before yesterday if two days from now will be Sunday? (*Hint:* Break it up, or draw a diagram.)

4. A caterpillar has to climb up the muddy wall of a well that is 12 metres deep. Each day the caterpillar advances four metres, but each night as he sleeps he slips back two metres. How many days will it take him to get out? (*Hint:* Draw it.)

5. A man has four chains, each three links long. He wants to join the four chains into a single, closed chain. Having a link opened costs two cents and having a link closed costs three cents. How can he have the chains joined for 15 cents? (*Hint:* Can only end links be opened?)

6. What is two-thirds of one-half? (*Hint:* Reverse course.)

7. I have three separate large boxes. Inside each large box are two separate medium-sized boxes, and inside each of the medium boxes are four small boxes. How many boxes do I have altogether? (*Hint:* Draw it.)

After working to solve these problems, consider these questions: Which problems were the easiest to solve, and which were the more difficult ones? Why? Were the hints helpful? Do you think there was more than one solution to any of the problems? Did your initial assumptions about the problem help or hinder your efforts to solve it? (*Note:* Answers to the problems are found at the bottom of the page.)

Answers to Try It! 1 problems:

1. Remove one lug nut from each of the other three tires on the car and use these three to attach the spare tire. This will hold until four more lug nuts can be purchased. 2. Dump the tools out of the toolbox and use it as a pail. 3. Thursday. 4. Five days; on the fifth day the caterpillar will reach the top and will not have to slide down again. 5. Open all three links on one chain (cost = 6 cents) and use them to fasten the other three chains together (cost = 9 cents; total cost = 15 cents). 6. It is the same as one-half of two-thirds, or one-third. 7. Thirty-three boxes (3 large, 6 medium, 24 small).

Unfortunately, it is sometimes the alternative you *didn't* think of that can end up being the most satisfactory decision or solution. So how can we learn to think critically and avoid blind spots that hinder us in our decision making and problem solving? We can start by considering the common obstacles to critical thinking.

Here are some decision-making and problem-solving pitfalls to look out for. Avoiding them will improve your critical thinking greatly.

- **Don't assume that giving something a name explains it.** The mere fact that we can give an idea or problem a name doesn't mean we know its causes and can explain it. Yet we often confuse the two.

  For instance, consider the following sequences of questions and answers:

  Q. Why do I have so much trouble falling asleep?
  A. Because you have insomnia.

  Q. Why is he so unsociable?
  A. Because he's an introvert.

  Q. Why did the defendant shoot those people?
  A. Because he's insane.
  Q. How do you know he's insane?
  A. Because only someone who was insane would shoot people in that way.[2]

  It's clear that none of these answers is satisfactory. All use circular reasoning, in which the explanation for the behaviour is simply the use of a label. But labels don't explain anything; they merely provide a convenient name.

- **Don't accept vague generalities dressed up as definitive statements.** Read the following personality analysis and think about how well it applies to you:

  > You have a need for other people to like and admire you and a tendency to be critical of yourself. You also have a great deal of unused potential that you have not turned to your advantage, and although you have some personality weaknesses, you are generally able to compensate for them. Nonetheless, relating to members of the opposite sex has presented problems for you, and although you appear to be disciplined and self-controlled to others, you tend to be anxious and insecure inside.

  If you believe that these statements provide an amazingly accurate description of your unique qualities, you're not alone: Most college or university students believe that the descriptions are tailored specifically to them.[3]

  But how is that possible? It isn't. The reality is that the statements are so vague that they are virtually meaningless. The acceptance of vague but seemingly useful and significant statements about oneself and others has been called the *Barnum Effect*, after showman and circus master P.T. Barnum, who coined the phrase "there's a sucker born every minute."

- **Don't confuse opinion with fact.** Opinions are not fact. Although you may be aware of this simple formula, almost all of us can be fooled into thinking that someone's opinion is the same as a fact. Sometimes it occurs when we listen to so-called authorities. For instance, the fact that a person has a distinguished title, such as "Doctor" or "Professor," doesn't mean that his or her statements are facts, as opposed to opinions.

A fact is information that is proven to be true. In contrast, an opinion represents judgments, reasoning, beliefs, inferences, or conclusions. If we accept some bit of information as a fact, we can use it to build our opinions. But if we are presented with an opinion, we need to determine the facts on which it is built in order to judge its reliability.

The difference between fact and opinion can sometimes be subtle. For instance, compare these two statements:

1. All college and university students need to take a writing course during their first term.

2. Many college or university students need to take a writing course during their first term.

The first statement is most likely an opinion, because it is so absolute and unqualified. Words such as "every," "all," and "always" are evidence of opinion. The second statement is more likely a fact, since it contains the qualifier "many." In general, statements that are qualified in some way are more likely to be facts.

Try "Fact versus Opinion" (see Try It! 2) to see the difficulties in distinguishing between the two.

- **Avoid jumping to conclusions.** Read this riddle and try to answer it:

  A father and his son were driving along the interstate highway when the father lost control of the car, swerved off the road, and crashed into a telephone pole. The father died instantly, and his son was critically injured. An ambulance rushed the boy to a nearby hospital. A prominent surgeon was summoned to provide immediate treatment. When the surgeon arrived and entered the operating room to examine the boy, a loud gasp was heard. "I can't operate on this boy," the surgeon said. "He is my son."[4]

  How can this be?

  If you find this puzzling, you've based your reasoning on the assumption that the surgeon is a male. But suppose you had assumed that the surgeon was a female. Suddenly, the riddle becomes a lot easier. It's far easier to guess that the surgeon is the boy's *mother* if we don't leap to embrace a faulty assumption.

  Why is it so easy to jump to conclusions? One reason is that we sometimes aren't aware of the assumptions that underlie our thinking. Another is our reliance on "common sense."

- **Don't believe in the myth of common sense.** Much of what we call common sense makes contradictory claims. Which are we to believe? For example, if you subscribe to the notion "Absence makes the heart grow fonder," you may assume that your high-school girlfriend, now at school across the country from you, will arrive home at Christmas even more in love with you than before. But what about "Out of sight, out of mind," which suggests a less positive outcome?

  Truisms, as such statements are called, are not factually true. Sure, being away from a loved one for a few days or a week can make you aware of just how important that person is to you and make it seem as if your heart has grown fonder. But living away from someone for an extended time is more likely to produce distance than romance.

Try It! 2

Fact versus Opinion

Read the following statements and try to determine which are facts and which are opinions.

1. College or university students should get at least seven hours of sleep every night.

2. The average college or university student sleeps less than seven hours a night.

3. Nikes offer better styling and comfort than any other brand of shoe.

4. Two out of five sports figures surveyed preferred Nikes over Converse shoes.

5. Currently, women's earning power is equal to men's.

6. Canadian government figures show full-time female workers earn 72.2 cents for every dollar earned by male workers.

7. In general, Canadian high-school students receive less classroom instruction in math and sciences than their counterparts in Europe and Asia do.

8. No secondary-school student in Canada should graduate without having studied math and sciences for at least four years.

9. Wayne Gretzky is the most outstanding, most exciting, and certainly most successful hockey player who ever stepped onto a rink.

• **Don't assume that just because two events occur together one causes the other.** Just because two events appear to be associated with one another—or, in the language of social science, are *correlated* with one another—we cannot conclude that one event has caused the other to occur. It's a basic rule: *Correlation does not prove causation.*

For example, suppose you read that a study showed that 89 percent of juvenile delinquents use marijuana. Does this mean that smoking marijuana *causes* juvenile delinquency? No, it doesn't. It is pretty safe to say that 100 percent of juvenile delinquents grew up drinking milk. Would you feel comfortable saying that milk causes delinquency? With correlations such as marijuana use and delinquent behaviour, it is very likely that there's some third factor—such as strife among family members—that causes people both to (1) try drugs and (2) engage in illegal acts. The bottom line: We don't know anything other than the fact that many young people charged with crimes said they had smoked marijuana. We do not know the cause of the correlation.

In short, we need to be careful in assuming causality. Even if two events or other kinds of variables occur together, it does not mean that one causes the other. (To apply what we've been discussing to some actual situations, complete Try It! 3, "What's Wrong with This Picture?")

One impediment to critical thinking is difficulty in distinguishing fact from opinion. For example, although many people are of the opinion that older people have a hard time learning new material, age need not be a deterrent to learning.

Try It! 3

What's Wrong with This Picture?
Identify the Faulty Reasoning

Each of the statements and situations below illustrates a failure of critical thinking. Analyze each of them and state why the conclusion might be wrong.

1. When asked why she often engages in shoplifting, Marian says, "I can't help it. I'm a kleptomaniac."

2. Zack reads in a newspaper horoscope that he "will have good luck toward the end of the week, especially in matters of chance, with a sharp downturn possible by early next week." He immediately buys 10 lottery tickets for Friday's drawing.

3. A political candidate makes this statement: "My party is 10 times more concerned about the lives and fortunes of the working person than is the opposing party."

4. Two students in a large lecture class—one evidently Asian and the other not—wait as their math professor grades their papers. The professor notes that Jackie Lee has done very well, while Darryl Roberts has not. As she finishes grading, the professor gives the good paper to the Asian-looking student and the other paper to the student who doesn't look Asian. The students look at the papers, and exchange them with the rightful owner.

Can you identify the faulty logic for each of the four scenarios? Do you think the people making the statements or taking the action are aware of their faulty thinking? Can you think of any instances in which you displayed similar faulty logic?

Speaking of Success

Jeff Goplin

Business Marketing Diploma, Northern Alberta Institute of Technology

When Jeff Goplin considered his postsecondary options, his foremost goal was to graduate and experience the world of work as soon as possible. With that end in mind, he was attracted to the Northern Alberta Institute of Technology and its practical hands-on two-year Business Marketing program. Jeff was extremely pleased with his courses, such as business statistics, marketing, market research, and selling, which he says were very relevant to achieving his goal.

Since shortly after graduation, Jeff has worked at Manpower Services, a world leader in the staffing industry, serving customers in more than 3700 offices in 59 countries. Now the regional marketing manager for Alberta, Jeff is responsible for Manpower's marketing throughout the province. Jeff is a strong proponent of his employer's global values and appreciates its corporate social responsibility, especially as it relates to Alberta's underemployed workers. Although Alberta's economy is strong and its unemployment rate is the lowest in Canada, there is a shortage of skilled workers. There are employers whose needs are not being met and workers who, for lack of training

THE NORTHERN ALBERTA INSTITUTE OF TECHNOLOGY

or education, are not able to access higher-paying jobs.

In addition to his work, Jeff is an active community member on behalf of underemployed persons. To this end, he sits on a number of workforce development and training boards and committees. In addition to the benefits gained by employers and workers, both Jeff and Manpower Services profit from this volunteer work. Jeff gains valuable experience and good contacts throughout the community; Manpower Services' profile is raised and goodwill is created for the organization.

When Jeff addresses college or university students, as he frequently does, he is an advocate for volunteer work in the community. He says this type of experience is very valuable for the workforce of tomorrow. However, Jeff also recommends taking some time before making the decision, to weigh the pros and cons of the situation. He advises students who want to offer their services in the community to get a clear understanding of the expectations and responsibilities associated with the position. He says that student volunteers need to know their limits before committing to a volunteer job so that they don't get too tired, their studies don't suffer, and the volunteer organizations and people served by them are not disappointed.

How can I improve the quality of my decisions?

- A structured process of decision making can clarify the issues involved, expand our options, and improve the quality of our choices.

- Good decision making begins with understanding your short- and long-term goals.

- Decision making is improved if you have a large number of alternatives.

- For difficult decisions, strategies include giving the decision time, acting out alternatives, tossing a coin to test our feelings, understanding that indecision is often a decision itself, and acting on gut feelings.

What strategies can I use for problem solving?

- Problem solving entails the generation of alternatives to consider.

- We need to first understand and define the problem and to determine the important elements in coming to a solution to a problem.

- Approaches to generating solutions include using trial and error, breaking problems into pieces, working backward, using pictures, considering the opposite, using analogies, taking another's perspective, and "forgetting" the problem.

- Problem solving ultimately requires the evaluation and refinement of the solutions that have been generated.

What are some problems that affect critical thinking, and how can I avoid them?

- Several types of obstacles pose threats to critical thinking, such as faulty assumptions, vague generalities, jumping to conclusions, and the myth of common sense.

- Awareness of the biases that may affect our thinking can help us avoid them.

P.O.W.E.R. Portfolio

Decision Making and Critical Thinking

1. How can you demonstrate critical thinking, one of the most important skills employers expect from employees? Here are several suggestions! Write a letter to the editor about a topical or controversial issue in your community. Make sure your commentary shows a depth of reasoning. Or include a discussion thread from an e-mail group you participate in. The subject area doesn't matter as much as the quality of your arguments. Or consider including an op-ed piece you wrote for your school or local newspaper, an analytical essay, a case history, or a video of a debate you participated in. Your reflective comments should indicate what you learned and the thinking process you went through.

2. Consider including your journal reflections on decision making from this chapter in your portfolio. The "look back" approach to decision making can have positive implications for future decisions.

3. Use a formal decision making technique, like SWOT (strengths, weaknesses, opportunities, and threats) analysis, a decision-making tree, or PMI (plus, minus, interesting) and work through a problem. Include your work in your portfolio, along with a commentary on the process. Information about these techniques is available at <www.psychwww.com/mtsite/page2.html>.

Resources

On Campus

Some colleges or universities offer courses in critical thinking, and they are a good bet to help increase decision-making and problem-solving skills. In addition, courses in logic and philosophy will help improve critical thinking skills.

If you are having a personal problem that is difficult to solve, you can turn to staff at the campus counselling centre, mental health centre, or residential life office. Even if the person with whom you speak initially is not the right one, he or she can direct you to someone who can help.

In Print

If you have trouble making good decisions, the H.W. Lewis book *Why Flip a Coin? The Art and Science of Good Decisions* (Wiley, 1998) is for you. The book shows how to make a rational decision based on the information at hand.

Thinking and Deciding by Jonathan Baron (Cambridge University Press, 3rd edition, 2000) is helpful for anyone interested in learning how to think and decide better. The book explores conventional ways of thinking and provides a toolkit for improved thought processing

Asking the Right Questions: A Guide to Critical Thinking, by M. Neil Browne and Stuart M. Keeley (Prentice Hall, 7th edition, 2003), focuses on the difference between memorization and the more difficult tasks of critical analysis and synthesis. It teaches students to respond to alternative points of view and develop a solid foundation for making personal choices about what information to accept and what to discard.

On the Web

The following sites on the World Wide Web provide the opportunity to extend your learning about the material in this chapter. Although the Web addresses were accurate at the time the book was printed, check the P.O.W.E.R. Learning website, <www.mcgrawhill.ca/college/power>, for any changes that may have occurred.

www.psychwww.com/mtsite/index.html
This Web site offers links to other sites that can help you with setting goals, time management, and stress control, and to numerous other helpful sites. It also includes shareware for setting up life plans.

www.kcmetro.cc.mo.us/longview/ctac/toc.htm
Core concepts in critical thinking are presented here with exercises and examples. The site contains a short history of logic and answers the question: "What is the point of studying critical thinking?"

http://www2.sjsu.edu/depts/itl
This award-winning site has three interactive tutorials on critical thinking, with exercises and tests so that you can evaluate your analytical ability.

The Case of . . .

Left Holding the Lease

Erica has a problem.

In the spring of her first year of college, she and her friend Jeri had found a two-bedroom apartment to share for the upcoming school year. The apartment was on the expensive side, but they had decided that it was worth it because it was so close to campus. She and Jeri had jointly paid the security deposit on the apartment. However, because Jeri hadn't been around when it came time to sign the lease, only Erica had signed it. Consequently, Erica was legally responsible for fulfilling the terms of the lease.

Now, only two weeks before the start of the fall term, Jeri tells Erica that she has realized she can't afford the rent on the apartment and that she has decided to live with her parents. Erica is simultaneously furious with Jeri and panicky at the thought of having to pay the rent herself, which she simply can't afford.

How is she going to deal with the problem?

1. Is the problem a purely financial and legal one, or are there personal and social considerations that should be taken into account in solving the problem?

2. Is the problem solely Erica's problem, or should Jeri take responsibility for solving it as well?

3. What alternatives does Erica have for dealing with the situation?

4. How should Erica go about evaluating the outcomes for each alternative?

5. Based on your analysis of the problem, what advice would you give Erica for dealing with the situation?

Making Academic Choices

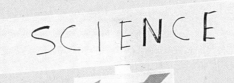

Making Academic Choices

Prepare: Becoming Familiar with Your Options and Requirements

Organize: Examining What You Have Done and What You Need to Do

Work: Choosing Next Term's Courses

Evaluate: Deciding Whether You Are in the Classes You Need

Rethink: Learning What You Love and Liking What You Learn

Choosing a Program or Major

Career Connections: Choosing a Job That's Right for You

Dealing with Academic Failure—and Success

Journal Reflections: Focus on Your Interests

Speaking of Success: Dr. Anthony Brissett

The Case of . . . No Clear Decision

"FREN257: Oral French."

Jesse Price's eyes skimmed over the title, automatically dismissing it from consideration. Then he returned to the course description in the list of general education options. Perhaps it was worth a try.

Although Jesse had gotten Bs and Cs in high-school French, he had dropped it as soon as he could, because he was focusing on sciences, where his marks were better. He needed the best grades possible to get into Aviation and Flight Technology—the competition to get into that program was fierce.

Now he was in AFT and he loved every minute of it, but he needed a general education elective, and the one he was considering was French! How would he survive postsecondary French? Could he even remember any vocabulary?

After talking it over with the course instructor, he felt a bit better; she indicated the course started with the basics and told him would surprise himself with what he would remember. He'd heard the course was interactive and fun— why not give it a shot? He decided to enroll. After all, it *did* fit his schedule and it *was* a break from all the technical courses in his program.

It turned out to be one of the best decisions he had ever made; he loved the course. The instructor was terrific, making French seem fascinating. He had never spent any time in francophone areas of Canada, but now he started to consider it. He found he had a real flair for pronunciation and enjoyed giving simple presentations about the field of aviation in French. It turned out that much of the vocabulary he was developing related to his career.

Jesse enjoyed his French course and did so well that he actually took another French course in his third semester. At graduation, he applied for an aircrew position in the Canadian Forces. While not yet bilingual, Jesse's proficiency and confidence in using French made him a much stronger candidate than he would have been otherwise. His interviewers were very impressed when Jesse was enthusiastic about taking more French courses during his military training.

Looking
Ahead

Our academic and professional careers are propelled by many forces, not the least of which is chance. Jesse Price, like many other students, found a new direction while leafing through the general education course list. Although he never would have predicted at the start of college that he would end up taking two French courses and possibly take more, his willingness to take an academic chance led to a new passion and to a career opportunity.

In this chapter we focus on choosing an academic course of study, one of the central challenges of college or university. Not only do the choices we make colour our entire postsecondary experience, but they also may determine the path we follow once we graduate.

This chapter begins by considering the many choices you'll have to make as a routine part of attending college or university, including the choice of courses, instructors, and programs or majors—each of which has long-term implications. You'll learn ways to select courses that meet your needs and meet requirements for future courses or programs.

Ultimately, the degree to which your postsecondary education benefits you is in your hands. By learning various strategies, you can act decisively to get the most out of your postsecondary experience. After reading this chapter, you'll be able to answer these questions:

- **How can I prepare for the academic choices that college or university demands?**

- **What is the best way to choose courses and ensure I'm getting the most out of my studies?**

- **How can I choose a major or program?**

- **How can I deal with academic success and failure?**

Making Academic Choices

For some readers of P.O.W.E.R. Learning, there may be little in the way of academic choice. In some college or university programs, most courses are compulsory, with just a couple of electives to be chosen. For other programs, the course calendar is like an Ikea catalogue; course offerings are briefly described and you must match the ones that sound most interesting to you with your personal interests and goals, as well as with the requirements of your program.

Choosing the right set of courses can be intimidating. But if you approach the problem thoughtfully, your final choices will make the best of the possibilities offered. Let's consider how to proceed, using the P.O.W.E.R. system as a guide (see the P.O.W.E.R. Plan).

Prepare: Becoming Familiar with Your Options and Requirements

Choosing which courses to take requires that you take several significant preparatory steps before you jump in. In addition, many academic decisions are very school-specific, so it is extremely important for you to be familiar with the policies and procedures of your particular college or university.

Familiarize Yourself with Your College or University Calendar A college or university calendar, sometimes called a catalogue or program guide, provides information about courses, programs or majors, tuition fees, important details (add/drop guidelines, course withdrawal, exam schedules), and the steps you need to take to graduate with a college certificate or diploma or a university degree.

All this information is also included on the college or university Web site. In addition, websites are updated regularly and recent events or unexpected changes are added throughout the year.

College or university calendars are actually legal documents that offer you a contract. If you are admitted to the college or university and you fulfill certain requirements (such as taking a particular set of courses, maintaining a certain level of grades, and—let us not forget—paying your tuition bills on time), you'll get something in return. That something is a diploma or degree.

Because they outline contractual obligations, college and university calendars are important documents. They provide an outline of what your institution expects and offers in a number of areas:

1. **Academic regulations.** Every college and university has strict rules, requirements, and policies; these are all spelled out in the college or university calendar. For example, to continue in school, you must maintain a particular grade average in all your courses; to drop a course, you need to do so by a certain date in the term; and to graduate, you need a certain number of courses or course credits.

PREPARE

Become familiar with your options and requirements

ORGANIZE

Examine what you have done and what you need to do

WORK

Choose next term's courses

EVALUATE

Decide whether you are in the classes you need

RETHINK

Learn what you love and like what you learn

P.O.W.E.R. Plan

2. **Academic programs.** Most of the college or university calendar is a description of the major areas of study offered by the school—its academic departments, programs or majors, and the requirements for each program or major.

   Requirements generally fall into two or three categories. First, typically, are schoolwide requirements that every student enrolled in a college or university must fulfill. Second are specific requirements for each particular program or major. A **major** is a specialization in a particular subject area, requiring a set course of study; to major in an area, you must take a specific number of courses or credits in that area. Finally, if the major falls within a broader academic unit (such as a school of education), that broader entity may have its own requirements for a degree. A **program** is typically found in colleges and involves a course of study with a set curriculum.

   For instance, an early childhood education major might be required to fulfill schoolwide requirements that apply to all students enrolled in the college or university, such as several English, writing, or general education courses. Then, because the early childhood education program may be housed in a more-general division of social sciences, there may be divisional requirements to fulfill (perhaps a course in social science methodology or a human services issues requirement). Finally, the early childhood education program will have its own separate requirements for its majors to complete, such as completing three field placements.

3. **Advance credit or transfer credit.** Most Canadian universities and colleges have transfer or articulation agreements that recognize academic knowledge and achievements undertaken at other postsecondary institutions. College and university calendars provide information for students transferring from other schools or intending to transfer to other colleges or universities in the future. Transfer students should pay careful attention to what courses they will and will not receive credit for. Partnership programs, offered by two separate institutions, may also have specific requirements students need to be aware of.

4. **Prior learning assessment and recognition (PLAR).** PLAR is the process of identifying, assessing, and recognizing what a person knows and can do. The award of transfer credit in given courses or programs may be based on formal or informal learning experiences including work experience, life experience, unstructured educational experiences such as self-study, and structured educational activity. An individual is assessed through a combination of demonstration, portfolios, interviews, assignments, challenge exams, and other assessment methods. This method of gaining academic recognition for prior learning is particularly helpful for immigrants to Canada with training, skills, and experience from their home countries, as well as

Advisors can play an important role in your academic career, providing valuable advice, helping you to overcome problems, and making sure that you meet all the requirements needed to graduate.

Major

A specialization in a particular subject area, requiring a set course of study (often found in universities)

Program

A course of study (often found in colleges and professional schools) with a set curriculum adult learners who are returning to college or university for formal credentials. Information about PLAR can be obtained from college or university calendars, school websites, or academic advisors.

5. **Course listings.** The college or university website and course calendar list all the courses the school offers, even though not all of them may be offered every term. Courses are listed by department, and the descriptions typically include the course name, the number of credits it provides, and a short description. Some courses have **prerequisites**—requirements you must fulfill before you can enroll in them. If the course has a prerequisite, this will also be stated. Sometimes the description will also name the instructors who teach the course and the time and place the class meets, although this information may be published separately.

Prerequisites
Requirements that must be fulfilled before a student may enroll in a course, program, or discipline

Get Academic Advice Every college or university has its own way of doing things, so be sure to find out the best practice at your school. In general, the following resources are very helpful:

- **Academic advisors** are important school employees. Most academic advisors want to empower students to do their own academic pathing. Your academic advisor performs many important functions within the college or university community, such as providing assistance for students who are off-track academically, in addition to counselling for emotional concerns or major issues between students, peers, parents, or professors. Before consulting an academic advisor about course selection concerns, be sure you have tried to find the answer on the school website, in the school catalogue, or in your program guide.

> "It can be no dishonor to learn from others when they speak good sense."
>
> Sophocles, *Antigone*

- **Program coordinators** can provide information to students about program requirements as well as answer many career-related questions.

- **Student advisors** are voices of experience. They have gone through many of the same situations and solved many of the same problems as younger students and can give good clear-headed advice.

Organize: Examining What You Have Done and What You Need to Do

Where Are You? If you've prepared well, you have a basic understanding of the courses you have already taken that fulfill the requirements for the diploma or degree you are seeking. To figure out what you need to do, you'll need to organize a list of the requirements you must fulfill to graduate. Try It! 1, "Create a List of Course Requirements," provides a form that you can complete if your college or university doesn't provide one for you. Even if you have yet to decide on a program or major, you may be taking some courses that satisfy one of the requirements for a program or major you are considering. Noting this on your list will help you plan as your academic career progresses.

If this is just the start of your postsecondary career, you'll probably have completed only a few requirements. Don't let the blanks on the form get you down; this is typical, and the credits have a way of adding up quickly.

Try It!
1

Create a List of Course Requirements

Use the form below to list all your course requirements. The form covers both prerequisite courses (i.e., courses you must take before you can take other requirements) and requirements imposed by your college or university, the division of which your department is a part, and your department. In addition, the form allows you to indicate both credit requirements and grade requirements.

List of Course Requirements

Type of Course	Credits Required	Credits Completed	Grade Required	Grade Achieved	Whose Requirement?		
					School	Division	Department
I. Prerequisite Courses							
Total Prerequisite Courses							
II. Required Courses							
Total Required Courses							

What does the information in the chart tell you? How can you use it to plan your future course selections? What courses do you want to take that are not requirements? How much leeway do you have to take nonrequired courses?

If you are further along in your college or university career, you may find that you have already fulfilled a significant number of requirements. In fact, you may not remember everything you've already done. If you have trouble remembering what courses you've taken, get a copy of your transcript from the **registrar,** the official designated to oversee the scheduling of courses, the maintenance of grades and transcripts, and the creation and retention of other official documents. A **transcript** is the official record of the courses you've taken and the grades you received in them. Many educational institutions charge a fee for official transcripts.

As you're recording the courses you've taken, remember that meeting graduation requirements may not be the same as meeting your major's requirements. For instance, some schools not only require that you take and pass certain courses, they require you to achieve a certain minimum grade in your courses as a whole. Or you may have to get a grade of C or better in a course for it to be counted toward your major. In this case, if you received a C– in the course, you'd still get credit toward graduation, but the course wouldn't count toward the number of credits you earned for your major.

Confusing? You bet. That's why it's important to keep track of where you stand from the very start of your postsecondary career. (It's a good idea to keep all relevant information together in a file folder or even a shoebox.) There's no worse surprise than finding out a month before you thought you'd be graduating that you lack some critical requirement. Don't count on others to keep track of this information for you. No one knows more about what you've done—or is more interested in it—than you.

Where Are You Going? You also need to determine what requirements you've yet to fulfill. Use this information to help determine which courses you should take in the upcoming term. Once you have declared a major you can add those requirements to your record.

Now that you know where you are and where you are going, you are ready to start selecting courses to take you there.

Work: Choosing Next Term's Courses

The course offerings for the next term are published in a *course schedule*. It is organized by department, with each course in the department having a number, such as "PSYC230: Sports Psychology." Generally, the higher the number, the more advanced the course. The course catalogue will usually tell you when and where the class meets (for large introductory courses there may be several sections) and whether the course has any prerequisites—requirements that must be fulfilled before you can enroll in a course or discipline.

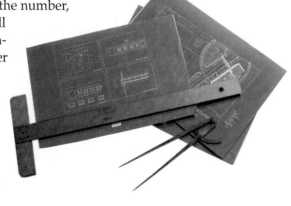

Go with What You Know Chances are, you already know of at least one or two courses you need to take in a given term. Perhaps this is the term you plan to fulfill your natural science or your foreign language requirement. There may be some courses you have been waiting to take, since some courses are only taught once a year. A good place to begin is to find out when these courses are given and where.

Draft a Personal Schedule for the Term First, write down when the courses you absolutely have to take are scheduled. If, as is the case for many introductory courses in large colleges or universities, you have a choice of times, choose one you prefer. In choosing times, take into

Registrar
The college or university official designated to oversee the scheduling of courses, the maintenance of grades and transcripts, and the creation and retention of other official documents

Transcript
An official record of courses taken and grades received by students

consideration whether you are a "morning person" who is at your best first thing in the morning, or whether you usually must drag yourself out of bed in the morning and don't fully function until 11 A.M. This will be the beginning of your time management for the upcoming term.

Next, choose courses that are not required. Keep in mind broad considerations about the kinds of courses you need to take for your major and for graduation, but also explore possible courses that simply sound interesting to you. College or university offers the opportunity to discover who you are and what you like and do best, but the only way that can happen is by taking intellectual risks.

To get started in deciding what courses to take for the upcoming term, complete Try It! 2, "Choose Your Courses."

Register for Courses   After laying the groundwork of course selection, the rest of the actual work of choosing courses for your classes consists of completing the school's paperwork to become formally enrolled in your chosen classes.

Meeting with your advisor is an essential step. Sometimes, in fact, it's mandatory, and you won't be allowed to register without your advisor's signature. But even if it's not required, it's a good idea to go over your proposed course of studies. You may have overlooked something, or your advisor may be able to suggest some alternative courses that will work better for you.

Remember, though, that the ultimate responsibility for taking the right courses rests with you. Not only can advisors sometimes make mistakes and overlook a requirement, but also only you ultimately know what's right for you.

Register
To enroll formally in courses

After meeting with your advisor, your next step will be to actually **register,** the formal act of enrolling in courses. Course registration varies significantly from one school to another. In some cases, it's a matter of listing course numbers on a form, along with some alternatives.

In some larger schools, you will be expected to register for your courses over the telephone or through the World Wide Web. If your college or university uses a telephone registration system, you will be given a specific time in which to call. When you do call, you'll receive voice prompts to enter your course choices using your telephone's touch-tone key pad (see Figure 11.1 on page 300).

If your college or university uses the newest form of registration, the World Wide Web, you will be prompted to enter course information on a Web form, and your registration will be accomplished completely online.

E valuate: Deciding Whether You Are in the Classes You Need

Picture this horror story:

You receive your grade report from the previous term. You're excited because you know you've done well. You're especially looking forward to seeing your French grade because you know you were on the borderline between an A– and a B+. Instead you're astounded to see that not only is there no grade listed for the French class, but you've received an F in a Spanish class that you didn't even take. That F pulls down your grade average, and at the bottom of your grade report is an announcement that you are on academic probation.

Here's the explanation: Because of an error during registration, you were never formally enrolled in the French course, even though you actually spent the entire term attending classes in the course. To compound the mistake, your instructor never

Try It!

2

Choose Your Courses

Use the form below to make your course selections for the coming term. The form will permit you to verify that you are meeting course requirements, avoiding schedule conflicts, and signing up for instructors you want.

Course Selections

Term: _____

Course Name and Number	Credits	Required Course or Just for Fun?	Pre-requisites Met?	Grade Required	Meeting Days and Time	Schedule Conflicts	Instructor	Instructor Okay?

After completing the chart, answer these questions: How does the next semester shape up for you? Will you be able to take the courses you *want* to take, as opposed to those you *need* to take? Have you made any choices that open you to new intellectual possibilities?

noticed that you weren't on her class roster. At the end of the term, when she was filling out her grade report, she didn't notice that your name wasn't listed. So no grade was reported for French.

At the same time, the instructor of the Spanish class in which you were erroneously enrolled had to give you a grade at the end of the semester. Because you never completed any assignments or took any tests, your average for the semester was 0— warranting an F for the term. That F is what appeared on your grade report.

The situation—which is far more likely to occur at a large university than a small college—might be seen as a comedy of errors if it weren't so painful. Fortunately, if this were actually your story, it would most likely have a happy ending—eventually. You would go to your college or university registrar, who would be able to tell you what to do to get the F erased and the appropriate grade added. Still, undoing the cascade of errors would take time and a considerable amount of effort. Difficulties such as these are encountered by a surprising number of students every term. Many problems, however, can be avoided with a bit of due diligence on the part of the student. One key is to evaluate your success in registering.

Figure 11.1

Telephone Course Registration Worksheet

Before you begin your telephone call, fill in this entire worksheet, listing all courses you wish to add, drop, or change including laboratory and discussion sections, and the appropriate "action codes" you will enter. Be sure to fill in all boxed areas properly and to enter '##' at the end of your call.

1. Call the system at (555) 444-3214 (From On-Campus, call 4-3214)

2. Enter your student ID number `1` `2` `6` - `0` `4` - `9` `8` `1` `1`

3. Enter your branch code `1`   (Undergraduate = 1, Graduate = 2)

4. Enter your personal ID number (PIN) `6` `7` `7` `5`

5. If the Schedule Confirmation you receive in the mail instructs you to get from your advisor a Registration Approval Code before

   add/drop, enter that code `☐` `☐` `☐` `☐`

6. For each add, drop, or change you want to make, enter the appropriate action code from the list below and the schedule number for the course you want affected by that action.

Action Code*	Schedule Number of Course Requested	Dept	Course #	Section #	Crd	Day/Time
`1` `0`	`7` `8` `2` `8` `4` `0`	Psych	102	1	3	T-T 11:15-12:30
`1` `0`	`6` `7` `2` `9` `9` `7`	Engl	231	1	3	M-W-F 9:05-9:55
`1` `0`	`2` `6` `0` `4` `6` `3`	Phed	102	2	1	M 4:00-4:50
`1` `0`	`1` `2` `0` `3` `0` `9`	Latn	124	1	3	T-T 9:00-10:15
`1` `0`	`8` `8` `0` `1` `8` `1`	Hist	102	1	3	M-W-F 10:10-11:05
`1` `0`	`7` `2` `4` `9` `6` `2`	Phys	101	3	3	T-T 2:30-3:45
`☐☐`	`☐☐☐☐☐☐`					
`☐☐`	`☐☐☐☐☐☐`					
`☐☐`	`☐☐☐☐☐☐`					
`☐☐`	`☐☐☐☐☐☐`					

7. After entering your course requests, enter ## instead of an action code to terminate your call.

*Action Code	Action
10	ADD a course or Swap between sections of a course (To SWAP, simply add the new section; the old section will automatically be dropped from your schedule.)
30	ADD a course with Pass/Fail option or CHANGE existing course to Pass/Fail
90	DROP a course
80	REMOVE Pass/Fail or Audit option from existing course
50	CHANGE variable credit for an existing variable credit course
40	ADD a course with AUDIT grading option or CHANGE existing course to AUDIT grading
60	LIST your course schedule (press any key to end listing)
*	ERASE an entry error before completion

Note: Action Codes 30 and 80 are not available to graduate students. 40 is not available to undergraduates.

Before the term starts, your school will provide you with a list of courses in which you are enrolled for the upcoming term. Immediately look it over. Use the following checklist to determine how successful your efforts to register have been:

- Are the courses to which you are assigned the ones you wanted?

- Are the times accurate? Are there any conflicts?

- Have any substitutions been made?

- Are you registered for the number of credits that you wanted to be registered for?

If there are any problems, try to correct the situation immediately. If there has been a clerical error, you should pay a visit to the registrar's office. Sometimes, though, you'll find that there was no mistake. Class sizes are almost always limited, and not every student who wants to enroll can do so, either because of physical limitations (the room can hold only a certain number of students) or because of educational considerations (learning may be maximized when only a small number of students are in the class).

When a course is overbooked, you have several alternatives. One is to sign up for another section of the course that is not overbooked. Another is to attempt to register for an entirely different course.

Finally, you may appeal directly to the course instructor. Instructors sometimes will permit particularly interested or motivated students to enroll in the class, even if the official capacity has been reached. You may find that approaching an instructor with a polite request may yield you a slot in the course after all.

If none of these alternatives works, you will have to add a course to the ones you have already registered for. How do you add courses after the registration period has ended? Typically, you'll need to complete a special form. Depending on the timing of your request, the form may require the signature of the instructor whose course you are adding.

"Help—I Can't Get into the Courses That I Need to Graduate!" For some students, their efforts to register result in utter disaster. Sometimes most or all of their first choices are unavailable, and they end up enrolled in only a few of the courses they had requested. Or perhaps they cannot get into the one crucial course required for graduation.

Whatever the problem, there are several steps you can take to improve the situation:

- **Don't despair—act!** Virtually no academic problem exists that can't be solved in some way. Focus your energies on finding a creative solution to the problem.

- **Identify classes that are still available and enroll in them.** Many classes offered at your college or university are probably still available. Registrars or departments often maintain lists of classes that have openings.

- **Talk with your advisor.** Perhaps what you think of as an absolute requirement can be waived or appealed. Or maybe some other course can substitute for a particular required course.

- **Speak with individual course instructors.** It may be that the instructor of the course you need will make an exception and permit you to enroll, given that you must take the course for some pressing reason.

- **Consider taking a must-have, required course at another school.** If you live in an area where there are other schools in the vicinity, it may be possible to enroll in a course that you simply *must* take at another school. It also may be possible to take the course using distance learning. In **distance learning,** courses are taught at some other institution, and students participate via either video technology or the World Wide Web.

Distance learning
The teaching of courses at another institution, with student participation via video technology or the World Wide Web

In distance education, you can take classes at another institution without physically having to be on that campus. David Morris and Marian Burdsall are both earning their M.B.A.s entirely online from Athabasca University in Alberta, while living in Kingston, Ontario. What do you think the future of distance education will be?

Before you take a course offered by a college or university other than your own, make sure that you'll receive credit for the course at your school. Also keep in mind that you'll probably have to pay for courses offered by other schools, over and above what you've already spent on your own school's tuition.

R ethink: Learning What You Love and Liking What You Learn

Take one step back. No, make that two steps back.

Stepping back and taking stock of where you are in your course of studies and where you're headed are absolutely essential tasks. In fact, they are among the most important things you can do during your postsecondary career. They can spell the difference between plodding through your courses, focused only on day-to-day deadlines and tribulations, and, alternatively, gaining a sense of satisfaction as you progress toward your own goals and see yourself growing as a person.

Taking stock of your course of studies is not something you need to do every day, or once a week, or even once a month. But you should do it, without fail, at least once every term. Circle a date on your calendar so you'll be sure to do it, and treat it no differently than any other deadline you simply can't miss.

When you do take stock, answer the questions in Try It! 3, "Reflect on Your College or University Experience." If you're satisfied with your answers, feel

Try It! 3

Working in a Group
Reflect on Your College or University Experience

As you proceed in higher education, it's a good idea to take a few moments at regular intervals (e.g., once a term, once a year) to rethink your entire postsecondary experience. With a small group of classmates, discuss your reactions to the following topics and questions:

Course Work

- Are my courses moving me toward my educational, career, and personal goals?
- Are the classes I'm taking helping me to meet my short-term and long-term goals?
- Are the classes I'm taking meeting my expectations?

Personal Commitment

- Am I working hard to get the most out of the classes I'm taking?
- Am I doing my best in every class?
- Am I keeping the goal of learning—apart from doing well in classes—in mind as I progress through my classes?

Personal Growth

- What personal growth am I experiencing?
- Am I becoming closer to the person I want to be?
- Are my critical-thinking abilities growing?

College

- Is my school providing me with the best educational experience possible?
- Am I learning not only in the classroom, but also outside the classroom?
- Am I learning from my fellow students as well as my instructors?

Changes

- Is there anything (my course selections, my major, or my school) that I should consider changing?
- Have I made the best choices in the past? How can I remedy mistakes that I have made?

affirmed in the choices you've made. You're on the right track, and you should feel secure in the knowledge that you're getting from college or university what you want and aspire to.

On the other hand, if you're less than satisfied with the answers you come up with, take action. Choose courses in the future that better match your goals. Consider changing your program or major to one that more closely reflects what you want to get out of your higher education. And, if you're truly unhappy with the way your postsecondary career is proceeding, consider changing schools.

Whichever course you choose, don't accept being dissatisfied with your college or university career. There are few times in our lives when we have the opportunity to partake of an experience that has the potential to raise us to new intellectual and emotional heights. Higher education should be intellectually enlightening and exciting. We should be able to see how our education is preparing us for the rest of our lives. The worst thing we can do is let the time slip away without being confident that our postsecondary experience is the best experience possible.

Taking stock of your courses and academic career also helps you with another important choice you will have to make: choosing your program or major.

Choosing a Program or Major

You attend a family gathering and encounter relatives you haven't seen for a while. What's the first question they ask when you say you're attending college or university? You can bet on it: "What's your major?"

Although you could argue that there are lots of other important questions that you could be asked—"What interesting things have you learned?" comes to mind—having a major focus of study *is* an important part of higher education. A program or a major, a field of specialization requiring a particular course of study, is important because it focuses what we study, leading us to become experts in a specific area.

Some students know what they want to major in when they begin college or university. In contrast, other students don't have a clue what they want to major in when they start school. That's fine. No one says you should know.

In fact, using your first year in college or university to explore a range of possibilities is a very good idea. You might find after taking a civics course that you have a passion for legal studies. Or a physics class may lead you to consider a program in engineering technology. College or university is meant to be a time of exploration, and leaving yourself open to the future—and the unknown—is a completely reasonable thing to do. (To begin your own exploration of majors, complete Try It! 4, "Identify Major Attractions," on page 306.)

But what if you don't have any idea which program or major you want to pursue? If you are still in your first year of school, you have plenty of time to decide. But here are some approaches that should help. You may also want to review the discussion of decision making in Chapter 10 as the time to declare a major (usually by the end of your second or the beginning of your third year) draws nearer.

1. **Celebrate your indecision.** If you don't have to make a decision for some time, take advantage of the situation. Enjoy the fact that you're uncommitted and that you have an uncommon degree of freedom.

2. **Focus on your interests.** Take a long look inward, paying attention to what your interests are. What do you most like to do in life? What are your strengths and weaknesses? What do you want to get out of life? The more you know about yourself, the easier it will be to narrow down the choices for a program or major.

3. **Seek the help of others.** College and university campuses provide many resources to help their students choose a program or major (and also to help narrow the choices for potential careers). Talk to other students majoring in areas that interest you. Find out what they like and don't like about the field and its requirements. You will probably find your interest grows or diminishes depending on how you feel about the issues they mention.

> "He who hesitates is sometimes saved."
>
> James Thurber, author

Speak with your advisor. If you've gotten to know your advisor, he or she can often provide reasonable, helpful information. For instance, you may be able to find out about the strengths and weaknesses of various departments.

You can also turn to your college or university counselling or career centre. Most schools have offices that can provide information about the various programs and majors, including information about career opportunities typically available to graduates. Sometimes it's possible to take tests that will help focus your choices, pinpointing your strengths and weaknesses.

4. **Be career-oriented, but not *too* career-oriented.** If you have a good idea about what career you want to embark on once you graduate, you can easily find out what skills are required to be successful in that field. Knowing what you'll need to gain entry into a field can help you determine a good major that will set you on the road toward your desired profession.

Don't narrow your options too much, however. Students sometimes fear signing up for classes that don't seem to lead directly toward a career. Or they may avoid courses that seem to point them in the direction of a career that would be "unacceptable" to their parents or friends. One of the greatest sources of indecision in choosing a major stems from the mistaken notion that when you choose your major, you're also choosing a career.

Don't fall into that trap. Follow your heart—not always your head—and pursue courses without regard to how they may broaden or narrow your future job opportunities. You may discover a passion—and an aptitude—that you never knew you had.

5. **Always keep in mind that education is a lifelong enterprise.** Educational opportunities will continue to present themselves not just through the undergraduate years, but for the rest of your life as well.

College counselling and career centres are excellent sources of information on potential majors and occupations.

Identify Major Attractions

The following chart is meant to focus your thinking on the kinds of courses and educational experiences that typify several potential fields of study. While this list is not exhaustive, it may lead you toward some unexplored territory. You should also feel free to add areas of academic study not mentioned here but offered in your college or univesity catalogue. The third column is for you to check off characteristics that appear to suit you.

Field of Study	Characteristics	Is This Me?
Arts (e.g., dance, drama, music, art, creative writing, graphic design, interior decorating, fashion design)	• High interest in creative expression. • Appreciation of nonverbal communication. • Understanding of aesthetics. • Commitment to perfection. • Ability to manipulate form and shape.	
Business (e.g., marketing, financial planning, accounting, management, purchasing, logistics)	• Interest in organization and order. • Ability to lead and manage people. • Interest in practical problem solving. • Ambition and interest in financial incentives. • Can-do attitude. • Ability to simplify complexity.	
Engineering sciences (e.g., engineering, computer science, tool and die maker)	• Intense interest in solving real problems. • "Tinkerer" mentality a plus. • Extreme ability to focus on minute details. • Commitment to exactness and perfection. • Strong logical ability. • Ability to work alone for long stretches.	
Helping professions (e.g., nursing, counselling, child and youth work, teaching, and many areas of medicine such as psychiatry, art therapy, occupational therapy)	• Interest in people. • Desire to solve real human problems. • Commitment to people more than to money. • Tolerance of "messy" situations with multiple, partial solutions. • Insight and creativity. • Ability to work with people.	
Humanities (e.g., English literature, history, theatre, film)	• Interest in human emotions and motivations. • Interest in cultural phenomena. • Ability to integrate broad areas of study and inquiry. • Good skills of human observation. • Interest in the panorama of human life.	

Consequently, no matter what your choice of major, you're not precluding the possibility of taking courses in other areas in the future. You may eventually end up in a graduate school pursuing a master's degree, a doctorate, or a law degree. You also may take continuing education courses periodically at a local college or university even after

Field of Study	Characteristics	Is This Me?
Languages and linguistics (e.g., translator, interpreter, journalist, anthropologist)	• Interest in words, word origins, and speech. • View of language as a science. • View of literature as human expression. • Appreciation of cultural differences as scientific phenomena.	
Physical education (e.g., kinesiology, health and fitness, recreation and leisure studies, physiotherapist)	• Interest in physical performance. • Enjoyment of sports and athletics. • Commitment to helping others appreciate physical activity. • Patience and perseverance. • Commitment to perfection through practice.	
Physical, biological, and natural sciences (e.g., physics, astronomy, chemistry, biology, some areas of medicine such as paramedicine, laboratory technology, respiratory technology)	• Enjoyment of research questions; high level of curiosity about natural phenomena. • Quantitative thinking a requirement; high comfort level with mathematics and statistics. • Minute-problem-solving skills; attention at great level of detail. • Strong logical ability. • Ability to work with others.	
Social sciences (e.g., psychology, communications, sociology, education, political science, economics)	• Interest in people as individuals or groups. • Ability to think quantitatively and qualitatively. • High comfort level with mathematics and statistics. • High level of creativity and curiosity. • Ability to work with others. • Interest in theory as much as problem solving.	
Spiritual and philosophical studies (e.g., grief counsellor, thanatology, pastoral counsellor, academic)	• Interest in the inner life. • Interest in highly theoretical questions. • Ability to think rigorously about abstract matters. • Appreciation of the human search for meaning.	

After you complete the chart, consider how you can use the information. Did you learn anything new about yourself or about various courses of study? Do your responses direct you toward a particular major? Do they direct you away from any major?

you graduate, because they will help you advance in your career or simply because they interest you.

In short, choosing a major or a program is not a decision that sets your life on an unchangeable course. Instead, it's one step in what can be a lifetime of learning.

Career Connections

Choosing a Job That's Right for You

It's a question nobody can resist asking, and one that you've probably asked: What kind of work are you going to do when you graduate?

While some postsecondary students wait until late to decide their careers, other students are focused on specific career paths right from the start. Whether you are undecided or wholeheartedly committed to a specific occupation, our world is changing rapidly and everyone should be prepared to continually develop their careers, whether that means changing jobs, being promoted, being downsized, or given special temporary projects.

In previous chapters, we've discussed various strategies for exploring professions. Here, in summary, are some steps to take to identify a career:

1. **Start with what you know about yourself.** There's no single perfect career choice. Some people search for the ideal career, assuming that they need to identify the one career for which they are destined. The reality is that many careers would make them equally happy and satisfied. You've already done a lot of mental work toward narrowing down a profession. Do you hate the sight of blood? Then you're probably well aware you're not cut out to be a veterinarian. Does the sight of a column of numbers bring an immediate yawn? Forget about accounting and statistics. Awareness of your likes and dislikes puts you on the road to identifying a future career. Knowing what you don't want to do helps identify what you do want to do and to narrow down the occupations that suit you.

2. **Gather information.** The more you know about potential careers, the better. Examine career-planning materials, read industry profiles, and visit relevant websites. Talk with career counsellors. Discuss your options with people who work in professions in which you're interested. Find out how they chose

their career, how they got their current job, and what advice they'd have for you. In addition, consider participating in an internship in a profession that you think might be attractive. As an intern, you'll gain first-hand experience—probably postsecondary credit as well—for the work that you do.

3. **Narrow down your choices.** Once you've gathered enough information to give yourself a reasonable comfort level, narrow down the choices. If it's early in your postsecondary career, you don't need to make up your mind. If it's late and you feel the pressure to choose, then make the decision. Just do it. Remember, there's no single, absolutely correct decision; there are many right decisions. There's nothing to prevent you from shifting careers later.

Whatever it is you ultimately choose as a career, think of it as only a first step. As the average life span continues to lengthen, most people will pass through several careers during their lives. By periodically taking stock of where you are and considering the things you want for your life, you'll be in a position to make career changes that bring you closer to your ideal. In short, any career choice you make now is likely to be just the first of many.

For over 10 years, the Bank of Montreal's Institute for Learning has been its corporate university, serving as the strategic training and education centre for North America and as a tangible symbol of BMO's dedication to lifelong learning. Tens of thousands of employees have received professional training and development in both face-to-face training and e-learning environments. Ranked as one of Canada's top 100 employers, BMO has spent more than half a billion dollars in the past decade on employee development.

Dealing with Academic Failure—and Success

Experiencing failure is not easy. If we take a course and fail it, it hurts, though we may pretend for a moment that it doesn't. But even if you feel tempted to shrug it off publicly, don't make that mistake privately. It's important to take responsibility for and accept our failures.

However, there's a difference between accepting failure and blaming ourselves. When we fail, it's reasonable to seek to understand what went wrong. It's helpful to figure out how we can do better in the future and to take steps to avoid further failure.

However, it's not useful to spend time and energy blaming ourselves. Self-criticism, denunciation, and rebuke directed at ourselves are behaviours that don't take us forward; they keep us mired in the past.

It's important, then, to forgive ourselves for our failures.

We should not make failure a part of our lives, but it's important to learn from it. We need to consider why a failure occurred, to analyze what we could have done—or avoided doing—to prevent it, and to seek ways of preventing a similar outcome in the future. Real failure occurs when we don't learn from our mistakes.

If you have failed a test, exam, or course, you can take several steps to save your grade:

1. Check with your instructor. Politely request a meeting with your professor to discuss the issue. Ask about possibilities for rewriting or making up the work. If you have a concern about marking procedures or grading criteria, explore these topics diplomatically.

2. If you feel your grade is wrong or unfair and you have not achieved a satisfactory resolution to your problem, consider lodging an academic appeal. The process varies from school

to school but usually involves further contact with your professor, the coordinator of the program, the chair of the department or division, and possibly the dean or an academic review committee. Make sure you have documentation and evidence that supports your claims. Don't throw anything away in anger or frustration. Your school calendar will outline the process for academic appeals.

3. Some schools have an ombudsperson who assists students who feel they have been treated unfairly. The ombudsperson is generally a neutral mediator who tries to facilitate equitable solutions to disputes of an academic or personal nature.

4. Academic probation is a penalty imposed on students who have not met the academic standards of their program or major. This may involve sitting out for a year, taking remedial or make-up classes, or writing a letter or essay detailing your strategies for future success. If you are required to be on academic probation, ensure you use your time to its fullest advantage.

> "Perseverance is not a long race; it is many short races one after another."
>
> Walter Elliott

To avoid a failing grade in a course, consider withdrawing from it. Check your course calendar to find the withdrawal deadline. Remember—there may be consequences (student status or student loan) associated with these actions!

Dealing with Success Some people have as much trouble dealing with academic success as they do dealing with failure. As we first noted in Chapter 1, fear of success is a very real factor in some people's lives. They feel that somehow they're not worthy of success—that their success is a fluke and undeserved.

It's simply not true. We all deserve success, and when we achieve it, we should celebrate it. If you're doing well academically, it's not an accident; it's because you've worked hard and put your intellectual capacities to full use.

Success occurs because we want it to and because we've worked to make it happen. It can happen every day if we allow it. Success is not just reaching an endpoint, such as when we're handed our diploma. Success is a process. Any achievement that brings us closer to fulfilling our goals and dreams should be counted as a success.

> "Our deepest fear is not that we are inadequate. Our deepest fear is that we are powerful beyond measure. It is our light, not our darkness, that most frightens us."
>
> Marianne Williamson

But in the same way that we need to learn from failure, we also need to learn from success. We need to consider what we did and didn't do to achieve success. We need to think about how we might repeat successful behaviours in the future—such as using a study strategy that works for us—and how we can elaborate and extend the strategy to make the likelihood of achieving success even higher.

Finally, we need to keep in mind that life is not an either/or proposition; we're not either successes *or* failures. Even as we fail in one area, we succeed in others. And even as we succeed in one domain, other areas in our lives may not be going so well. Keeping success and failure in perspective is a critical aspect of doing our best in both academic and nonacademic realms.

Speaking of Success

Dr. Anthony Brissett

Dental Assisting Diploma, George Brown Community College
B.N. Sc., George Brown Community College
M.D., Wayne State University

When Dr. Anthony Brissett began the Dental Assisting Program at George Brown College in 1986, he did not know that the career path he was embarking on would lead him to become a highly-skilled doctor specializing in otolaryngology (head and neck surgery), a well-trained surgeon practicing in several top American hospitals, a capable researcher with an interest in wound healing and scarring, a dedicated volunteer who provides cleft-lip and palate surgery to patients in developing countries, and an assistant professor and the director of the Facial Plastic Surgery Center at the prestigious Baylor College of Medicine in Houston, Texas.

As a high-school student, Anthony was not academically inclined, but his parents, first-generation Canadians, wanted him to attend college. So he enrolled in the Dental Assisting Program at George Brown Community College in Toronto, in large part because it was just a one-year program. While at George Brown, Anthony began to develop and mature personally and academically. He credits his courses and faculty at George Brown with providing a solid educational foundation and awakening his intellectual curiosity. After graduating from the Dental Assisting Program, Anthony

George Brown
The Toronto City College

completed the Nursing Program at George Brown and thought he would continue his education by enrolling in a Master's program in nursing. However, on the advice of his professors, he switched disciplines, and graduated from Wayne State Medical School with honours. From there he went to the celebrated Mayo Clinic in Rochester, Minnesota, to do his residency and then completed a fellowship in facial plastic and reconstructive surgery at the University of Minnesota in Minneapolis.

Anthony states that every step of the way his academic choices allowed him to gain more confidence, deepen his knowledge, to search for and meet new challenges, and to use his gift. The recipient of the 2002 Ontario Premier's Award for Health Sciences, an award given to distinguished alumni of Ontario community colleges, Anthony views his background in dental assisting and nursing as essential building blocks to his later academic and career success. In turn, he has demonstrated his appreciation for George Brown by establishing a scholarship benefiting dental assisting and nursing students.

While Anthony's academic and professional success is unquestioned, it has come with a high cost. Leaving his parents, siblings, friends, and immediate support group in Canada has been difficult but in the long run worthwhile, as he is now in a position to achieve satisfaction by contributing the most he can to society.

How can I prepare for the academic choices that college or university demands?

- Making course choices involves finding out as much as possible about what your college or university has to offer. The school catalogue is the best initial source of this information.

- The most personal source of information and guidance in college or university are academic advisors, who have training and experience in advising students on courses, instructors, requirements, and regulations.

What is the best way to choose courses and ensure I'm getting the most out of my studies?

- In choosing courses, you should check out your selections with your academic advisor and then register for the courses. You should be prepared to choose different courses or sections if your initial selections are unavailable.

- You should verify that you have received your chosen courses, that the schedule of courses makes sense, and that your course schedule will help provide the number of credits needed to graduate.

- Be prepared to deal with errors during registration or to cope with the unavailability of courses that you need to take.

- Reflect on your postsecondary experience regularly, verifying that course choices, academic performance, personal growth, choice of major, and your overall educational experience are satisfactory.

How can I choose a major or program?

- Choosing a major or program first involves accepting a period of indecision, finding out more about yourself, seeking the help and advice of others, considering going beyond the traditional structure of your major or program, trying out unusual courses, and taking career plans into account.

How can I deal with academic failure and success?

- Failure and success are part of everyone's life.

- We need to learn to take responsibility for both our failures and our successes.

P.O.W.E.R. Portfolio

Choosing Your Courses and Major

1. Include a program brochure or course outline for your major in your portfolio, along with your course requirements, to show the academic

and professional progress you are making. Your reflection could be an overall assessment of each course completed: what you learned, the biggest surprise, any disappointments, what you need to learn. Have projects, essays, assignments, and tests handy in case you want to include them later. This can be particularly helpful in the future, if you subsequently apply for advanced standing or prior learning assessment (PLA) for a different course or program.

2. Include your transcripts as you receive them. They demonstrate one (important) aspect of your progress to your final goal. As you compile your transcripts, note any patterns or trends. How do these trends relate to your choice of a program or major, or your readiness for your academic or career goals?

Resources

On Campus

The obvious choice for information about courses is your advisor. Sometimes your advisor will be associated with a general program, such as liberal arts; sometimes with a particular division or school, such as technology; or sometimes with a campuswide academic advising centre. Your course instructors also can often give good advice about what courses to sign up for. Finally, don't forget about your fellow students; they can be an excellent source of information about the most interesting and exciting courses. In fact, some schools publish students' course evaluations, which can provide valuable insights about particular courses and instructors.

In Print

Probably the most popular guide to careers is *What Color Is Your Parachute? 2004: A Practical Manual for Job-Hunters & Career-Changers*, by Richard Nelson Bolles (Ten Speed Press, 2003). In it you'll find ways to make decisions about choosing (and changing) professions, as well as ways to obtain a job.

On the Web

The following sites on the World Wide Web provide the opportunity to extend your learning about the material in this chapter. Although the Web addresses were accurate at the time the book was printed, check the P.O.W.E.R. Learning website, <www.mcgrawhill.ca/college/power>, for any changes that may have occurred.

www.cdm.uwaterloo.ca
This career development eManual from the University of Waterloo contains a wealth of career development information, including self-assessment, occupational research, decision-making strategies for education and career, and career and life planning.

www.jobhuntersbible.com/intro/wciyp.shtml
Richard Nelson Bolles's site accompanies his book, *What Color Is Your Parachute? 2004: A Practical Manual for Job-Hunters & Career-Changers*, and contains a wealth of career information as well as links to most of the popular online tests.

www.macleans.ca/universities/index/jsp
Maclean's Guide to Canadian Universities 2004 presents up-to-date information about colleges and universities, including rankings based on student questionnaires and other criteria.

www.assessment.com/
MAPP, the motivational appraisal of personal potential, is an online career assessment tool that provides individuals with comprehensive information on motivations and links with matching careers, based on survey responses.

The Case of . . .

No Clear Decision

As Tarik Chabar began his second semester of General Arts and Science at a large community college, he was still unsure of what to do. It was time to apply to a career program or to university, but Tarik couldn't seem to make up his mind what he wanted to do.

Tarik had thought seriously about several possibilities, including radiography, computer programming, and business purchasing programs, but nothing seemed to offer exactly what he was looking for. Part of the problem, of course, was that he didn't really know what he was looking for. In fact, Tarik was a lot clearer about what he *didn't* want to study than what he *did* want to study.

The clock was ticking, and Tarik felt lost. His parents offered many suggestions, but that just seemed to increase the pressure. And he knew that application deadlines were approaching and programs would be filling up. If he didn't make his own decision soon, circumstances might prevent him from making one he was happy with.

1. What seems to be Tarik's main problem in coming to grips with academic decision making?

2. How can Tarik's prior consideration of programs such as communications and business purchasing help him move closer to a decision?

3. How would you advise Tarik to make use of his understanding of what he doesn't want to study?

4. How can Tarik find out more about himself? Why is this important in choosing a community college career program or university major?

5. Do you think Tarik is taking this decision too seriously or not seriously enough? What advice would you give him about the importance of the academic decisions facing him?

Getting Along with Others

12

Becoming Comfortable in a Multicultural, Diverse World

Building Cultural Competence

Prepare: Accepting Multiculturalism and Diversity as a Valued Part of Your Life

Career Connections: Cultural Competence in the Workplace

Organize: Exploring Your Own Prejudices and Stereotypes

Journal Reflections: Thinking about Race, Ethnicity, and Culture

Work: Developing Cultural Competence

Evaluate: Checking Your Progress in Attaining Cultural Competence

Rethink: Understanding How Your Own Racial, Ethnic, and Cultural Background Affects Others

Building Lasting Relationships

Speaking of Success: Jenny Zhang

The Case of . . . Answering for All

Cablinasian.

That's the word coined by star golfer Tiger Woods to describe his racial heritage. "Cablinasian" means a mix of Caucasian, Black, Indian, and Asian, and it was a label he didn't find on forms asking for his racial identity when he began college.

But Woods did not want to fit himself into some arbitrary racial category. His mother is from Thailand and his father is an African-American, and none of the standard racial categories were appropriate to describe him.

But to Woods, it didn't matter. His background is less important than who he is now and where he is going in the future. "I'm just who I am," he told one interviewer, "whoever you see in front of you."[1]

Looking
Ahead

Whether you have skin that is black or white or brown, are Jewish or Muslim or Greek Orthodox, were born in Calgary or Vietnam or Bosnia, are able-bodied or have a disability, higher education presents new opportunities with regard to diversity and your relationships with others. Because almost every postsecondary institution draws students from a wider sphere than the average high school, college or university permits you to encounter people with very different backgrounds from your own. If you take the opportunity to form relationships with a wide variety of individuals, you will stretch your understanding of the human experience and enrich your life.

In this chapter, we consider how social diversity and relationships affect your postsecondary experience. We examine the increasing multicultural diversity of Canadian society and college and university campuses and consider the meanings and social effects of race, ethnicity, and culture. We look at practical strategies for acknowledging—and shedding—prejudice and stereotypes and for being receptive to others on their own merits.

Next we discuss relationships from a broader perspective, exploring ways that you can build lasting friendships with others. Finally, the chapter discusses the conflicts that can arise between people and what you can do to resolve them.

After reading this chapter you'll be able to answer these questions:

- **Why is the increasing racial, ethnic, and multicultural diversity of society important to you?**

- **How can you become more at ease with cultural differences and diversity?**

- **How can you build lasting relationships and deal with conflict?**

Becoming Comfortable in a Multicultural, Diverse World

No matter where we live, our contacts with others who are racially, ethnically, religiously, and physically different from us are increasing. The Internet and World Wide Web are bringing people from across the globe into our homes, as close to us as the computer sitting on our desk. Businesses now operate globally, so coworkers are likely to come from many different countries and cultures. Being comfortable with people whose backgrounds and beliefs differ from our own is not only a social necessity, but it is also virtually a requirement for career success.

Canada has the most culturally diverse population in the world. Noted author and commentator Gwynne Dyer declares, "Canada is becoming the world in one country."[2] He states that Canada's current immigration patterns mirror the distribution of the global population, with 25 percent of immigrants coming from East Asia, 25 percent from South and Southeast Asia, 10 percent from the Middle East, 10 percent from Africa and the Caribbean, 10 percent from Latin America, and about 20 percent from Europe and the United States. University and college enrollments reflect these changes, especially in large cities like Toronto, Montreal, and Vancouver. For example, visible minorities have grown from 3 percent of the population of Toronto to more than 50 percent in the past 30 years. You can examine the multiculturalism of your campus by completing Try It! 1, "Determine the Multicultural Diversity of Your Campus Community."

Race, Ethnicity, and Culture

Are you black or African-Canadian? Caucasian or white or Euro-Canadian? Salvadoran-Canadian or Latino? Native Canadian or Aboriginal?

The language we use to describe our ethnic and racial group membership, and those of other people, is in constant flux. And what we call people matters. The subtleties of language affect how people think about members of particular groups, and how they think about themselves.

Our cultural heritage plays an important role in shaping who we are.

Try It! 1

Determine the Multicultural Diversity of Your Campus Community

Try to assess the degree of diversity that exists at your college or university, and the overall attitude toward diversity on your campus, by answering these questions. When thinking of diversity, remember to include the many different ways in which people can be different from one another, including race, ethnicity, culture, sexual orientation, physical disabilities, and so on.

Overall, how diverse would you say your campus is?

What is the nature of your college or university's student diversity in terms of statistics regarding student membership in different racial, ethnic, or cultural groups?

What is the nature of your college or university's faculty diversity in terms of statistics regarding faculty membership in different racial, ethnic, or cultural groups?

Are many courses available that directly address multiculturalism or diversity as issues? (A good place to check is your school's catalogue listing of courses in the social sciences and humanities.)

Does your college or university have an explicit statement of policy and principles relating to diversity or the avoidance of discrimination?

Was diversity discussed during your orientation to the campus?

Look back at your answer to the first question ("Overall, how diverse would you say your campus is?") and answer the question again. Did your response change?

Race
Biologically determined physical characteristics that distinguish one group from another

Ethnicity
Shared national origins or cultural patterns

One of the difficulties in understanding diversity is that many of the terms we use are ill defined and often are overlapping. The term **race** is generally used to refer to obvious physical differences that set one group apart from others. According to such a definition, whites, blacks, and Asian-Canadians are typically thought of as different races, determined largely by biological factors.

Ethnicity refers to shared national origins or cultural patterns. In Canada, for example, Ukrainian-, Irish-, and Italian-Canadians are categorized as ethnic groups. However, ethnicity—like race—is very much in the eye of the beholder.

For instance, an Indo-Canadian who is a third-generation citizen of Canada may feel few ties or associations to India. Yet whites may view her as "South Asian."

Finally, **culture** comprises the learned behaviours, beliefs, and attitudes that are characteristic of an individual society or population. Culture also encompasses the products that people create, such as architecture, music, art, and literature. Culture is created and shaped by people, but at the same time it creates and shapes people's behaviour.

Race, ethnicity, and culture shape each of us to an enormous degree. They profoundly influence our view of others, as well as who we are. They affect how others treat us, and how we treat them in turn. They determine whether we look people in the eye when we meet them, how early we arrive when we're invited to dinner at a friend's house, and even, sometimes, how well we do in school.

Culture
The learned behaviours, beliefs, and attitudes—as well as the products people create—that are characteristic of an individual society or population

Cultural competence
Knowledge and understanding about other races, ethnic groups, cultures, and minority groups

Building Cultural Competence

We're not born knowing how to drive a car or cook. We have to learn how to do these things. The same is true of developing a basic understanding of other races, ethnic groups, cultures, and minority groups. Called **cultural competence,** this knowledge of others' customs, perspectives, background, and history can also teach us a great deal about ourselves.

The building of cultural competence proceeds in several steps, as outlined in the P.O.W.E.R. Plan to the right.

P repare: Accepting Multiculturalism and Diversity as a Valued Part of Your Life

In the title of her book on social diversity, psychologist Beverly Tatum asks, *Why Are All the Black Kids Sitting Together in the Cafeteria?*[3] She might just as well have asked a similar question about the white kids, the Chinese-Canadian kids, and so forth. It often appears as if the world comes already divided into separate racial, ethnic, and cultural groups.

It's more than appearances. We form relationships more easily with others who are similar to us than with those who are different. It's easier to interact with others who look the same as we do, who come from similar backgrounds, and who share our race, ethnicity, and culture because we can take for granted certain shared cultural assumptions and views of the world.

But this doesn't mean that easy and comfortable are good. We can learn a great deal more, and grow and be challenged, if we seek out people who are different from us. If you look beyond surface differences and find out what motivates other people, you can become aware of ways of thinking about family, relationships, earning a living, and the value of education

PREPARE

Accept diversity as a valued part of your life

ORGANIZE

Explore your own prejudices and stereotypes

WORK

Develop cultural competence

EVALUATE

Check your progress in attaining cultural competence

RETHINK

Understand how your own racial, ethnic, and cultural background affects others

P.O.W.E.R. Plan

Career Connections

Cultural Competence in the Workplace

Cross-cultural issues are a part of Canada's workplaces.[4] Employers must deal with issues ranging from arranging a private space for Muslim employees to pray to deciding whether the partner of a gay or lesbian worker should be covered by the worker's benefit insurance.

The gulf in the workplace between people with different cultural backgrounds may be wide. For instance, in Japan, the cultural expectation is that people should stress their incompetence; for a new immigrant, having to outline his or her accomplishments in a job interview would be considered highly immodest.

Canada requires immigration for its population to grow since our birth rate is very low. In addition, Canada needs more skilled workers to have enough replacements for retiring baby boomers.

The increasingly diverse and multicultural Canadian workplace means that increasing your cultural competence is necessary. It will help you perform on workgroup teams that comprise people of different races and ethnic backgrounds; it will help you supervise people whose native language and customs may be different from yours; and it will help you to work for a boss from another country and cultural background.

> Photonics is the science of harnessing light at a microscopic level to make communication networks more efficient. It is an emerging trillion-dollar industry, and it has a critical shortage of trained personnel. Photonics Research Ontario says Canada does not have the capacity to produce enough skilled workers to meet demands. Currently Eastern European universities produce the most capable graduates, but since it takes two years or more for skilled workers to immigrate to Canada independently, shortages still exist. Therefore, Canadian businesses are urging the government to speed up the process, allowing more skilled workers into Canada to fill job vacancies.

that are very different from your own. It can be liberating to realize that others may hold very different perspectives from your own and that there are many ways to lead your life.

Letting diversity into your own life may not be simple or easy, but it's incredibly helpful in and important to achieving your own growth and understanding. Understanding diversity also has very practical implications: As we discuss in Career Connections, "Cultural Competence in the Workplace," learning to accept and work with people who are different from you is a crucial skill that will help you in whatever job you hold.

◘ rganize: Exploring Your Own Prejudices and Stereotypes

Arab, lesbian, African-Canadian, tattooed, female—quick: What comes into your mind when you think about each of these labels? If you're like most people, you don't draw a blank. Instead, a collection of images and feelings comes into your mind, based on what you know, have been told, or assume about the group.

The fact that we don't draw a blank when thinking about each of these terms means that we already have a set of attitudes and beliefs about them and the groups they represent. Acknowledging and then examining these preexisting assumptions is a first step toward developing cultural competence. We need to explore our own prejudices and stereotypes to know where we're starting from.

Prejudice refers to evaluations or judgments of members of a group that are based primarily on membership in the group, rather than on an individual's particular characteristics. For example, the auto mechanic who doesn't expect a woman to understand the repair he is undertaking or the supervisor who finds it unthinkable that a father might want to take childcare leave are engaging in gender prejudice, evaluating individuals based on their being male or female and not on their own specific characteristics or abilities. Similarly, prejudice can be directed toward individuals because of their race, ethnic origin, sexual orientation, age, physical disability, or even degree of physical attractiveness.

Prejudice is maintained by **stereotypes,** beliefs and expectations about members of a group that are held simply because of their membership in the group. For example, do you think that women don't drive as well as men? Do you agree that "white men can't jump"? Do you believe that people raised in the jungles of South America are less intelligent than those raised in a Western society? Do you think that people on welfare are lazy? If you answered yes to any of these questions, you hold stereotypes about the group being referred to. It is the degree of generalization involved that makes stereotypes inaccurate. Some white men *can't* jump. But the fact is, many can—and do—and the stereotypes ignore this diversity.

To develop cultural competence, it's important to identify our prejudices and stereotypes and to fight them. Sometimes they are quite subtle and difficult to detect. For instance, a wealth of data taken from observation of elementary school classrooms shows that teachers often are more responsive to boys than to girls. The teachers don't know they're doing it; it's a subtle, but very real, bias.

Why does this happen? In part it's because we're exposed to stereotypes from a very young age. Parents and relatives teach them to us, sometimes unwittingly, sometimes on purpose. The media illustrate them constantly, and often in very subtle ways. For instance, African-Canadians and Aboriginal people are often portrayed as unemployed or as criminals, and women are less likely than men to be shown as employed.

But it's not only stereotypes that lead us to view members of other groups differently from those of our own. For most people, their own membership in a cultural or racial or ethnic group is a source of pride and self-worth. There's nothing wrong with this. However, these feelings can lead to a less desirable outcome: the

Journal Reflections

Thinking about Race, Ethnicity, and Culture

1. Overall, what are your feelings about race, ethnicity, and culture?

2. Were race and ethnicity discussed in your family? In what ways?

3. In what ways has your race or ethnicity affected your schooling?

4. In what ways has your race or ethnicity affected your social life?

5. If you are a member of a majority group, imagine yourself as a member of a minority group. In what ways would your childhood and adolescence have been different? If you are a member of a minority group, perform this exercise in reverse.

6. Are you proud of your ethnicity? Why? What traces of ethnicity do you show?

7. What are some cultural differences between you and members of *other* races or ethnicities?

8. How many "cultures" can you identify among your fellow students? Among your friends?

9. Have you taken steps to learn more about persons of another race, ethnicity, or culture? What steps might you take in the future?

Check Your Stereotype Quotient

Do you hold stereotypes about other people? How pervasive do you think they are? Respond to the following informal questionnaire to get a sense of your susceptibility to stereotyping.

1. When you see five African-Canadian students sitting together in the cafeteria, do you think that they are exhibiting racism? How is your reaction similar or different when you see five white students sitting together in the cafeteria?

2. When you are speaking with a person who has a speech-related disorder such as stuttering, are you likely to conclude that the person is less intelligent than a fluent speaker?

3. When an elderly woman can't remember something, do you assume her forgetfulness is because she is old or perhaps has Alzheimer's disease?

4. When an attractive blonde female student states an opinion in class, are you surprised if the opinion is intelligent and well expressed?

5. If a person with a mobility disorder turns down your offer for assistance, would you be offended and resentful?

Prejudice

Evaluations or judgments of members of a group that are based primarily on membership in the group, and not on the particular characteristics of individuals

belief that their own group is superior to others. As a result, people inflate the positive aspects of their own group and belittle groups to which they do not belong. The bottom line is continuing prejudice.

To overcome stereotypes and to develop cultural competence, we must first explore and identify our prejudices. To begin that process, complete Try It! 2, "Check Your Stereotype Quotient."

W ork: Developing Cultural Competence

Stereotypes

Beliefs and expectations about members of a group that are held simply because of their membership in the group

Although it's neither easy nor simple to increase your understanding of and sensitivity to other cultures, it can be done. Several strategies are effective:

- **Study other cultures and customs.** Take an anthropology course, study religion, or learn history. If you understand the purposes behind different cultural customs, attitudes, and beliefs, you will be able to understand the richness and meaning of other people's cultural heritage.

6. When you meet a student with a Vietnamese or Chinese last name, are you surprised if he or she speaks fluent, unaccented Canadian English?

7. When an African-Canadian student whom you don't know joins an athletic team you're on, are you happy because you believe he or she will be a good athlete?

8. If you see a group of three large males walking toward you in the distance at night, are you more nervous if they're members of a different race from yours than if they're members of your own race?

9. If a male student and a female student each ask you the same question about a technical topic you understand thoroughly, do you respond differently or in the exact same way?

Do you think you would have answered any of these questions differently five years ago? Do you think you will answer any of them differently five years from now? What experiences would make you change your responses?

Working in a group, compare your responses with those of your classmates. What similarities and differences do you see? Do you have the sense, not just from this exercise but from your general experience, that stereotypes are still prevalent?

Many colleges and universities offer workshops on multiculturalism, diversity, and prejudice reduction. Student religious groups and ethnic associations and clubs often hold open houses, discussions, and celebrations and invite all interested people to attend. These can help too. The important point is that understanding comes from knowledge, and you won't be able to fully appreciate others without learning about their background.

"We also know that racial discrimination is perhaps the epitome of human indignity and that if we tolerate it even privately—in our own hearts—then we have diminished our own stature."

Pierre Trudeau

- **Travel.** There is no better way to learn about people from other cultures than to see those cultures firsthand. College and university vacations offer you the time to travel, and relatively inexpensive charter flights can take you to Europe, Asia, and other places around the globe. Sometimes, in fact, it's cheaper to take a transoceanic flight than to travel to closer locations within Canada.

Travel provides us with an opportunity to become immersed in very different cultures and to see the world—and ourselves—through different eyes.

If you can't afford air fare, take a car or bus ride to the United States or Mexico. Travel need not be international, however. If you are from the Atlantic provinces, head west. If you are from British Columbia or Alberta, consider heading east. A visit to Quebec can be an eye-opening and culturally enriching experience, whether you choose to visit the bright lights of Montreal or the relative quiet of Trois-Pistoles. No matter where you go, simply finding yourself away from home can aid your efforts to learn about other cultures by putting you in a new context.

- **Don't ignore people's backgrounds.** None of us is blind to a person's colour, or blind to ethnicity, or to culture. It's impossible to be completely unaffected by people's racial, ethnic, religious, and cultural backgrounds. So why pretend to be? Cultural heritage is an important part of other people's identity, and to pretend that their background doesn't exist and has no impact on them is unrealistic at best, and insulting at worst. It's important, though, to distinguish between accepting the fact that other people's backgrounds affect them and pigeonholing people and expecting them to behave in particular ways.

- **Don't treat people as representatives of the groups to which they belong.** If you're a member of a minority group, you've probably been asked how members of your group think, feel, or behave with respect to a particular issue. Somehow, as a member of the group, you're expected to know how every other member feels about a topic.

Of course, that's impossible; no single individual can speak for an entire group. Furthermore, group members are likely to display little uniformity on most issues and in most behaviours, and so this type of question is ultimately impossible to answer. In short, it makes little sense to treat others as if they were representatives of the racial, ethnic, religious, or cultural group to which they belong.

> "...all individuals should have an equal opportunity to make for themselves the lives that they are able and wish to have, consistent with their duties and obligations as members of society..."
>
> *Canadian Human Rights Act*

- **Accept differences.** Different does not mean better. Different does not mean worse. Different just means not looking, acting, or believing exactly the same as you. We shouldn't attach any kind of value to being different; it's neither better nor worse than being similar.

Even people who seem obviously different on the surface probably share many similarities with you. Like you, they are students; they have fears and anxieties like yours; and they have aspirations and dreams, just as you do.

The important point about differences is that we need to accept them. All people want to be accepted for who they are—their abilities and talents, their attitudes and beliefs, their interests and accomplishments—not just because they are similar to you. In Canada, individuals are protected by federal and provincial legislation against discrimination. The idea behind human rights legislation is that people should not be placed at a disadvantage because of their age, sex, race, religion, or other grounds covered by federal and provincial Acts.

Evaluate: Checking Your Progress in Attaining Cultural Competence

Because cultural groups are constantly changing, developing cultural competence is an ongoing process. To evaluate where you stand, ask yourself the following questions:

- Do I make judgments about others based on external features, such as skin colour, ethnic background, religious attire, cultural customs, gender, weight, or physical appearance?

- Who are my friends? Do they represent diversity or are they generally similar to me?

- Do I openly express positive values relating to diversity? Do I sit back passively when others express stereotypes and prejudices, or do I actively question their remarks?

- Am I educating myself about the history and varying experiences of different racial, ethnic, religious, and cultural groups?

- Do I give special treatment to members of particular groups, or am I evenhanded in my relationships?

- Do I recognize that, despite surface differences, all people have the same basic needs?

- Do I feel so much pride in my own racial, ethnic, religious, and cultural heritage that it leads me to look less favourably on members of other groups?

- Do I seek to understand events and situations through the perspectives of others and not just my own?

Rethink: Understanding How Your Own Racial, Ethnic, and Cultural Background Affects Others

If you are a member of a minority group, you probably don't need to be told that your race, ethnicity, religious, and cultural background affects the way that others treat you. But even if you are a member of a majority group, the way in which others respond to you is, in part, a result of others' assumptions about the groups of which you are a part.

In short, both how we view others and how we ourselves are viewed are affected by the groups to which we—and others—belong. But keep this in mind. No matter how different other students are from you in terms of their race, ethnicity, religious, and cultural background, they undoubtedly share many of the same concerns you do. Like all of us, they question themselves, wonder whether they will be successful, and fret about what they will do for the rest of their lives. Bridging the surface difference between you and others can result in the development of close, lasting social ties—a topic we consider next.

Building Lasting Relationships

Few of us lead our lives in isolation. There's a reason for this. Relationships with others are critical aspects of our sense of well-being. The support of friends and relatives helps us feel good about ourselves. In fact, studies have found that our physical and psychological health may suffer without friendships. The social support of others acts as a guard against stress and illness. And if we do get sick, we recover more quickly if we have a supportive network of friends.

Our relationships with others also help us understand who we are. To understand our own abilities and achievements, we compare them with those of others who are similar to ourselves. Our attitudes, beliefs, and values are influenced—and shaped—by others. We are who we are largely because of the people with whom we come in contact. (To learn more about your views of friendship, complete Try It! 3, "Define Friendship.")

Making Friends

Although some of us naturally make friends with ease, for others making friends is more difficult. But building relationships is not a mystery. Here are several ways to go about it:

- **Invest time in others.** There's no better way to demonstrate that you are interested in being friends than investing time. Relationships need to be nourished by the commitment of time. You can't expect friendships to flourish unless you spend time with people.

- **Reveal yourself.** Good friends understand each other. The best way to make that happen is to let others get to know you. Be open and honest about the things you like and dislike. Talk about where you come from, what your family is like. Find out about the other person. Having a deeper understanding of where someone comes from not only helps build bridges between people of different racial and ethnic backgrounds, it also helps build friendships. By honestly communicating your beliefs and attitudes, you give others the chance to learn those things you have in common—which, despite surface differences, may be substantial when it comes to basic values and approaches to the world.

- **Let others know you like them.** It may seem scary, but don't be coy and try to pretend you are uninterested in the friendships of others. Take the risk of being rebuffed. You don't have to announce outright that you like someone. Instead, reveal your interest in a friendship by inviting the person to do something with you or simply by engaging in conversation, sharing something about your life. Your actions will speak louder than words.

- **Accept others as they are, not as you would like them to be.** One mark of friendship is accepting of people the way they are, warts and all, and

Define Friendship

Everyone has a personal understanding of what friendship is, but different people may define it differently. Answer the following questions to sharpen your personal definition of friendship.

1. How important are close personal relationships to you?

2. Approximately how much time do you spend on your friendships (being with, talking with, or corresponding with your friends)? Do you tend to initiate your contacts with your friends (e.g., are you the one to pick up the phone?), do your friends tend to initiate them, or is it about 50–50?

3. How honest are you with your close friends? Do you have any friend with whom you would share even your most secret ideas, acts, and fantasies?

4. What is your style of making friends (e.g., just letting it happen or perhaps opening up to someone in the hope of reciprocation)? How do you know when an acquaintanceship has moved to a true friendship?

5. Has a friend of yours ever changed in a fairly substantial way during your friendship? What has been your reaction?

6. All things considered, how would you define *friendship,* and how would you describe what makes a good friend?

After completing these questions, ask yourself the following ones: Are you generally satisfied with your friendships? Would you like to change them in some way?

Working in a group, compare your definitions of friendship, considering similarities and differences.

not the way you would like them to be. Do not impose conditions on accepting others. Keep in mind that no one is perfect and that everyone has both good and bad qualities.

- **Show concern and caring.** This is really the substance of friendship and the basis for the trust that develops between friends. Don't be afraid to show your interest in the fortunes of others and to share the sadness when they suffer some setback or loss.

- **Not everyone makes a good friend.** People who belittle you, consistently make you feel bad or unhappy, or behave in ways that violate your own personal standards are not friends, no matter what they may tell you. Choose your friends based on the good feelings you have when you are with them and the concern and caring they show for you. Friendship is a two-way street.

The R-Word: Relationships

Relationships move beyond friendship. They occur when two people feel emotionally attached, fulfill each other's needs, and generally feel interdependent. When a true relationship exists, several components are present:

- **Trust.** Relationships must be built on a foundation of trust. We need to be able to count on others and feel that they will be open with us.

- **Honesty.** No relationship can survive if the partners are not honest with one another. Each partner must share a commitment to the truth. Your life does not have to be a completely open book—it's the rare individual who has no secrets whatsoever—but it is important to be honest about your fundamental beliefs, values, and attitudes. Those in good relationships accept one another, blemishes and all, and a relationship based on untruths or even half-truths lacks depth and meaning.

- **Mutual support.** Healthy relationships are characterized by mutual support. A partner's well-being should have an impact on you, and your well-being should affect your partner. In good relationships, the partners seek out what is best for each other, and they act as advocates for and defend each other.

- **Loyalty.** The mark of a good relationship is loyalty. Loyalty implies that relationship partners are supportive of each other, even in times of adversity and difficulty.

- **Acceptance.** Your best friend watches every reality show going, and is incredibly caught up by the action and personalities on each episode. You can't stand to watch this type of TV show. Do you decide that you can no longer be friends? Of course not.

    In good relationships small annoyances don't get in the way of the deeper connection between you and another person. We don't have to like everything others do to maintain relationships with them. We don't even have to appreciate or approve of every aspect of their personalities.

What you *don't* say matters. Close, lasting relationships are often built on good listening skills.

What is crucial is the willingness to accept others as they are, without constantly yearning for changes. All of us want to be accepted by others as we are, not as they'd like us to be; we should offer the same approval to those with whom we maintain relationships.

- **Willingness to embrace change.** Change is part of everyone's life. As people grow and develop, they change. So do relationships.

  We need to accept change as a fundamental part of relationships and build on that change. In fact, we need to welcome change. Although change brings challenges with it, it also helps us to understand ourselves and our own place in the world more accurately.

  It is only natural that some relationships will fade over time. People do outgrow one another. That's inevitable. What's important is not to live in fear that your relationship is so fragile that you have to avoid or ignore changes in who you and your partner are. Instead, both partners in a relationship should do their best to accept changes and development in the relationship as a part of life.

Communicating in Relationships

Communicating well in personal relationships is a blend of talking and listening. Not only does it help to do both well, it is also important to know when it's time to listen and when it's time to speak up. Listening is an often overlooked skill in personal relationships. We may be so busy trying to communicate our feelings and interests that we overlook the need of the other person to be heard. As friendships develop into personal relationships, simply talking isn't enough. How you express yourself, especially in moments of difficulty, can be very important to getting your message across.

Being a Good Listener: The Power of Supportive Silence

When it comes to building relationships, how you listen is sometimes more important than what you say. The silence involved in listening is a powerful force, one that can bind us more closely to others.

We've already discussed in Chapter 7 the art and science of listening as it applies to academic success. The same principles that promote learning about lecture topics also promote learning about our friends. You can't call yourself a good friend without knowing what others are like and what they are thinking. Good listening is one of the ways to enhance your understanding of others.

> "Maybe the single most important thing I have learned is that I don't need to become friends with every one out there."
>
> Alicia Fuchs, Student, Trinity Western University

When we are heard, we appreciate it because we get the message that our listeners care about us, not just about themselves. Similarly, when we listen, we show that we have respect for those who are speaking, are interested in their ideas and beliefs, and are willing to take the time to pay attention to them.

You can improve your ability to listen in five ways:

1. **Stop talking!** Are you the kind of person who revels in telling stories about what happened to you? Do you wait eagerly for others to finish what they are saying so that you can jump in with a response? Do you even accidentally cut other people off or finish their sentences while they are speaking?

   No one likes to be interrupted, even in casual conversation. In more personal relationships, it really is a sign of not respecting what the other person has to say and, thus, is disrespectful of *them*.

   One way to break the habit of overtalking is to consciously slow the conversation down. Wait several seconds (mentally count to three) before making a response.

2. **Demonstrate that you are listening.** Linguists call them "conversational markers"—those nonverbal indications that we're listening. They consist of head nods, uh-huh's, okay's, and other signs that we're keeping up with the conversation. Eye contact is important too. Listening this way shows that we're paying attention and are interested in what the other person is saying.

3. **Use reflective feedback.** Carl Rogers,[5] a respected therapist, developed a very useful way to lend support to someone and draw him or her out. In **reflective feedback,** a listener rephrases what a speaker has said, trying to echo the speaker's meaning. For example, a listener might say, "as I understand what you're saying . . . ," or "you seem to feel that . . . ," or "in other words, you believe that . . . ."

   In each case, the summary statement doesn't just "play back" the speaker's statements literally. Instead, it is a rephrasing that captures the essence of the message in different words.

   Reflective feedback has two big benefits. First, it provides speakers with a clear indication that you are listening and taking what they're saying seriously. Second, and equally important, it helps ensure that you have an accurate understanding of what the speaker is saying. If your reflective feedback is inaccurate, you can be certain that the speaker will attempt to correct your erroneous impression.

4. **Ask questions.** Asking questions shows that you are paying attention to a speaker's comments. Questions permit you to clarify what the speaker has said, and they can move the conversation forward. Further, people feel valued when others ask them about themselves.

5. **Admit when you're distracted.** We've all had those moments: Something is bothering you and you can't get it out of your mind, or you've simply got to finish something and don't really have time to chat. If at the same time someone wants to engage you in conversation, your distraction will undoubtedly show, making the other person feel you are not interested in her or him.

   The way to deal with this situation is to admit that you're distracted. Simply saying, "I'd love to talk, but I've got to finish reading a chapter" is enough to explain the situation to a classmate who wants to talk about his date. If you don't say anything, you will probably feel resentment, anger, or some other negative emotion, which will surely be conveyed to your friend.

Reflective feedback

A technique of verbal listening in which a listener rephrases what a speaker has said, trying to echo the speaker's meaning

Loneliness

Loneliness is a subjective state. We can be totally alone and not feel lonely, or we can be in the midst of a crowd and feel lonely. Loneliness occurs when we don't experience the level of connection with others that we desire. There are also different types of loneliness. Some of us feel lonely because we lack a deep emotional attachment to a single person, which can occur even if we have many friends. Others feel loneliness because they believe they don't have enough friends or relatives.

Although people may feel lonely because they have an insufficient number of relationships, the reality is that no standard indicates the "right" number of relationships. Is it enough to have one or two close friends? Does having many acquaintances replace having a single, enduring, close relationship? Obviously, there are no hard-and-fast rules, and you shouldn't think that there's a single standard against which to measure yourself and the number, and kind, of relationships that you have. It's something you need to decide.

What is clear is that certain situations produce loneliness. First-year college and university students almost always report higher degrees of loneliness than students in subsequent years of study.

Loneliness is not inevitable. Several strategies for dealing with loneliness follow:

- **Become involved in campus activities.** Join a club. Volunteer to help some social organization. Try out for a play. You'll soon get to know others who have similar interests.

- **Find a study partner.** Ask one of your classmates to study with you. You can review your class notes, work together on a project, or study for tests together. Working together will not only help you to master the class material, it will also help you make what can become an important social connection.

- **Understand how certain circumstances lend themselves to feeling lonely.** Why are first-year students lonely? It's because they haven't had time to meet people and become well-enough acquainted enough with anyone to develop a true friendship. Furthermore, many of the people whom they may have relied on previously are no longer present. The combination of no new friends and unavailable old friends can easily lead to loneliness. Simply knowing the reasons for your loneliness can help you deal with it.

- **Know that you're not alone in your loneliness.** If you're feeling lonely, you may find yourself looking at your classmates and noticing groups of people engaged in social activities. This can make you feel even more isolated. Don't be fooled by such social illusions into believing that you are the only one experiencing loneliness. Remember that for every person you notice who is socializing, there are others who are not doing so.

- **Take advantage of orientation and first-year student social events.** Even if you don't consider yourself particularly good at socializing, it's

Loneliness
A subjective state in which people do not experience a desired level of connection with others

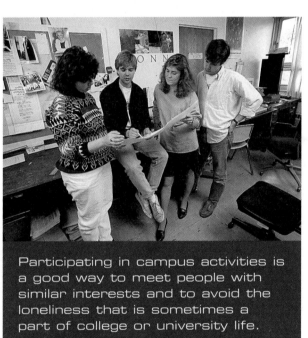

Participating in campus activities is a good way to meet people with similar interests and to avoid the loneliness that is sometimes a part of college or university life.

important to make the effort. If you're shy—and even if you're not—consider it a social success if you meet just one new person at such an event.

- **Take a job on campus.** Campus jobs not only provide income, but social connections as well. Through work you can meet members of the college or university staff and make connections with other students.

- **Remember that loneliness is a subjective—and typically temporary—state.** Whether you experience isolation depends on how you interpret your current state. If you interpret your feelings of isolation as due to your personal failings ("I'm alone because I'm not a very likable or interesting person"), you'll experience loneliness. If you view your isolation as a consequence of temporary, short-term factors ("Everyone has a lot of work this semester and few opportunities to socialize"), you're less likely to feel loneliness. In short, try to pinpoint why you're feeling lonely, and don't blame yourself for your sense of loneliness.

What if your feelings of loneliness are extreme and you experience a sense of complete isolation and alienation from your classmates? If the feeling persists, it's wise to talk to someone at your campus counselling centre, a health service provider, or your advisor. Although everyone feels isolated at times, such feelings shouldn't be extreme. Counsellors can help you deal with them.

It's Not Just Talk: Avoiding and Handling Conflicts in Relationships

Listening communicates a great deal in personal relationships, but, as discussed previously, it is also important to put yourself forward. Generally, close relationships are built on good communication, so day-to-day there may be no problem in this regard. But when misunderstandings or conflicts occur—as they definitely will from time to time—communication can fall apart. In these situations your ability to communicate in words is tested, and more-sensitive listening and more-careful ways of saying what you think and feel are needed.

The Subject Is "I," and Not "You" Suppose a close friend says something with which you disagree: "All you guys are the same—you expect to get everything your way!" You might respond by directing anger at the other person, directly or indirectly accusing them of some imperfection. "You never have any ideas! You're just looking for something to complain about!" Such responses (and, as you will notice, the initial statement) typically include the word *you.* Consider these possible responses to indicate disagreement: *"You* really don't understand"; *"You're* being stubborn"; and "How can *you* say that?"

The problem with such statements is that each includes the word you, putting the speaker on the defensive. These types of statements cast blame, make accusations, express criticism, and make assumptions about what's inside the other person's head. And they lead to defensive replies that will probably do little to move the conversation forward: "I do so understand"; "I'm not being stubborn"; and "I can say that because that's the way I feel."

A far more reasonable tactic is to use "I" statements. **"I" statements** cast responses in terms of yourself and your individual interpretation. Instead of saying, for example, "You really don't understand," a more appropriate response would be, "I feel we have a misunderstanding." "You're being stubborn" could be rephrased as "I feel as though you're acting in a stubborn

"I" statements
Statements that cast responses in terms of yourself and your individual interpretation

Try It!

4

🕊 Working in a Group
Switch "You" to "I"

Working in a group or in pairs, turn the following "you" statements into less aggressive "I" statements.

You Statements

1. You just don't get it, do you?

2. You never listen to what I say.

3. You don't see where I'm coming from.

4. You don't really believe that, do you?

5. You never try to see my point of view.

6. Please stop interrupting me and listen to what I'm saying for a change.

7. Stop changing the subject!

8. You're not making sense.

9. You keep distorting what I say until I don't even know what point I'm trying to make.

10. You use too many "you" statements. Use more "I" statements when you're talking to others.

way." And "how can you say that" becomes "I don't understand why you're saying that." In each case, "I" statements permit you to state your reaction in terms of your perception or understanding, rather than as a critical judgment about the other person. (Practise using "I" statements in Try It! 4, "Switch 'You' to 'I'.")

Resolving Conflict: A Win–Win Proposition Even with careful attention to putting our own feelings forward instead of making accusations, whenever two people share their thoughts, concerns, fears, and honest reactions with each other, the chances are that sooner or later some sort of conflict will arise.

Conflict is not necessarily bad.

Often, people are upset simply by the fact that they are having a conflict. It is as though they believe conflicts don't occur in "good" relationships. In fact,

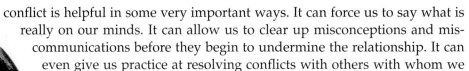

conflict is helpful in some very important ways. It can force us to say what is really on our minds. It can allow us to clear up misconceptions and miscommunications before they begin to undermine the relationship. It can even give us practice at resolving conflicts with others with whom we might not share such good relations.

Like anything else, though, there are good ways to resolve conflict, and there are bad ways. Good ways move people forward, defining the problem and promoting creative problem solving. Bad ways make the situation worse, driving people apart rather than bringing them together. The following are some fundamental principles of conflict resolution that you can use when conflict occurs in personal and professional relationships:

- **Stop, look, and listen.** In the heat of an argument, all sorts of things that otherwise would go unsaid get said. If you find yourself making rash or hurtful statements, stop, look at yourself, and listen to what you and the other person are saying.

    Stopping works like a circuit breaker that prevents a short circuit from causing a deadly fire. You've probably heard about counting to 10 when you are angry. Do it. Take a break and count to 10 . . . or 20 . . . or more. Whether you count to 10 or 100, stopping the action gives you time to think and not to just react.

- **Defuse the argument.** Anger is not an emotion that encourages rational discourse. When you're angry and annoyed with someone, you're not in the best position to evaluate logically the merits of various arguments or excuses others may offer. It may feel exhilarating to get our fury off our chests in the heat of an argument, but you can bet it isn't taking anyone any closer to resolving the problem.

    Don't assume that you are 100 percent right and the other person is 100 percent wrong. Make your goal *solving the problem* rather than winning the argument.

- **Get personal.** Perhaps you've heard others suggest that you should avoid getting personal in an argument. In one sense that's true: You don't want to accuse people you're arguing with of having character flaws that make some aspect of their behaviour unacceptable.

    At the same time, you should be willing to admit personal responsibility for at least part of the conflict. The conflict would not exist without you, so you need to accept that the argument has two sides and that you are not automatically blameless.

- **Listen to the real message.** When people argue, what they say is often not the real message. There's typically an underlying communication—a meta-message—that is the source of the conflict.

    It's important, then, to dig beneath what you're hearing. If someone accuses you of being selfish, the real meaning hidden in the accusation may be that you don't give anyone else a chance to make decisions. Remember, arguments are usually about behaviour, not underlying character and personality. What people *do* is not necessarily synonymous with what they *are*.

    If you rephrase the person's statement in your own mind, it moves from an insult ("You're a bad person") to a request for a change of behaviour ("Let me participate in decision making"). You're much more likely to respond reasonably when you don't feel that your personal essence is under attack.

- **Show that you're listening.** It's not enough only to listen to the underlying message that someone is conveying. You also need to acknowledge the message. For example, saying something like "Okay, I can tell you are concerned about sharing the work/the responsibility on our group project, and I think we should talk about it" acknowledges that you see the issue and admit that it is worthy of discussion. This is a far more successful strategy than firing back a countercharge each time your partner makes a complaint.

- **If you are angry, acknowledge it.** Don't pretend that everything is fine if it isn't. Ultimately, relationships in which the partners bottle up their anger suffer more than those in which the partners express their true feelings. If you're angry, say so.

- **Ask for clarification.** As you're listening to another person's arguments, check your understanding of what is being said. Don't assume that you know what's intended. Saying something like "Are you saying . . ." or "Do you mean that . . ." is a way of verifying that what you *think* someone means is really what is meant.

- **Make your requests explicit.** If you're upset that your roommate leaves clothes lying around your apartment or dorm room, remarking that he or she is a "pig" shows more than that you are angry. It also shows that your intent is to hurt rather than to solve the problem.

  It's far better to be explicit in your concerns. Say something like "It would make me feel better if you would pick up your clothes from the floor." Couching your concern in this way changes the focus of the message from your roommate's personality to a specific behaviour that potentially can be changed.

- **Always remember that life is not a zero-sum game.** Many of us act as if life were a **zero-sum game,** a situation in which when one person wins, the other person automatically loses. It's what happens when you make a bet: If one person wins the bet, the other person loses.

  Life is not like that. If one person wins an argument, it doesn't mean that others automatically have to lose it. And if someone loses an argument, it doesn't mean that others have automatically won. In fact, all too often conflict escalates so much that the argument turns into a lose–lose situation.

  However, life can be a win–win situation. The best resolution of conflict occurs when both parties walk away with something they want. Each may not have achieved *every* goal they had, but they at least have enough to feel satisfied. (For practice in resolving conflict, do Try It! 5, "Resolve That Conflict.")

Zero-sum game
A situation in which when one person wins, the other person automatically loses

Changing Relationships: Surviving Endings

Not all relationships last a lifetime. Sometimes they just wind down, as the two people involved slowly lose interest in maintaining their partnership. At other times, they break apart, as disagreements build and there is not a strong enough bond to hold the two parties together. Or there may be an abrupt rupture if some event occurs that destroys one partner's feeling of trust.

Caring for others is rewarding, but risky. When relationships don't work out, their endings can be painful, even devastating, for a time. Even when

Resolve That Conflict

Find and resolve as many conflicts as you can in the following discussion at a student newspaper meeting:

Shira: I'd like to run the women's basketball conference finals article as the lead story on this week's sports page.

Todd: Wait a minute. Women's basketball doesn't precede men's basketball. We always lead with the men's team.

Sara: Yeah, and the NBA and even the NHL are mentioned before women's sports. The Lions are in the conference finals, and the men's game this week is meaningless.

Dushan: Meaningless? There'll be 200 more fans at the men's game than at the girls' game.

Shira: That's *women's game*! Well, that's partly the problem. With the women's sports columns stuck after NASCAR racing and the World Wrestling Entertainment (WWE), who can find out about how well our teams are doing?

Sara: I agree! And you know men's teams are funded like, 10 times more than women's— they can't afford to advertise like the guys can. With such little publicity, the women's team hasn't drawn as many supporters, but now we're in the finals … I think the school paper should lead the way in raising the profile of women's sports.

Dushan: You never pass up a chance to complain about the WWE. Why don't you get it? Guys *like* the WWE and they *like* to read columns about racing. Kevin Bidwell is gonna croak if I give him the ladies' game as his assignment this weekend.

Shira: Why don't *you* get it? The last I heard, female students' tuitions paid for this paper too! More than 50 percent of the students here are female, but 85 percent of the writers and editorial staff are male. That's why the coverage is so biased! Why not let one of us write the article? Why does Kevin always get the big story? What Sara and I say has no weight when you male editors wield all the power here!

Todd: How about reason A: your familiarity with sports jargon is severely limited, and B: Kevin is the sports editor, and his stories always lead. That's the way it works around here. If you don't like it, you can always go to student council.

Shira: Oh, right. As if Kyle Douglas is going to listen to us. Student council is no better than here. Only the VP for internal affairs is female; everyone else is male. This place is a bastion for male, hierarchical thinking.

Dushan: Whoa, Nellie McClung. Haven't you heard that feminism is dead? Expired. Deceased. Finito. Next item on the agenda?

Can you think of several approaches for resolving each of the various conflicts? Which of the resolution possibilities you've devised do you think would work best? Are there any approaches that should be avoided?

relationships evolve naturally, and change is expected, the transformation in a relationship may not be easy. Couples break up. Best friends grow apart. Parents die. Children grow up and move away from home. Siblings get new jobs on the other side of the country.

One sure cure exists for the heartache of a lost relationship: time. You can do some other things, however, as you wait for time to pass and for the pain to ease:

Speaking of Success

Jenny Zhang

International Business, Centennial Community College, Toronto, Ontario

Jenny Zhang is currently studying international business at Centennial College in Toronto. Her long-term goal is to become involved in the growing trade between Canada and China. A recent immigrant from Jiangsu, China, Jenny took one semester of English as a Second Language before passing the Centennial College's English test and beginning the International Business program where she studies with English-speaking Canadians as well as with other immigrants and international students. Jenny is enjoying her program and achieving an A average in subjects such as finance, marketing, mathematics of finance, computers, introduction to Canadian business, operations management, and international business.

The biggest challenge in higher education in Canada for Jenny is language, especially spoken English. She feels her listening has improved since beginning classes in her post-secondary program, but as with many second-language learners, Jenny finds it difficult to practise speaking. Because there are so many group projects and presentations in community college business courses, Jenny is confident that with increased practise, she will achieve more progress. Jenny sometimes gets nervous when making presentations, but has found her professors to be very helpful. She knows that her classmates are a supportive audience and want her and her team members to succeed. In addition, she is very familiar with using presentation software, such as PowerPoint, to enhance her presentations.

Although adjusting to a new country and new culture takes time, Jenny and her husband are enjoying their new life in Canada. Jenny says her International Business courses are much more practical and useful for her career. And she says she is confident about overcoming adjustment difficulties in her schooling and life in Canada. Her advice for other new Canadian postsecondary students is to have a career goal. She recommends that students know why they are studying and what they will do in the future; in that way education is more meaningful. In addition, she encourages students whose first language is not English to get active and to enjoy their new lives in Canada. Jenny says if people are enjoying themselves, their learning will be better.

1. **Do something—anything.** Mow the lawn, clean out the closets, go for a run, or see a movie. It won't completely get your mind off your loss, but it beats languishing on your bed, thinking about what you might have done differently or what could have been.

2. **Accept that you feel bad.** If you're not experiencing unhappiness over the end of a relationship, it means that the relationship wasn't terribly meaningful in the first place. Understand that unhappiness normally accompanies the end of a relationship, and allow yourself some satisfaction over the fact that you were able to maintain a relationship that, at least at one point, was meaningful.

3. **Talk to a friend or relative.** Talking about your sadness will help you to deal with it better. Other people can help you feel better about yourself, offer different perspectives, and simply support you by listening. Make use of your network of existing relationships to get you through a difficult period.

4. **Write about the relationship.** If you have a journal, writing about the relationship and its aftermath can be therapeutic. You can say whatever you want without fear of being contradicted.

5. **Talk to a professional.** If your sadness over a relationship feels totally overwhelming or continues for what you perceive to be too long a time, talk to a counsellor or other professional. He or she can help you gain a better understanding of the situation and perhaps help you understand why you are taking it so hard. And remember that, ultimately, the pain *will* disappear: Time does heal most wounds.

Looking
Back

Why is the increasing racial, ethnic, and multicultural diversity of society important to you?

- The multiculturalism and diversity of Canada—and of Canadian campuses—is increasing rapidly, and the world is becoming closer as television, radio, the Internet, the World Wide Web, and international commerce bring other peoples and cultures into our lives, and vice versa.

- Being aware of diversity can allow you to accept the challenge and opportunity of living and working with others who are very different.

How can you become more at ease with differences and diversity?

- Cultural competence begins with accepting diversity by seeking out others who are different, as well as exploring your own prejudices and stereotypes.

- You can learn about other cultures by travelling to other countries and geographic areas. It also helps to accept differences simply as differences.

How can you build lasting relationships and deal with conflict?

- Relationships not only provide social support and companionship, but they also help people understand themselves.

- The central components of good relationships are trust, honesty, mutual support, loyalty, acceptance, and a willingness to embrace change.

- Listening is an important skill for relationship building, demonstrating that the listener really cares about the other person.

- Conflict is inevitable in relationships, and sometimes it is useful because it permits us to clear up misconceptions and miscommunications before they escalate.

- Although the end of a relationship can be very painful, the pain does subside over time.

P.O.W.E.R. Portfolio

Getting Along with Others

1. Consider including any evidence of skill or training in conflict resolution, multicultural education, peer mediation, justice circle involvement, or diversity awareness workshops. Evidence could include certificates, photographs, brochures, letters, or notes taken during courses. Include a reflective passage to indicate your understanding and learning.

2. Do in-depth research on a Canadian who has succeeded despite physical or social barriers, for example, Rick Hansen, Susan Aglukark, Tomson Highway, Milton Acorn, or Jeff Healey. In doing so, try to focus on what qualities that individual has that have contributed to his or her success. What have you learned about yourself because of this research?

3. Reflect on the multicultural diversity at your school and do an "environmental scan." Is there room for improvement? What ideas do you have to create change for the better? Are there groups or individuals deserving of credit or praise? Write a proposal to a committee or group (or your student newspaper) with your suggestions. Include your proposal and rationale in your portfolio.

Resources

On Campus

One of the most frequent sources of difficulties for first-year students involves roommate problems. If you and your roommate are having problems getting along, begin by speaking with your resident advisor or residence director. If the problem persists, talk with a member of the residential life office. You can also speak with a counsellor at the counselling office.

Anyone who feels he or she is facing discrimination based on race, gender, ethnic status, or national origin should contact a university official *immediately*. Often there is a specific office that handles such complaints. If you don't know which campus official to contact, speak to your academic adviser or someone in the dean's office and you'll be directed to the appropriate person. The important thing is to act and not to suffer in silence. Discrimination is not only immoral, but it's also against the law.

In Print

Beverly Daniel Tatum's *Why Are All the Black Kids Sitting Together in the Cafeteria?* (Basic Books, 5th edition, 2003) explores race, racism, and the everyday effect of prejudice.

In *Emotional Intelligence* (Bantam, 1997), Daniel Goleman discusses how we can learn to become more sensitive and emotionally aware of others.

Finally, Stewart Levine's *Getting to Resolution: Turning Conflict into Collaboration* (Berrett-Koehler, 2000) suggests a variety of practical approaches to resolving conflict.

On the Web

The following sites on the World Wide Web provide the opportunity to extend your learning about the material in this chapter. Although the Web addresses were accurate at the time the book was printed, check the P.O.W.E.R. Learning website, <www.mcgrawhill.ca/college/power>, for any changes that may have occurred.

www.islandnet.com/~wwlia/ca-hr.htm
This site, from the Canadian Human Rights Law Centre, has links to the Canadian Human Rights Commission, as well as provincial commissions and other interesting and informative human rights resources.

www.couns.msu.edu/self-help/pamphlets.htm#relationship
This site has a great selection of pamphlets, some of which deal with conflict resolution, relationship issues, and diversity.

http://mentalhelp.net/psyhelp/chap13/
As a portion of Mental Health Net's Psychological Self-Help site, this is a good starting point for developing skills in conflict resolution.

The Case of . . .

Answering for All

Kenisha Kinkaid stood out in any crowd. Being six-feet tall, she towered above most of her classmates. Even when she was seated at a desk, she looked tall. And since she was an African-Canadian, her skin colour set her apart from her classmates, almost all of whom were white.

Although most people were polite and nice to her, Kenisha felt isolated from most of her peers and instructors. While she had one or two good friends from high school with whom she kept in touch, she was not close to many people on campus. Her isolation came to a head, however, in the most public of places: her Canadian Literature class. It happened when her instructor, a white man, was leading a discussion on *Land to Light On*, a novel by noted black writer Dionne Brand. The instructor turned to Kenisha and asked her to comment on a passage from the novel.

"Does it ring true to you, Kenisha, as an African-Canadian?" asked her instructor, who then went on to inquire, "What do African-Canadians think about the perspective that Brand is taking?"

Kenisha was taken aback. What was she supposed to say? She hardly felt like a representative of all black people. She barely knew how she felt, let alone everyone else who was African-Canadian. Furthermore, her roots were in Nova Scotia, not the Caribbean. What an absurd situation to be placed in—her instructor asking her to answer for thousands of other people. She felt awful—embarrassed, upset, and angry with her instructor for putting her on the spot.

1. Why was the instructor's question so troubling to Kenisha? If the instructor really wanted Kenisha's opinion about the passage, what should he have said?

2. Would the question have had a different effect if the instructor had also been African-Canadian? Why or why not?

3. What are some cultural assumptions that the instructor is making about Kenisha? about African-Canadians? about white people?

4. What response might Kenisha make in this situation to make her feelings clear without causing excessive conflict?

Money Matters

13

Managing Your Money

Career Connections: Budgeting on the Job

Prepare: *Identifying Your Financial Goals*

Organize: *Determining Your Expenditures and Income*

Journal Reflections: My Sense of Cents

Work: *Making a Budget That Adds Up*

Evaluate: *Reviewing Your Budget*

Rethink: *Reconsidering Your Financial Options*

Credit Cards

Student Housing

Paying for Your Postsecondary Education

Speaking of Success: Murray Baker

The Case of . . . Overdrawn, Overwrought, and Over Her Head

Why do tours of Ottawa have to be boring? thought Derek Johnson as he picked up the Kilpatricks at their hotel. His parents, now living in Nanaimo, had asked him to show their friends around the capital district. Three hours later, the Kilpatricks told Derek that he was the best tour guide they'd ever had. A plan started forming. With summer and the heaviest tourist season coming up in a few months, perhaps Derek could skip looking for a job and go into business for himself.

With a $5000 young entrepreneur loan from Industry Canada, Derek leased a passenger van and started squiring small specialty tours around Ottawa, up into the Gatineau Hills, and even to Algonquin Park. That summer he made enough money to pay next year's tuition, and he lined up enough business to pay the bills over the fall and winter. Derek was ecstatic—he made great tips; his tours were unique; his customers felt like VIPs. He took a few business courses and by the following summer, his organization and marketing were much improved. Derek was able to lease two vans, rent a small office, and hire another driver and tour guide. He discovered he liked being his own boss and that his young and fresh perspective on touring was a hit with customers.

Five years later Derek's firm, *Bytown Bus*, has served more than 300 000 visitors and he has a staff of 10 energetic, enthusiastic tour guides who are committed to providing the best and most entertaining tours of the Ottawa area. Derek doesn't drive the vans much any more—but he certainly enjoys driving his Lexus LX 470!

Looking
Ahead

Money problems aren't often solved as readily as they were for Derek Johnson. And, even under the best of circumstances, our finances present us with challenges that affect many facets of our lives. Money often plays a large role in where we go to school, where we live, and what jobs we take. It is the source of many of our problems and much of our stress, forcing us to find a balance between what we need and what we want.

This chapter will show you how to manage your money. It begins by discussing the process of preparing a budget and identifying your financial goals—the basis for money management. The chapter goes on to examine ways you can keep track of your expenditures and estimate your financial needs and resources, and it discusses ways to exercise control over your spending habits and save money.

Education is one of the largest financial expenditures anyone encounters in life. Knowing the best ways to meet the costs of a postsecondary education—finding loans, grants, and scholarships—can give your finances a big boost and help you avoid graduating with thousands of dollars of debt. You will also learn what to do if your personal finances get out of control and how to stop the downward spiral of unpaid bills, defaulted loans, and unfavourable credit ratings. The chapter ends by suggesting ways to develop a financial philosophy.

After reading this chapter you'll be able to answer these questions:

- **What purpose does a budget serve and how can you prepare and stick to one?**

- **What help is available to pay for your higher education?**

- **What can you do if you fall into financial difficulty?**

Managing Your Money

Money management is a huge issue for Canadian postsecondary students. Most college students are worried about having enough money to complete their higher education. While over half of all students receive financial assistance from their families and almost half receive government funding (from bursaries, loans, or scholarships) the majority of Canadian students work in the summer to help pay for school, and 60 percent of students hold part-time or full-time jobs during the year to finance their education. However, the reality is that in 2003, six out of 10 students enrolled in community colleges anticipate graduating with debt; over 50 percent expect their debt loads will be $10,000 or more

In addition to tuition fees and the costs of textbooks and other related school supplies that every postsecondary student expects to pay, almost one in five Canadian college students have dependants. Students with dependants, especially child dependants, know that almost everything about college is costlier—from housing to food to clothing to transportation to daycare expenses. It's no wonder almost 30 percent of Canadian college students are very worried about having enough money to complete school.[1]

If you have money concerns—and there's virtually no one who doesn't have at least *some* worries about finances—the solution is to develop a budget. A **budget** is a formal plan that accounts and plans for expenditures and income. Taking your goals into account, a budget helps determine how much money you should be spending each month, based on your income and your other financial resources. Budgets also help prepare for unexpected occurrences that would reduce your income, such as the loss of a part-time job or an illness, or for sudden, unanticipated expenses, such as a major car repair or needing to purchase a new computer.

Although all budgets are based on an uncomplicated premise—expenditures should not exceed income—budgeting is not simple, particularly when

Budget
A formal plan that accounts for expenditures and income

> "Education costs money, but then so does ignorance."
>
> Claus Moser

Keeping to a budget is a constant balancing act. For example, even though you know you'll need to purchase books at the start of each semester, you can't predict exactly how much they'll cost.

Career Connections

Budgeting on the Job

If you've ever held a job, the salary you received was determined, in part, by your employer's budget.

Although they may not always be accessible to every employee, budgets are part of the world of work. Regardless of who the employer is—be it a small dry-cleaning store or the massive federal government—the organization undoubtedly has a budget outlining anticipated income and expenditures. Managers are expected to keep to the budget, and if their expenditures exceed what is budgeted, they are held accountable.

For this reason, the ability to create and live within a budget is an important skill to acquire. Not only will it help keep your own finances under control, but it will also prepare you to be financially responsible and savvy on the job—qualities that are highly valued by employers.

With e-business, e-banking, and e-trading, computerized finances are available to almost everyone in Canada. Numerous budgeting software applications are used by Canadian companies and you can get a head start by learning a software program and maintaining your finances on your computer.

> Entrepreneurship is the generator of most new jobs in Canada today. However, if you plan to start a business or buy a business, you need to create a business plan that includes a detailed budget. The Canada Businesses Services Centre has an Interactive Business Planner at: <www.cbsc.org/ibp/>. Similar versions are available online or on CD-ROM from most major banks.

you are a student. Several times during the year require especially large expenditures, such as the start of a semester, when you must pay your tuition and purchase books. Furthermore, income is erratic; it is often lower during the school year and higher during the summers. But a budget will help you deal with the ups and downs of income and expenditures, smoothing the curves and extending your view toward the horizon. Learning budgeting skills also helps prepare you for the world of work, of which budgeting is an important aspect, as discussed in Career Connections, "Budgeting on the Job."

Most of all, a budget provides security. It will let you take control of your money, permitting you to spend it as you need to without guilt because you have planned for the expenditure. It also makes it easier to put money aside because you know that your current financial sacrifice will be rewarded later, when you can make a purchase that you've been planning for.

Budgeting is very personal: What is appropriate for one person doesn't work for another. For a few people, keeping track of their spending comes naturally; they enjoy accounting for every dollar that passes through their hands. For most people, though, developing a budget—and sticking to it—does not come easily.

However, if you follow several basic steps—illustrated in the P.O.W.E.R. Plan—the process of budgeting is straightforward.

repare: Identifying Your Financial Goals

Your first reaction when asked to identify your financial goals may be that the question is a no-brainer. You want to have more money to spend. But it's not that simple. You need to ask yourself why you want more money. What would you spend it on? What would bring you the most satisfaction? Purchasing a DVD player? Paying off your debt? Saving money for a vacation? Starting a business? Paying for college or university rather than taking out loans?

You won't be able to develop a budget that will work for you until you determine your short- and long-term financial goals. To determine them, use Try It! 1, "Identify Your Financial Goals," on page 350.

Organize: Determining Your Expenditures and Income

Have you ever opened your wallet for the $10 that was there yesterday and found only a loonie? Spending money without realizing it is a common affliction.

There's only one way to get a handle on where your money is going. Keep track of it. To get an overview of your expenditures, go through any records you've kept to identify where you've spent money for the last year—old cheques, rent and utility receipts, and previous college tuition can help you.

In addition, keep track of everything you spend for a week. Everything. When you spend $1.25 for a candy bar from a vending machine, write it down. When you buy lunch for $2.97 at a fast-food restaurant, write it down. When you buy a 49-cent postcard, write it down.

Record your expenditures in a small notebook that you carry with you all the time. It may be tedious, but you're doing it for only a week. And it will be eye-opening. People are usually surprised at how much they spend on little items without even thinking about it.

Finally, make a list of everything you think you'll need to spend over the next year. Some items are easy to think of, such as rent and tuition payments, because they occur regularly and the amount you pay is fixed. Others are harder to budget for because they can vary substantially. For example, the price of gasoline changes frequently. If you have a long commute, the changing price of gasoline can cause substantial variation in what you pay each month. Similarly, the cost of books varies considerably from one term to another. (Use Table 13.1 on page 352 to estimate your expenditures for the coming year.)

Determine Your Income Sources You probably have a pretty good idea of how much money you have each month. But it's as important to list each source of income as it is to account for everything you spend.

🏃🏃 **Working in a Group:** Identify Your Financial Goals

STEP 1: Use the planning tool below to identify and organize your financial goals.

Short-Term Goals

What would you like to have money for in the short term (over the next three months)? Consider these categories:

Personal necessities (such as food, clothes, household supplies, daycare costs, shelter, transportation, loan payments, debts, medical expenses):

Educational necessities (such as tuition, fees, books, school supplies):

Social needs (for example, getting together with family, friends, and others; charitable contributions; clubs; teams; entertainment):

Lifestyle improvements (for example, optional but desirable personal or educational tools, computer hardware and software, living space improvements, transportation improvements, clothing):

Other:

Mid-Range Goals

What would you like to have money for soon, but not immediately (three months to a year from now), but not immediately? Use the same categories:

Personal necessities:

Educational necessities:

Social needs:

Lifestyle improvements:

Other:

Long-Range Goals

What would you like to have money for one to three years from now? Use the same categories:

Personal necessities:

Educational necessities:

Social needs:

Lifestyle improvements:

Other:

STEP 2: Now put each of your lists in <u>priority</u> order, arranging items in each list across the categories.

Short-Term Priorities:

Mid-Range Priorities:

Long-Range Priorities:

After you've completed prioritizing your financial goals, consider these questions: What does the list tell you about what is important to you? Did you find any surprises? Would you classify yourself as a financial risk taker or someone who values financial security?

Working in a group, compare your priorities with those of your classmates. What similarities and differences can you find, and what can you learn from others' priorities?

To Try It! online, go to **www.mcgrawhill.ca/college/power**.

Table 13.1

Estimated Expenditures for the Next 12 Months

Category	0–3 months from now	3–6 months from now	6–9 months from now	9–12 months from now
Personal Necessities				
Food				
Clothing				
Shelter (rent, utilities, etc.)				
Household supplies				
Transportation (car payments, gas, repairs, bus tickets, etc.)				
Loan and debt payments				
Medical expenses				
Childcare costs				
Other				
Educational Necessities				
Tuition and fees				
Books				
Computer costs				
Other				
Social Needs				
Relationships				
Clubs and teams				
Charitable contributions (church, food drives, donations, etc.)				
Presents (weddings, birthdays, etc.)				
Other				
Entertainment				
Movies and shows				
Trips				
Recreation and sports				
Eating out				
Gambling (lottery tickets, Pro-Line, etc.)				
Bars/Parties				
Lifestyle Improvements				
Educational				
Living space				
Computer				
Transportation				
Clothing				
Other				
TOTAL				

Table 13.2

Estimated Income in the Next 12 Months

Category	0–3 months from now	3–6 months from now	6–9 months from now	9–12 months from now
Wages				
Family support				
Financial aid				
Loan income				
Scholarship payments				
Other				
Interest and dividends				
Gifts				
Other				
TOTAL				

Add up what you make from any jobs you hold. Also list any support you receive from family members, including occasional gifts you might get from relatives. Finally, include any financial aid (such as tuition reductions, loan payments, or scholarships) you receive from your college or university. Use Table 13.2 to record this information. When you do, be sure to list the amounts you receive in terms of after-tax income.

ork: Making a Budget That Adds Up

If you've prepared and organized your budget, actually constructing your budget is as easy as adding 2 + 2. Well, not exactly, the numbers will be larger. But all you need to do is add up your list of expenses, and then add up your sources of income. In a perfect world, the two numbers will be equal.

But most of the time, the world is not perfect. Most of us find that expenditures are larger than our income. After all, if we had plenty of excess cash, we probably wouldn't be bothering to make a budget in the first place.

If you find you spend more than you make, there are only two things to do: decrease your spending or increase your income. It's often easiest to decrease expenditures, because your expenses tend to be more under your control. For instance, there are many things you can do to save money, including the following:

- **Control impulse buying.** When you shop for groceries, always take a list with you, and don't shop when you're hungry.

- **Make and take your own lunch.** Brown-bag lunches can save you a substantial amount of money over purchasing your lunches, even if you go to a fast-food restaurant or snack bar.

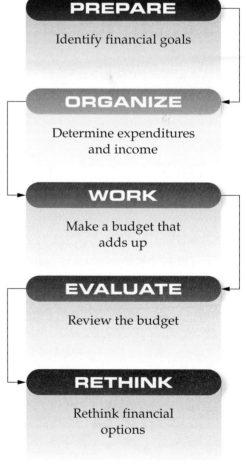

PREPARE

Identify financial goals

ORGANIZE

Determine expenditures and income

WORK

Make a budget that adds up

EVALUATE

Review the budget

RETHINK

Rethink financial options

P.O.W.E.R. Plan

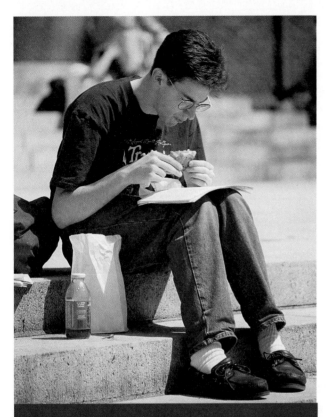

Bag it! One way to cut down on expenditures is to reduce everyday expenses, such as by making your own lunch, rather than grabbing a bite at a campus snack bar. Even small savings like this can add up fast.

- **Read the daily newspaper and magazines at the library.** College libraries subscribe to virtually every daily newspaper and magazine that you could want.

- **Check bills for errors.** Computers make mistakes, and so do the people who enter the data into them. So make sure that your charges on any bill are accurate.

- **Cut up your credit cards and pay cash.** Using a credit card is seductive; when you take out your plastic, it's easy to feel as if you're not really spending money. If you use cash for purchases instead, you'll see the money going out.

- **Make major purchases only during sales.** Plan major purchases so they coincide with sales.

- **Share and trade.** Pool your resources with friends. Car pool, share resources such as computers, and trade CDs.

- **Live more simply.** Do you really need a cellular phone or beeper? Is cable TV an absolute necessity? Is it really necessary to eat out once a week? Do you buy clothes because you need them or because you want them?

- **Do well in your classes.** One of the best ways to save money is to get good grades, because you avoid the hidden costs of poor performance. If you are forced to repeat a class because of a low grade, you'll have to take another course in the future as a substitute, and that may be an added expense. Doing well avoids the possibility of additional tuition costs.

There are as many ways to save money as there are people looking to save it. But keep in mind that saving money should not necessarily be an end in itself. Don't spend hours thinking of ways to save a dime, and don't get upset about situations where you are forced to spend money. The goal is to bring your budget into balance, not to become a tightwad who keeps track of every penny and feels that spending money is a personal failure. To help you get started, get a sense of your current style of saving money in Try It! 2, "Determine your Saving Style."

Finally, it's important to remember that budgets may be brought into balance not only by decreasing expenditures, but also by increasing income. The most direct way to increase income is to get a part-time job if you don't already have one.

Many students work during school. Although it adds to the time-management challenges you will face, working does not mean that your grades will necessarily suffer. In fact, many students who work do better in school than those who don't work, because those with jobs need to be more disciplined and focused. In addition, a part-time job in an area related to your future career may prove to be helpful in getting a job after you graduate.

Personal Styles: Determine Your Saving Style

Read each of the following statements and rate how well it describes you, using this scale:

1 = That's me

2 = Sometimes

3 = That's not me

	1	2	3
1. I count the change I'm given by cashiers in stores and restaurants.			
2. I always pick up all the change I receive from a transaction in a store, even if it's only a few cents.			
3. I don't buy something right away if I'm pretty sure it will go on sale soon.			
4. I feel a real sense of accomplishment if I buy something on sale.			
5. I always remember how much I paid for something.			
6. If something goes on sale soon after I bought it, I feel cheated.			
7. I have money in at least one interest-bearing bank account.			
8. I rarely lend people money.			
9. If I lend money to someone repeatedly without getting it back, I stop lending it to that person.			
10. I share resources (e.g., CDs, books, magazines) with other people to save money.			
11. I'm good at putting money away for big items that I really want.			
12. I believe most generic or off-brand items are just as good as name brands.			

Add up your ratings. Interpret your total score according to this informal guide:

12–15: Very aggressive saving style

16–20: Careful saving style

21–27: Fairly loose saving style

28–32: Loose saving style

33–36: Nonexistent saving style

What are the advantages and disadvantages of your saving style? How do you think your saving style would affect your ability to keep to a budget? If you are dissatisfied with your saving style, how might you be able to change it?

To Try It online, go to **www.mcgrawhill.ca/college/power.**

Considering part-time work is often a better strategy for dealing with budget shortfalls than taking out a loan. Because student loans are relatively simple to get, it's easy to use them as a crutch. Loans can be a help in an emergency or if you couldn't afford to attend college without them. If you do take out a loan, remind yourself: one day soon you'll have to pay it back, with interest.

E valuate: Reviewing Your Budget

Budgets are not meant to be set in stone. You should review where you stand financially each month. Only by monitoring how closely actual expenditures and income match your budget projections will you be able to maintain control of your finances.

You don't need to continually keep track of every penny you spend to evaluate your success in budgeting. As you gain more experience with your budget, you'll begin to get a better sense of your finances. You'll know when it may be possible to consider splurging on a gift for a friend, and when you need to operate in penny-pinching mode.

The important thing is to keep your expenditures under control. Review, and if necessary revise, your budget to fit any changes in circumstances. Maybe you receive a raise in a part-time job. Maybe the financial aid office gives you more support than you expected. Or maybe you face a reduction in income. Whatever the change in circumstances, evaluate how it affects your budget, and revise the budget accordingly.

R ethink: Reconsidering Your Financial Options

If all goes well, the process of budgeting will put you in control of your financial life. Your expenditures will match your income, and you won't face major money worries.

In the real world, of course, events have a way of inflicting disaster on even the best-laid plans:

- You lose your job and can't afford to pay next semester's tuition.

- Your roommate moves out and leaves you with an $800 phone bill. You don't have $800.

- Your parents, who have promised to pay for your education, run into financial difficulties and say they can't afford to pay your tuition any longer.

- Your car breaks down, and repairing it will cost $1,500. If you don't have a car, you can't get to campus. But if you pay for repairs, you can't afford tuition.

All of us face financial difficulties at one time or another. Sometimes it happens suddenly and without warning. Other times people sink more gradually into financial problems, each month accumulating more debt until they reach a point at which they can't pay their bills.

However it happens, finding yourself with too little money to pay your bills requires action. You need to confront the situation and take steps to solve the problem. The worst thing to do is nothing. Hiding from those to whom you owe money makes the situation worse. Your creditors—the institutions and people to whom you owe money—will assume that you don't care, and they'll be spurred on to take harsher actions.

These are the steps to take if you do find yourself with financial difficulties (also see Table 13.3):

- **Assess the problem.** Make a list of what you owe and to whom. Look at the bottom line and figure out a reasonable amount you can put toward each debt. Work out a specific plan that can lead you out of the situation.

Assess the Problem	Make a list of what you owe and to whom.
	Figure out a reasonable amount you can put toward each debt.
	Work out a specific plan.
Contact Each of Your Creditors	Start with your bank, credit card companies, and landlord.
	Explain the situation.
	Show them your plan to pay off debt.
See a Credit Counsellor	If you cannot work out a repayment plan on your own, visit a credit counselling service.
Stick to the Plan	Once you have a plan, make a commitment to stick to it.
	Your bank or creditor can help you identify a credit counsellor.

Table 13.3

Steps in Dealing with Financial Difficulties

- **Contact each of your creditors**. Start with your bank, credit card companies, and landlord, and continue through each creditor. It's best to visit personally, but a phone call will do.

When you speak with them, explain the situation. If the problem is due to illness or unemployment, let them know. If it's due to overspending, let them know that. Tell them what you plan to do to pay off your debt, and show them your plan. The fact that you have a plan demonstrates not only what you intend to do, but also that you are serious about your situation and capable of financial planning.

If you've had a clean financial record in the past, your creditors may be willing to agree to your plan. Ultimately, it is cheaper for them to accept smaller payments over a longer time than to hire a collection agency.

- **See a credit counsellor.** If you can't work out a repayment plan on your own, visit a credit counselling service. These are nonprofit organizations that help people who find themselves in financial trouble. Visit Industry Canada's Business and Consumer website for information about credit counselling services in your area at <http://strategis.ic.gc.ca/epic/internet/inoca-bc.nsf/en/ca01514e.html>.

- **Stick to the plan.** Once you have a plan to get yourself out of debt, follow it. Unless you diligently make the payments you commit to, you'll find your debt spiraling out of control once again. It's essential, then, to regard your plan as a firm commitment and stick to it.

Credit Cards

"Congratulations! You've been preapproved for a Gold credit card! Just send us your signature on the enclosed authorization form, and we'll rush you your card."

Have you ever received such a letter in the mail? If so, you're far from the only one. Millions of people in Canada are regularly enticed to receive credit cards in just such a manner, and college or university students are especially attractive targets. In fact, during orientation or frosh week, several major credit card companies hold special promotions on campus in hopes of signing up new cardholders. In many cases, it doesn't even matter whether you have income; the mere fact that you're a postsecondary student is sufficient to win you approval to receive a card.

Credit cards are not necessarily bad. In fact, used appropriately, they can help get you through brief periods when you must make a purchase—such as a car tire to replace an unexpected flat—but temporarily don't have enough money to do so. But there are several questions you should ask when deciding whether to get and use a credit card:

1. **Is there an annual fee?** Many cards charge an annual fee, ranging from $20 a year to $100 a year, although some are free. You need to determine if the advantages of the card are worth the cost of an annual fee.

2. **What is the interest rate?** Interest rates—the percentage of the unpaid balance you are charged on credit cards—vary substantially. Some interest rates are as low as 12 percent per year, while some are as high as 25 percent per year. If the rate is 25 percent, you may be charged $250 each year if you owe an average of $1000. Furthermore, although some interest rates are *fixed,* meaning that they don't vary from month to month, others are *variable,* which means they change each month. How much they change is tied to various factors in the overall economy. To get a better sense of how interest rates add up, look again at Try It! 3, "Maintain Your Interest."

3. **Do I need a credit card?** There are good reasons for getting a credit card, and bad reasons.

The Pluses of Credit Cards

- **Establishing a good credit history.** If you've ever owed money to a bank or your college or university, a computer file exists describing your payment history. If you have never missed a loan payment and always pay on time, you have a good credit history. If you haven't paid on time or have missed payments, your history has negative marks against it. Negative information can stay in a file for seven years, so it's important to establish and keep a clear credit history. Using a credit card moderately, never exceeding your credit limit, and paying on time will help you establish a good credit history. (You can get a copy of your credit report; complete Try It! 4, "I Know What You Did Last Summer," on page 360.)

> "Invest in yourself, in your education. There's nothing better."
>
> Sylvia Porter

- **Emergency use.** Few of us carry around enough cash to deal with emergencies. A credit card can be a life saver if we're on a trip and the car breaks down and needs emergency repairs.

- **Convenience.** Sometimes it's just easier to make purchases using a credit card. For instance, we can make purchases from catalogues over the telephone or on the Internet if we have a credit card. Furthermore, credit cards not only provide a record of purchases, but they also give us consumer protection should a product prove to be defective and we need a refund.

Try It!
3

Maintain Your Interest

Suppose you saw a $275 television set on sale "for a limited time" for $240. The $35 discount tempts you. The trouble is you don't have $240 to spare. But you do have a credit card—and you decide to buy the TV with the card and pay it off over time.

The advantages of this strategy are that you get the discount and have immediate use of the television set. The main disadvantage is that you will end up paying more than the $240 figure that you have in mind as the bargain price for the TV. In fact, depending on how high your credit card's interest rate is, how long you take to pay your bill in full, and how large each monthly payment is, you may wipe out most or all of the $35 savings that caused you to make the purchase in the first place. The more slowly you pay off the loan, the more money you pay for the television set.

For example, suppose you use a card with an annual interest rate of 12 percent, compounded monthly, meaning that the interest charge is applied each month, rather than at the end of the year—making the true annual rate 12.68 percent. (Some cards even compound on a daily basis, resulting in a real interest rate that is even higher.) At the end of a year, assuming you pay $10 per month toward the $240 purchase, you will have paid $120 and still have $143.61 to pay. At the end of 2 years, you would end up paying $35 in interest on top of the $240 purchase price.

The 12-month calculation is illustrated in the first table below. To see how much of a factor the interest rate is, complete the second table, which shows the same purchase on a credit card with a 20 percent annual (approximately 1.67 percent monthly) interest rate, compounded monthly. (These calculations can also be figured automatically on several websites, including **<www.bankrate.com>** and **<www.quicken.com>**.)

Credit Card Payments: 12% Interest, Compounded Monthly (1% per month)

	Month 1	2	3	4	5	6	7	8	9	10	11	12
Unpaid Balance	$240.00	$232.40	$224.72	$216.97	$209.14	$201.23	$193.24	$185.18	$177.03	$168.80	$160.49	$152.09
Plus Interest of	2.40	2.32	2.25	2.17	2.09	2.01	1.93	1.85	1.77	1.69	1.60	1.52
Minus Payment of	10.00	10.00	10.00	10.00	10.00	10.00	10.00	10.00	10.00	10.00	10.00	10.00
Balance Due	$232.40	$224.72	$216.97	$209.14	$201.23	$193.24	$185.18	$177.03	$168.80	$160.49	$152.09	$143.61

Credit Card Payments: 20% Interest, Compounded Monthly (approx. 1.67% per month)

	Month 1	2	3	4	5	6	7	8	9	10	11	12
Unpaid Balance	$240.00	$234.01	$227.92	$221.72	$215.42							
Plus Interest of	4.01	3.91	3.81	3.70								
Minus Payment of	10.00	10.00	10.00	10.00	10.00	10.00	10.00	10.00	10.00	10.00	10.00	10.00
Balance Due	$234.01	$227.92	$221.72	$215.42								

How much would the $240 TV set cost if you bought it with this higher-rate card, paying $10 per month for 12 months and then paying the remaining balance by cheque? How does this compare with the nondiscounted purchase price of $275?

To Try It! online, go to **www.mcgrawhill.ca/college/power**.

I Know What You Did Last Summer: Learn What Your Credit History Shows

Big Brother is alive and well, at least in terms of your credit history. If you've ever had a credit card in your own name, taken out a student loan, or sometimes just received an unsolicited offer for credit in the mail, there's probably a computer file describing who you are, where you live, and your financial history. It shows how big your credit lines are on every credit card you have, if you've ever been late on a payment, and a considerable amount of additional information.

Even worse—many people's credit histories are riddled with errors. That's why it's important to periodically check the record. To get a copy of your credit file, write a letter to one of the organizations listed below, stating you would like a complimentary copy of your credit report. Include your full name (including middle name), your date of birth, your current address, and any other addresses for the previous five years. You may include your telephone number, and social insurance number as well, but these are not necessary. You also need to include photocopies of both sides of two pieces of signed identification, like a driver's licence, credit card, or passport. Send the letter to Equifax Canada Ltd., Consumer Relations Department, Box 190 Jean Talon Station, Montreal, Quebec, H1S 2Z2; or Trans Union of Canada, P.O. Box 228 LCD1, Hamilton, Ontario, L8L 7W2. For further information, call Equifax at 1-800-465-7166 or Trans Union at 1-800-663-9980.

Once you get your credit report, check it carefully. If you find any mistakes, contact the credit bureau and explain the error. They are legally responsible for investigating the report and correcting the file. It's also a good idea to check your file at least once a year.

The Minuses of Credit Cards

There can be significant drawbacks to the use of credit cards. Potential problems include the following:

- **Interest costs can be high.** Unless you pay off your entire balance each month, your account will be charged interest. Here is an amazing statistic—if you use a credit card to purchase a $2,000 computer and make minimum payments at 18% interest, it will take 23 years to pay the balance. If you invested the same minimum payment amount, and invested it in a modest return mutual fund, 23 years later you would have nearly $40,000![2]

- **It's too easy to spend money.** Credit cards are so convenient to use that you may not realize how much you are spending in a given period. Furthermore, spending can become addictive or can be viewed as a recreational activity. In addition, the more credit cards students possess, the more their debt. The average debt of Canadian students possessing one credit card stands at $900, but rises to $1,600 among students with two cards, and $2,500 among students with three or more credit cards.[3]

- **If you're late in making your payments or exceed your credit limit, your credit rating will be damaged.** Credit card companies have long memories, and any mistakes you make will be reflected in your credit record for close to a decade. This may prevent you from buying a car or house in the future and jeopardize your ability to take out student loans.

Heed this advice: Even if you are in a serious relationship or would trust your roommates with your most prized possessions, *do not lend your credit or debit cards!* You are the one who is ultimately responsible for debts accrued in your name. It is not worth losing a friendship over bad debts. Be cautious with your credit cards!

Student Housing

While many Canadian college and university students live at home or in residence, a large number of students must or prefer to live independently off-campus. This has many advantages, such as providing an opportunity for additional self-responsibility, greater freedom, and more privacy, but there are a few factors that need to be considered to avoid financial difficulties.

Finding a Place Most colleges and universities have student-housing offices that offer information on both on-campus and off-campus housing. Housing listings are usually available online. If you are visiting your school's campus, bulletin boards often have ads by landlords, local families with rooms to let, and other students looking for roommates. Family friends, neighbours, and older students from your home town may have information about student housing, so word of mouth is an excellent way to learn about affordable housing near your college or university. Bear in mind that commercial apartment finders have direct or indirect fees that could make your apartment more expensive.

Location Finding a house or an apartment near your school may be very convenient, but it can also be quite expensive, as many owners count on renting to students and rents may be somewhat higher than for similar apartments not so close to campus.

Additional Costs Basic rent is only a part of what students need to consider when deciding on a house or apartment to rent. If utilities, such as heat, water, and electricity are not included in the rent, they may add a lot, depending on how the apartment is heated and how many showers you and your roommates take per day! Options, such as cable or satellite TV, Internet hook-up, and parking add to the total monthly bills and all the extra costs may add as much as 25 to 50 percent to your rent. In addition, landlords may require a 12-month lease when students may only need their apartment for eight or nine months of the year. Unless you can sublet your apartment, you may be on the hook for three or four months of rent over the summer.

Legalities Even if you know your roommates really well, make sure all occupants' names and signatures are on the lease. If your name is the only one on the lease, you may be responsible for any damage charges, the full rent, and any additional charges.

Be sure you give your landlord proper notice when you move out. Even if you have a lease, you should inform him or her in writing—depending on your province—30 or 60 days before leaving.

If you give your landlord first and last month's rent, you are entitled to interest on your last month's rent. Even though you may have to ask for this interest, your landlord is required to give it to you.

Some landlords require a security deposit in case damage occurs during the course of a tenancy. Report any damage you notice upon moving in, or you may be required to pay for repairs you are not responsible for. You are responsible for damage done by you or your guests; so be sure that parties don't get rowdy or out of hand.

If you have a dispute with your landlord or neighbours, contact your campus-housing mediator who can help resolve and offer advice regarding differences of opinion about leases, bylaws, rights, and responsibilities. If you have no housing mediator at your school, contact legal aid or local law school to help you.[4]

Paying for Your Postsecondary Education

Tuition costs vary greatly from one program to another and one school to another, but they are substantial everywhere. In the past 10 years tuitions costs have just about doubled.[5] Tuition costs between $1200 and $2500 per year at the average community college or CÉGEP (depending on the province) and between $3000 to $5000 per year at the average university (although Quebec's and British Columbia's tuition fees are slightly lower). Professional programs, such as nursing or medicine, have higher fees. All schools have auxiliary fees, which can range from $200 to $700. Specific majors or programs may also include lab or extra fees, as well. In addition, books and school supplies may add several hundred dollars to your cost. Finally, if you live in residence, you can count on an additional $5000 to $7000, depending on whether you have a single or double room and the type of meal plan you choose. Living on your own, off-campus, can push that fee even higher.

Nothing about college or university is cheap. It takes enormous expenditures of three often-scarce commodities to attend a postsecondary institution: energy, time, and money. Many find that, of these, the easiest to find is—perhaps surprisingly—money. So many sources of aid for education exist that no one should feel that he or she can't afford a postsecondary education.

While it's not simple to get financial aid, it is a fact that if you are persistent, you can find many sources of funding for your education.

To find money to attend college or university, you will need to spend ample amounts of the other two scarce commodities: time and energy. The entire process of securing financial aid takes a considerable amount of preparation. You need to first identify potential sources of funds and then apply for them. You should assume the process will take from several weeks to as long as several months, depending on the type of aid you're applying for. The steps you need to take to find funding are summarized in the P.O.W.E.R. Plan.

Identifying the Different Types of Funding Available

Funding for college or university comes in three basic categories: loans, grants, and scholarships. Although each supplies you with funds for your higher education, they do so in very different ways.

- **Loans.** When you receive a **loan**, a bank, credit union, or other agency provides funds that must be repaid within a specified time. A loan carries a particular interest rate, which is stated as an annual percentage rate. The interest rate is the cost of borrowing. Think of a loan as renting money. As long as you have the use of someone else's money, you have to pay them "rent" for the privilege. Banks and other lending agencies make money through the interest they charge on loans, just as credit card companies do.

  For example, suppose a bank gives you a $5000 loan that has an interest rate of 8 percent per year. Not only must you pay back the $5000 over a specified period, but you must pay the bank interest of 8 percent on the balance that you owe on the loan. Obviously, the higher the interest rate, the more you are paying for the privilege of borrowing the bank's money.

  Three factors must be considered when you receive a loan: the stated amount of the loan (called the **principal**), the interest rate (stated as a percentage), and the length of the loan (referred to as the **term** of the loan). All three factors are important because they determine how much your payments will be when you pay the loan back.

Several kinds of loan programs exist for college and university students.

- **CSLP.** Although some students arrange student loans privately through their own banks, or set up student lines of credit, the Canada Student Loan Program (CSLP), sponsored by the federal government, is the most popular student loan program, because payments and interest are deferred until after you are out of school. Approximately 350 000 students in Canada receive subsidized loans every year. The Canada Student Loan is actually about 60 percent of the loan's total; a Provincial Student Loan accounts for the remaining 40 percent. You should know some of the details about the CSLP:

  - **Repayment.** You must start paying back your loan on the first day of the seventh month after your last day of school; however, interest is calculated starting the same month you complete school. You can calculate what your student loan repayments will be using interactive software at **<www.canlearn.ca/english/csl/hrd-cloan/loanen.shtml>**.

    > "Interest works night and day, in fair weather and in foul."
    > Henry Ward Beecher, author

  - **Interest relief.** People with difficulty repaying student loans have options; for example, you can apply for interest relief—a hiatus or break from loan payments for a short time (usually three months). People requiring additional relief can contact the National Student Loans Centre for information about other repayment options.

Loan
Funds provided by a bank, credit union, or other agency that must be repaid within a specified time

Principal
The stated amount of a loan

Term
The length of time for which money is lent

– **Defaulting.** Defaulting on student loans occurs when you stop making or miss payments. This can lead to serious financial repercussions. One negative consequence is getting a bad credit rating, which can stay with you for a very long time and can affect your ability to buy a car, obtain a mortgage, or borrow money in the future.

• **Grants, bursaries, and scholarships.** These financial awards do not have to be repaid. Obviously, it's more advantageous to receive a grant, bursary, or scholarship than a loan. And not surprisingly, it's harder to qualify for these awards than for loans. Some **grants**, **bursaries**, and **scholarships** are awarded by community service groups, labour unions, or individuals and families; criteria for receiving these awards may include financial need, merit, or specified field of study. Contact your financial aid office for information about awards that may be offered at your school. Amazingly, many scholarships and bursaries go unclaimed every year, because students don't know about them.

In addition, the Canadian government has grant and scholarship programs that can help reduce the costs of paying for higher education for certain students:

– **Canada study grants.** These grants assist postsecondary students with special needs. These grants are targeted at students with permanent disabilities, high-need part-time students, women in certain doctoral programs, and student loan recipients who have dependants. Once you apply for your Canada student loan, you can submit your application for a Canada study grant at your school's financial aid office or your provincial or territorial student assistance office.

– **The Millennium Scholarship.** These scholarships, from the Government of Canada, are awarded on financial need; you must be eligible for a Canada student loan to receive this scholarship. Information about Millennium Scholarships can be obtained at your school's financial aid office.

Other ways of relieving the financial burden of your postsecondary education include

• **Work-study programs.** Work-study programs provide student jobs in educational institutions. Typically, students work 10 to 12 hours per week in various capacities. Work-study placements may be tied to financial need and academic success. Contact your financial aid office for information on work-study opportunities at your campus.

• **Cooperative education.** Co-op programs are set up in many colleges and universities. Cooperative education provides opportunities for students to integrate periods of academic study with curriculum-related, productive work experiences. These programs allow students to test their skills, adjust to the work environment, and earn money.

Researching Possible Sources of Financial Aid

As you can see, several sources of financial aid are available. However, finding those sources can be time consuming. Your college or university financial aid office should be your first stop for researching sources of funding. The library and World Wide Web also contain many types of information about possible funding. A few sites are particularly useful: <http://youth.hrdc-

drhc.gc.ca/ythlink/sec1ind.shtml>, a government website listing numerous awards, bursaries, fellowships, and scholarships, and the scholarship search websites at **<www.scholarshipscanada.com/>** and **<www.studentawards.com /english/can/register.asp>**.

Whatever the potential source of financial aid, you'll be asked to bare your financial soul. There will also be forms galore. Before actually completing the forms, it will be important to gather the information you will need. If you are being supported by your parents, much of it may have to come from them, and they will have to complete some of the forms.

Keep track of deadlines! If you miss a deadline for applying for financial aid, you'll be out of luck; no exceptions are made. You'll just have to wait for another aid cycle.

Finally, make sure you know what your needs are. The typical costs of school include not only tuition but also fees, books, and supplies, as well as associated costs, such as transportation, housing, food, and child care.

Applying for Financial Aid

It may seem that for every dollar in aid you get, there is a different line to complete on a complicated form. Prepare yourself for a blizzard of paperwork.

You need follow only two basic steps to receive financial aid:

1. **Apply.** To get a student loan, fill out an application form, which you can get at the financial aid office at the school you are applying to or at your provincial or territorial student assistance office. Some applications can be made online. Campusaccess.com has put together a detailed, informative section to make sense of all the different programs available to Canadian students. You can find information on financial aid programs, both federal and provincial, as well as scholarships at **<www.campusaccess.com/campus_web/educ/e2fin.htm>**.

2. **Wait.** It takes time for loan applications to be processed and financial aid decisions to be made. Apply 10 weeks in advance of the semester you are applying for. Be prepared to wait, and have contingency funding in place in case of administrative delays.

Show Me the Money: Building a Financial Philosophy

It's hard to forget the famous line from *Jerry McGuire,* the movie in which Tom Cruise plays a sports agent: "Show me the money." That direct statement—however crude—might be used to illustrate one financial philosophy: Life revolves around money.

Many would disagree. For instance, authors Vicki Robin and Joe Dominguez argue in their book *Your Money or Your Life*[6] that, while most people find money to be a controlling force in their lives and, consequently, their major source of stress, it needn't be. Yes, the authors concede, acquiring and spending money can become an obsession, and when this is the case the simple pleasures of life are lost. But Robin

> "I'm so poor I can't even pay attention."
>
> Ron Kittle

and Dominguez outline an alternative approach in which we reprioritize our values, live frugally, and ultimately achieve financial independence.

🏃 **Working in a Group:** Discover Your Personal Financial Philosophy

Begin to create a personal financial philosophy by completing this exercise.

A. Attitudes toward Money

	Strongly Disagree	Disagree	Neutral	Agree	Strongly Agree
1. Money is essential for happiness.					
2. Having money guarantees happiness.					
3. Money makes no difference to my happiness.					
4. More money equals more happiness.					
5. Beyond having enough to live modestly on, money doesn't make much of a difference.					
6. I frequently worry about money.					
7. I frequently daydream about having a lot of money.					
8. If I suddenly had to live on very little money, I could adjust easily.					
9. If I suddenly won a lot of money, I would go on a spending spree.					
10. If I suddenly won a lot of money, I would share it with my relatives.					
11. If I suddenly won a lot of money, I would give a large percentage to charity.					
12. If I found a substantial amount of cash in a bag, I would try hard to find its rightful owner.					
13. If I could carry only a briefcase full of $100 bills or my pet dog out of a burning building, I would take the dog.					
14. I plan to make a lot of money in my career.					
15. I plan to make only enough money to live in reasonable comfort.					
16. It's great to have money.					
17. Money is a necessary evil.					
18. Money is the root of all evil.					

Whether you choose to follow the path of Jerry McGuire or that of Vicki Robin and Joe Dominguez, the important thing is to develop your own personal financial philosophy. You can get a start in developing your financial philosophy by completing Try It! 5, "Discover Your Personal Financial Philosophy," which can help assess how money affects your life. It will help you consider the role that money plays in your life. How much does money motivate what you

B. Sources of Satisfaction

1. Which activities that you engaged in over the past five years have given you the greatest satisfaction?

2. How much money did those activities cost?

3. How would you spend your time if you could do anything you chose?

4. How much money would this cost each year?

C. Personal Financial Philosophy

Consider your attitudes toward money and the sources of your satisfaction. Sum up your personal financial philosophy here:

After you've completed these questions, separate into small groups and compare your answers with those of other students. How does your financial philosophy compare to that of other students? What are the major similarities and differences, and how do you think they came about?

do? Are you interested in becoming rich, or do you tend to think more in terms of simply having enough to have a comfortable life, without lots of luxuries? What activities bring you the greatest satisfaction in life? Do those activities require a certain level of income?

Ultimately, consider how college or university relates to issues involving finances. Higher education is undoubtedly one of the biggest investments that you'll ever make. If you only think of it in terms of its eventual financial payoff—getting a better job and leading a more affluent life—you'll be missing some central aspects of the process of educating yourself.

Looking Back

What purpose does a budget serve and how can you prepare and stick to one?

- Concerns about money can be significantly lowered through the creation of a budget by which expenditures and income can be planned, accounted for, and aligned with your goals.

- Budgets provide security by helping you control your finances and avoid surprises.

- The process of budgeting involves identifying your financial goals, keeping track of current expenses and estimating future expenses, and making the necessary adjustments to keep income and expenditures in balance.

What help is available to pay for your college education?

- Loans for education are available with reasonable interest rates and conditions, especially the ability to defer paying the loans back until after graduation.

- Grants and bursaries offer money without requiring repayment. They are harder to receive than loans because they are typically reserved for people with exceptional financial or other needs.

- Scholarships are usually awarded by colleges and other institutions based on either financial need or academic, athletic, or other abilities.

What can you do if you fall into financial difficulty?

- If financial difficulties arise, contact your creditors and arrange a plan for paying off the debt. If you need help in designing a repayment plan, nonprofit credit counsellors can help.

P.O.W.E.R. Portfolio

Money Matters

After completing Try It! 5, expand your thoughts into a submission for your portfolio. Your entry could be a reflective rationale, a poem, a motto, or anecdotes about your perspective on money. You could be artistic and create a collage to express your financial philosophy. Overall, your philosophy should be reflected in what you do, so try to provide some evidence for your entry. For example, Marc, who believes in *voluntary simplicity*, rejects the waste of *conspicuous consumption*. As proof of his philosophy, Marc can include a paper he

Speaking of Success

Murray Baker

B.A. (Honours), History, University of Western Ontario

Vancouver-based author, researcher, and speaker Murray Baker wrote his best-selling book, *The Debt-Free Graduate*, while working as the coordinator of first-year programs at the University of Western Ontario. With students and friends struggling to pay off loans, Murray saw the toll financial difficulties and stress levels associated with student debt take.

Now with yearly printings, *The Debt-Free Graduate*, which was written in Murray's spare time, has led to a new career for him. After its publication in 1996, Murray had requests for TV and radio interviews and invitations for speaking engagements. In 1997, he decided to pursue writing and speaking full-time, feeling he could make more of a difference in that role. Murray, who has just completed a U.S. edition of his book, has now given more than 200 interviews, and has written numerous articles for magazines and newspapers. In addition, he maintains a comprehensive website on student finances at **<www.debtfreegrad.com>**.

Financial advising may be a long way from being a history major; however, Murray says investing and finance always interested him and he pursued what had been a hobby to create a product he enjoyed that helped people. Murray believes there is significant transferability from his liberal arts education to his current career—particularly in the areas of researching, writing, speaking, critical thinking, and analytical reasoning. He says that while at Western he wouldn't have dreamed he'd end up as a professional speaker, but debating and analytical skills (developed during university seminars) have helped him in speaking on-air and in front of crowds.

Avoidance is one of the chief reasons students end up with financial problems, Murray believes. Student debt is a serious issue and side-stepping it gets students into a lot of financial difficulty. While he doesn't think every student can graduate debt-free, Murray believes all students can take control of their personal finances and reduce the debt they owe on graduation.

Murray is a strong advocate of proactive financial planning for students. The "get the loan, put it in the bank, and hope the school year is finished before the money runs out" approach to money management is ineffective. Murray recommends that students create budgets, and use them as road maps, avoiding consequences such as having to take on overly demanding part-time work, dropping out of school, or making forced errors, such as cash advances on credit cards. He also suggests students invest student loans in safe short-term investments, such as Canada Savings Bonds or GICs. Students can gain modest returns on their money (as opposed to little or no return in a bank account) and start to learn how to handle their finances. With this experience, students will graduate with sound financial knowledge, which will serve them well when they do start to earn money.

wrote in SOSC255: Human Ecology, indicating the steps he has taken to live frugally; brochures and pictures of a *Simpler Living* conference he attended; and ways he and other concerned classmates have improved recycling on his campus. Jenn, on the other hand, believes money is a commodity that will grow and benefit those who deal wisely with it. She has participated in an investment club that finance students at her college started. She includes records of her dealings and a tally sheet showing the profits her group has made; a list of peer counselling appointments where she assisted fellow students with income taxes; and a financial report from the precision skating club she belongs to and for which she serves as treasurer.

Resources

On Campus

If you are receiving financial aid, you should know whether a particular office is devoted to the complexities of scholarships, loan processing, and other forms of aid. The personnel in the office can be very helpful in maximizing your financial aid package as well as in solving financial problems related to your schooling. If you have a problem with your finances, see them sooner rather than later.

In Print

David Chilton's *The Wealthy Barber: Everyone's Commonsense Guide to Becoming Financially Independent* (Prima Lifestyles, 1997) is Canada's best-selling book ever, aside from The Bible. *The Barber* offers the average person all the information needed to make a lifetime of good financial decisions.

Another excellent resource is Murray Baker's *The Debt-Free Graduate: How to Survive College Without Going Broke* (Career Press, 2000). The book is very helpful in preparing information for students about how to be financially fit.

On the Web

The following sites on the World Wide Web provide the opportunity to extend your learning about the material in this chapter. Although the Web addresses were accurate at the time the book was printed, check the P.O.W.E.R. Learning website, <www.mcgrawhill.ca/college/power>, for any changes that may have occurred.

www.debtfreegrad.com/
A comprehensive site from Murray Baker with lots of information on student money matters, from banking to eating well on a budget. The site includes cost calculators, loan repayment schedules, and links to financial aid centres as well.

http://canadaonline.about.com/cs/educationfinances/
Education Finances in Canada has a list of numerous links on tuition, savings, student loans, RESPs, scholarships, and debt to finance a Canadian education.

http://canadaonline.about.com/od/budgets/index.htm
This is a very helpful Canadian site on budgets and personal financial planning resources to help in preparing a personal budget, managing money, and planning your future.

www.stretcher.com/index.cfm
The Dollar Stretcher is a website devoted to saving money that offers many helpful hints on how to cut costs.

The Case of . . .

Overdrawn, Overwrought, and Over Her Head

Her life was a house of cards, and someone had just pulled one out from the bottom.

At least that's what it felt like to Tara Kenko. The month had started out badly when Tara found that she had made a mistake in her chequing account and had only $439, instead of the $939 she thought she had. After paying her share of the rent—$210—there wasn't enough money left to make her car payment. So she just put the bill aside, figuring that she'd take care of it later in the month when she got paid.

Things went from bad to worse two days later when her car refused to start. She had to have it towed to a mechanic, who told her that it would cost about $350 to get it fixed. She didn't have that, either, but she figured she could put it on her credit card even though her unpaid balance was already high. But later, when she went to pick up her car and pay for the repair, which turned out to be closer to $400 than the $350 she expected to pay, her card was rejected. She called the credit card company from the repair shop and was told that she had exceeded her authorized credit limit and that her card was frozen. Because the mechanic wouldn't let her take her car until she paid for the repairs, she was forced to leave it and catch a bus to campus.

The final straw came in her chemistry class. The instructor announced that students in the class would have to buy yet another book for the latest assignment. Having already spent $150 for books in that class alone, Tara was both angry and dismayed. She had no idea how she was going to find the money to pay for the book, let alone her regular car payment and the car repairs. She was in financial trouble, and she didn't know what to do.

1. What should Tara do now to start addressing her problem?

2. Can you suggest some approaches Tara can take to deal with the problem of the new book for her chemistry class?

3. How do you think the mistake may have occurred in Tara's chequing account? What advice would you give her to avoid a similar mistake in the future?

4. Given that Tara does not have a lot of leeway in her finances for multiple disasters such as the ones that befell her this month, what general course would you advise her to take as a way to plan her expenditures more effectively?

5. What steps might Tara take to decrease her expenses? What might she do to increase her income?

Stress, Health, and Wellness

14

Living with Stress

Handling Stress

Prepare: *Readying Yourself Physically*

Organize: *Identifying What is Causing You Stress*

Work: *Developing Effective Coping Strategies*

Evaluate: *Asking If Your Strategies for Dealing with Stress are Effective*

Rethink: *Placing Stress in Perspective*

Keeping Well

Career Connections: Anticipating Job Stress

Staying Safe on the Job

Drug Abuse

Journal Reflections: College Drinking Experiences

Sexual Health and Decision Making

Speaking of Success: Krista Bailey

The Case of . . . Grievous Bodily Harm

ouis Denby's day began badly: He slept through his alarm and had to skip breakfast to catch the bus to campus. Then, when he went to the library to catch up on the reading he had to do before taking a test the next day, the one article he needed was missing. The librarian told him that replacing it would take 24 hours. Feeling frustrated, he walked to the computer lab to print out the paper he had completed at home the night before.

The computer wouldn't read his disk. He searched for someone to help him, but he was unable to find anyone who knew any more about computers than he did.

It was only 9:42 a.m., and Louis had an awful headache. Apart from that pain, he was conscious of only one feeling: stress.

Have you had days like Louis's? Are most of your days like his? Then you're no stranger to stress. It's something that all college or university students experience to varying degrees throughout their academic careers. In fact, almost a third of first-year college or university students report feeling frequently overwhelmed with all they need to do.[1]

Coping with stress is one of the challenges that postsecondary students face. The many demands on your time can make you feel that you'll never finish what needs to get done. This pressure produces wear-and-tear on your body and mind, and it's easy to fall prey to ill health as a result.

However, stress and poor health are not inevitable outcomes of college. In fact, by following simple guidelines and deciding to make health a conscious priority, you can maintain good physical and mental health.

This chapter covers the ways you can keep fit and healthy during—and beyond—college. It offers suggestions on how you can cope with stress, improve your diet, get enough exercise, and sleep better. It also will help you consider particular threats to mental and physical health that you're likely to face while you are in college, including alcohol and drugs, pregnancy, sexually transmitted diseases, and rape.

In sum, after reading this chapter you'll be able to answer these questions:

- **What is stress and how can I control it?**

- **What is involved in keeping fit and healthy, and why is it important for me to do so?**

- **What are the main threats to my health and well-being?**

- **What are the components of sexual health?**

Living with Stress

Stressed out? Tests, papers, due dates, job demands, roommate problems, childcare difficulties, financial hassles, relationship blues, political activities, committee work—it's no surprise that each of these can produce stress. But it may be a surprise to know that so can graduating from high school, starting your dream job, falling in love, getting married, and even winning the lottery.

Virtually *anything*—good or bad—is capable of producing stress if it in some way presents us with a challenge. **Stress** is the physical and emotional response we have to events that threaten or challenge us. It is rooted in the primitive fight or flight response wired into all animals—human and nonhuman. You see it in cats, for instance, when confronted by a threat. Their backs go up, their hair stands on end, their eyes widen, and, ultimately, they either take off or attack. The challenge stimulating this revved-up response is called a *stressor*. For humans, stressors can range from a first date to losing our chemistry notes to living through an ice storm.

Stress
The response to events that threaten or challenge us

Because our everyday lives are filled with events that potentially can be interpreted as threatening or challenging, stress is commonplace in most people's lives. There are three main types of stressors:

1. **Cataclysmic events** are sudden, powerful events that occur quickly and affect many people simultaneously. Tornadoes, hurricanes, and plane crashes are examples of cataclysmic events. Although they may produce powerful immediate consequences, ironically they produce less stress than other types of stressors. The reason? Cataclysmic events have a clear end-point, which can make them more manageable. Furthermore, because they affect many people simultaneously, their consequences are shared with others, and no individual feels singled out.

   Cataclysmic events
   Sudden, powerful events that occur quickly and affect many people simultaneously

2. **Personal stressors** are major life events that produce a negative physical and psychological reaction. Failing a course, losing a job, and ending a relationship are all examples of personal stressors. Sometimes positive events—such as getting married or starting a new program—can also act as personal stressors. Although the short-term impact of a personal stressor can be difficult, the long-term consequences may decline as people learn to adapt to the situation.

   Personal stressors
   Major life events that produce stress

3. **Daily hassles** are the minor irritations of life that, singly, produce relatively little stress. Being late for a class, receiving a tuition bill riddled with mistakes, and being interrupted by noises of major construction while trying to study are examples of daily hassles. However, daily hassles add up, and eventually they can produce even more stress than a single larger-scale event. Figure 14.1 indicates the most common daily hassles in people's lives.[2]

   Daily hassles
   The minor irritants of life that, by themselves, produce little stress, but that can add up and produce more stress than a single larger-scale event

What Is Happening When We Are Stressed Out

Stress does more than make us feel anxious, upset, and fearful. Beneath those responses, we are experiencing many different physical reactions, each placing a high demand on our body's resources. Our hearts beat faster, our

Figure 14.1

Daily Hassles

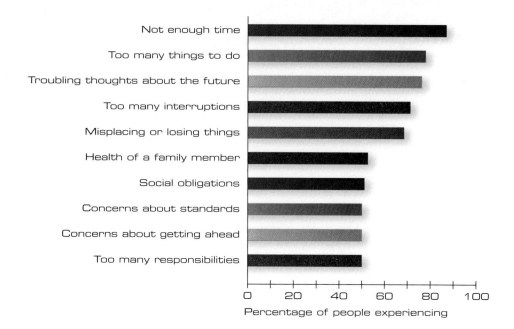

Not enough time

Too many things to do

Troubling thoughts about the future

Too many interruptions

Misplacing or losing things

Health of a family member

Social obligations

Concerns about standards

Concerns about getting ahead

Too many responsibilities

0 20 40 60 80 100

Percentage of people experiencing

breathing becomes more rapid and shallow, and we produce more sweat. Our internal organs churn out a variety of hormones. In the long run, these physical responses wear down our immune system, our body's defence against disease. We become more susceptible to a variety of diseases, ranging from the common cold and headaches to strokes and heart disease. In fact, surveys have found that the greater the number of stressful events a person experiences over the course of a year, the more likely it is that he or she will have a major illness (see Try It! 1, "Assess Your Susceptibility to Stress-Related Illness," on page 378).

Handling Stress

Coping
The effort to control, reduce, or tolerate the threats that lead to stress

Stress is an inevitable part of life. In fact, a life with no stress at all would be so boring and uneventful, that you'd quickly miss the stress that had been removed.

That doesn't mean, though, that we have to sit back and accept stress when it does arise. **Coping** is the effort to control, reduce, or tolerate the threats that lead to stress. Using the P.O.W.E.R. principles, we can ward off stress and actively deal with it.

Prepare: Readying Yourself Physically

Being in good physical condition is the primary way to prepare for future stress. Stress takes its toll on your body, so it makes sense that the stronger and fitter you are, the less negative impact stress will have on you. For example, a regular exercise program reduces heart rate, respiration rate, and blood pressure at times when the body is at rest—making us better able to withstand the negative consequences of stress. Furthermore, vigorous exercise produces *endorphins*, natural painkilling chemicals in the brain. Endorphins produce feelings of happiness—even euphoria—and may be responsible for the "runner's high," the positive feelings often reported by long-distance runners following long runs. Through the production of endorphins, then, exercise can help our bodies produce a natural coping response to stress.

If you now drink a lot of coffee or pop, a change in your diet may be enough to bring about a reduction in stress. Coffee, most soft drinks, chocolate, and a surprising number of other foods contain caffeine, which can make you feel jittery and anxious even without stress; add a stressor, and the reaction can be very intense and unpleasant. Simply reducing the amount of caffeine you take in can make you better prepared to deal with stress.

Eating right can alleviate another problem: obesity. Around 30 percent of Canadians between 20 and 64 are obese,[4] defined as having body weight more than 20 percent above the average weight for a person of a given height. Lest you think obesity is a problem only for older adults, experts estimate that 10 to 25 percent of all young adults have a weight problem.[5] Obesity can bring on stress for several reasons. For one thing, being overweight drags down the functioning of the body, leading to fatigue and a reduced ability to bounce back when we encounter challenges to our well-being. Also, about 30 percent of individuals who are 50 kg overweight have elevated blood pressure.[6] In addition, feeling fat in a society that acclaims the virtues of slimness can be stressful in and of itself.

rganize: Identifying What Is Causing You Stress

You can't cope effectively with stress until you know what's causing it. In some cases, it's obvious—a series of bad test grades in a course, a child whose behaviour at school is worrisome and causing you to miss classes, a job supervisor who seems to delight in making things difficult. In other cases, however, the causes of stress may be more subtle. Perhaps your relationship with your boyfriend or girlfriend is rocky, you are undergoing culture shock, or moving away from home was more difficult than you had expected and you have a nagging feeling that something is wrong.

Whatever the source of stress, you can't deal with it unless you know what it is. To organize your assault on stress, take a piece of paper and list the major circumstances that are causing you stress. Just listing them will help put you in control, and you'll be better able to figure out and apply strategies for coping with them.

Sources of Stress
1. Biology professor talks so fast that notetaking is nearly impossible
2. Difficulty paying rent this month.
3. Not enough time to study for Tuesday's psych test

Assess Your Susceptibility to Stress-Related Illness

Are you susceptible to a stress-related illness? The more stress in your life, the more likely it is that you may experience a major illness.

To determine the stress in your life, take the stressor value given beside each event you have experienced and multiply it by the number of occurrences over the past year (up to a maximum of four), and then add up these scores.[3]

87 Experienced the death of a spouse

77 Got married

77 Experienced the death of a close family member

76 Were divorced

74 Experienced a marital separation

68 Experienced the death of a close friend

68 Experienced pregnancy or fathered a pregnancy

65 Had a major personal injury or illness

62 Were fired from work

60 Ended a marital engagement or a steady relationship

58 Had sexual difficulties

58 Experienced a marital reconciliation

57 Had a major change in self-concept or self-awareness

56 Experienced a major change in the health or behaviour of a family member

54 Became engaged to be married

53 Had a major change in financial status

52 Took on a mortgage or loan of more than $10 000

52 Had a major change in use of drugs

50 Had a major conflict or change in values

50 Had a major change in the number of arguments with spouse

50 Gained a new family member

50 Entered college or university

50 Changed to a new school

50 Changed to a different line of work

W ork: Developing Effective Coping Strategies

A wide variety of tactics can help you deal with stress. Among the most effective approaches to coping are these:

- **Take charge of the situation.** Stress is most apt to arise when we are faced with situations over which we have little or no control. Take

49 Had a major change in amount of independence and responsibility

47 Had a major change in responsibilities at work

46 Experienced a major change in use of alcohol

45 Revised personal habits

44 Had trouble with school administration

43 Held a job while attending school

43 Had a major change in social activities

42 Had trouble with in-laws

42 Had a major change in working hours or conditions

42 Changed residence or living conditions

41 Had spouse begin or cease work outside the home

41 Changed choice of major field of study

41 Changed dating habits

40 Had an outstanding personal achievement

38 Had trouble with boss

38 Had a major change in amount of participation in school activities

37 Had a major change in type and/or amount of recreation

36 Had a major change in religious activities

34 Had a major change of sleeping habits

33 Took a trip or vacation

30 Had a major change in eating habits

26 Had a major change in the number of family get-togethers

22 Were found guilty of minor violations of the law

Scoring: If your total score is above 1435, you are in a high-stress category and therefore more at risk for experiencing a stress-related illness. However, a high score does not mean that you are sure to get sick. Many other factors determine ill health, and high stress is only one cause. Other positive factors in your life, such as getting enough sleep and exercise, may help to prevent illness. Still, having an unusually high amount of stress in your life is a cause for concern, and you may want to take steps to reduce it.

charge of the situation and you'll increase your sense of mastery and reduce the experience of stress. For example, if several assignments are all due on the same day, you might try negotiating with one of your instructors for a later due date.

- **Don't waste energy trying to change the unchangeable.** There are some situations that you simply can't control. You can't change the fact that you have come down with a case of mono, and you can't change your performance on a test you took last week. Don't hit your head against a brick

> "I continually try to remind myself that a PhD in English is not worth getting unhealthy over."
>
> Colleen Shea, Student, Queen's University

wall and try to modify things that can't be changed. Use your energy to address the situation as a problem to be solved: Seek out ways to improve the situation, not to rewrite history.

- **Look for the silver lining.** Stress arises when we perceive a situation as threatening. If we can change how we perceive that situation, we can change our reactions to it. For instance, if your computer science instructor requires you to learn a difficult spreadsheet program in a very short time, the saving grace is that you may be able to use the skill to your advantage in getting a job. (You can practise finding the silver lining in Try It! 2, "Look for the Silver Lining.")

Social support
Assistance and comfort supplied by others in times of stress

- **Talk to your friends. Social support,** assistance and comfort supplied by others, can help us through stressful periods. Turning to our friends and family and simply talking about the stress we're under can help us tolerate it more effectively. Contact your campus student life or counselling office for school, community, and professional social support resources.

- **Relax.** Because stress produces constant wear and tear on the body, practices that lead to the relaxation of the body might lead to a reduction in stress. Using any one of several techniques for producing physical relaxation can prevent stress. Among the best relaxation techniques are the following:

Meditation
A learned technique for refocusing attention and producing bodily relaxation

  - **Meditation.** Though often associated with its roots in the ancient Eastern religion of Zen Buddhism, meditation, a learned technique for refocusing attention and producing bodily relaxation, is practised in some form by members of virtually every major religion. Meditation reduces blood pressure, slows respiration, and in general produces relaxation in the body.

    How do you meditate? The process is actually rather simple. As summarized in Table 14.1, it includes sitting in a quiet room with eyes closed or focused on a point about 2 metres away from you and paying attention to your breathing. Though the specifics of what you do may vary slightly, meditation works by helping you concentrate on breathing deeply and rhythmically, sometimes murmuring a word or sound repeatedly.

Table 14.1

Methods of Meditation

Step 1	Pick a focus word or short phrase that's firmly rooted in your personal belief system or a neutral word like *one* or *peace* or *love*.
Step 2	Sit quietly in a comfortable position.
Step 3	Close your eyes.
Step 4	Relax your muscles.
Step 5	Breathe slowly and naturally, repeating your focus word or phrase silently as you exhale.
Step 6	Throughout, assume a passive attitude. Don't worry about how well you're doing. When other thoughts come to mind, simply say to yourself, "Oh, well," and gently return to the repetition.
Step 7	Continue for 10 to 20 minutes. You may open your eyes to check the time, but do not use an alarm. When you finish, sit quietly for a minute or so, at first with your eyes closed and later with your eyes open. Then do not stand for one or two minutes.
Step 8	Practise the technique once or twice a day.

Look for the Silver Lining

Consider the following list of potentially stressful situations. Try to find something positive—a silver lining—in each of them. The first two are completed to give you an idea of where to look for the silver lining.

Situation	Silver Lining
1. Your car just broke down and repairing it is more than you can afford right now.	1. This is the perfect time to begin exercising by walking and using your bicycle.
2. Your boss just yelled at you and threatened to fire you.	2. Either this is a good time to have an honest discussion with your boss about your job situation, OR this is a good time to get a more interesting job.
3. You have two papers due on Monday and there's a great concert you wanted to go to on Saturday night.	3.
4. You just failed an important test.	4.
5. You're flat broke, you have a date on Saturday, and you wanted to buy some things beforehand.	5.
6. Your last date went poorly and you think your girlfriend/boyfriend was hinting that it was time to break up.	6.
7. Your parents just told you that they can't afford to pay your tuition next semester.	7.
8. You just got cut from a sports team or club activity you loved.	8.
9. Your best friend is starting to turn weird and seems not to enjoy being with you as much as before.	9.
10. You just realized you don't really like your academic major, and you're not even sure you like your school much any more.	10.

- **Progressive relaxation.** Progressive relaxation does some of the same things that meditation does, but in a more direct way. To use progressive relaxation, you systematically tense and then relax different groups of muscles. For example, you might start with your lower arm, tensing it for five seconds and then relaxing it for a similar amount of time. By doing the same thing throughout the parts of your body, you'll be able to learn the "feel" of bodily relaxation. You can use the technique when you feel that stress is getting the better of you. (Use Try It! 3, "Use Progressive Relaxation," to experience progressive relaxation for yourself.)

- **Remember that wimping out doesn't work—so keep your commitments.** Suppose you've promised a friend that you'll help out on moving day and yourself that you'll spend more time with your children. You've also been elected to the student body governing board, and you've made a commitment to bring more speakers to campus. Now you are facing all the demands connected to these commitments and feeling stressed.

Use Progressive Relaxation

You can undertake progressive relaxation almost anywhere, including the library, a sports field, or a classroom, since tensing and relaxing muscles is quiet and unobtrusive. Although the following exercise suggests you lie down, you can use parts of it no matter where you are.

1. Lie flat on your back, get comfortable, and focus on your toes.

2. Become aware of your left toes. Bunch them up into a tight ball, then let them go. Then let them relax even further.

3. Now work on your left foot, from the toes to the heel. Without tensing your toes, tighten up the rest of your foot and then let it relax. Then relax it more.

4. Work your way up your left leg all the way to your groin, first tensing and then relaxing each part. You may move up as slowly or as quickly as you want, using big leaps (e.g., the entire lower leg) or small steps (e.g., the ankle, the calf, the front of the lower leg, the knee, etc.).

5. Repeat the process for the right leg.

6. Now tense and relax progressively your groin, buttocks, abdomen, lower back, ribs, upper back, and shoulders.

7. Work your way down each arm, one at a time, until you reach the fingers.

8. Return to the neck, then the jaw, cheeks, nose, eyes, ears, forehead, and skull.

By now you should be completely relaxed. In fact, you may even be asleep—this technique works well as a sleep-induction strategy.

To vary the routine, play with it. Try going from top to bottom, or from your extremities in and ending with your groin. Or target any other part of your body to end up at, and take the most circuitous route you can think of.

You may be tempted to cope with the feeling by breaking some or all of your commitments, thinking, "I just need to sit at home and relax in front of the television!" This is not coping. It is escaping, and it doesn't reduce stress. Ducking out of commitments, whether to yourself or to others, will make you feel guilty and anxious, and will be another source of stress—one without the satisfaction of having accomplished what you set out to do. Keep your promises.

 valuate: Asking Whether Your Strategies for Dealing with Stress Are Effective

Just as the experience of stress depends on how we interpret circumstances, the strategies for dealing with stress also vary in effectiveness depending on who we are. So if your efforts at coping aren't working, it's time to reconsider your approach. If talking to friends hasn't helped ease your stress response, maybe you need a different approach. Maybe you need to see the silver lining or cut back on some of your commitments. If one coping strategy doesn't work for you, try another. What's critical is that you don't become paralyzed, unable to deal with a situation. Instead, try something different until you find the right combination of strategies to improve the situation.

R ethink: Placing Stress in Perspective

It's easy to think of stress as an enemy. In fact, the coping steps outlined in the P.O.W.E.R. Plan at the right are geared to overcoming its negative consequences. But consider the following two principles, which in the end may help you more than any others with understanding how to deal with stress:

- **Don't sweat the small stuff . . . and it's all small stuff.** Stress expert Richard Carlson[7] emphasizes the importance of putting the circumstances we encounter into the proper perspective. He argues that we frequently let ourselves get upset about situations that are actually minor. So what if someone cuts us off in traffic, or does less than his or her share on a group project, or unfairly criticizes us? It's hardly the end of the world, and the behaviour of the other people involved in such situations reflects negatively on them, not us. One of the best ways to reduce stress, consequently, is to maintain an appropriate perspective on the events of your life, sorting out what is and is not important.

- **Make peace with stress.** Think of what it would be like to have no stress—none at all—in your life. Would you really be happier, better adjusted, and more successful? The answer is "probably not." A life that presented no challenges would probably be, in a word, boring. So think about stress as an exciting, although admittedly sometimes difficult, friend. Welcome it, because its presence indicates that your life is stimulating, challenging, and exciting—and who would want it any other way?

PREPARE

Ready yourself physically

ORGANIZE

Identify what is causing you stress

WORK

Develop effective coping strategies

EVALUATE

Ask yourself whether your strategies for dealing with stress are effective

RETHINK

Place stress in perspective

P.O.W.E.R. Plan

Keeping Well

Eat right. Exercise. Get plenty of sleep.

Pretty simple, isn't it? We learn the fundamentals of fitness and health in the first years of elementary school.

Yet for millions of us, wellness is an elusive goal. We eat on the fly, stopping for a bite at the drive-in window of a fast-food restaurant. Most of us don't exercise enough, either because we feel we don't have enough time or because it's not much fun for us. And as for sleep, we're a nation in which getting by with as little sleep as possible is seen as a badge of honour.

> "The first wealth is health."
>
> Emerson

You can buck the trends, however; you can begin to eat properly, exercise effectively, and sleep better by following several basic rules.

Eating Right

- **Eat a variety of foods.** Strive to eat a range of different foods. If you make *variety* your goal, you will end up eating the right foods. Although many popular diets recommend reducing carbohydrates in favour of high-fat, high-protein foods, most nutritionists recommend eating a selection of foods that contain all the vitamins, minerals, and fibre a healthy body needs.

- **Eat plenty of fruits, vegetables, and grain products.** Enough said.

- **Avoid foods that are high in sugar and salt content.** Read labels on supermarket packages carefully and beware of hidden sugars and salts. Many ingredients that end in *-ose* (such as dextrose, sucrose, maltose, and fructose) are actually sugars; salt can lurk within any number of compounds beginning with the word *sodium*. Your best bet is to trust the nutrition labels that the Canadian government requires food manufacturers to put on their products.

- **Seek a diet low in fat and cholesterol.** The fat that is to be especially avoided is saturated fat—the most difficult for your body to rid itself of. Be especially careful to avoid trans fat, which is found in many processed snacks and junk food.

- **Less is more.** You don't need to walk away stuffed from every meal. Moderation is the key. To be sure you don't eat more than your body is telling you to eat, pay attention to internal hunger cues.

The lure of fast foods is difficult to resist, and eating a balanced, nutritious diet is a challenge for most college students.

- **Schedule three regular meals a day.** Eating should be a priority—a definite part of your daily schedule. Avoid skipping any meals. Breakfast is particularly important; get up early enough to eat a full meal.

- **Be sensitive to the hidden contents of various foods.** Soft drinks and chocolate can contain substantial quantities of caffeine, which can disrupt your sleep and, along with coffee and tea, become addictive. Many cereals—even those labelled "low fat"—contain a substantial amount of sugar or salt. Pay attention to labels.

- **Beware of eating disorders.** Between 1 percent and 4 percent of college- or university-age women, and a smaller percentage of men, suffer from an eating disorder. Those with *anorexia nervosa* may refuse to eat, while denying that their behaviour and appearance—which can become skeletonlike—are unusual. Some 15 to 20 percent of those with anorexia literally starve themselves to death. *Bulimia* is a disorder in which individuals binge on incredibly large quantities of food, such as a gallon of ice cream and a whole pie, but later feel so much guilt and depression that they induce vomiting or take laxatives to rid themselves of the food. Eating disorders represent serious threats to health and require aggressive medical intervention.

Making Exercise a Part of Your Life

Exercise produces a variety of benefits. Your body will run more efficiently, you'll have more energy, your heart and circulatory system will run more smoothly, and you'll be able to bounce back from stress and illness more quickly.

- **Choose a type of exercise that you like.** Exercising will be a chore you'll end up avoiding if you don't enjoy what you're doing.

- **Incorporate exercise into your life.** Take the stairs instead of elevators. Leave your car at home and walk to campus or work. Join an intramural team. When you're on campus, take the longer way to reach your destination.

- **Make exercise a group activity.** Exercising with others brings you social support and turns exercise into a social activity. You'll be more likely to stick to a program if you have regular workouts scheduled with a friend.

- **Vary your routine.** You don't need to do the same kind of exercise day after day. Choose different sorts of activities that will involve different parts of your body and keep you from getting bored.

These students from Capilano College and the Royal Military College battle for the national soccer championship despite the snow. Intramural and varsity sports have the advantage of mixing regular exercise with an enjoyable social activity.

One note of caution: Before you begin an exercise program, it is a good idea to have a physical checkup, even if you feel you're at the peak of health. This is especially true if you're starting an exercise program after years of inactivity. You also might consult a trainer at the gym to set up a program that gradually builds you up to more vigorous exercise.

Getting a Good Night's Sleep

Do you feel as if you don't get enough sleep? That's not surprising. Most college and university students are sleep deprived, a condition that causes them to feel fatigued, short-tempered, and tense. Insufficient sleep also leads to declines in academic and physical performance. You can't do your best at anything if you're exhausted—or even tired. Some scientists believe that long-term sleep debt could be a factor in the national epidemics of diabetes and obesity; in addition, inadequate sleep could weaken the immune system,

Career Connections

Anticipating Job Stress

Stress is one of the prime hazards of the world of work. Consider these statistics from the Canadian Mental Health Association:[10]

- Workplace stress is the most common form of stress experienced by Canadians.
- Forty-three percent of all Canadian adults aged 30 and over feel overwhelmed by their jobs.
- Canadian workers view job stress as more prevalent than work-related injury or illness.
- Canadians are not alone. Job-related stress has been identified by the World Health Organization as a "worldwide epidemic."
- Not all stress is bad; without some degree of stress, people become bored and depressed. However, ill health can occur when our response to stress is not channelled properly.
- It is estimated that 40 percent of worker turnover is due to job stress.
- Job stress is a major factor in employee absenteeism. Statistics Canada calculates the annual cost of work time lost to stress at $12 billion.
- Workplace stress has been shown to cause backaches, migraines, and to lead to substance abuse, all of which contribute to poor job performance.
- Chronic stress can lead to hypertension, depression, and susceptibility to other common physical illnesses.
- Less obvious results of workplace stress are the feelings of frustration, anger, and hopelessness that affect stressed employees.

Consequently, considering potential stress should be an important consideration when choosing a profession.

MDS Nordion recently received a Healthy Workplace Award from the National Quality Institute for its first-rate health and wellness system. Two focuses of the program are encouraging employees to strike a better balance between work and family life, and stress reduction. The result is less attrition, fewer absences, less time lost to injuries.

leading to colds and other infections. To make matters worse, research studies in Britain have shown that prolonged sleep deprivation mimics a rapid aging process.[8]

Often the solution to the problem is simply to allow yourself more time to sleep. Most people need around eight hours of sleep each night, although there are wide individual differences. Realistically, there will be times when you are up late with your kids, spend the night away from home, lose track of time playing on the Internet until the wee hours, or have to pull an all-nighter. When you're behind on sleep, a nap can work wonders in boosting your alertness. A short nap can equal one hour of sleep you didn't get the night before![9] In addition to sleeping more, there are also some relatively simple changes you can make in your behaviour that will help you to sleep better. They include the following:

- **Exercise during the day.** Regular exercise will help you sleep more soundly at night, as well as help you cope with stress that might otherwise keep you awake.

- **Have a regular bedtime.** By going to bed at pretty much the same time each night, you give your body a regular rhythm and make sleep a habit.

- **Use your bed for sleeping and not as an all-purpose area.** Don't use your bed as a place to study, read, eat, or watch TV. Let your bed be a trigger for sleep.

- **Avoid caffeine after lunch.** The stimulant effects of caffeine (found in coffee, tea, and some soft drinks) may last as long as 8 to 12 hours.

- **Drink a glass of milk at bedtime.** Drinking a glass of milk before you go to bed will help you get to sleep. The reason? Milk contains a natural chemical that makes you drowsy.

- **Avoid sleeping pills.** Despite advertisements to the contrary, you're better off not taking sleeping pills. Although they may be temporarily effective, in the long run they impair your ability to sleep because they disrupt your natural sleep cycles. Alcohol is similarly ineffective.

- **Sleep in the dark.** Falling asleep with the lights or TV on can be unhealthy. Too few hours spent in darkness might boost cancer risk. Cancer researchers speculate that there might be a connection between the epidemic of breast cancer and hormone cycles disrupted by late-night light. For more information on breast cancer and its link to hormone cycles, check out **<www.hopkinsmedicine.org/breastcenter/artemis/200111/feature.html>**.

- **Don't try to force sleep on yourself.** It turns out that one of the reasons that we have trouble sleeping is that we try too hard. To follow this advice, try to relax when you go to bed—and don't try to go to sleep. If you're wide awake after 10 minutes or so, get up and do something else. Only go back to bed when you feel tired. Do this as often as necessary.

Staying Safe on the Job

Tim Hickman, a 21-year-old Fanshawe College student was killed in 1996, 10 days after an explosion at a London arena left him badly burned. He had been refilling an ice-resurfacing machine when it caught on fire and engulfed him in flames. The city, which was subsequently convicted of health and safety violations, has begun to rectify the conditions that resulted in Tim Hickman's death.

Dozens of young Canadians are hurt on the job every day and, as in Tim Hickman's case, some of those injuries result in death. New employees are especially vulnerable, with some accidents occurring within the first week of starting a job. If you have a part-time job, be aware of any concerns and make sure equipment operating instructions and emergency/safety procedures are explained to you. Make sure you are WHMIS (Workplace Hazardous Materials Information System) trained if you deal with hazardous materials.

For more information on young worker safety, check out the P.O.W.E.R. Learning Online Learning Centre at **<www.mcgrawhill.ca/college/power>**.

Drug Abuse

For better or worse, drugs are part of our lives. It's virtually impossible to be unaware of the extent of the Canadian and international problem of illegal drug use, which involves millions of individuals who have used illegal substances at least once. Patterns of drug use and the ability to avoid abusing drugs are often established in college or university. These patterns can have a big impact on your academic career and your life, so it is a good idea to learn what you can now, before negative patterns of abuse, and in some cases, addiction, take hold.

Alcohol and Its Allure

The drug most likely to be found on college or university campuses is alcohol. It may surprise you to know that though it initially seems to raise your spirits, alcohol is actually and ultimately a depressant. As the amount of alcohol you consume increases, its depressive effects become more obvious. You've probably seen other negative effects. Drinkers show poor judgment, their memory is impaired, and their speech becomes slurred and eventually incoherent. If you drink enough, you'll pass out. And if you consume enough alcohol in a short period, you can die of alcohol poisoning.

Binge drinking
Having at least four (for females) or five (for males) drinks in a single sitting

Alcoholics
Individuals with serious alcohol-abuse problems who become dependent on alcohol and continue to drink despite serious consequences

Journal Reflections

College Drinking Experiences

Examine your own feelings about alcohol use by answering these questions.

1. Why do you think people use alcohol? Why do you use (or don't use) alcohol?

2. What do you think the minimum age to legally drink alcohol should be, and why?

3. What is your opinion on people who only drink to get drunk? On binge drinking?

4. Have you ever suspected any of your friends or acquaintances of being alcoholics? Why?

5. Have you ever witnessed or been part of a scene in which drunkenness played a part in obnoxious behaviour? Rowdiness? Drinking and driving? Death? Violence? Abuse of others? What are your comments?

The potential negative consequences of drinking have done little to prevent the use of alcohol on university and college campuses, many of which have pubs, bars, or licensed facilities in student activity centres. (To assess your drinking style, complete Try It! 4, "Personal Styles: Consider Your Drinking Style.") About 68 percent of Canadian university students describe themselves as regular drinkers.[11] The average university student in Canada has 6.5 alcoholic drinks per week.[12]

Some students drink even more and the extent of alcohol consumption can reach astonishing levels. According to a national survey of alcohol and drug use on Canadian campuses, 63 percent of Canadian university students had engaged in **binge drinking**, defined as having at least four (for females) or five (for males) drinks in a single sitting.[13] Around 38 percent reported binging on more than eight drinks.[14] Such heavy drinking doesn't just affect the drinker. Most college students report having had their studies or sleep disturbed by drunken students. Students in residence reported the highest levels of binge drinking;[15] the problem is enough of a concern that *substance-free* residences or *substance-free* floors in residences are growing in popularity on Canadian campuses.

Approximately 10 percent of Canadian adults are alcoholics or problem drinkers, and Canadian college and university students make up their fair share of the total.[16] **Alcoholics,** individuals with serious alcohol-abuse problems, become dependent on alcohol, experiencing a physical craving for it. They continue to drink despite serious consequences. Furthermore, they develop a tolerance for alcohol and must drink increasing amounts to experience the initially positive effects that alcohol brings about.

The long-term consequences of high levels of alcohol consumption are severe. Heavy drinking damages the liver and digestive system, and can even affect brain cells. In fact, virtually every part of the body is eventually affected by heavy alcohol use.

Nicotine

Despite millions of dollars spent on anti-smoking education, bylaws prohibiting

Personal Styles: Consider Your Drinking Style

If you drink alcohol, do you have a style of use that is safe and responsible? Read the statements below and rate the extent to which you agree with them, using the following scale:

1 = Strongly disagree

2 = Disagree

3 = Neutral

4 – Agree

5 = Strongly agree

	1	2	3	4	5
1. I usually drink alcohol a few times a week.					
2. I sometimes go to class after I've been drinking alcohol.					
3. I frequently drink when I am alone.					
4. I have driven under the influence of alcohol.					
5. I have used fake or borrowed ID to buy alcohol.					
6. I'm a totally different person when I am drinking alcohol.					
7. I often drink so much that I feel drunk.					
8. I wouldn't want to go to a party where alcohol wasn't allowed.					
9. I avoid people who don't like to drink alcohol.					
10. I sometimes urge others to drink more alcohol.					

The lower your score (i.e., the more 1's and 2's) the better able you are to control your alcohol consumption and the more likely it is that your alcohol use is responsible. The higher your score (i.e., the more 4's and 5's) the greater is your use and reliance on alcohol, and the more likely it is that your alcohol consumption may be reckless. If your score is over 40, you may have an alcohol problem and should seek professional help to control your alcohol usage.

smoking in public venues, and graphic warnings on cigarette packages, smoking remains a significant health problem. Smoking causes lung damage and increases the risks of developing cancer, emphysema, and a host of other diseases.

Why do people smoke, when the evidence is so clear about its risks? They start to smoke for a variety of reasons. Smoking is sometimes viewed as a kind of initiation into adulthood, a sign of growing up. In other cases, teenagers see smoking as "cool," a view glorified by movies and television.

The problem is that, no matter what the reason a person tries a few cigarettes, smoking usually quickly becomes a habit because a major ingredient of tobacco—nicotine—is an addictive drug. An *addictive drug* produces a biological or psychological dependence. The absence of the drug leads to a craving for it that may be nearly irresistible.

Smoking cigarettes is one of the hardest addictions to break. Among the suggestions for quitting are the following:

- **Remain smoke-free one day at a time.** Don't think to yourself about not smoking tomorrow, or next week, or for the rest of your life. Instead, think of what you're doing as not smoking for the rest of the day. You can worry about tomorrow . . . tomorrow.

- **Visualize the consequences of smoking.** Visualize blackened, rotting lungs filled with smoke. Then think about the fresh, pink lungs that you'll have after you've stopped smoking.

- **Exercise.** The all-purpose antidote, exercise, will make you feel better physically and take your mind off smoking.

- **Use nicotine patches or nicotine gum.** "The Patch" and nicotine gum can provide enough nicotine to satisfy your craving for the drug, while permitting you to stop smoking. Physicians can also sometimes prescribe drugs that help reduce the craving for nicotine.

- **Avoid smokers.** It's nearly impossible to avoid the urge to smoke when others are lighting up. If you're trying to quit, stay away from people who are smoking.

- **Enlist the social support of family and friends.** Tell others that you're trying to quit, and accept their encouragement and praise.

- **Reward yourself.** Every few days, give yourself some kind of reinforcement for spending a period of time smoke-free. Go to a movie, buy a CD. Think about how you can afford these more easily since you aren't buying cigarettes anymore.

- **Join a quit-smoking program.** Many college and university health services hold periodic programs to help students who want to stop smoking. By enrolling in one, you'll receive the support of others who are in the same boat as you are.

- **Keep trying.** If after quitting you start smoking again, just consider that lapse as part of the process of quitting. Many people quit several times before they manage to quit for good.

Illegal Drugs

"Just say 'no.'"

If it were only so easy. Decisions about drugs are quite a bit more complicated than simplistic antidrug slogans would have you believe. They involve complex decisions about your body, peer pressure, and your personal values.

Several things are clear, however. Despite the prevalence of illicit drug use among college and university students—surveys show that approximately 30 percent of Canadian university students report using cannabis in the previous 12 months and 10 percent acknowledge using illicit drugs other than cannabis[17]—the benefits of drug use are difficult to enumerate. Apart from a temporary high, the advantages of using drugs are nil, and the use of illegal drugs is among the riskiest activities in which people can engage. Not only does drug use make you vulnerable to arrest, it also poses short- and long-term health risks. The escape from one's responsibilities that drugs provide is likely to make it even harder to later deal with those responsibilities—which aren't going to go away.

> "Every form of addiction is bad, no matter whether the narcotic be alcohol or morphine or idealism."
>
> Carl Jung

Not all illegal drugs are the same, and they produce widely varying effects and consequences. For information on the most common drugs and their effects, please go to the Online Learning Centre at www.mcgrawhill.ca/college/power. But they all share a common result—a reduction in your awareness of what is happening around you and an escape from the realities of life.

People often fall into drug use without much thought. But doing so is still a personal choice. Preaching and slogans are not going to help you to make a sensible decision. You need to employ every critical thinking skill you can to determine exactly what you want—and don't want—to introduce into your body. Give some thought to why escape is attractive and consider seeking counselling instead. Allow yourself to consider the long- and short-term effects of drug use—both the physical effects as well as the potential effects on your own aspirations and dreams. Let yourself think about the legal consequences of drug use. A drug conviction can lead to expulsion from college or university and refusal by many employers to hire you. Furthermore, random drug tests are starting to become a part of corporate life in Canada, and your ability to get and keep a job may be placed at risk if you use drugs—even only occasionally.

Drugs that produce addiction, such as cocaine, methamphetamines, and heroin, present a further set of problems. The lives of people with drug addictions become centred on the drug. They enter into a pattern of alternating highs—when on the drug—and lows. During their lows, much of their thinking is focused on obtaining the drug and looking forward to their next high.

Addiction's Warning Signs   Addictions to drugs—and alcohol—can begin subtly, and you may not be aware of the extent of the problem. Here are some signs that indicate when use becomes abuse:

- Feeling you need to be high to have a good time.

- Being high more often than not.

- Getting high to get yourself going.

- Going to class or work high.

- Missing class or work because you are high.

- Being unprepared for class because you are high.
- Feeling regret over something you did while you were high.
- Driving while high.
- Having a legal problem due to being high.
- Behaving, while high, in a way you wouldn't otherwise.
- Being high in nonsocial, solitary situations.
- Thinking about drugs or alcohol much of the time.
- Avoiding family or friends while using liquor or drugs.
- Hiding drug or alcohol use from others.

Any one of these symptoms indicates that you have a drug or alcohol problem. If you do have a problem, seek professional help. Addictions to illegal drugs or alcohol are extremely difficult to deal with on your own. No matter how good your intentions, few people can overcome the cravings brought about by an addiction to a particular substance without help.

Here are some places to which you can turn:

1. **College and university health services, counselling centres, and mental health centres.** Most schools provide services to help you overcome an addiction. They can evaluate the extent of the problem and refer you to the proper place for further help. (To learn about your own campus resources, complete Try It! 5, "Tap Into Campus Resources.")

2. **Drug treatment centres and clinics.** Sometimes located in hospitals and sometimes independently run, drug treatment centres or clinics can provide help. You can also check your telephone book for a local listing of Alcoholics Anonymous or Narcotics Anonymous.

Sexual Health and Decision Making

Relationships, contraception, AIDS, rape—sexual health relates to a host of issues, involving not just your body but your heart and mind as well. In fact, it is often said that our most important sexual organ is our brain. It determines what we view as sexually arousing, and it's what we use to make decisions and choices about our sexuality.

Although the focus of the brief discussion of sexual health here is on strategies for protecting yourself (from pregnancy, sexually transmitted diseases, and rape), sexual decisions are also a reflection of your basic values. You can't make responsible decisions about sex without knowing what is important to you and how you view yourself. So you don't want to wait until a sexual encounter begins before thinking through your views of sexuality and what is and is not right for you.

Most campuses have health centres where students can see a nurse or doctor, access medical counselling, obtain birth control at reduced rates, or receive treatment, support, and information about issues such as abuse, date rape, and sexually transmitted diseases.

Tap into Campus Resources

Try It!

5

Complete the following chart to identify the campus office locations and their services that deal with alcohol and drug problems.

Campus Resource	Where Is It?	What Service Does It Provide?	How Do You Get in Touch?
Health Centre			
Mental Health Centre			
Campus Chaplain			
Drug and Alcohol Education Centre(s)			
Counselling Centre			
Residential Life Office			
Ombudsperson			
Campus Security Services			
(add other office here)			
(add other office here)			
(add other office here)			
(add other office here)			

Preventing Unwanted Pregnancy

One and only one means of preventing pregnancy is totally effective. Don't have sexual intercourse. **Abstinence,** refraining from intercourse, only works, however, if you practise it without fail—something that many people find difficult. But it certainly is possible. Despite the folklore that insists "everybody's doing it," they're not. In fact, if you think critically about what others say about their sexual activity, you'll conclude that the possibility of misrepresentation of sexual activity is high.

Those who do want to have a sexual relationship can still avoid pregnancy. Many possibilities exist, including the following:

Abstinence
The avoidance of sexual contact

Relationships and sexuality raise substantial issues, involving your attitudes, beliefs, values, and emotions, as well as your body, in a complex intermix. Making responsible decisions requires that you know who you are and what's important to you.

- **Birth control pills.** Composed of artificial hormones, birth control pills are among the most effective ways of preventing pregnancy—as long as they are taken as prescribed. Except for women with particular medical conditions, the side effects are minimal.

- **Condoms.** Condoms are thin sheaths that fit over the penis. By preventing sperm from entering the vagina, they are highly effective in preventing pregnancy, if used properly and consistently. If they are positioned properly and are used with a contraceptive jelly that kills sperm, condoms are highly effective. Condoms, which can also protect against STDs, are readily available. A female condom is now available; although not as familiar or popular as other female contraceptive methods, it has the potential to be highly effective.

- **Depo-Provera injections.** A relatively new form of female birth control, Depo-Provera injections are long-lasting doses of progesterone that are given every three months. This contraceptive method is very effective (99.7 percent) and provides protection after 24 hours, but it does have some side effects that warrant investigation.

- **Implants.** One of the newest forms of birth control, Norplant implants work through a simple surgical procedure in which six tiny tubes are inserted into a woman's upper arm. Implants last for five years, preventing pregnancy for the entire time. With few side effects, implants are highly effective, but they are only practical for women who want to avoid pregnancy for extended times.

- **Intrauterine device, or IUD.** IUDs are small pieces of plastic inserted by a medical practitioner into a woman's uterus. Although highly effective, some have been found to produce unacceptable side effects, including infections and scarring that can make it impossible for a woman to get pregnant when she wants to.

- **Diaphragms and cervical caps.** Diaphragms and cervical caps are circular, dome-shaped pieces of thin rubber that a woman inserts into her vagina, covering the cervix. A sperm-killing cream or jelly must be used simultaneously, and the diaphragm and cervical cap must be removed after sexual intercourse. Although side effects are few, the risk of pregnancy is somewhat higher than with the other forms of birth control we've discussed; some 18 percent of women using them become pregnant. Diaphragms and cervical caps are prescribed by health care practitioners.

- **Contraceptive foam, jelly, gel.** These spermicides are most effective when combined with a condom, diaphragm, or other barrier method. When used with a condom, they are effective in preventing STDs. They are easily obtainable.

- **Contraceptive sponge.** The sponge, shaped like a large mushroom cap, is inserted into the vagina. It can be left in place for 24 hours, during which time it can be used for multiple acts of intercourse. Although it has few side effects, it has a failure rate of between 17 and 25 percent.

- **Emergency contraceptive pills.** Also known as the morning after pill, emergency contraceptive pills are taken within 72 hours of having unprotected sex. As a last resort, two doses of two pills (estrogen and progestin) are taken 12 hours apart. Severe nausea may result.

- **Rhythm.** The only form of birth control (besides abstinence) that involves no chemical or mechanical intervention, rhythm consists of refraining from intercourse during times in a woman's menstrual cycle when pregnancy is possible. With a failure rate of 20 percent, rhythm requires scrutiny of calendars, body temperature, or cervical mucus—all of which can be indicators of the time of the month to avoid intercourse.

- **Withdrawal and douching: ineffective birth control.** Withdrawal, in which a man removes his penis from a woman's vagina before climaxing, and douching, flushing the vagina with a liquid, just don't work. They should not be used for birth control because they are so ineffective.

- **Sterilization.** Sterilization is a surgical procedure that causes a person to become permanently incapable of having children. Vasectomies (for men) or tubal ligations (for women) are sometimes possible to reverse, but this method is not recommended for people who may decide to have children (or more children).

What You Can Do If You Are Pregnant

More than 40 percent of all pregnancies in Canada are unintended.[18] Usually unplanned pregnancies occur when contraception fails or people use it incorrectly. If you are one of the hundreds of thousands of Canadian women who unintentionally become pregnant every year, three options are available to you:

1. **Keeping your baby.** About half of unintentionally pregnant Canadian women keep their babies.[19] Not all unplanned babies are unwanted. But questions abound for the woman who is intending to keep her baby. Is the baby's father going to be involved in the child's life? To what degree? The baby is entitled to some financial support from the father, even if your relationship is over. Social assistance is an option for single parents; however, in Canada, 60 percent of single mothers and their families live in poverty.[20] Lifestyle, friends, relationships, and transportation are all subject to change when you become a parent.

2. **Adoption.** Although research indicates only about 2 percent of women in Canada choose to give their babies up for adoption,[21] it is an option that may be right for both you and your baby. New practices, such as open adoptions, allow birth mothers to choose adoptive parents for their child and permit ongoing contact.

3. **Abortion.** About 22 percent of pregnancies in Canada end in an induced abortion, a medical procedure that is legally available in all provinces and territories, except Prince Edward Island.[22] In 1995, almost 107 000 abortions were performed in Canada.[23] In 1995, 52 percent of all abortions in Canada were obtained by females between 20 and 29. Twenty percent were obtained by women younger than 20. Three types of medical abortions are used, depending on how long the woman has been pregnant. Dilation and curettage (D&C) accounts for

90 percent of all medical abortions performed in the first 12 weeks of pregnancy. The dilation-evacuation-curettage (DEC) procedure is used after the 12th week, along with a late-term method, hormone-saline injection. The "abortion pill" RU-486, which is widely available in Europe, is currently undergoing clinical testing in Canada.

Medical abortions are medically very safe; however, emotional responses to abortion vary, depending on the woman and her values, religion, relationship with the child's father, and support systems. If you are contemplating abortion, you should carefully consider your psychological state and seek counselling and support if you need it afterward.

What You Can Do to Avoid Sexually Transmitted Diseases

Sexually transmitted diseases (STDs)

Medical conditions acquired through sexual contact

Sexually transmitted diseases (STDs) threaten the general health, well-being, and reproductive ability of a sizable number of Canadians. It is difficult to determine how many Canadians have STDs, as many of the symptoms are mild enough to avoid detection (and reporting). While rates of chlamydia, syphilis, and gonorrhea are declining somewhat in Canada, viral STDs, such as herpes simplex, human papilloma virus (HPV), and HIV/AIDS are increasing.[24] For a list of common STDs, please go to the Online Learning Centre at www.mcgrawhill.ca/college/power.

There are many varieties of STDs, although all share a similar origin: sexual contact. Depending on the type of disease, symptoms may include warts in the genital area, pelvic infection, painful urination, infertility, blindness, and even death.

Acquired immune deficiency syndrome (AIDS)

A lethal, sexually transmitted disease that causes the destruction of the body's immune system

The STD that has had the greatest impact in the past two decades is **acquired immune deficiency syndrome (AIDS)**. Although it started as a disease that most often affected homosexuals, AIDS quickly spread among heterosexuals. Some populations are particularly affected, such as intravenous drug users. Worldwide, more than six million people have already died from the disease. Some estimates suggest that 40 million people now carry the AIDS virus.

Although AIDS is the best-known STD, the most common is *chlamydia*, a disease that if left untreated can cause sterility in some victims. *Genital herpes* is a virus that appears as small blisters or sores around the genitals. Although the sores heal after several weeks, the disease can remain dormant and reappear periodically. Other STDs, although somewhat less common, also afflict millions of people.

It's no secret how to avoid AIDS and other STDs. Abstinence—the avoidance of sexual contact—is completely effective. However, many people are unwilling to make such a choice. Several alternative approaches, called "smart sex" practices, reduce the risk of contracting STDs. They include the following:

- **Know your sexual partner—well.** You should not have sexual contact with a person who is only a casual acquaintance. You want to know the person well enough to have a discussion with him or her in which you both talk about your sexual histories.

- **Prevent the exchange of bodily fluids during all sex acts.** Avoid semen and unprotected anal and vaginal intercourse and oral sex.

- **Use condoms.** Condoms not only prevent the spread of AIDS and other STDs, but they also prevent pregnancy.

- **Be faithful to a single partner.** People in long-term relationships with only one other individual are less likely to contract AIDS and other STDs than those with multiple sexual partners.

Date Rape

We usually think of rape as a rare crime, committed by strangers. However, after the age of 18, 1 in every 4 women and 1 in 10 men will be sexually assaulted; 14 to 25 percent of female students will be victims of sexual assault during their university careers. Unfortunately, not only is rape surprisingly common, but rapists usually know their victims. The University of Alberta Health Centre reports that more than 80 percent of rapes that occur on university and college campuses are committed by someone the victim knows, and 50 percent occur on dates. Many of these assaults, categorized as **date rape**, happen during the first eight weeks of classes and most involve the use of alcohol. Between 15 and 30 percent of women attending university report experiencing acquaintance rape.[25]

What leads to rape? Most often, rape has less to do with sex than with power and anger. Rapists use forced sex to demonstrate their power and control over the victim. The rapist's pleasure comes not so much from sex as from forcing someone to submit.

In addition, rapes sometimes are brought about by the common—but untrue—belief that when people offer resistance to sex, they don't really mean it. If a man holds the view that when a woman says no to sex, she really means yes, he is likely to ignore the woman's protests that she doesn't want sex, resulting in rape. Some men may even believe that it is unmasculine to accept no for an answer, perhaps because they feel it is a rejection of them as men.

Whatever the causes, rape is devastating to the victim. Victims experience extreme anxiety, disbelief, fear, and shock. These reactions may linger for years, and rape victims may experience suspiciousness and a fear of entering into relationships.

Both men and women must be sensitive to the issue of date rape. Among the suggestions for reducing its incidence are the following:

- **Set limits.** Everyone has the right to set limits, and these should be communicated clearly, firmly, and early.

- **No means no.** When a partner says no, it means nothing other than no.

- **Be assertive.** You should never passively accept being pressured into an activity in which you don't want to engage. Remember that passivity may be interpreted as consent.

- **Communicate.** Partners should talk about their views of sexual behaviour and what is and is not permissible.

- **Keep in mind that alcohol and drugs cloud judgment.** Nothing hinders communication more than alcohol and drugs.

- **Be careful when you go to bars and parties.** Never accept drinks or opened cans from others or leave drinks unattended, as they can easily be spiked with date rape drugs, such as Rohypnol or GHB.

Date rape
Forced sex in which the rapist is a date or romantic acquaintance

Speaking of Success

Krista Bailey

Emergency Medical Technician Certificate, Saskatchewan Institute of Applied Science and Technology
Emergency Medical Technician, Paramedic Diploma, Saskatchewan Institute of Applied Science and Technology

Determination and enthusiasm describe Krista Bailey and undoubtedly these characteristics help her save lives in her demanding career as a paramedic with Edmonton Emergency Medical Services.

Born and raised in Saskatchewan, Krista was the assistant aquatic director and senior guard at the Regina YWCA when a friend invited her to ride along on a shift with an ambulance crew. Krista was hooked and enrolled in the Saskatchewan Institute of Applied Science and Technology's Emergency Medical Technician (EMT) program.

One of her most memorable calls as an EMT involved a 2-year-old girl named Karlee Kosolofski, who survived after being found outdoors, frozen solid. Karlee was clinically dead when taken to the hospital, but the emergency medical treatment the girl received and her survival taught Krista to "never give up."

After four years of working as an EMT, Krista went back to SIAST to become a paramedic, graduating in 1995. Her advanced standing as a paramedic gave her more opportunities to lead the calls she attended and to administer drugs and perform restricted procedures. In addition, Krista took on responsibilities as a field trainer and a relief supervisor.

SIAST
SASKATCHEWAN INSTITUTE OF
APPLIED SCIENCE AND TECHNOLOGY

In January 2001, Krista moved to Edmonton. She was drawn to the city for its active lifestyle. Krista appreciates the bike paths and opportunities to roller blade and run on her time off. However, Edmonton is also a larger centre with a much busier emergency medical service and because of Alberta's medical direction, the responsibilities of paramedics are greater and more comprehensive. Changing provinces meant becoming certified in Alberta, and Krista passed the exams with honours.

Shortly after beginning to work for Edmonton Emergency Medical Services, Krista and partner, Justin Mazzolini, attended a call that was eerily similar to Karlee Kosolofski's case seven years earlier. A 13-month-old toddler, Erika Nordby, had been found frozen solid. Krista says she felt "a sense of peace" while dealing with Erika. "Everyone did their jobs and did them well." Erika not only lived, but she also exceeded all expectations of the medical team that treated her at the University of Alberta Hospital.

Krista, who is now a superintendent with Edmonton EMS, enjoys her job, as there is always a lot to learn. There are plenty of opportunities for in-service professional development, but formal education is on the back burner for the present, as Krista is beginning a new stage of her life as a wife and mother. Undoubtedly, Krista's calm and positive attitude will lead to continued success in all her important roles.

Looking
Back

What is stress and how can I control it?

- Stress is a common experience, appearing in three main forms: cataclysmic events, personal stressors, and daily hassles. Excessive stress is not only unpleasant and upsetting, it also has negative effects on the body and mind.

What is involved in keeping fit and healthy, and why is it important for me to do so?

- For all people, keeping fit and healthy is both essential and challenging. It is vital to learn to eat properly, especially by eating a variety of foods on a regular schedule and by restricting your intake of fat, cholesterol, and salt.

- Exercise is valuable because it improves health and well-being. Choosing exercises that we like, making everyday activities a part of exercise, and exercising with others can help form the habit of exercise.

- The third key element of good health is sleeping properly. Good exercise and eating habits can contribute to sound sleep, as can the development of regular sleeping habits and the use of sleep-assisting practices.

- Coping with stress involves becoming prepared for future stress through proper diet and exercise, identifying the causes of stress in your life, taking control of stress, seeking social support, practising relaxation techniques, training yourself to redefine and reinterpret stressful situations, and keeping your promises.

What are the main threats to my health and well-being?

- One of the major threats that postsecondary students (and others) face is the improper use of drugs. The most commonly abused drug is alcohol, which is a depressant (despite an initial reduction of inhibitions and feeling of euphoria) and can lead to a physical or psychological dependence. Nicotine is the second most commonly abused drug.

- The use of illegal drugs presents not only potential dangers related to law-breaking and prosecution, but short- and long-term health risks as well. Drugs cause a reduction in awareness and involvement in life, and some drugs can be dangerously addictive.

What are the components of sexual health?

- Sexual health is as important as other forms of health. People must make their own individual decisions about their sexuality and how they will express it.

- Many forms of contraception are available, ranging from abstinence to surgical implants. Each form has different procedures, risks, and effectiveness.

- The incidence of sexually transmitted diseases (STDs) is high in Canada, with about 25 percent of the population experiencing an STD at some point in life.

- Rape is a surprisingly common crime, with most victims knowing the rapist—often in a circumstance known as date rape.

P.O.W.E.R. Portfolio

Stress, Health, and Growth

1. How do you deal with stress in your life? Is it by playing sports? working out at the gym? playing guitar? canoeing in wilderness preserves? practising yoga? Reflect on how your stress-management approach has helped you deal with the pressures of university or college. If you can describe *and* demonstrate how you manage stress in the fast-paced academic world, with multiple assignments, self-directed study, strict time frames, and critical evaluation, you may be able to convince an employer that you are ready for the pressures of a career! Consider including photographs of various activities, such as rock climbing, skiing, construction projects, gardens, or musical events to add variety and creativity to your portfolio.

2. Include a reflective analysis on the theme of health and wellness, including a personal assessment. Consider adding visual elements as well.

3. What training have you done or certificates and/or licences have you attained that would demonstrate your awareness of health and safety—WHMIS, CPR, first aid, bronze medallion, Smart Serve? Include evidence of these with a reflective statement on the importance of safety in various situations.

4. Create a PowerPoint presentation or poster session on some aspect of this chapter and include the disk in your portfolio along with a photograph and reflection.

Resources

On Campus

Your campus health service/medical provider is the first line of defence if you become ill. The staff can provide you with advice and often medical care. Furthermore, colleges and universities often have health education offices that help educate students on safer sex practices, on how to eat in healthier ways, and generally on how to increase wellness. Finally, schools sometimes offer stress reduction workshops to help students cope more effectively.

In Print

The title says it all: *The New York Times Book of Health: How to Feel Fitter, Eat Better, and Live Longer* (Times Books, 1998), by Jane Brody, provides an up-to-date, common-sense guide to living well.

Why Zebras Don't Get Ulcers: An Updated Guide to Stress, Stress-Related Diseases, and Coping (Owl Books, 3rd edition, 2004), by Robert M. Sapolsky, offers an entertaining guide to both the reasons we experience stress and ways of coping with it.

Sue Johanson's *Sex, Sex, and More Sex* (Regan Books, 2004) provides clearheaded, no-nonsense answers to some of the most frequently asked questions about sex, intimacy, and relationships. Readers of all ages and sexual orientations will discover that no question or topic is taboo for Canada's "sex lady."

On the Web

The following sites on the World Wide Web provide the opportunity to extend your learning about the material in this chapter. Although the Web addresses were accurate at the time the book was printed, check the P.O.W.E.R. Learning website, <www.mcgrawhill.ca/college/power>, for any changes that may have occurred.

www.hc-sc.gc.ca/hppb/nutrition/pube/foodguid/index.html
Canada's *Food Guide to Healthy Eating* offers suggestions on healthy eating, vitamin supplements, and a food checklist.

www.uofaweb.ualberta.ca/healthinfo/
A comprehensive site on all aspects of student health concerns including interactive software on AIDS, alcohol, birth control, stress, STDs, and nutrition that can be downloaded.

http://canadaonline.about.com/aboutcanada/canadaonline/library/weekly/aa050997.htm
This Canada Online stress-management site gives lots of helpful information and links to a large variety of stress-busting sites.

www.campusaccess.com/campus_web/health/h3fit_expert.htm
Campusaccess has a fitness site with experts who will answer questions about bodybuilding, nutrition, vitamins, etc. It also links to the Campusaccess home page, which has many interesting sections relating to college life and postsecondary concerns.

www.mirror-mirror.org/eatdis.htm
This guide to eating disorders provides definitions, coping strategies, links to related organizations, and personal messages from survivors as well as information related to eating disorders.

The Case of . . .

Grievous Bodily Harm

It started out innocently as a thank-you bash for volunteers after an all-day orientation event to raise money for charity. Andrea and her roommate, Jessalyn, both unfamiliar with their campus and both a little shy, went together for "mutual support."

The party was great—school spirit was high and people were so friendly. Andrea and Jessalyn gradually started mixing with other students from their own programs. Andrea was happy when the DJ started playing dance music, and danced steadily for about 45 minutes with a nice guy named Casey. As she drank the beer that Casey had brought her, Andrea waved across the room at Jessalyn. She was feeling a little light-headed and very relaxed.

The next morning, Andrea awoke in a strange bed, naked and feeling desperately sick. Beside her was a stranger. He said his name was Casey, said they'd hit it off at the party the night before and had come back to his place to continue to party— privately. Andrea just stared at him in disbelief. What was he talking about? Who was he? Why was she here? Where were her clothes? What time was it? What had happened to her?

As Andrea tried to get up and go into the bathroom, Casey started to touch her— he said she'd been a little unresponsive the night before, said he'd like to see a little more action. What was he saying … that she had had sex with him? Andrea couldn't believe it; she was a virgin! Her face burning with embarrassment and tears filling her eyes, Andrea bolted into the bathroom, quickly dressed, and left, not saying a word. As she left the building, she realized she was in the residence beside her own. At least she'd be home soon.

As she let herself into her room, Jessalyn called out, "Hey, how are you? You left so suddenly with that guy—you must have really hit it off with him."

Andrea started to cry. "You saw me leave with him? You know I don't pick up guys at parties."

"Hey, An. I thought you really liked him. When you left, he was all over you, and you seemed okay with it," her roommate replied.

As she continued crying, Andrea sobbed, "You know me better than that, Jess. I wouldn't leave you without letting you know when I'd be home or where I was going. He says we had sex, but I can't remember a thing. I just want to have a bath, go to bed, and wake up knowing that this was just a bad dream."

1. What happened to Andrea?

2. What should Andrea and Jessalyn do now?

3. What were some warning signs that Andrea and Jessalyn could have tuned in to?

4. What should happen to Casey?

5. What is the school's responsibility in this situation?

Conclusion

Near the beginning of P.O.W.E.R. Learning, you assessed your employability skills and gave examples of evidence you could use to demonstrate those skills. Please take the time to reassess your employability skills and see if your abilities or proficiency have improved over the duration of this course or this semester.

A Final Word

Throughout this book you've seen how the principles of P.O.W.E.R. Learning can be applied to a variety of situations, ranging from reading and writing to coping with stress. You can use the framework in any situation where you need to organize your thinking and behaviour in a systematic way. It's a tool you can call on throughout life.

College or university is the beginning of a journey through adulthood. This book has been designed to help you with the immediate demands and challenges of higher education, but at the same time to prepare you for life after school. It has tried to show you that it is you who must make things happen to fulfill your own aspirations and successfully meet goals.

Ultimately, however, there are some key ingredients to success that no book can teach you, and that only you can provide—integrity and honesty, intellectual curiosity, and love. We, the authors, hope this book will help you as you consider what your contribution to the world will be and as you work to make that contribution.

Endnotes

Chapter 1

1. Gottesman, G. (1994). *College Survival*. New York: Macmillian, p. 70.

2. The Conference Board of Canada. (2000). *Employability Skills 2000+*. The Conference Board of Canada, 255 Smyth Road, Ottawa ON K1H 8M7; Tel: 613-526-3280; Fax: 613-526-4857. [Online]. Available: <www.conferenceboard.ca/nbec>.

3. Adapted from Good, L.R., & Good, K.C. (1973). "An Objective Measure of the Motive to Avoid Success." *Psychological Reports*, 33, 1009–1010.

Chapter 2

1. Adapted, in part, from Ferner, J.D. (1980). *Successful Time Management*. New York: Wiley, p. 33.

2. Adapted from Ferner, J.D. (1980). *Successful Time Management*. New York: Wiley, p. 33.

3. Cline, B. (2000, February). "Succession to the Throne." *Your Office*, 7. [Online]. Available: <www.youroffice.ca/mag_0001/0001cover-1.html>.

Chapter 3

1. Adapted from Middlesex Community College. (n.d.). *Modality Preference Inventory*. Middlesex Community College, 100 Training Hill Rd., Middletown, CT 06457. [Online]. Available: <www.mxctc.commnet.edu/clc/survey.htm>.

2. Adapted from Clark, D. (2000). *Learning Style Indicator: What Kind of Learner Are You?* [Online]. Available: <www.nwlink.com/~donclark/hrd/kolb.html>.

3. Sternberg, R.J. (1997). *Thinking Styles*. Cambridge, U.K.: Cambridge University Press.

4. Rosenberg, M. (1979). *Conceiving the Self*. New York: Basic Books.

Chapter 4

1. <www.techweb.com/encyclopedia/printDefinition?term=URL>.

2. From Petroff, L., & Teixeira, C. (2000). *Portugal*. Canada Heirloom Series Volume VII, Canada at the Millennium: A Trans-cultural Society. [Online]. Available: <http://collections.ic.gc.ca/heirloom_series/volume7/volume7.htm>.

3. From Richardson, C., and Friesen, J. (2004, May 9). "Buying an Essay Way Out," *The Eyeopener Online*: <www.theeyeopener.com/storydetail.cfm?storyid=786>.

Chapter 5

1. Pauk, W. (1974). *How to Study in College*. Boston: Houghton Mifflin.

2. Raloff, J. (2000, October 7). "Even Nunavut Gets Plenty of Dioxin." *Science News*, 158, 230. Copyright Science Service, Incorporated, 2000, October 7. Reproduced with permission of the copyright owner. Further reproduction or distribution is prohibited without permission.

3. 3M United States. (2001). *Articles and Advice: Minutes and Group Recordings*. [Online]. Available: <www.3m.com/meetingnetwork/readingroom/meetingguide_minutes.html>.

Chapter 7

1. Bransford, J.D., & Johnson, M.K. (1972). "Contextual Prerequisites for Understanding: Some Investigation of Comprehensions and Recall." *Journal of Verbal Learning and Verbal Behavior*, 11, 171–221.

2. Learning Disabilities Resource Community: Letter of Intent. (2000, July 19). Submitted to the Office of Learning Technology. [Online]. Available: <http://snow.utoronto.ca/initiatives>.

Chapter 8

1. Elbow, P. (1998). *Writing with Power* (2nd ed.). New York: Oxford University Press.

2. Higher Education Research Institute, University of California, Graduate School of Education & Information Studies. (1999). *The American Freshman: National Norms for Fall 1998*. [Online]. Available: <www.gseis.ucla.edu/heri/press98.html>.

3. Bottom Line: One Cliché is Absolutely the Worst (2004, March 25). [Online]. Available: <www.freep.com/features/living/cliche25_20040325.htm>. Retrieved: 2004, March 26.

4. Wydro, K. (1985). *Think on Your Feet: The Art of Thinking and Speaking Under Pressure*. Englewood Cliffs, NJ: Prentice Hall.

Chapter 9

1. Smith, M.U. (1992). "Expertise and the Organization of Knowledge: Unexpected Differences Among Genetic Counselors, Faculty, and Students on Problem Categorization Tasks." *Journal of Research in Science Teaching*, 29, 179–205.

2. <www.usu.edu/arc/online_learning_center/index.htm>.

3. Halpern, D.F. (1996). *Thought and Knowledge: An Introduction to Critical Thinking*. Mahwah, NJ: Erlbaum, p. 48.

4. Abel, T., Alberini, C., Ghiradi, M., Huang, Y.Y., Nguyen, P., and Kandel, E.R. (1995). "Steps Toward A Molecular Definition of Memory Consolidation." In D.L. Schacter (Ed.), *Memory Distortions: How Minds, Brains, and Societies Reconstruct the Past*. Cambridge, MA: Harvard University Press.

Chapter 10

1. Adapted from Halpern, D.F. (1996). *Thought and Knowledge: An Introduction to Critical Thinking* (3rd ed.). Mahwah, NJ: Erlbaum.

2. Ibid., and Bransford, J.D., & Stein, B.S. (1993). *The Ideal Problem Solver* (2nd ed.). New York: W.H. Freeman.

3. Adapted from Levy, D.A. (1997). *Tools of Critical Thinking*. Boston: Allyn & Bacon, p. 20.

4. Forer, B. (1949). "The Fallacy of Personal Validation: A Classroom Demonstration of Gullibility." *Journal of Abnormal and Social Psychology*, 44, 118–123.

Chapter 12

1. Nolan, M.F. (1997, April 26). "Tiger's Racial Multiplicity." *Boston Globe*, A11.

2. Dyer, G. (2001). "Visible Minorities." *Canadian Geographic*, 121(11), 44.

3. Tatum, B.D. (1997). *Why Are All the Black Kids Sitting Together in the Cafeteria? And Other Conversations about Race*. New York: Basic Books.

4. Statistics Canada. (1997). *Immigrant Population by Place of Birth, Showing Period of Immigration for Canada*, 1996 Census. [Online]. Available: <www.statcan.ca/english/census96/nov4/imm2a.htm>.

5. Farber, B.A., Brink, D.C., & Raskin, P.M. (Eds.). (1996). *The Psychotherapy of Carl Rogers: Cases and Commentary*. New York: Guilford Press; and Rogers, C.R. (1951). *Client-Centered Therapy*. Boston: Houghton Mifflin.

Chapter 13

1. Millennium Scholarships press release: <www.millennium scholarships.ca/en/research/archive>.

2. <www.rbcroyalbank.com/agriculture/reference/risk_management/risk_may_2001_001.html>.

3. <www. millenniumscholar-ships.ca/en/foundation/publications/archivepress/nov262001/>.

4. <www.canlearn.ca/living/housing/clindex.cfm?langcanlearn=en>.

5. CanLearn Interactive. (2001). CanLearn Interactive. [Online]. Available: <www.canlearn.ca/>; and individual college and university home pages.

6. Dominquez, J., & Robin, V. (1993). *Your Money or Your Life: Transforming Your Relationship with Money and Achieving Financial Independence*. New York: Penguin USA.

Chapter 14

1. Sax, L.J., Astin, A.W., Korn, W.S., & Mahoney, K. (1990). *The American Freshman: National Norms for Fall 1999*. Los Angeles: Higher Education Research Institute, UCLA.

2. Chamberlain, K., & Zika, S. (1990). "The Minor Events Approach to Stress: Support for the Use of Daily Hassles." *British Journal of Psychology*, 81, 469–481.

3. Source of table: Marx, M.B., Garrity, T.F., & Bowers, F.R. (1975). "The Influence of Recent Life Experience on the Health of College Freshmen."

Journal of Psychosomatic Research, 19, 87–98 (Questionnaire on p. 97).

4. Birmingham, C.L., Muller, J.L, Palepu, A., Spinelli, J.J., & Anis, A.H. (1999). "The Cost of Obesity in Canada." *Canadian Medical Association Journal*, 160, 483–486.

5. Obesity Canada. (2001). *Fact sheet*. [Online]. Available: <www.obesitycanada.com>.

6. Myers, M.D. (2001). *Complications of Obesity*. [Online]. Available: <www.weight.com/complications.html>.

7. Carlson, R. (1997). *Don't Sweat the Small Stuff…And It's All Small Stuff*. New York: Hyperion.

8. Brink, S. (2000, October 16). "Sleepless Society." *US News and World Report*.

9. Ibid.

10. Canadian Mental Health Association. (2001). *Ten Facts about Workplace Stress*. [Online]. Available: <www3.sympatico.ca/cmha.toronto/mhw4.html>.

11. de la Hey, M. (2000). "Survey Highlights Problem of Binge Drinking at Canadian Universities." *Journal of Addiction and Mental Health*. [Online]. Available: <www.camh.net/journal/journalv3no4/survey_highlights_binge.html>.

12. Ibid.

13. Ibid.

14. Centre for Addiction and Mental Health. (2000). *First National Survey of Drug Use Among University Students Released by the Centre for Addiction and Mental Health Shows "Heavy" Drinking to be a Significant Concern*. [Online]. Available: <www.camh.net/press_releases/can_campus_survey_pr29300.html>.

15. Ibid.

16. Addiction Research Foundation. (1994). *Facts about… Alcohol*. [Online]. Available: <www.canoe.ca/Health Reference/arf_facts1.html>.

17. Centre for Addiction and Mental Health. (2000). *First National Survey of Drug Use Among University Students Released by the Centre for Addiction and Mental Health Shows "Heavy" Drinking to be a Significant Concern*. [Online]. Available: <www.camh.net/press_releases/can_campus_survey_pr29300.html>.

18. Childbirth by Choice Trust. (1999). *Fact Sheet: Unwanted Pregnancy*. [Online]. Available: <www.cbctrust.com/unwanted.html>.

19. Ibid.

20. Childbirth by Choice Trust. (1999). *The Economics of Contraception, Abortion, and Unintended Pregnancy*. [Online]. Available: <www.cbctrust.com/ECONOMIC.html>.

21. Childbirth by Choice Trust. (1999). *Fact Sheet: Unwanted Pregnancy*. [Online]. Available: <www.cbctrust.com/unwanted.html>.

22. Trouton, K., & Dzakpasu, S. (1998). *Fact Sheet: Induced Abortion*. [Online]. Available: <www.hc-sc.gc.ca/hpb/lcdc/brch/factshts/inabor_e.html>.

23. Ibid.

24. Maticka-Tyndale, E. (1997). "Reducing the Incidence of Sexually Transmitted Disease Through Behavioural and Social Change." *Canadian Journal of Human Sexuality*, 6(2). [Online]. Available: <www.hcsc.gc.ca/hpb/lcdc/publicat/ cjhs/cjhs2.html>.

25. University of Alberta Health Centre. (1997). *Sexual Assault and the Law in Canada*. [Online]. Available: <www.ualberta.ca/dept/health/public_html/heathinfo/SACan.html>.

Acknowledgments

P. 22: Adapted from Good, L. R., & Good, K. C. (1973). "An Objective Measure of the Motive to Avoid Success." *Psychological Reports*, 33, 1009–1010. © Psychological Reports 1973. Adapted by permission.

P. 23: Logo of University of Guelph. Reprinted by permission of the University of Guelph.

P. 29: Cartoon © 1999 William Haefeli from cartoonbank.com. All Rights Reserved.

P. 31: Cartoon © 1999 Alex Hamlett from CartoonStock.com. All Rights Reserved.

Pp. 63–64: The Learning Styles Modality Preference Inventory, Middlesex Community College, available online at <www.mxctc.commnet.edu/clc/survey. htm>. Used by permission.

Pp. 68–71: Multiple Intelligence Inventory and the Eight Styles of Learning. Reprinted with permission of Gregory R. Gay, Learning Disabilities Resource Centre (LDRC) website at <www.ldrc.ca>.

P. 82: Rosenberg, M. (1979). *Conceiving the Self*. Reprinted by permission of The Morris Rosenberg Foundation.

P. 83: Cartoon, CALVIN AND HOBBES © 1992 Watterson. Reprinted with permission of UNIVERSAL PRESS SYNDI-

P. 87: Figure 3.3: Maslow, Abraham (1970). MOTIVATION AND PERSONALITY, 3rd ed. Copyright 1954, 1987 by Harper & Row Publishers, Inc. Copyright 1970 by Abraham H. Maslow. Reprinted by permission of Addison-Wesley Education Publishers, Inc.

P. 101: Technology in Canada, 2002, adapted from Statistics Canada website, <www.statcan.ca/english/Pgdb/famil09c.htm>, date of extraction September 7, 2004.

P. 115: Cartoon © The New Yorker Collection 1998 Arnie Levin from cartoonbank.com. All Rights Reserved.

P. 123: Excerpt from Granatstein, J. L. "Mackenzie King." *Maclean's*, III, p. 24–25.

P. 143: Raloff, Janet. (2000). "Even Nunavut Gets Plenty of Dioxin." *Science News*, Issue 15, p. 230. Reprinted with permission from *Science News*, the weekly newsmagazine of science, copyright 2000 by Science Service Inc.

P. 153: Logo of Niagara College. Reprinted by permission of Niagara College.

P. 180: Exercise adapted from *The College Learner: How to Survive and Thrive in an Academic Environment*, by Mary Renck Jalong, Mahoney Twiest, and Gail J. Gerlack with Diane H. Skoner. Englewood Cliffs: Merill/Prentice Hall. 1996. From <www.bucks.edu/%7especpop/Evaltest.htm>.

P. 183: Logo of the Okanogan Valley College of Massage Therapy. Reprinted by permission of the Okanogan Valley College of Massage Therapy.

P. 191: Excerpt from Bransford, J. D., & Johnson, M. K. (1972). "Contextual Prerequisites for Understanding: Some Investigations of Comprehension and Recall." *Journal of Verbal Learning and Verbal Behavior*, 11, 717–721. Reprinted by permission of Academic Press.

P. 209: Logo of University of King's College in Halifax. Reprinted by permission of University of King's College in Halifax.

P. 230: Exercise from <http://writing.englishclub.com/ee/lth_shortessays.html>.

P. 238: Logo of Red River College of Applied Arts, Science and Technology. Reprinted by permission of Red River College of Applied Arts, Science and Technology.

P. 252–253: Exercise from Halpern, Diane F. (1996). *Thought and Knowledge: An Introduction to Critical Thinking*, 3rd edition, 48. Reprinted by permission of Lawrence Erlbaum Associates, Inc., Mahwah, NJ.

P. 263: Logo of Nova Scotia Community College. Reprinted by permission of Nova Scotia Community College.

Pp. 280, 289: Exercise adapted in part from Bransford, J. D., & Stein, B. S. (1993). *The Ideal Problem Solver*, 2/e. © 1993, 1984 by W. H. Freeman & Company. Used with permission. And adapted in part from Halpern, Diane F. (1996). *Thought and Knowledge: An Introduction to Critical Thinking*, 3rd edition, 48. Reprinted by permission of Lawrence Erlbaum Associates, Inc., Mahwah, NJ.

P. 285: Logo of The Northern Alberta Institute of Technology. Reprinted by permission of The Northern Alberta Institute of Technology.

P. 311: Logo of George Brown—The Toronto City College. Reprinted by permission of George Brown—The Toronto City College.

P. 369: Logo of University of Western Ontario. Reprinted by permission of University of Western Ontario.

Pp. 378–379: Exercise from Marx, M. B., Garrity, T. F., & Bowers, F. R. (1975). "The Influence of Recent Life Experience on the Health of College Freshmen." *Journal of Psychosomatic Research*, 19, 87–98. Copyright 1975. Reprinted with permission from Elsevier Science.

P. 400: Logo of Saskatchewan Institute of Applied Science and Technology. Reprinted by permission of Saskatchewan Institute of Applied Science and Technology.

Photo Credits

p. 1 Chuck Savage/Corbis Stock Market

p. 11 Solstice Photography/Brand X Pictures

p. 15 NASA/Photo Researchers

p. 23 CP Picture Archive (Marianne Helm, Calgary Herald)

p. 27 Gerald Haling/Photo Researchers

p. 33 Superstock

p. 43 Michael Newman/Photo Edit

p. 49 Peter Menzel/Stock Boston

p. 50 Photo credit: Karen Baer. Courtesy of Darryl Weeks, Outside Music

p. 59 Paul S. Howell/Getty Images News Services

p. 61 Rick Smolan/Stock Boston

p. 73 Andersen Ross/Getty Images

p. 84 Greg Gibson/AP Photo

p. 93 Courtesy Tom Currie

p. 97 Royalty-Free/CORBIS

p. 102 Photodisc

p. 105 Photodisc

p. 112 Image courtesy of Seneca College Learning Commons

p. 114 Index Stock

p. 115 Bob Daemmrich/Stock Boston

p. 127 Courtesy Shawn Thomson

p. 133 Matthias Tunger/Digital Vision

p. 137 Kaluzny & Thatcher/Stone

p. 141 Robert Ullmann

p. 153 Courtesy Kofi Boateng

p. 159 PNC/Getty Images

p. 164 Jeff Maloney/Getty Images

p. 168 Ian Shaw/Stone

p. 176 Matthias Tunger/Digital Vision

p. 183 Courtesy Asta Kovanen

p. 187 Scott T. Baxter/Getty Images

p. 196 L. Korvoord/Image Works

p. 207 Mary Steinbacher/PhotoEdit

p. 208 Randy Duchane/Corbis Stock Market

p. 209 Courtesy Rachel Trail

p. 213 Sotographs/Getty Images News Service

p. 214 PhotoDisc

p. 216 EsbinAnderson/Image Works

p. 224 Didier Givois/Photo Researchers

p. 226 Michael Newman/PhotoEdit

p. 234 David Shopper/Stock Boston

p. 238 Courtesy of TSN The Sports Network

p. 245 Robert Smith/Index Stock

p. 250 Chuck Savage/Corbis Stock Market

p. 255 PhotoDisc

p. 256 John A. Rizzo/Getty Images

p. 261 John Touscany/Index Stock

p. 263 Courtesy Elaine Hudson

p. 267 PhotoDisc

p. 270 Spencer Platt/Getty Images News Service

p. 272 Superstock

p. 283 SW Productions/Getty Images

p. 285 Courtesy Jeff Goplin

p. 291 George Zimbel

p. 294 Will & Deni McIntyre/Photo Researchers

p. 302 CP Picture Archive (Phill Snel, Maclean's)

p. 305 CP Picture Archive (Jonathan Hayward, Canadian Press)

p. 311 Courtesy Dr. Anthony Brissett

p. 317 Gaye Hilsenrath/Index Stock

p. 319 Henley/Corbis Stock Market

p. 326 Sonda Dawes/Image Works

p. 330 Bill Aron/PhotoEdit

p. 333 Richard Pasley/Stock Boston

p. 339 Courtesy Jenny Zhang

p. 345 Jack Hollingsworth/Brand X Pictures

p. 347 Tom Stewart/CORBIS/MAGMA

p. 354 (top) Margot Granitsas/Image Works; (bottom) PhotoDisc

p. 356 CP/Doug Ives

p. 358 Digital Vision/Digital Vision

p. 369 Courtesy Murray Baker

p. 373 Gregg Adams/Stone

p. 374 Corbis

p. 384 Jeff Zaruba/Corbis Stock Market

p. 385 CP Picture Archive (Ian MacAlpine, Kingston Whig Standard)

p. 395 David Hanover/Stone

p. 400 Courtesy Krista Bailey

Index

3M, 154

ABBCC structure, 221
abortion, 395
abstinence, 393
abstract conceptualization, 72
abstracts, 111
academic advisers, 295
academic choices
   college adviser, 295
   college calendars, 292–395
   course requirements,
     293–295, 296
   evaluation, 298–302
   major, choice of, 304–307
   options, familiarity with,
     293–295
   organization, 295–297
   personal schedule, draft of,
     297–298
   preparation, 293–295
   program, choice of, 304–307
   register for courses, 298
   rethinking, 302–304
   take stock, 302–304
   unavailable courses,
     301–302
   university adviser, 295
   university calendars,
     293–295
   what you know, 297
   what you need to do,
     295–297
   work of, 297–298
academic failure, 309–310
academic honesty, 9, 174–175
academic programs, 294
academic regulations, 293–295
academic success. See success
accommodators, 73
accomplishments, evaluation of,
   14–15
accreditation exams, 175
acronym, 252
acrostics, as memory aids, 253
active experimentation, 72
active listening. See listening skills
activists, 73
addiction, 387–392
adoption, 395
advance credits, 294
advance organizers, 190,
   191–192, 193
AIDS (acquired immune
   deficiency syndrome),
   396–397
alcoholics, 387, 388
analogies, 278
analytic learning style, 62–65, 66
anorexia nervosa, 384
APA (American Psychological
   Association) style, 121
argument, 221
assimilators, 73
attention span, 194, 195
audience
   speeches, for, 229
   writing, for, 217–220
auditory learning style, 62

background, 221
Baker, Murray, 369
balancing school and work,
   45–46

Bank of Montreal, 308
Barnum Effect, 281
binge drinking, 388
Boateng, Kofi, 153
Bondar, Roberta, 23
brainstorming, 216, 217, 219
Brissett, Anthony, 311
browsers, 114
bubble chart goal, 52
budget
   defined, 347
   evaluation, 356
   expenditures, 349, 352
   financial goals, 348,
     350–351
   income, 349
   process, 348–353
   purpose of, 347–348
   rethink, 356
   workplace, in the, 348
bulimia, 384
bursaries, 364
Bytown Bus, 346

call number, 112
Cambrian College, 127
Canada Businesses Services
   Centre, 348
Canada Student Loan Program
   (CSLP), 363
Canada Study Grant, 364
Canadian Professional Logistics
   Institute, 231
career planning, 46, 308
career possibilities, 273
career time line, 47
cataclysmic events, 374
catalogues, 111–113
causation, 283
CBE (Council of Biology Editors)
   style, 121
Centennial Community College,
   339
character, 9
cheating, 174–175
childcare, and time management,
   43–45
citation systems for sources,
   121–124
college adviser, 295
college calendars, 293–295
common sense, myth of, 282
communication, 3
communication, control of, 42
   relationships, in, 331
competency assessments, 175
computers
   familiarity with, 99
   learning about, 105
   presentation programs, 101
   spell checkers, 100
   spreadsheet programs, 102
   word-processing programs,
     99
concept map, 203
concept mapping, 150–152,
   201–202
conclusions, 223
   jumping to, 282
concrete experience, 72
Conference Board of Canada, 51,
   118
conflict resolution, 338
contraception, 392–395

convergers, 73
conversational markers, 332
cooperative education, 364
coping with stress, 376, 380–381
copy-and-paste plagiarism, 124
Cornell notetaking, 138
correlation, 283
counterarguments, 223
course listings, 295
course requirements, 296
cover letter, 231
cramming, 167–168, 261
credit cards, 357–361
credit counsellor, 357
credit counsellors, 357
credit history, 358, 360
creditors, 357
critical thinking, 200
   defined, 15
   notetaking, 147–149
   pitfalls to avoid, 279–283
CS (Chicago/Turabian Style) style,
   121
cultural competence
cultural heritage
   acknowledging, 326
   defined, 320
   differences, acceptance of,
     326–327
   evaluation, 327
   organization, 322–324
   prejudice, identify your
     own, 322–324
   preparation, 320–321
   representativeness,
     assumption of, 326
   rethinking, 327–328
   stereotypes, identify your
     own, 322–324
   strategies to develop,
     324–327
   study other cultures,
     324–325
   travel, 325–326
   work, 324–327
   workplace, in, 322, 326
culture, 4, 320, 324–325
   See also cultural competence
Currie, Todd, 93
cyber-cheating, 124
cyberspace, 98
cycle of failure, 83–85

daily hassles, 375
daily to-do list, 35, 39–40, 46–48
date rape, 397
deadlines, 11
debt, 356–357
decision making
   academic choices. See
     academic choices
   action, 275
   assessment of alternatives,
     271–272
   career possibilities, 273
   choosing among
     alternatives, 272–275
   coin toss, 272
   defined, 269
   evaluation, 275
   flexible alternatives,
     270–272
   freewriting, 270–272
   goals, 269–270, 275–276

gut feelings, 275
indecision, 274
mental movies, 272
options, reconsideration of,
   275–276
organization, 270–272
outcomes, consideration of,
   275
pitfalls to avoid, 279–283
preparation, 269–270
rethinking, 275–276
sexual health. See sexual
   health
work of, 272–275
dictionaries, 111, 194, 198
differences, acceptance of,
   326–327
distance learning, 301
distractions, 41–42
divergers, 73
diversity
   cultural competence. See
     cultural competence
   focus on, in Canada, 3
   valued part of life, 320–321
domain name, 104
drug abuse
   addiction, 391–392
   alcohol, 387–388
   binge drinking, 388
   illegal drugs, 390–391
   nicotine, 388–390
Dyer, Gwynne, 319

e-learning, 105–110
e-mail, 98, 103, 104
eating right, 384–385
educated guessing, 174
effort, 12
emotional intelligence, 91
Employability Skills Profile 2000+,
   19–20, 118
encyclopedias, 111
endorphins, 376
Enterprise Rent-A-Car, 91
entrepreneurship, 348
essay questions, 165–166,
   170–172
essays. See writing process
ethics, 9
ethnicity, 320
evaluation
   academic choices, 298–302
   cultural competence, 327
   decision making, 275
   financial aid, 356
   memory skills, 260–261
   notetaking, 147–149
   P.O.W.E.R. Learning process,
     13–15
   personal mission statement,
     89–92
   public speaking, 230
   reading, 200
   research, 124–126
   stress strategies, 382
   test-taking, 175–179
   time management, 46–48
   tuition costs, 356
   writing, 228
exams, 162–163
   See also tests
exercise, 385
experiential learning, 72–73

extemporaneous talks, 236–237
extroverts, 67

fact vs. opinion, 281, 283
failure, 182, 309–310
family-owned businesses, 46
Fanshawe College, 50
faulty logic, 284
fear of success, 17, 22
feelers, 71
fight or flight response, 375
    See also stress
fill-in questions, 174
filter, 104
financial aid
    application for, 365
    bursaries, 364
    Canada Student Loan
        Program (CSLP), 363
    Canada Study Grant, 364
    cooperative education, 364
    deadlines, 365
    evaluation, 356–348
    grants, 364
    loans, 363
    Millennium Scholarship,
        364
    scholarships, 364
    work-study programs, 364
financial goals, 348, 350–351
financial philosophy, 366–367
financial trouble, 356–357
finding information. *See* research
first drafts
    blank page, the, 223–224
flash cards, 154
flexible alternatives, 270–272
flexible outline, 225
flow, 224–225
    inner critic, 224
    reading aloud, 226
    revisions, 225–227
    start anywhere, 224
    voice, 225
foreign languages, vocabulary
    learning, 254
forgetting, value of, 247–248
freewriting, 216–217, 218,
    270–272
friendships, 328–330
frontmatter, 190–191

gap analysis, 51
Gardner, Howard, 65
generalities, 281
George Brown Community
    College, 311
goal setting model, 54
goals
    attainable, 7
    decision making, 269–270
    financial, 348, 350–351
    goal setting models
        worksheet, 51–55
    informed choices, 29
    long-term, 6
    measurable, 7
    notetaking, of, 135–137
    ownership, 8
    reading assignment, 190
    realistic, 7
    setting, 6–9
    short-term, 6
    time management, 29
    writing, 215–216
Goplin, Jeff, 285
grants, 364
Grynor, Emm, 50

gut feelings, 275

Hawking, Stephen, 84
health
    drug abuse. *See* drug abuse
    eating right, 384–385
    exercise, 385
    sexual. *See* sexual health
    sleep, 385–387
    stress. *See* stress
    workplace safety, 387
hearing, 204
Hudson, Elaine, 263
hyperlinks, 115

"I" statements, 334–337
illegal drugs, 390–392
impulse buying, 353
indecision, 274
indexes to information sources,
    111–112
information
    alternative types, 126
    authority of, 125
    biases and assumptions,
        identification of, 126
    currency of, 125
    evaluation, 124–126
    finding. *See* research
    folders, 120
    missing, 125
    multiple points of view, 126
    processing vs. copying,
        140–147
    self-improvement, 126
    sources. *See* research
    use of. *See* research
inner critic, 224
instructor's learning styles, 75–78
intellectual organization, 10–11
interest rates, 357, 358–359
interlibrary loan, 114
Internet, 117–118
    browsers, 114
    career research, 99
    citation of sources, 124
    computers, necessity of, 99
    copy-and-paste plagiarism,
        124
    cybercheating, 124
    defined, 98
    e-mail, 103, 104
    links (hyperlinks), 115
    metasearch tools, 115
    online courses, 105–110
    search engines, 115–118
    URL (uniform resource
        locator), 114
    Web addresses, 114
    Web pages, 114
    World Wide Web, 114
introverts, 67
intuitors, 67

jingles, as memory aids, 253
judgers, 71

keyword technique, 254
kinesthetic learning style, 62
knowledge, 3
Kolb's Learning Style Inventory,
    63–64, 72–73
Kovanen, Asta, 183

labels, 281
laptop programs, 140

lateral bubble chart, 52
learning disabilities, 202–203
learning style
    analytic, 62–65, 66
    auditory, 62
    changing, 75
    clues to, 64
    cooperative work, 78
    defined, 61
    experiential learning, 72–73
    focus, 62
    indicator, 73–77
    instructors', 75–78
    Kolb's Learning Style
        Inventory, 63–64, 72–73
    less-preferred styles,
        improvement of, 78
    personality, and, 67–72
    receptive, 62
    relational, 65, 66
    senses, 62
    tactile, 62
    tips, 64
    visual, 62
librarian, 114, 120
Library of Congress classification
    system, 112
library research
    abstracts, 111
    basic collection, 110–112
    call number, 112
    catalogues, 111–113
    dictionaries, 111
    encyclopedias, 111
    indexes to information
        sources, 111–112
    interlibrary loan, 114
    microform, 110
    periodicals, 110
    recalling material, 114
    reserve collections, 111
    stacks, 113–114
lifetime learning, 4
Liftking, 46
linear goal setting model, 53
links (hyperlinks), 115
listening skills
    distractions, 332
    focus, 205–206
    hearing, 204
    improvement of, 332
    listening, defined, 204
    meta-message, 206
    nonverbal messages, 206
    notetaking, 206
    problem instructor, 207–208
    questioning. *See* questioning
    reflective feedback, 332
    relationships, in, 331–332
    seat, 204
    silence, 206
    tips, 204–207
    workplace, in, 205
lists, 255
loans, 363
logistics processes, 231
loneliness, 333–334
long-term goals, 6
Lu, John, 237

machine-scored tests, 170
mailbox name, 104
major
    attractions, identification of,
        306–307
    choice of, 304–307
    defined, 294
Maslow, Abraham, 86
master calendar, 35–37

matching questions, 166, 174
McMaster University, 23
meditation, 380
memory
    associations, 249–250
    biology of, 247
    consolidation, 261
    cramming, 261
    essential things, 249
    evaluation, 260–261
    forgetting, value of,
        247–248
    in-text review questions and
        tests, 260
    notetaking, 250–251
    organization, 249–250
    preparation, 249
    rethinking, 261
    retrieval, 247
    rhymes, 253
    self-test, 260
    strategies. *See* memory
        strategies
    work. *See* memory strategies
    workplace, in the, 260
memory strategies, 252
    acronym, 252
    acrostics, 253
    body movement, 256
    draw and diagram, 257
    foreign languages, 254
    jingles, 253
    keyword technique, 254
    lists, 255
    method of loci, 255
    mnemonics, 251, 252
    multiple senses, 256–258
    overlearning, 258
    peg method, 255–257
    positive thinking, 258
    rehearsal, 251
    rhymes, 253
    sequences, 255
    visualization, 257–258, 259
message board, 105
meta-message, 141, 206
method of loci, 255
microform, 110
Millennium Scholarship, 364
minutes of meetings, 154
mission statement. *See* personal
    mission
MLA (Modern Languages
    Association) style, 121
mnemonics, 251, 252
money management
    budget. *See* budget
    credit cards, 357–361
    debt, 356–357
    financial aid. *See* financial
        aid
    financial philosophy,
        366–367
    financial trouble, 356–357
    interest rates, 357, 358–359
    tuition costs. *See* tuition
        costs
motivation
    defined, 11
    keeping motivation alive,
        13
    needs, 86–87, 88
    organization, and, 86–87
    work, to, 11–13
multiculturalism
    cultural competence. *See*
        cultural compete
    focus on, in Canada, 4
    valued part of life, 320–321
multimedia, 152

multiple intelligences, 65–67, 68–71
multiple senses, 256–258
multiple-choice questions, 166, 172–174
Myers-Briggs Type Indicator, 67, 72

National Student Loans Centre, 363
negative thinking, 17
netiquette, 104
Niagara College, 153
nicotine, 388–390
"no", 40–41
nonverbal behaviour
    listening and, 206
    public speaking and, 235–236
nonverbal messages, 206
Northern Alberta Institute of Technology, 285
note cards, 120–121
notetaking
    abbreviations, 141–142
    annotating textbook material, 154
    broad view, 150–151
    class discussions, 144–147
    colours, 139
    complete assignments before class, 135–137
    concept mapping, 150–152
    Cornell, 138
    critical thinking, 147–149
    evaluation, 147–149
    flash cards, 154
    goals of, 135–137
    information on board or overheads, 144–147
    key ideas, 141
    laptop/notebook computers, 140
    lecture styles, 137, 147
    listening skills and, 206
    memory, 149–152, 250–251
    meta-message, 141
    minutes of meetings, 154
    multimedia, 152
    notebooks, 139–140
    organization, 137–140
    outline form, 142–144
    preclass warmup, 137
    preparation, 135–137
    problem instructors, 147
    processing vs. copying information, 140–147
    rethink as soon as possible, 149
    rethinking as active process, 150–152
    short phrases, 141–144
    study notes, 152–155
    technology, 152
    textbooks, necessity of, 140
    tools, 137–140
    work, 140–147
    writing instruments, 137
Nova Scotia Community College, 263
nutrition, 384–385

Okanagan Valley College of Massage Therapy, 183
ombudsperson, 309–310
online courses, 105–110
opinion vs. fact, 281
oral presentations. See public speaking

organization
    academic choices, 295–297
    cultural competence, 322–324
    decision making, 270–272
    memory, 249–250
    motivation, and, 86–87
    needs, 88
    notetaking, 137–140
    P.O.W.E.R. Learning process, 9–11
    personal mission statement, 86–87
    public speaking, 230
    reading, 192–194
    research, 119–120
    stress, dealing with, 377
    tests, 168–169
    time management, 35–40
    tuition costs, 364
    writing, 220–223
outline
    flexible, 225
    goal setting model, 53
    notetaking, 142–144
    writing process, 220–221
overlearning, 258
overtalking, 332

P.O.W.E.R. Learning
    defined, 4
    employability skills, 24
    evaluation, 13–15
    organization, 9–11
    preparation, 6–9
    process, 5
    rethinking, 15–17
    work, 11–13
    work world, 18
papers. See writing process
Passionate Vision, 23
Pauk, Walter, 139
peg method, 255–257
perceivers, 71
perfectionism, 17
periodicals, 110
personal hierarchy of needs, 88
personal mission statement
    assessment, 89–92
    creating, 87–89
    evaluation, 89–92
    options, reconsidering, 91–92
    organization, 86–87
    preparation, 85–86
    purpose of, 88–89
    rethinking, 91–92
    self-actualization, 86–87
    values, identification of, 85–86
    work, 87–89
personal self, 78
personal stressors, 375
personality assessments in workplace, 91
personality styles, 67–72
Photonics Research Ontario, 322
physical organization, 10
physical self, 78
plagiarism, 121–125
positive thinking, 258
postsecondary education, benefits of, 3–4
pragmatists, 73
pregnancy
    identify your own, 322–324
    options, 397
    prevention of, 393–395
    unplanned, 397
prejudice, defined, 322, 324

Premiere Image International Inc., 260
PREP formula, 236
preparation
    academic choices, 293–295
    cultural competence, 320–321
    decision making, 269–270
    memory, 249
    notetaking, 135–137
    P.O.W.E.R. Learning process, 6–9
    personal mission statement, 85–86
    public speaking, 229
    reading, 190–192
    research, 110
    stress, dealing with, 376–377
    tests, 162–168
    tuition costs, 362–364
    writing, 215–220
prerequisites, 295
presentations. See public speaking
prime time, 35
principal, loan, 363
prior learning assessment and recognition (PLAR), 294–295
priorities, 33, 34
prioritize, 200
problem instructors
    listening and, 207–208
    notetaking and, 147
problem solving
    analogies, 278
    another perspective, 278
    break down problem, 277
    defined, 276
    defining the problem, 276–277
    opposites, consideration of, 278
    pitfalls to avoid, 279–283
    potential solutions, assessment of, 279
    process of, 279
    redefine problem, 278
    strategies, 277–278
    trial and error, 277
    walk away, 278
    work backward, 277
procrastination, 42–45
professional tests, 175
program
    attractions, identification of, 306–307
    choice of, 304–307
    defined, 294
    progressive relaxation, 381–382
program coordinator, 295
public speaking
    anecdote, 231
    audiences, 229
    beginnings, 231
    challenges of, 230–235
    cliches, 233
    evaluation, 230
    extemporaneous talks, 236–237
    humour, 231
    nonverbal behaviour, 235–236
    notes, and, 233–234
    oral transition points, 231–232
    organization, 230
    practice, 229, 234
    PREP formula, 236

    preparation, 229
    quotation, 231
    rethinking, 230
    stage fright, 235
    visuals, 234
    work, 230

questioning
    attitude, 206
    class, in, 207
    purpose of, 206–207
    self-defeating thoughts, 207
    strategies, 207
quiz, 162–163
    See also tests

race, 320
RCMP, 205
reading skills
    advance organizers, 190, 191–192, 193
    attention span, 194, 195
    breaks, 196
    concept mapping, 201–202
    dictionary, 194, 198
    distractions, 196
    evaluation, 200
    focus, 196
    frontmatter, 190–191
    goal of assignment, 190
    highlight key points, 197
    learning disabilities, 202–203
    level of understanding, 200
    organization, 192–194
    point of view, 190
    preparation, 190–192
    reading style, 189
    rephrase key points, 197
    rereading, 201
    retention, 189–190
    rethinking, 201–202
    small bites, 196
    speed, 189–190
    time for reading, 194
    tools for reading, 192–194
    underline key points, 197
    unfamiliar words, 198
    visuals for understanding and recall, 197–198
    work, 194–199
    writing while reading, 196–199
reading style, 189
recalling material, 114
receptive learning style, 62
Red River College, 237
reflective feedback, 332
reflective observation, 72
reflectors, 73
register for courses, 298
registrar, 56, 297
rehearsal, 251
relational learning style, 65, 66
relationships
    acceptance, 330–331
    change, willingness to embrace, 331
    communication in, 331
    components of, 330–331
    conflict, dealing with, 334–337, 338
    ending, 337–338
    friendships, 328–330
    honesty, 330
    "I" statements, 334–337
    listening skills and, 331–332
    loneliness, 333–334

loyalty, 330
mutual support, 330
trust, 330
zero-sum game, 337
relaxation techniques, 160
Rempel, Krista, 400
rereading, 201
research
basic tool, 120–121
careers on the Internet, 99
citation of sources, 121–124
evaluation, 124–126
information folders, 120
Internet, 114–120
key issues, 119–120
key sources, 119–120
library, 110–114
missing information, 125
note cards, 120–121
organization, 119–120
plagiarism, 121–125
preparation, 110
rethinking, 126
using information found,
120–121
writing topics, 220
your own words, 121
reserve collections, 111
responsibility, 13, 92
resumes, 231
retention, and reading, 189–190
rethink
academic choices, 302–304
cultural competence,
327–328
decision making, 275–276
mechanics, the, 228
memory skills, 261
message, the, 228
method, the, 229
notetaking, 149–152
P.O.W.E.R. Learning process,
15–17
personal mission statement,
91–82
public speaking, 230
reading, 201–202
research, 126
stress, 383
tests, 179–182
time management style,
48–49
tuition costs, 356
writing, 228–229
retrieval, 247
revisions
basic rules, 226–227
logic check, 227
long view, 226
neatness, 227
punctuation check, 227
reading aloud, 226
rewriting, 225–226
ruthlessness, 226–227
sequence check, 227
spelling check, 227
rhymes, 253–319
Rogers, Carl, 332

Saskatchewan Institute of Applied
Science and Technology,
400
savings style, 355
scaffolding, 220
scholarships, 364
search engines, 115–118
self-actualization, 86–87
self-concept
acceptance, 79

coherent view, 79
defined, 78
others' views, 80–81
personal self, 78
physical self, 78
roles, 79
self-fulfilling prophecies,
78–80
social self, 78
strengths and weaknesses,
79
understanding your, 79–80
self-congratulation, 13–14
self-efficacy, 82
self-esteem, 83–85
achieving ideal level of,
83–85
cycle of failure, 83
defined, 81
importance of, 81–83
lifelong undertaking, 84
measurement of, 82
self-efficacy, 82
self-fulfilling prophecies, 78–80
self-responsibility, 92
self-test, 166, 260
Seneca College, 93
sensors, 67
sexual health
abstinence, 393
AIDS (acquired immune
deficiency syndrome),
396–397
contraception, 393–395
date rape, 397
pregnancy options, 395–396
pregnancy prevention,
393–395
sexually transmitted
diseases, 396–397
sexually transmitted diseases,
396–397
short-answer questions, 174
short-term goals, 6
silence, 42, 206
sleep, 385–387
Smith, Shannon, 260
social self, 78
social support, 380
sources. See research
spam, 104
speaking
extemporaneous talks,
236–237
PREP formula, 236
public. See public speaking
spell checkers, 100
stacks, 113–114
stage fright, 235
stereotypes
defined, 323, 324
identify your own, 322–324
stress
cataclysmic events, 375
commitments, 381–382
coping, 376
coping strategies, 378–382
daily hassles, 375
defined, 375
evaluation of strategies, 382
fight or flight response, 375
meditation, 380
organization, 377
personal stressors, 375
perspective, in, 383
physical reactions to, 375
physical readiness for,
376–377
preparation, 376–377
progressive relaxation,

381–382
relaxation, 380–381
rethinking, 383
silver lining, look for,
380–381
social support, 380
source of, 377
stressor, 375
susceptibility to illness,
378–379
take charge, 378–379
work of dealing with,
378–382
stressor, 375
student advisor, 295
Student Affairs Office, 24
student housing, 361–362
study groups, 43, 164
study notes
annotating textbook
material, 154
defined, 152
flash cards, 154–155
laptop computers, 155
material you can write on,
154–155
material you cannot write
on, 155
success
dealing with, 310
effort equals, 12
fear of, 17, 22
succession planners, 46
tactile learning style, 62

tactile learning style, 62
task completion, 10
Tatum, Beverly, 320
teaching styles, 75–78
technology, 3, 98
notetaking, 152
Telus, 273
term of loan, 363
test anxiety, 160, 167
test-taking. See also tests
academic honesty, 174–175
allocation of time, 170
cheating, 174–175
checking your work,
175–176
easy questions first, 170
educated guessing, 174
essay questions, 170–172
evaluation, 175–179
fill-in questions, 174
legible writing, 170
matching questions, 174
multiple-choice questions,
172–174
out of time, 176
principles, 169–174
short-answer questions, 174
stopping, 176
true-false questions, 174
tests, 177–179
See also test-taking
accreditation exams, 175
anxiety about, 167
competency assessments,
175
cramming, 167–168
defined, 162–163
essay questions, 165–166
failure, 182, 309–310
listening, 170
machine-scored, 170
matching questions, 166
multiple-choice questions,
166

organization, 168–169
panicking, 169
preparation, 162–168
professional, 175
purpose of, 161–162
question types, 165–167
quiz, 162–163
results, 179–182
rethinking, 179–182
review of notes, 162
self-test, 166
strategies, 162–168
study groups, 164
test-taking test, 177–179
tools, 169
true-false questions, 166
work of. See test-taking
theorists, 73
thesis, 221
statement, 222
thinkers, 71
thinking, 3
Thomson, Shawn, 127
time log, 29–31
creating, 30
time management
avoiding distractions,
41–42
balancing school and work,
45–46
black holes, 31–32
childcare, 43–45
colour-coding, 35
communications, control of,
42
daily to-do list, 35, 39–40,
46–48
doing less, 48–49
doing more, 49
evaluation, 46–48
goal of, 29
inevitable surprises, 40, 42
master calendar, 35–37
organization, 35–40
personal style of, 48–49
preparation, 29–35
prime time, identification of,
35
priorities, 33, 34
procrastination, 42–45
reading, 194
rethinking, 48–49
saying no, 40–41
silence, 42
test-taking, 170
time log, 29–31
weekly timetable, 35, 37–40
work of, 40–46
timetable, 35
to-do list, 35
Toyota, 175
Trail, Rachel, 209
transcript, 297
transfer credits, 294
travel, 325–326
true-false questions, 166, 174
truisms, 282
tuition costs
cooperative education, 364
evaluation, 356–348
financial aid. See financial
aid
organization, 364
postsecondary education,
value of, 356
preparation, 362–364
rethinking, 356

unfair treatment, 309–310
university adviser, 295

university calendars, 293–295
University of Guelph, 23
University of King's College, 209
University of Toronto, 23
University of Western Ontario, 23, 369
URL (uniform resource locator), 114

values, identification of, 85–86
visual learning style, 62
visualization, 257–258, 259
voice, 225

Web addresses, 114
Web pages, 114
Web searches, 117–118
weekly timetable, 35, 37–40
wellness. *See* health
word-processing programs, 118
work, 364
    academic choices, 297–298
    backward, 277
    cultural competence, 324–327

decision making, 272–275
memory. *See* memory strategies
motivation, 11–13
notetaking, 140–147
P.O.W.E.R. Learning process, 11–13
personal mission statement, 87–89
public speaking, 230
reading, 194–199
stress, dealing with, 378–382
test-taking, 169–164
time management, of, 40–46
tuition costs, 364
writing, 223–227
work-study programs, 364
worker shortages, 46
Workopolis.com, 118
workplace
    budget, 348
    cultural competence, 322
    listening skills, 205
    memory, 260
    personality assessments, 91

safety, 387
World Wide Web, 114, 117–118
    See also Internet
writing
    process. *See* writing process
    rewriting, 225–226
    voice, 225
    while reading, 196–199
writing process
    ABBCC structure, 221
    appearance of your paper, 227
    argument, 221
    audience, 217–220
    background, 221
    body, 221–223
    brainstorming, 216, 217, 219
    conclusion, 223
    counterarguments, 223
    evaluation, 228
    first drafts, 223–225
    freewriting, 216–217, 218
    goals, 215–216
    mechanical aspects, 228
    organization, 220–223
    outline, 220–221

preparation, 215–220
research. *See* research
rethinking, 228–229
revisions, 225–227
short chunks at a time, 220
thesis, 221
topic choice, 216–217
work, 223–227

zero-sum game, 337
Zhang, Jenny, 339